The
ultimate guide to
Sugarcraft

The *ultimate guide to* Sugarcraft

Principal teacher: Nicholas Lodge
Teachers: Book 1: Janice Murfitt,
Book 2: Ann Baber, Lindsay John Bradshaw, Anne Smith, Cynthia Venn

MURDOCH BOOKS

Published in 2011 by Murdoch Books Pty Limited.

Murdoch Books Australia
Pier 8/9, 23 Hickson Road, Millers Point NSW 2000
Phone: +61 (0)2 8220 2000 Fax: +61 (0)2 8220 2558
www.murdochbooks.com.au

Murdoch Books UK Limited
Erico House, 6th Floor North, 93–99 Upper Richmond Road
Putney, London SW15 2TG
Phone: + 44 (0) 20 8785 5995 Fax: + 44 (0) 20 8785 5985
www.murdochbooks.co.uk

Chief Executive: Juliet Rogers
Publishing Director: Chris Rennie

Publisher: Lynn Lewis
Senior Designer: Heather Menzies
Cover Designer: Clare O'Loughlin
Designers: Richard Slater, Maggie Aldred
Editor: Deborah Gray
Editorial Coordinator: Liz Malcolm
Photographer: Graham Tann
Production: Joan Beal

National Library of Australia Cataloguing-in-Publication Data:
Title: The Ultimate Guide to Sugarcraft
ISBN: 978-1-74266-156-8 (pbk.)
Subjects: Sugar art. Icings, cake. Cake decorating.
Dewey Number: 641.86539

Printed by 1010 Printing International Limited. PRINTED IN CHINA.
Reprinted 2011.

CONTENTS

Authors 6

AUTHORS

NICHOLAS LODGE

Nicholas Lodge became interested in the art of sugarcraft at an early age, designing his first cake at the age of ten. After finishing school, he studied at the National Bakery School in London where he was a distinguished student.

Nicholas then worked for one of Britain's leading commercial cake decorating companies, working on commissions for many leading stores and hotels. At the age of 21, Nicholas became Tutorial Manager at a well-known cake decorating school where he taught at all levels, including instructing many overseas students.

Today, Nicholas continues to teach, lecture and demonstrate sugarcraft, as well as carry out cake commissions. He runs a cake decorating school in the USA, and also finds time to travel extensively, lecturing and teaching in the USA, Australia, South Africa and Japan.

As well as providing the framework for this book and overseeing its completion, Nicholas has contributed the beautiful chapters on the various aspects of flowerwork.

JANICE MURFITT

Janice Murfitt is the author of numerous cookery books, and has always been keenly interested in all aspects of cookery, particularly cake decorating and icing. An enthusiastic traveller, Janice has combined this interest with her love of cookery and is an avid collector of local recipes from many countries.

Janice began her career as a home economist in London, producing recipes, food for photography, advertising commercials and educational films on food. For several years, she worked in the cookery department of a well-known magazine, writing features and creating recipes. She now works as a freelance creative home economist.

ANN BABER

Ann Baber's versatile sugarcraft skills are renowned in the cake decorating world. Ann is an expert cake decorator, who is particularly skilled in working with chocolate and marzipan, as well as a capable businesswoman running her own cake decorating business. Ann has contributed lessons on marzipan figure modelling, making chocolate eggs and figures and decorating with chocolate, all of which are important inclusions in this book.

LINDSAY JOHN BRADSHAW

Qualified as a chef, baker, confectioner and teacher, Lindsay John Bradshaw is a specialist in cake and confectionery design. He teaches and demonstrates throughout the United Kingdom. His lessons on filigree, advanced figure piping and freestanding runouts are valued contributions to this volume.

ANNE SMITH

Anne Smith's training is in the arts and her skills as a sculptor, potter and needlewoman provide a firm foundation for her fine work in sugarpaste. She has contributed the lessons on pastillage and sugar moulding to this book.

CYNTHIA VENN

Cynthia Venn's cake decorating skills are well known and admired in the world of sugarcraft. A teacher and a contributor to magazines, she has established a following in the application of needlework techniques to cake decorating. She has won numerous national competitions. Cynthia has contributed the lessons on tube and brush embroidery, lace extension work, bas relief, appliqué and smocking.

BOOK ONE

LESSON PLANS

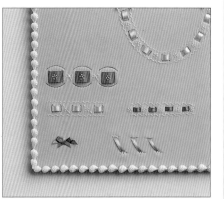

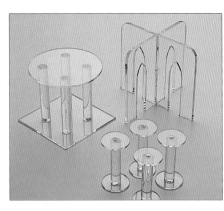

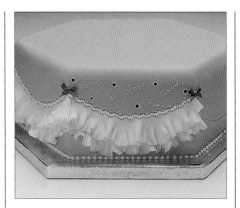

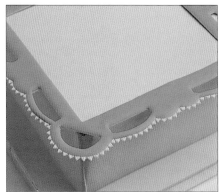

LESSON 1

Equipment

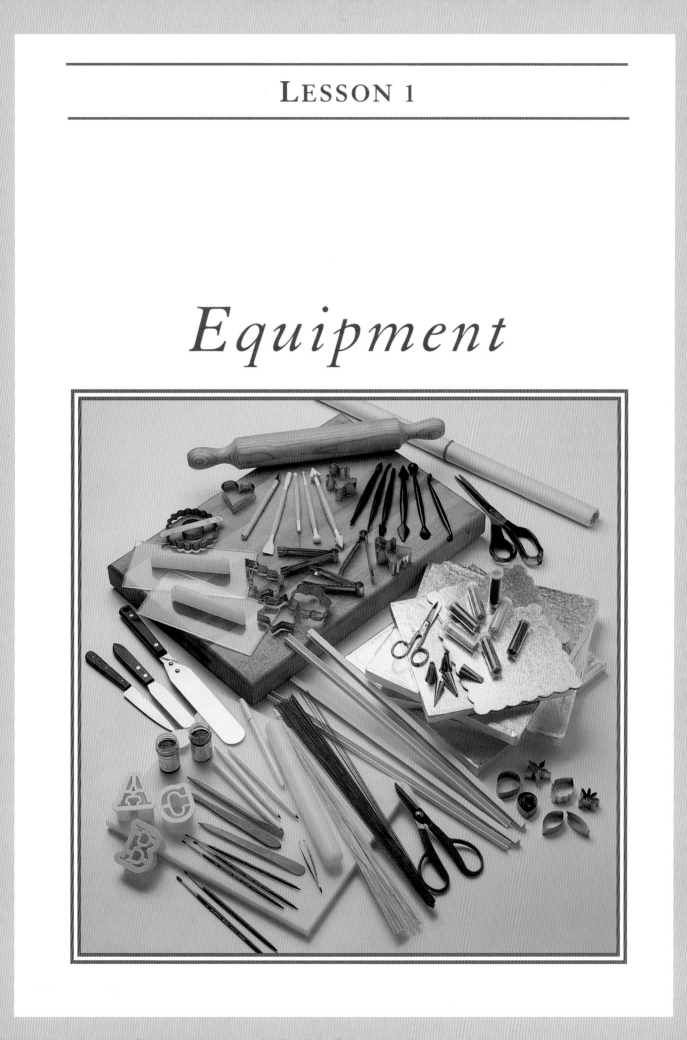

Equipment

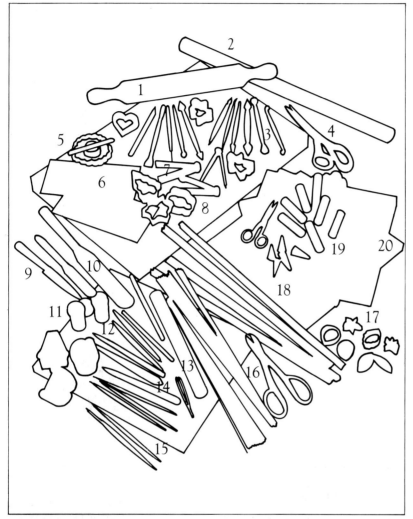

1. Rolling pin and worksurface
2. Greaseproof (waxed) paper
3. Metal modelling tools
4. Scissors
5. Garrett frill cutter
6. Smoothers
7. Crimpers
8. Selection of pastry and cookie cutters
9. Kitchen knife
10. Palette knives
11. Paste colours
12. Sugarcraft pens
13. Small non-stick rolling pin and board
14. Wooden modelling tools
15. Paintbrushes
16. Floristry wire and wire cutters
17. Flower cutters
18. Piping tubes
19. Petal dust
20. Cake boards and cards

Brushes

Use sable-hair brushes for the best effect and have several different sizes to hand.

Cake boards

These come in a wide variety of shapes and sizes designed to correspond with the various cake tins (pans) on the market. These are covered in greater detail in chapter (13)

Cocktail sticks

Used to add colouring paste to icing and in modelling work. Japanese birch are the best quality sticks that are available.

Colours

Dry dusting colours, paste colours and liquid food colouring are all needed for the various techniques covered in this and the companion volume.

Crimpers and leather embossing tools

Used for decorating sugarpaste and marzipan. See below for further details.

Cutters

A wide selection of cutters is useful. Flower, pastry, sweet (candy) and biscuit (cookie) cutters are used for making plaques and cutouts, while frills and flounces are made with Garrett cutters.

Dummies

Used for practice and competition work. See below for further details.

Electric mixer

Useful in cake preparation and for making royal icing.

Ball tools

A selection of different sizes are required although a glass-headed pin stuck into a piece of dowelling can be used in place of a small ball tool.

Bowls

A selection of various sizes, preferably glass, all clean and free of grease.

Florist's wire

You will need varying gauges for flower work, and modelling.

Icing bag stand

Not essential but keeps the worksurface clean and stops the tubes, once filled from drying out.

Knives

A good kitchen knife with a fine sharp blade is essential, you may also wish to use a scalpel for fine cutting and trimming work.

Measuring jug

The 500ml (1pint) is most useful.

Modelling tools

These may be bought from specialist suppliers although you will be able to improvise with various common household tools.

Moulds

Used in sugarcraft work and chocolate work and come in a wide variety of shapes and sizes for many different occasions.

Palette knife

Crank-handled and straight palette knives are used for lifting, smoothing and trimming.

Paper and card

Greaseproof (waxed) and silicone paper is used for icing bags and runouts. Card is used to make templates.

Dummy Cakes

There are three main types of dummy cake used for practising and for competition work. The polystyrene dummies come in a range of different shapes and sizes, they generally work well but are very light weight. This can be overcome by hollowing out the inside and filling with wall plaster or plaster of Paris. Royal icing is usually used to attach the dummy to the cake board, allow to dry for a few hours before coating. Alternatively, if the dummy is to be sugarpasted, stick to the board with clear piping jelly. Piping jelly may also be used to attach the paste to the dummy. When cleaning the dummy, remove from the board and soak in warm water, never attempt to cut the icing from the dummy with a sharp knife as this will damage the polystyrene.

Dummies can also be created from a stack of cake boards stuck together with royal icing or glue. Because of the ridges along the edges, this dummy type is most suitable for royal icing rather than paste. Board dummys cannot be washed but layers of practice coating may be built up.

Finally there is the wooden dummy. If you plan on doing a good deal of competition work or practising then it is worth investing in a good quality wooden dummy. These are suitable for all types of work and are easy to wash and reuse. Most dummies do have an attached wooden board which can be a disadvantage if you wish to practise collars or extension work but most dummies can be unscrewed and used separately using an ordinary cake-board.

Piping tubes

Various sizes and shapes are available in both nickle plate and plastic. The former are more expensive but tend to be more accurate and defined.

Rolling pin

An extra long or non-stick pin is necessary and a smaller stainless steel or non-stick pin is useful for making plaques and for fine work.

Scissors

One good pair of large scissors and a pair of sharp fine bladed scissors are also required.

Scrapers

Plain and serrated plastic side scrapers are used for or putting royal icing on the sides of cakes.

Scriber

Fine lines are scratched or scribed onto the cake using a scriber.

Sieve

Keep a small fine mesh sieve for sieving icing sugar only.

Smoothers

These are used to smooth the surface of marzipanned or sugarpasted cakes although some people prefer to use their hands.

Spacers

These help to maintain uniform thickness when rolling out sugarpaste or marzipan.

Spatula

Plastic or rubber for use in cake and icing preparation and wooden for mixing royal icing.

Food Colouring

Food colouring comes in four main forms: powder, liquid, paste and pens.

Powder is mainly used as petal dust as for adding colour to flowers and frills. It can be used to colour the icing itself but the intensity is not so strong as with paste or liquid colouring so it is uneconomical to use in large quantities. However, it should be used for lace and filigree work as paste contains glycerine and liquid would make the icing too soft for fine work. Powders should also be used when colouring white chocolate as other types would cause it to thicken.

Liquid colourings are readily available but are less concentrated than paste consequently making sugarpaste more sticky and royal icing too soft if used in any quantity. Use for pastel shades only and use paste for dark colours.

Paste colours are generally the best to use for colouring royal icing or sugarpaste. Pastes are glycerine based and come in a good colour range. Use a cocktail stick to add the colour to the icing and use sparingly.

Sugarcraft pens are also available and are used for marking outlines, and writing on surfaces. They are used like a felt pen.

Straight edge

Used when flat icing the top of a cake with royal icing.

Tweezers

Use fine pointed tweezers with grooved ends.

Turntable

Preferably a quality turntable; a tilting one is best for some jobs.

Wooden dowelling

Used for pulled flower work and modelling.

Work surface

Melamine, non-stick plastic, marble or wooden surfaces are best. Be sure that they are thoroughly clean and grease-free.

Care of Equipment

Wash each piece of equipment thoroughly after use in warm, mild detergent taking care to ensure that all items are free of grease. Rinse before drying. Store in a dry, dust-free environment, rewash before use if necessary.

Crimper Plaque 2

The numbers along the edge of the plaque relate to the particular set of crimpers shown above.

No. 1 Single open scallop
No. 2 Single closed scallop
No. 3 Double open scallop
No. 4 Double closed scallop
No. 5 Diamond
No. 6 Chevron
No. 7 Straight edge
No. 8 Heart
No. 9 Holly

Crimper Plaque 1

The plaque shows a full set of crimpers with their corresponding effects. Crimpers are a quick and versatile method of decoration for marzipanned and sugarpasted surfaces. Crimping must always be worked on soft paste so is generally worked as soon as the cake is covered. When using crimpers dip in cornflour (cornstarch) to prevent them sticking to the paste while working. Pinch the crimper slightly so the edges are about 5mm (¼in) from the closed position, place on the sugarpaste surface and bring your thumb and first finger together. Squeeze the crimper to create the desired effect.

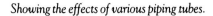

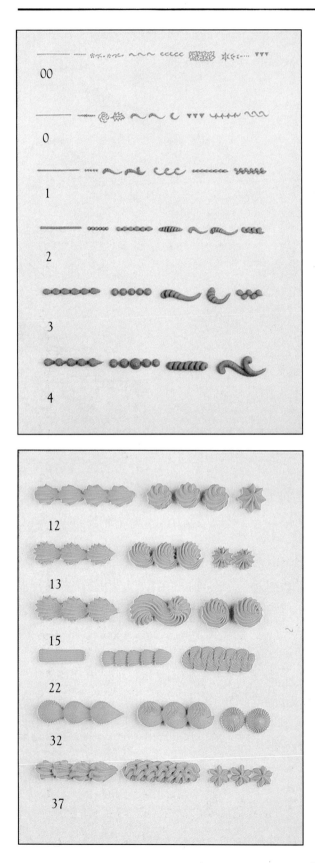

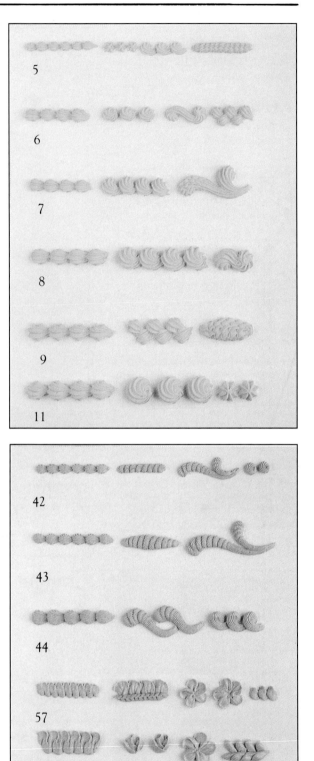

LESSON 2

Sponge Cakes

Basic Sponge Cake

This is a traditional sponge cake made by creaming together the butter and sugar to incorporate the air. The result is very similar to the one-bowl sponge but the texture is slightly firmer, making it easier to ice and decorate.

Place the butter or margarine and sugar in a mixing bowl. Mix together with a wooden spoon, then beat for 2 to 3 minutes until light and fluffy. Alternatively, use an electric mixer for about 1 minute.

Add the eggs a little at a time, beating well after each addition, until all the egg has been incorporated and the mixture is soft and glossy. If it looks slightly curdled, beat in 15-30ml (1-2 tablespoons) of flour.

Sift the flour into the bowl and add flavourings if wished. Using a spatula or a large spoon, carefully fold in the flour, cutting through and turning the mixture until all the flour has been incorporated into the batter.

Place the mixture into the prepared greased and lined tin; smooth the top with a spatula and give the tin a sharp tap to remove any air pockets and to level the mixture.

Place the cake mixture in the centre of a pre-heated oven 160°C (325°F/Gas 3) for the specified cooking time (see Basic Sponge chart). Test the cake by pressing the centre with the fingers. The cake should be golden brown and feel firm and springy when cooked.

Loosen the edges with a palette knife, invert onto a cooling rack and remove the lining paper. Turn the cake the right way up and leave until cold completely.

INGREDIENTS

See Basic Sponge Chart page 33

Flavourings for a 2-egg quantity of Basic Sponge Cake (increase the amounts for larger quantities of cake mixture):
15ml (1 tablespoon) cocoa blended with 15ml (1 tablespoon) boiling water
10ml (2 teaspoons) instant coffee blended with 5ml (1 teaspoon) boiling water
5-10ml (1-2 teaspoons) finely grated orange, lemon or lime rind
2.5ml (½ teaspoon) vanilla, almond or peppermint essence (extract) 25g (1oz/1 tablespoon) chocolate dots (chips) or grated chocolate
50g (2oz/¼ cup) glacé (candied) cherries, chopped

Making a Basic Creamed Sponge Cake

Preparing the Tin

1. Place the tin over a piece of greaseproof paper. Use a pencil to draw around the outside of the tin. Cut out the marked shape using a pair of sharp scissors.

2. Brush the tin lightly with oil and fit the greaseproof paper disc over the base of the tin. Brush the paper with oil.

3. Cream together the butter and sugar in a mixing bowl using a wooden spoon.

4. Beat the mixture until light and fluffy.

5. Add the eggs a little at a time, beating well after each addition.

6. Beat until smooth and glossy.

7. Sift the flour into the bowl.

8. Using a spatula or metal spoon to fold the flour carefully into the mixture until all the flour is incorporated.

9. Place the mixture into the tin and spread evenly using a small palette knife.

10. Mixture level, ready to bake.

11. Loosen the edge of the cake away from the tin using a small palette knife.

12. Turn the cake out onto a cooling rack.

13. Carefully peel off the lining paper.

14. Invert the cake and cool on the wire rack.

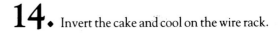

Whisked Sponge Cake

A light, fat-free sponge suitable for making into Swiss rolls (jelly rolls), small and large iced and decorated sponge and novelty cakes.

Place the eggs and sugar in a heat-proof bowl over a saucepan of hot but not boiling water. Whisk the mixture until thick and pale. Remove the bowl from the saucepan and continue whisking until, when lifted, the whisk leaves a trail of mixture on the surface.

Sift the flour and baking powder onto the surface of the mixture and add any flavourings. Using a spatula or a large spoon, carefully fold in the flour, cutting through and turning the mixture until all the flour has been incorporated.

Pour the mixture into the prepared greased and lined tin (see chart) and gently level the top with a spatula.

Place the cake in the centre of a pre-heated oven 180°C (350°F/Gas 4) for the specified cooking time (see chart). Test the cake by pressing the centre with the fingers. The cake should be golden brown feel firm and springy when cooked.

Loosen the edges with a palette knife and invert onto a cooling rack. Carefully remove the lining paper, turn the cake the right way up and leave until cold.

INGREDIENTS

See Whisked Sponge Cake Chart page 33

Flavouring for a 2-egg quantity of Whisked Sponge Cake (increase the amounts for larger quantities of cake mixture)
Chocolate: replace 15g (½oz/2 tablespoons) flour with cocoa powder
Coffee: add 10ml (2 teaspoons) instant coffee powder to the flour
Citrus: add 5ml (1 teaspoon) grated orange, lemon or lime rind
Nut: replace 25g (1oz/¼ cup) flour with finely ground nuts

Making a Swiss Roll

Preparing the Tin

1. Place the tin in the centre of a piece of greaseproof paper, 2.5cm (1in) larger all round than the tin. Cut from the corner of the paper to the corner of the tin using a pair of sharp scissors.

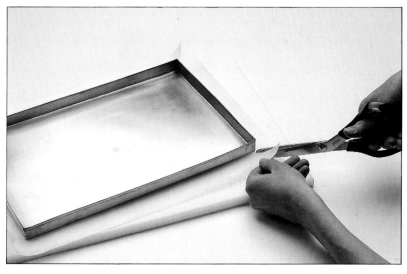

2. Lightly brush the tin with oil and fit the paper into the tin. Brush the paper lightly with oil.

3. Whisk the eggs and sugar in a bowl over a saucepan of hot water until light and thick.

4. Lift the whisk to show a trail on the surface.

5. Sift the flour onto the surface of the mixture.

6. Fold the flour carefully into the mixture.

7. Spread the mixture carefully into the corners of the tin.

8. Level mixture in the tin ready to bake.

9. Sprinkle a piece of greaseproof paper with caster (superfine) sugar.

10. Invert the cake on to the sugared paper.

11. Carefully peel off the lining paper.

12. Trim 5mm (¼in) off each side of the cake using a sharp knife.

13. Spread the trimmed cake evenly with warmed apricot jam.

14. Roll the cake towards you into a firm roll starting with the aid of the paper, from the short edge.

One-Bowl Sponge Cake

A quick and easy cake to make simply by mixing the ingredients together in one bowl. Different flavourings can be added to give variety. The mixture may be cooked in many different tin shapes and sizes (see chart).

Place the flour, baking powder, sugar, margarine and eggs into a mixing bowl. Mix together with a wooden spoon, then beat for 2 to 3 minutes until smooth and glossy. Alternatively, use an electric mixer and beat for 1 minute only. Add any flavourings if wished and mix until well blended.

Place the mixture into the prepared greased and lined tin; smooth the top with a spatula and give the tin a sharp tap to remove any air pockets and to level the mixture.

Place the cake mixture in the centre of a pre-heated oven 160°C (325°F/Gas 3) for the specified cooking time (see chart). Test the cake by pressing the centre with the fingers. The cake should be golden brown and feel firm and springy when cooked.

Loosen the edges with a palette knife, invert onto a cooling rack and remove the lining paper. Turn the cake the right way up and leave until completely cold.

INGREDIENTS
See One-Bowl Sponge Cake Chart page 33

Flavourings for a 2-egg quantity of One-Bowl Sponge Cake (increase the amounts for larger quantities of cake mixture)
15ml (1 tablespoon) cocoa blended with 15ml (1 tablespoon) boiling water
10ml (2 teaspoons) instant coffee blended with 5ml (1 teaspoon) boiling water
5-10ml (1-2 teaspoons) finely grated orange, lemon or lime rind
2.5ml (½ teaspoon) vanilla, almond or peppermint essence (extract) 25g (1oz/1 tablespoon) chocolate dots (chips) or grated chocolate
50g (2oz/¼ cup) glacé (candied) cherries, chopped

Genoese Sponge Cake

A rich sponge cake made with melted butter which gives a moist, light texture. It will cut well into different shapes for small, large or novelty cakes, and is easy to ice.

Place the eggs and sugar in a heatproof bowl. Put the bowl over a saucepan of hot, but not boiling water and whisk immediately. Whisk until thick and pale, for about 3 to 4 minutes. Remove the bowl from the saucepan and continue whisking until, when the whisk is lifted, the mixture leaves a trail on the surface.

Sift the flour onto the surface of the mixture and add any flavourings if desired. Pour the melted butter around the edge of the mixture.

Using a spatula or large spoon, carefully fold in the flour and butter, cutting through and turning the mixture gently until all the flour has been incorporated.

Pour the mixture into the prepared greased and lined tin (see chart) and gently level the top with a spatula. Place the cake mixture in the centre of a pre-heated oven 180°C (350°F/Gas 4) for the specified cooking time (see chart). Test the cake by pressing the centre with the fingers. The cake should be golden brown and feel firm and springy when cooked.

Loosen the edges with a palette knife and invert onto a cooling rack. Carefully remove the lining paper, turn the cake the right way up and leave until cold.

INGREDIENTS

See Genoese Sponge Cake Chart page 34

Flavourings for a 2-egg quantity of Genoese Sponge Cake (increase the amounts for larger quantities of cake mixture)
Chocolate: replace 15g (½oz/2 tablespoons) flour with cocoa powder
Coffee: add 10ml (2 teaspoons) instant coffee powder to the flour
Citrus: add 5ml (1 teaspoon) grated orange, lemon or lime rind
Nut: replace 25g (1oz/¼ cup) flour with finely ground nuts

Quick Madeira Cake

A good, plain cake which can be made as an alternative to a light or rich fruit cake. It is firm and moist and makes a good base for icing and decorating.

Place the flour, baking powder, sugar, margarine, eggs and milk into a mixing bowl. Mix together with a wooden spoon, then beat for 2 to 3 minutes until smooth and glossy. Alternatively, use an electric mixer and beat for 1 minute only. Add any flavourings if wished and mix until well blended.

Place the mixture into the prepared greased and lined tin (see chart); smooth the top with a spatula and give the tin a sharp tap to remove any air pockets and to level the top.

Place the cake mixture in the centre of a pre-heated oven 160°C (325°F/Gas 3) for the specified cooking time (see chart). Test the cake by pressing the centre with the fingers. The cake should be golden brown.

Loosen the edges with a palette knife, invert onto a cooling rack and remove the lining paper. Turn the cake the right way up and leave until completely cold.

INGREDIENTS

see Quick Madeira Cake Chart page 33

Flavourings for a 3-egg quantity of Madeira Cake (increase the amounts for larger quantities of cake mixture)
Cherry: 185g (6oz/¾ cup) glacé (candied) cherries, halved
Coconut: 60g (2oz/⅔ cup) dessicated (shredded) coconut
Nut: replace 125g (4oz/1 cup) flour with ground almonds, hazelnuts, walnuts or pecan nuts
Citrus: replace milk with lemon, orange or lime juice and 5ml (1 teaspoon) of grated lemon, orange or lime rind

American Sponge Cake

This white sponge cake makes a good base for a celebration cake; it can be marzipanned, iced and decorated.

For Ingredients see American Sponge Cake Chart page 34
Place the butter and sugar in a mixing bowl. Mix together with a wooden spoon, then beat for 2 to 3 minutes until light and fluffy. Alternatively, use an electric mixer for 1 minute.

Sift together the flour and baking powder. Gradually add the flour to the mixture with the water, beating well after each addition, until all the flour and water have been fully incorporated, to form a smooth lump-free batter.

Place the egg whites in a clean, grease-free bowl and whisk until stiff, but not dry. Add one-third of the egg whites to the mixture. Using a spatula or a large metal spoon, carefully fold in the egg whites, cutting through and turning the mixture until all the egg whites have been incorporated. Repeat this process with the remaining egg whites.

Pour the mixture into the prepared greased and lined tin (see chart) and gently level the top with a spatula. Place the cake mixture in the centre of a pre-heated oven 180°C (350°F/Gas 4) for the specified cooking time (see chart). Test the cake by pressing the centre with the fingers. The cake should be golden brown and feel firm and springy when cooked.

Loosen the edges with a palette knife and invert onto a cooling rack. Carefully remove the lining paper, turn the cake the right way up and leave until cold.

Simple Decorations

There are many simple ways in which a basic sponge cake can be decorated without spending a lot of time. It is always a pleasure to add a finishing touch to a cake to turn it into something a little more special.

Icing (confectioner's) sugar is one ingredient which, when used carefully, can transform the appearance of a cake. Simply dredging the surface with icing sugar makes a sponge cake more appealing. Try placing a patterned doily on top of a cake, or arranging 1cm (½in) strips of paper in lines or a lattice pattern on top of the cake; then dredge thickly with icing sugar. Carefully remove the doily or paper strips, revealing the pattern, in sugar. This looks most effective on a chocolate or coffee cake.

Fruit rinds cut into shapes using tiny cutters make an effective edible decoration. Cut thin strips of lemon, orange or lime rind from the fruits, taking care not to include the white pith. Using tiny aspic or cocktail cutters, cut out various shapes. Arrange these shapes on glacé-icing or cakes iced with buttercream to form flowers, stems and leaves, or just as a continuous border using the same shape but different coloured rinds.

Flowers seem a natural decoration to go on a cake; tiny fresh flowers positioned at the last minute look so pretty. Also attractive are sugar-frosted flowers, which are preserved with egg white and sugar; they will last for several weeks once they are completely dry.

To sugar-frost flowers, ensure they are fresh and dry and trim the stems to the length required. Pull the petals apart if you wish to frost each one of them separately.

Place some caster (superfine) sugar in a shallow bowl. Using a fine paint brush, paint each petal on both sides with egg white which has been lightly beaten. Brush the centre and stem, then carefully spoon over the sugar to coat evenly.

Place the flowers on a cooling rack covered with kitchen paper and leave in a warm, dry place until the flowers are completely dry and set hard.

Store in a box lined with kitchen paper for up to three weeks.

Glacé Icing

This icing is simply made from icing (confectioner's) sugar and boiling water, see page 83 for recipe. Pour over the top of the cake. Spread evenly to the edge and decorate with fruit rinds, cherries, angelica, nuts or flowers.

Feather icing is very pretty; working with a white and coloured glacé icing. Place the coloured icing into a paper piping bag and snip the point off the end. Spread the top of the cake evenly with white icing and quickly pipe evenly spaced lines of coloured icing across the top of the white icing.

Draw a cocktail stick backwards and forwards through the icing across the lines to form a feather design. Leave to set.

Purchased decorations are instant decorations and, chosen carefully, can make a pretty finish to a cake. Angelica can be cut into stems, leaves and diamond shapes. Glacé cherries in various colours can be cut in half or sliced into rings or into thin wedges and arranged as petal shapes for flowers. Sugar flowers, jelly diamonds, (gumdrops) crystallized flower petals all make attractive decorations on top of icing swirls or as a border design. Coloured dragées, sugared mimosa balls, hundreds and thousands (sprinkles), coloured sugar

strands make quick, colourful coatings, toppings and designs.

For children's cakes, sweets (candies) are always a favourite; white and chocolate buttons, coloured (jelly) beans and liquorice sweets can all be used for simple finishes.

Basic Sponge and One-Bowl Sponge Chart

Tin (Pan) Sizes	17.5cm (7in) shallow square tin 20cm (8in) round sandwich (shallow) tin	1kg (2lb) loaf tin 22.5cm (9in) ring mould (tube pan)	940ml (30fl oz/3¾ cups) pudding basin or (bowl) or mould	Two 17.5cm (7in) shallow square tins Two 20cm (8in) sandwich (shallow) tins	1 litre (32fl oz/4 cups) pudding basin (bowl) 17.5cm (7in) mould	1kg (2lb) loaf tin 27.5cm x 17.5cm (11in x 7in) oblong tin	Two 20cm (8in) round sandwich (shallow) tins Two 22.5cm (9in) round sandwich (shallow) tins	22.5cm (9in) deep round or square cake tin
Self-raising Flour	125g (4oz/1 cup)	125g (4oz/1 cup)	125g (4oz/1 cup)	185g (6oz/1½ cups)	185g (6oz/1½ cups)	185g (6oz/1½ cups)	250g (8oz/2 cups)	250g (8oz/2 cups)
Baking Powder	5ml 1 teaspoon	5ml 1 teaspoon	5ml 1 teaspoon	7.5ml 1½ teaspoons	7.5ml 1½ teaspoons	7.5ml 1½ teaspoons	10ml 2 teaspoons	10ml 2 teaspoons
Caster (superfine) Sugar	125g (4oz/½ cup)	125g (4oz/½ cup)	125g (4oz/½ cup)	185g (6oz/¾ cup)	185g (6oz/¾ cup)	185g (6oz/¾ cup)	250g (8oz/1 cup)	250g (8oz/1 cup)
Soft Margarine	125g (4oz/½ cup)	125g (4oz/½ cup)	125g (4oz/½ cup)	185g (6oz/¾ cup)	185g (6oz/¾ cup)	185g (6oz/¾ cup)	250g (8oz/1 cup)	250g (8oz/1 cup)
Medium Eggs	2	2	2	3	3	3	4	4
Approximate Cooking Time	35 to 40 minutes	30 to 35 minutes	50 to 55 minutes	30 to 35 minutes	60 to 70 minutes	45 to 55 minutes	35 to 40 minutes	55 to 65 minutes

Whisked Sponge Chart

Tin (pan) Sizes	27.5cm x 17.5cm (11in x 7in) Swiss (Jelly) roll tin	17.5cm (7in) shallow square tin 20cm (8in) round sandwich (shallow) tin	32.5cm x 22.5cm (13in x 9in) Swiss (jelly) roll tin Two 17.5cm (7in) shallow square tins	20cm (8in) round cake tin	Two 20cm (8in) round sandwich (shallow) tins Two 17.5cm (7in) shallow square tins	17.5cm (7in) square cake tin
Medium Eggs	2	2	3	3	4	4
Caster (superfine) Sugar	50g (2oz/¼ cup)	50g (2oz/¼ cup)	90g (3oz/⅓ cup)	90g (3oz/⅓ cup)	125g (4oz/½ cup)	125g (4oz/½ cup)
Plain (all-purpose) Flour	50g (2oz/½ cup)	50g (2oz/½ cup)	90g 3oz/¾ cup)	90g (3oz/¾ cup)	125g (4oz/1 cup)	125g (4oz/1 cup)
Baking Powder	2.5ml (½ teaspoon)	2.5ml (½ teaspoon)	2.5ml (½ teaspoon)	2.5ml (½ teaspoon)	2.5ml (½ teaspoon)	2.5ml (½ teaspoon)
Approximate Cooking Time	10 to 15 minutes	20 to 25 minutes	10 to 15 minutes	30 to 35 minutes	20 to 25 minutes	30 to 35 minutes

Quick Madeira Chart

Tin (pan) Sizes	15.5cm (6in) square 17.5cm (7in) round	17.5cm (7in) square 20cm (8in) round	20cm (8in) square 22.5cm (9in) round	22.5cm (9in) square 25cm (10in) round
Plain (all-purpose) Flour	250g (8oz/2 cups)	375g (12oz/3 cups)	500g (1lb/4 cups)	560g (1lb 2oz/4¼ cups)
Baking Powder	5ml (1 teaspoon)	7.5ml (1½ teaspoons)	10ml (2 teaspoons)	12.5ml (2½ teaspoons)
Caster (superfine) Sugar	185g (6oz/¾ cup)	315g (10oz/1¼ cups)	440g (14oz/1¾ cups)	500g (1lb/2 cups)
Soft Margarine	185g (6oz/¾ cup)	315g (10oz/1¼ cups)	440g (14oz/1¾ cups)	500g (1lb/2 cups)
Medium Eggs	3	5	7	8
Milk or Citrus Juice	30ml (2 tablespoons)	45ml (3 tablespoons)	52.5ml (3½ tablespoons)	60ml (4 tablespoons)
Approximate Cooking Time	1¼ to 1½ hours	1½ to 1¾ hours	1¾ to 2 hours	1¾ to 2 hours

Genoese Sponge Chart

Cake Tin (pan) Sizes	32.5cm x 22.5cm (13in x 9in) Two 17.5cm (7in) square Two 20cm (8in) round sandwich	Two 20cm (8in) shallow square Two 22.5cm (9in) round sandwich (shallow)	22.5cm (9in) deep square 25cm (10in) deep round
Medium Eggs	4	6	8
Caster (superfine) Sugar	125g (4oz/½ cup)	185g (6oz/¾ cup)	250g (8oz/1 cup)
Plain (all-purpose) Flour	125g (4oz/1 cup)	185g (6oz/1½ cups)	250g (8oz/2 cups)
Unsalted (sweet) Butter, melted	50g (2oz/¼ cup)	90g (3oz/⅓ cup)	125g (4oz/½ cup)
Approximate Cooking Time	15 minutes to 20 minutes	25 to 30 minutes	35 to 40 minutes

American Sponge Chart

Tin (pan) Sizes	17.5cm (7in) square 20cm (8in) round 22.5cm (9in) ring (tube) tin	20cm (8in) square 22.5cm (9in) round	22.5cm (9in) square 25cm (10in) round
Butter, softened	125g (4oz/½ cup)	250g (8oz/1 cup)	375g (12oz/1½ cups)
Caster (superfine) Sugar	185g (6oz/¾ cup)	375g (12oz/1¼ cups)	560g (1lb 2oz/2 cups)
Plain (all-purpose) Flour	220g (7oz/1¾ cups)	440g (14oz/3½ cups)	655g (1lb 5oz/5¼ cups)
Baking Powder	10ml (2 teaspoons)	20ml (4 teaspoons)	30ml (6 teaspoons)
Water	125ml (4fl oz/½ cup)	250ml (8fl oz/1 cup)	375ml (12fl oz/1½ cups)
Vanilla Essence (extract)	2.5ml (½ teaspoon)	5 ml (1 teaspoon)	7.5ml (1½ teaspoon)
Medium Egg Whites	4	8	12
Approximate Cooking Time	35 to 45 minutes	60 to 65 minutes	60 to 65 minutes

LESSON 3

Fruit Cakes

Rich Fruit Cake

This recipe makes a very moist, rich cake suitable for any celebration. The cake can be made in stages, if time is short or if you are making more than one cake, see page 46 for chart of ingredients.

The fruit may be prepared and soaked overnight and the cake made the following day. Once the mixture is in the tin, the surface may be covered with cling film and the cake stored in a cool place overnight if cooking is not possible on the day. The quantities have been carefully worked out so that the depth of each cake is the same. This is important when making tiers for a wedding cake, as they must all be the same depth.

Place in a large mixing bowl the raisins, sultanas, currants, apricots, glacé cherries, mixed peel, nuts, lemon rind and juice, brandy, whisky or sherry.

Mix all the ingredients together until well blended, then cover the bowl with cling film. This mixture of fruit can be left overnight if required.

In another mixing bowl place the flour, ground almonds, mixed spice, sugar, butter, treacle and eggs.

Mix together with a wooden spoon, then beat for 2 to 3 minutes until smooth and glossy, or beat for 1 to 2 minutes using an electric mixer or food processor.

Place the mixed fruit into the bowl with the cake mixture. Stir gently until all the fruit has been mixed into the cake mixture.

Spoon the mixture carefully into the prepared tin and spread evenly over the base and into the corners. Give the tin a few sharp bangs to level the mixture and to remove any air pockets. Smooth the surface with the back of a metal spoon dipped in hot water, making a slight depression in the centre. The cake surface may be covered with cling film and left overnight in a cool place if required.

Place the cake in the centre of a pre-heated oven 140°C (275°F/Gas 1) for the specified cooking time (see chart page 46).

Test the cake to see if it is cooked 15 minutes before the end of the cooking time. If cooked, the cake should feel firm and when a fine skewer or cocktail stick is inserted into the centre, it should come out quite clean.

If the cake is not cooked, re-test it at 15 minute intervals. Remove the cake from the oven and allow it to cool in the tin.

Turn the cake out of the tin but do not remove the lining paper as it helps to keep the cake moist. Spoon another half quantity of brandy, whisky or sherry according to the quantities used in the chart, over the top of the cake and wrap in double thickness foil.

Store the cake in a cool, dry place on its base with the top uppermost for a week. Unwrap the cake and spoon over the remaining brandy, whisky or sherry (unless the cake is to be stored for three months in which case add the liquid a little at a time at monthly intervals). Re-wrap well and invert the cake and store it upsidedown to keep the top flat. The cake will store for up to 3 months.

Making a Rich Fruit Cake

1. Place all the dried fruits into a large mixing bowl.

2. Add the lemon rind juice and stir in the brandy, whisky, sherry if desired until evenly mixed, and set aside.

3. Place the remaining ingredients (sugar, flour, ground almonds, mixed spice, treacle (molasses), butter) into another bowl ready to add the eggs.

4. Stir all the ingredients together using a wooden spoon until mixed.

5. Beat the mixture together until well mixed, smooth and glossy.

6. Add the mixed fruit to the cake mixture.

7. Stir the fruit into the mixture.

8. Place the mixture in the prepared tin. Smooth the top of the cake mixture with the back of a wet metal spoon. Bake.

9. Cool the cooked cake in the tin.

10. Turn out the cold fruit cake onto a wire rack.

11. Wrap the cake, with the lining paper on, in foil ready to store.

12. Unwrap the foil. Remove the lining paper from the fruit cake.

Light Fruit Cake

This is a very light, moist fruit cake. As there is less fruit in the cake, it has a tendency to dome during cooking, so make a deep depression in the centre before putting in the oven. The cake will keep for up to 4 weeks, see chart of ingredients page 44.

Prepare the required size deep cake tin according to the chart page 44.

Place in a large mixing bowl the mixed dried fruit, cherries, almonds, orange rind, and sherry. Mix all the ingredients together until well blended. In another mixing bowl, place the flour, mixed spice, sugar, butter or margarine and eggs.

Mix together with a wooden spoon until smooth and glossy, or beat for 1 to 2 minutes with an electric mixer or food processor.

Place the mixed fruit in the bowl with the cake mixture, stir gently until all the fruit has been mixed evenly into the cake mixture.

Spoon the mixture into the prepared cake tin and spread evenly over the base and into the corners. Give the tin a few sharp bangs to level the mixture and remove any air pockets. Smooth the surface with the back of a metal spoon, making a fairly deep depression in the centre.

Bake in a pre-heated oven 140°C

(275°F/Gas 1), following the chart cooking time guide. Test the cake 15 minutes before the end of the given cooking time. If cooked, a fine skewer or cocktail stick inserted into the centre of the cake will come out clean. If the cake is not cooked, re-test at 15 minute intervals.

Leave to cool in the tin, turn out and leave the lining paper on to ensure the cake keeps moist. Wrap in foil and store in a cool place for up to 4 weeks.

Glacé Fruit Cake

This recipe makes a light-coloured cake with a moist texture which is due to the addition of ground almonds to the mixture. The cake will store well for several weeks and may be marzipanned and iced, or left plain.

Prepare the cake tin. Sift the flour and baking powder into a bowl, add the ground almonds, sugar, butter and eggs. Mix together with a wooden spoon and beat for 2 to 3 minutes until smooth and glossy, or beat for 1 to 2 minutes using an electric mixer or food processor.

Add the fruit and nuts to the mixture and stir gently until well mixed. Spoon the mixture into the prepared tin and spread evenly over the base and into the corners. Give a few sharp bangs to level the mixture and make a slight depression in the centre of the cake.

Bake in the centre of a pre-heated oven 140°C (275°F/Gas 1) for about 2¼ to 2½ hours. Test the cake by pressing the centre with the fingers. The cake should feel firm and springy when cooked. Leave to cool in the tin, then turn out and wrap the cake in foil and store in a cool place for up to one week before decorating.

Makes one 20cm (8in) square cake or a 22.5cm (9in) round cake.

INGREDIENTS

375g (12oz/3 cups) plain (all-purpose) flour
5ml (1 teaspoon) baking powder
185g (6oz/1½ cups) ground almonds
375g (12oz/3 cups) caster (superfine) sugar
375g (12oz/3 cups) butter, softened
4 large eggs
375g (12oz/3 cups) chopped mixed glacé fruits
125g (4oz/1 cup) chopped Brazil nuts

Wheaten Fruit Cake

This wholesome fruit cake is made from a mixture of dried fruits, honey and wholewheat flour. It is easy to make and produces a moist cake which will keep for several weeks. Decorate it with fruit and nuts, or cover it with marzipan and icing.

Prepare the tin. Place the butter, honey and orange juice into a large saucepan. Heat gently until the butter has melted, then bring to the boil. Remove the saucepan from the heat then stir in the fruit until well mixed, then leave until lukewarm.

Place the flour, mixed spice and eggs into a large mixing bowl. Stir the bicarbonate of soda quickly into the fruit mixture, then add to the flour mixture in the bowl.

Mix together with a wooden spoon, then stir until well mixed. Spoon the mixture into the prepared tin and spread evenly over the base and into the corners. Give a few sharp bangs to level the mixture and make a slight depression in the centre.

Bake in the centre of a pre-heated oven 140°C (275°F/Gas 1) for about 2 hours. Test the cake 15 minutes from the end of the cooking time. When cooked, a fine skewer or cocktail stick inserted into the centre of the cake will come out clean. If the cake is not cooked, re-test at 15 minute intervals. Leave to cool in the tin, then turn out and wrap in foil for up to 2 weeks.

Makes one 17.5cm (7in) square cake or a 20cm (8in) round cake.

Ingredients
125g (4oz/1 cup) butter
60ml (4 tablespoons) clear honey
250ml (8fl oz/1 cup) orange juice
375g (12oz/3 cups)
chopped dried apricots
250g (8oz/1½ cups)
chopped dried figs
250g (8oz/1½ cups)
chopped stoned dates
315g (10oz/1¾ cups) raisins
375g (12oz/3 cups) 85%
wholewheat plain flour
10ml (2 teaspoons)
ground mixed spice
4ml (¾ teaspoon) bicarbonate of
soda (baking soda)
2 eggs, beaten

Preparing a Deep Tin

For rich fruit cakes, use good quality fixed-based deep cake tins (pans). Ensure you have the correct-sized tin for the quantity of cake mixture as this will affect the depth and cooking time of the cake. Always measure the tin across the base, not the top.

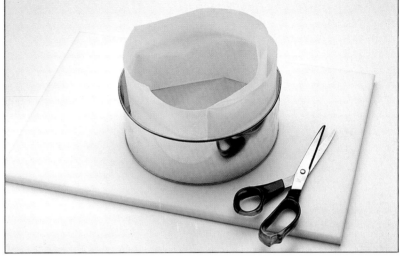

Double-line the inside of the tin with greaseproof or non-stick silicone baking paper and the outside with double-thickness brown paper. Stand the tin on a baking sheet lined with 3 or 4 thicknesses of brown paper. This prevents the side and base of the cake from being overcooked.

Place the tin on double-thickness greaseproof or non-stick silicone baking paper and draw around the base. Cut out the marked shape with a pair of scissors.

Cut a strip of double-thickness greaseproof or non-stick paper long enough to wrap around the outside of the tin with a small overlap and to stand 2.5cm (1in) above the top of the tin.

Brush the base and sides of the tin with melted fat or oil. Place the cut-out shape in the base of the tin and smooth out the creases.

Place the double strip of paper inside the tin, pressing well against the sides and making sharp creases where it fits into corners.

Brush the base and side paper well with melted fat or oil. Place a double-thickness strip of brown paper around the outside of the tin and tie securely with string.

Line a baking sheet with 3 or 4 layers of brown paper and stand the tin on top.

Decorating Ideas

Rich fruit cakes which are full of flavour are often enjoyed without marzipan and icing. Included in this section is a very rich fruit cake suitable for all celebration cakes. The light fruit cake is ideal for an everyday fruit cake as it is less expensive to make, and

Here are some simple decorations to give these cakes the finishing touches they deserve.

Apricot glaze brushed generously over the top of any fruit cake gives the top a glossy finish; when brushed over fruit or nut toppings it keeps them secure and moist.

Try arranging a variety of nuts over the top of the cake: a mixture of Brazil nuts, walnuts, almonds, pecan and hazelnuts. Brush the top of the cake before and after the nuts are applied.

Glacé fruits make a colourful and festive decoration; buy the pieces of fruit individually, or an assortment in a box: cherries in a variety of colours, pineapple slices, peaches, plums, pears, nectarines. Slice them thinly and arrange in rows across the top of the cake, brushing with apricot glaze before and after decorating.

The wheaten fruit cake lends itself to a topping of chopped apricots, figs and nuts drizzled with honey, or covered with raw sugar marzipan cutouts.

Purchased decorations provide the quickest and easiest way of decorating a fruit cake which has been already covered in marzipan and icing. They are available as seasonal decorations

and every kind of celebration occasion you can think of. Used sparingly and with a little thought, they can add colour and design to a cake. Ribbons of all shades, textures and width also look pretty around the

outside of a cake, or tied into tiny bows or loops. Teamed up with fresh flowers, this is a simple way to decorate a cake.
(See photographs on page 35 and 45 for decorating ideas)

Light Fruit Cake Chart

Cake Tin (pan) Size	17.5cm (7in) square 20cm (8in) round	20cm (8in) square 22.5cm (9in) round	22.5cm (9in) square 25cm (10in) round
Mixed Dried Fruit	500g (1lb/3 cups)	750g (1½lb/4½ cups)	1kg (2lb/6 cups)
Glacé (candied) Cherries, quartered	90g (3oz/⅓ cup)	125g (4oz/½ cup)	185g (6oz/¾ cup)
Flaked Almonds	60g (2oz/½ cup)	90g (3oz/¾ cup)	125g (4oz/1 cup)
Orange Rind, coarsely grated	10ml (2 teaspoons)	15ml (3 teaspoons)	20ml (4 teaspoons)
Orange Juice	30ml (2 tablespoons)	45ml (3 tablespoons)	60ml (4 tablespoons)
Sherry	30ml (2 tablespoons)	45ml (3 tablespoons)	60ml (4 tablespoons)
Plain (all-purpose) Flour	375g (12oz/3 cups)	500g (1lb/4 cups)	625g (1¼lb/5 cups)
Ground Mixed Spice	10ml (2 teaspoons)	15ml (3 teaspoons)	20ml (4 teaspoons)
Soft light brown Sugar	315g (10oz/1¼ cups)	440g (14oz/1¾ cups)	530g (1lb 1oz/2⅓ cups)
Butter or Margarine, softened	315g (10oz/1¼ cups)	440g (14oz/1¾ cups)	530g (1lb 1oz/2⅓ cups)
Medium eggs	4	5	6
Approximate Cooking Time	2¾ to 3¼ hours	3¼ to 3¾ hours	3½ to 4 hours

it can also replace the rich cake if preferred. If you prefer a lighter cake, the glacé fruit cake is ideal – light in colour and texture – and for the health conscious, there is the wheaten fruit cake, rich in mixed dried fruits, wholemeal flour and honey.

Storing Fruit Cakes

Leave the lining paper on the cakes, then wrap in a double layer of foil, waxed paper or greaseproof paper, and store in a cool, dry place. Never seal a cake in an airtight container as this may encourage mould growth.

Rich fruit cakes keep well, although they are moist, full of flavour and at their best when first made. The cakes do mature with keeping, but all fruit cakes are best eaten within 3 months. If you are going to keep a fruit cake for several months, pour on the alcohol a little at a time at monthly intervals, turning the cake each time.

Light fruit cakes are stored in the same way as rich fruit cakes, but as they contain less fruit, their keeping qualities are not so good. These cakes are at their best when first made, or within one month of baking.

Once the cakes have been marzipanned and iced they must be stored in cardboard boxes, to keep them dust-free, in a warm, dry atmosphere. Avoid damp and cold conditions as they cause the icing to stain and colourings to run.

Servings:
Working out the number of servings from a round or square cake is extremely simple. It depends if you require just a small finger of cake, or a more substantial slice. Whether the cake is round or square, cut across the cake from edge to edge into about 2.5cm (1in) slices, or thinner if desired. Then cut each slice into 4cm (1½in) pieces, or to the size you require. It is then easy to calculate the number of cake slices you can cut from a given size cake. A square cake is larger than a round cake of the same size, and will yield more slices. On a round cake the slices become smaller at the curved edges, so keep this in mind when calculating the servings.

Rich Fruit Cake Chart

Cake Tin (Pan) Size	13cm (5in) square / 15cm (6in) round	15cm (6in) square / 17.7cm (7in) round	17.5cm (7in) square / 20cm (8in) round
Raisins	125g (4oz/⅔ cup)	185g (6oz/1 cup)	250g (8oz/1½ cups)
Sultanas	125g (4oz/⅔ cup)	185g (6oz/1 cup)	250g (8oz/1½ cups)
Currants	125g (4oz/⅔ cup)	125g (4oz/⅔ cup)	155g (5oz/1 cup)
Dried apricots, chopped	60g (2oz/⅓ cup)	90g (3oz/½ cup)	125g (4oz/¾ cup)
Glacé (candied) cherries, quartered	90g 3oz/¾ cup)	90g (3oz/¾ cup)	150g (5oz/¾ cup)
Cut mixed peel	30g (1oz/3tbsp)	45g (1½oz/3½tbsp)	60g (2oz/⅓ cup)
Mixed chopped nuts	30g (1oz/¼ cup)	45g (1½oz/⅓ cup)	60g (2oz/½ cup)
Lemon rind, coarsely grated	5ml (1 teaspoon)	7.5ml (1½ teaspoons)	10ml (2 teaspoons)
Lemon juice	15ml (1 tablespoon)	22.5ml (1½ tablespoons)	30ml 2 tablespoons)
Brandy, whisky, sherry	15ml (1 tablespoon)	30ml (2 tablespoons)	45ml (3 tablespoons)
Plain (all-purpose) flour	185g (6oz/1½ cups)	220g (7oz/1¾ cups)	280g (9oz/2¼ cups)
Ground mixed spice	5ml (1 teaspoon)	10ml (2 teaspoons)	15ml (3 teaspoons)
Ground almonds	30g (1oz/¼ cup)	45g (1½oz/⅓ cup)	60g (2oz/½ cup)
Soft dark brown sugar	125g (4oz/½ cup)	155g (5oz/½ cup + 2 tbsp)	220g (7oz/¾ cup)
Butter or margarine, softened	125g (4oz/½ cup)	155g (5oz/½ cup + 2tbsp	220g (7oz/¾ cup)
Black treacle (molasses)	7.5ml (½ tablespoon)	15ml (1 tablespoon)	22.5ml (1½ tablespoons)
Medium eggs	2	3	4
Approximate cooking time	2 to 2¼ hours	2¼ to 2½ hours	2½ to 2¾ hours

Cake Tin (pan) Size	20cm (8in) square / 22.5cm (9in) round	22.5cm (9in) square / 25cm (10in) round	25cm (10in) square / 27.5cm (11in) round	27.5cm (11in) square / 30cm (12in) round
Raisins	280g (9oz/1⅔ cups)	375g (12oz/2¼ cups)	500g (1lb/3 cups)	560g (1lb 2oz/3¼ cups)
Sultanas	280g (9oz/1⅔ cups)	375g (12oz/2¼ cups)	500g (1lb/3 cups)	560g (1lb 2oz/3¼ cups)
Currants	250g (8oz/1½ cups)	350g (10oz/2 cups)	375g (12oz/2¼ cups)	440g (14oz/2¾ cups)
Dried apricots, Chopped	155g (5oz/1 cup)	185g (6oz/1 cup)	220g (7oz/1¼ cups)	250g (8oz/1⅓ cups)
Glacé (candid), cherries quartered	175g (6oz/¾ cup)	220g (7oz/¾ cup)	225g (8oz/1 cup)	280g (9oz/1 cup)
Cut mixed peel	90g (3oz/½ cup)	125g (4oz/⅓ cup)	185g (6oz/1 cup)	250g (8oz/1¼ cups)
Mixed chopped nuts	90g (3oz/¾ cup)	125g (4oz/1 cup)	185g (6oz/1 cup)	250g (8oz/2 cups)
Lemon rind, coarsely grated	12.5ml (2½ teaspoons)	15ml (3 teaspoons)	15ml (1 tablespoon)	22.5ml (1½ tablespoons)
Lemon juice	37.5ml (2½ tablespoons)	45ml (3 tablespoons)	60ml (4 tablespoons)	75ml (5 tablespoons)
Brandy, whisky, Sherry	60ml (4 tablespoons)	75ml (5 tablespoons)	90ml (6 tablespoons)	105ml (7 tablespoons)
Plain (all-purpose) flour	345g (11oz/2¾ cups)	470g (15oz/3¾ cups)	575g (1lb 3oz/4¾ cups)	685g (1lb 6oz/5¼ cups)
Ground mixed spice	15ml (1 tablespoon)	22.5ml (1½ tablespoons)	30ml (2 tablespoons)	45ml (3 tablespoons)
Ground almonds	75g (2½oz/⅔ cup)	90g (3oz/¾ cup)	100g (3½oz/⅔ cup)	155g (5oz/1¼ cups)
Soft dark brown sugar	280g (9oz/1 cup + 2tbsp)	410g (13oz/1⅔ cups)	530g (1lb 1oz/2 cups +tbsp)	625g (1lb 4oz/2½ cups)
Butter or margarine, softened	280g (9oz/1 cup + 2tbsp)	410g (13oz/1⅔ cups)	530g (1lb 1oz/2 cups + 2tbsp)	625g (1lb 4oz/2½ cups)
Black treacle (Molasses)	30ml (2 tablespoons)	37.5ml (2½ tablespoons)	45ml (3 tablespoons)	60ml (4 tablespoons)
Medium eggs	5	7	8	9
Approximate cooking time	3 to 3¼ hours	3½ to 3¾ hours	3¾ to 4 hours	4¾ to 5 hours

LESSON 4

Marzipan

Marzipan

Marzipan is a paste made from ground almonds and sugar. The consistency, texture and colour varies according to how the paste is made, but the end result is used for giving cakes a smooth, flat surface before applying icings or sugarpaste.

For added colour marzipan can be tinted or coloured and used for cut-out or moulded decorations.

Homemade marzipan has a taste of its own and can be easily made in manageable quantities. Take care not to over-knead or handle the marzipan when making it as this encourages the oils from the ground almonds to flow and they will eventually seep through the iced surface of the cake, causing staining.

Commercial marzipan is available as white, yellow and raw sugar marzipan. Use the white marzipan for all cakes as it is the most reliable type to use, especially when cakes are being iced in pastel shades or white. The yellow marzipan has added food colouring but may be used for covering rich fruit cakes; the yellow colour can show through if the icing is thinly applied, or may cause yellow staining. This marzipan does not take colour so well and is not really recommended for modelling work.

Raw sugar marzipan may be used in place of other marzipan if you are health conscious. Being dark, it is difficult to colour and to use for decorations. It is available from most health food shops.

Always use fresh, pliable marzipan to obtain the best results, especially for covering a cake.

Be sure to dry the marzipanned cake before applying the icing. Set marzipan ensures a good cake shape during icing and prevents any moisture seeping through from the cake and staining the surface.

Always store the marzipanned cake on a clean cake board in a warm, dry room.

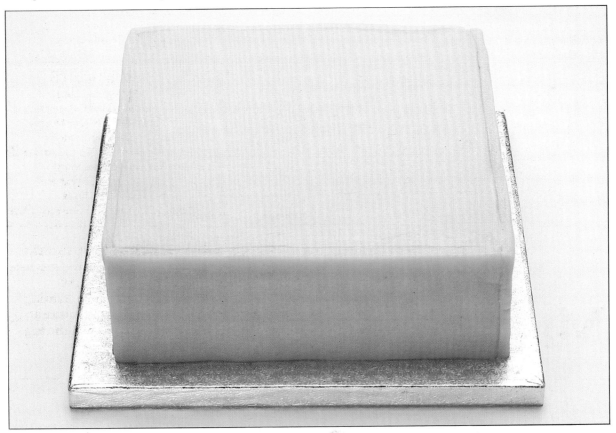

Marzipan Chart

Cake Size	13cm (5in) square 15.5cm (6in) round	15.5 (6in) square 17.5cm (7in) round	17.5cm (7in) square 20cm (8in) round	20cm (8in) square 22.5cm (9in) round	22.5cm (9in) square 25cm (10in) round	25cm (10in) square 27.5cm (11in) round	27.5cm (11in) square 30cm (12in) round
Apricot Glaze	15ml (1 tablespoon)	22.5ml (1½ tablespoons)	30ml (2 tablespoons)	37.5ml (2½ tablespoons)	45ml (3 tablespoons)	45ml (3 tablespoons)	60ml (4 tablespoons)
Marzipan	375g (12oz)	750g (1½lb)	875g (1¾lb)	1kg (2lb)	1.25kg (2½lb)	1.5kg (3lb)	1.75kg (3½lb)

Boiled Marzipan

This marzipan is soft and pliable but not so easy to work with as the kneaded marzipan. It has a good flavour and is used for covering cakes and for simple modelling.

Put the sugar and water in a medium-sized saucepan over a low heat, stirring occasionally until the sugar has dissolved.

Add the cream of tartar and bring quickly to the boil. Boil continuously until the sugar syrup has reached soft ball stage, or registers 116° (240°F).

Remove the saucepan from the heat, stir in the ground almonds and essence until well blended and the mixture turns opaque.

Place the egg whites in a bowl and whisk lightly, add them to the marzipan, stir, and return to the heat to cook for a further 2 minutes.

Lightly dust a work surface with icing sugar, place the marzipan in the centre, cover with cling film until completely cold.

Knead the marzipan until soft and pliable and free from any cracks. Store in a polythene bag in a cool, dry place until required.

Makes 500g (1lb) marzipan

INGREDIENTS
250g (8oz/1 cup)
caster (superfine) sugar
155ml (5fl oz/²⁄₃ cup) water
pinch cream of tartar
185g (6oz/1½ cups) ground almonds
2ml (¼ teaspoon)
almond essence (extract)
1-2 egg whites
icing (confectioner's) sugar, to dust

Kneaded Marzipan

This marzipan is quick and easy to make. Take care not to over-knead the mixture as this causes the oil from the ground almonds to flow, which may cause staining when the icing is applied. If you require a lighter-coloured marzipan, use just the egg white instead of a whole egg.

Place the ground almonds and sugars into a bowl. Stir until evenly mixed.

Make a well in the centre and add the lemon juice, almond essence and enough egg or egg white to mix to a soft but firm dough.

Lightly sprinkle a surface with sieved icing sugar and knead the marzipan until completely smooth and free from cracks.

Wrap in cling film or store in a polythene bag until ready for use.

Tint with food colouring if required and use for modelling or as a top covering for cakes.

Makes 500g (1lb) marzipan.

INGREDIENTS
250g (8oz/2 cups) ground almonds
125g (4oz/½ cup)
caster (superfine) sugar
125g (4oz/1 cup) icing
(confectioner's) sugar, sieved
5ml (1 teaspoon) lemon juice
few drops almond essence (extract)
1 small egg, or
1 large egg white

Raw Sugar Marzipan

This marzipan is very similar to kneaded marzipan but is made with raw, soft brown sugar. This gives it a rich flavour and makes it brown in colour. It is not easy to colour the marzipan, although it will take dark colourings. Use it for covering cakes.

Place the ground almonds and soft brown sugar into a bowl. Stir until evenly mixed.

Make a well in the centre and add the lemon juice, almond essence and enough egg or egg white to mix to a soft but firm dough.

Lightly sprinkle a surface with sieved icing sugar and knead the marzipan until smooth and completely free from cracks.

Wrap in cling film or store in a polythene bag until ready for use.

Makes 500g (1lb) marzipan

INGREDIENTS
250g (8oz/2 cups) ground almonds
250g (8oz/1 cup) raw soft dark or light brown sugar
5ml (1 teaspoon) lemon juice
few drops almond essence (extract)
1 small egg, or
1 large egg white

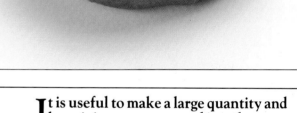

Apricot Glaze

It is useful to make a large quantity and keep it in a screw-topped jar when marzipanning a number of cakes.

Place the jam and water in a saucepan. Heat gently until the jam has melted. Boil rapidly for half a minute, then strain through a sieve. Rub through as much of the fruit as possible and discard the skins, as these cause the glaze to ferment.

Pour the glaze back into the clean hot jar, which has been heated in the oven, and seal with the lid. Use as required.

Makes 500g (1lb) glaze.

INGREDIENTS
500g (1lb) apricot jam (jelly)
45ml (3 tablespoons) water

Marzipanning a Cake

A well marzipanned cake is essential if the top icing is to be smooth, even and blemish-free. The method of application is the same for all varieties of marzipan.

Unwrap the cake and remove the lining paper. Place the cake on the cake board and roll the top with a rolling pin to flatten slightly.

Brush the top of the cake with apricot glaze. Sprinkle the work surface with sieved icing sugar.

Using two-thirds of the marzipan, knead it until smooth. Roll out to a 5mm (¼in) thickness to match the shape of the top of the cake.

Make sure the marzipan moves freely on the work surface inverting the cake on the centre of the marzipan shape.

Trim off the excess marzipan to within 1cm (½in) of the cake, then using a small flexible palette knife, push the marzipan until it is level with the side of the cake.

Turn the cake rightsideup and place in the centre of the cake board. Brush the sides of the cake with warm apricot glaze.

Knead the trimmings together, taking care not to include any crumbs from the cake. Measure and cut a piece of string the length of one side of a square cake or the circumference of a round cake. Measure and cut

another piece of string the depth of the side of the cake from the board to the top.

Roll out the marzipan to 5mm (¼in) thickness and cut out one side piece for a round cake and four pieces for a square cake, to match the length and width of the string. Knead the trimmings together and re-roll if necessary.

Carefully fit the marzipan on the side of the cake and smooth the joins with a palette knife. Leave in a warm, dry place for at least 24 hours to dry before icing.

1. Roll the top of the fruit cake to flatten the fruit.

2. Brush the top with warm apricot glaze.

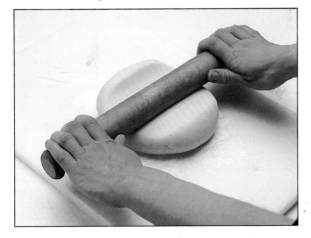

3. Roll out the marzipan on a lightly sugared surface.

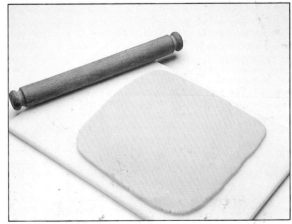

4. Marzipan rolled out to 5mm (¼in) thickness.

5. Fruit cake inverted on to centre of marzipan. Trim the marzipan to within 1cm (½in) of the cake.

6. Use a small palette knife and press the excess marzipan into the side, making it level with the edge of the cake.

7. Inverted cake on the cake board, with a flat square top.

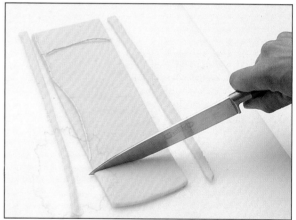

8. Use two pieces of string to measure the width and length of the side of the cake and cut the marzipan strip to size.

9. Fit the marzipan strip on to the side of apricot glazed cake.

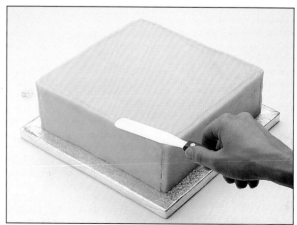

10. Use a small palette knife to smooth all the joins together.

Marzipanning a Cake for Sugarpaste

1. Brush the top and sides of the cake with warmed apricot glaze. Sprinkle the work surface lightly with sieved icing (confectioner's) sugar.

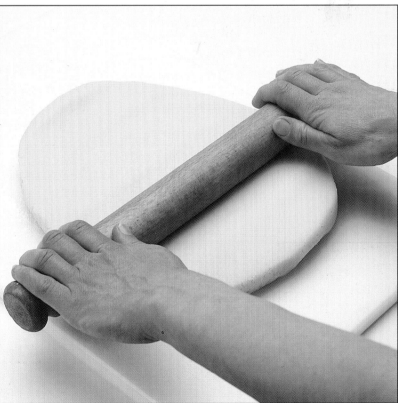

2. Knead the marzipan into a smooth ball. Roll out in the shape of the cake to a 5mm (¼in) thickness, and large enough to cover the whole cake.

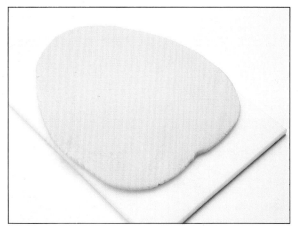

3. Make sure the marzipan moves freely, then roll the marzipan loosely around the rolling pin.

4. Place the supported marzipan over the cake and carefully unroll so that the marzipan falls evenly over the cake.

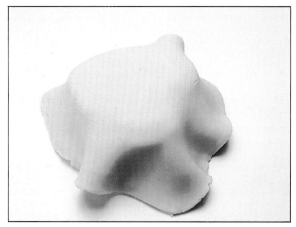

5. Smooth the marzipan over the top and down the sides, allowing the marzipan to fit at the base of the cake without stretching.

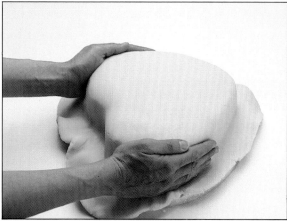

6. Using clean, dry hands, gently rub the top of the cake in circular movements to make a smooth, glossy finish to the marzipan.

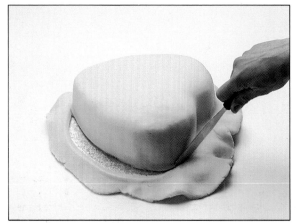

7. Using a sharp knife, trim the excess marzipan from the base of the cake, cutting down on to the board.

8. Leave in a warm, dry place for at least 24 hours before icing.

Decorating Ideas

Marzipan is smooth, soft, easy to work and an ideal base for royal icing and sugarpaste. It can be coloured in various shades with food colourings, cut into shapes moulded into flowers, animals and figures.

Cutouts

This is a simple way of decorating a cake with coloured marzipan cut into a variety of shapes. Tint several pieces of marzipan with food colourings to the required colours, see below. Roll out evenly on a sugared surface until about 3mm (⅛in) thick. Using small aspic, cocktail or biscuit cutters, cut out a variety of shapes. Arrange the cutout shapes in an attractive design on the cake and secure with apricot glaze.

Small flower and leaf cutters may be used to make a flower design; an arrangement of stems and other leaves can be cut out from thin strips of coloured marzipan.

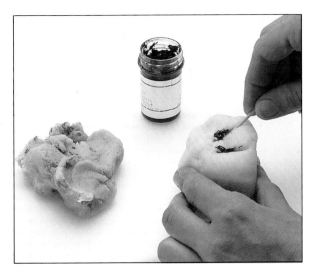

Used as a cake covering on its own, it combines colour, texture and flavour without the sweetness of icing (confectioner's) sugar. Once the cake has been covered in marzipan it can be decorated very simply by crimping the edges, applying cutouts, inlays and marzipan marquetry.

Crimper Designs

These quick, easy and effective designs are created with crimping tools which are available from most kitchen shops or cake decorating suppliers. They come in different shapes: straight, curve, scallops, ovals, 'V', hearts, diamonds, zig-zag.

To obtain an even crimped design, it is helpful to place an elastic band over the crimpers to prevent them springing apart and to adjust the size of the opening to give the required pattern. Try out the design on a spare piece of marzipan before decorating the cake.

Frilling Marzipan

Roll out thin strips of marzipan, making sure the strips move freely. Roll a cocktail stick or the end of a fine paintbrush backwards and forwards creating a thin frilled edge. Make several pieces and apply around the base or sides of the cake, securing with the apricot glaze.

Marquetry

Marquetry in marzipan can be used for making colourful and effective cutouts; it looks a very complicated process but when you know how, it really is quite easy.

Use two or more coloured pieces of marzipan and ensure they are all the same size for each strip. Place the pieces together in a line and roll out evenly to about 3mm (⅛in) thickness, making one piece of marzipan with coloured strips; trim to shape. Cut out the shapes required using shaped cutters or make a cardboard template by tracing around a shape. Try cutting out pieces of marzipan from a shape and replace the cutout piece with other coloured pieces of marzipan.

Christmas Cracker

Make a basic Swiss Roll (Jelly Roll) using a 3-egg quantity of mixture baked in a 32.5cm x 22.5cm (13in x 9in) shallow Swiss Roll (Jelly Roll) tin; fill with apricot jam and roll up.

Colour 375g (12oz) marzipan with red food colouring. On a lightly sugared surface, roll out the marzipan thinly and trim to an oblong 30cm x 25cm (12in x 10in). Brush the Swiss Roll with apricot glaze and place across the width of the marzipan oblong. Enclose the swiss roll in the marzipan trim and press the joins together. Roll over so that the join is underneath and place on a cake board. Smooth the surface and squeeze the ends to form a cracker shape. Using a pair of scissors dipped in icing (confectioner's) sugar, snip both ends of the cracker to form a frill, or flute the ends of the cracker with your fingers dipped in cornflour (cornstarch).

Colour 125g (4oz) marzipan with green food colouring. Roll out thinly and cut out six holly leaves using a holly cutter. Mark the veins with a knife and bend each leaf over a piece of dowel; leave to dry. Arrange on top of the cracker with a few berries made from the trimmings of the red marzipan secure with apricot glaze. Trim the frills with thin strips of green marzipan or ribbons. Leave to set.

LESSON 5

Sugarpaste

Commercial Sugarpaste

Although there are many recipes for homemade sugarpaste, there are certainly times when ready-made pastes are better or more convenient to use.

There are several types of sugarpaste on the market, basically the same kind of recipe but packaged under different names. Textures may vary and some are easier to work with than others. It is a good idea to try a small quantity first to see if it is suitable for the job you require, before purchasing a large quantity.

Sugarpaste is available from large supermarkets and cake decorating shops from 250g (8oz) packs up to 5kg (12lb) boxes, it may be tinted any shade and used very successfully for covering cakes, and for modelling into sugar decorations.

Keep the sugarpaste sealed in a polythene bag; knead in a little boiled water if the outside becomes dry and crumbly, or cut off the dried outer edges.

Fondant Icing

This is a cooked fondant icing which needs careful attention when boiling the sugar syrup. The longer it is kneaded, the whiter and silkier it becomes. When used to cover small or large sponge cakes, it produces a smooth satin finish and may be shaped into small decorations.

Put the white fat, lemon juice and water into a medium-sized saucepan. Heat gently, stirring occasionally, until the fat has melted. Stir in 250g (8oz/2 cups) of sugar and keep stirring until the sugar has dissolved. Leave the saucepan over a low heat until the mixture boils. Remove the saucepan from the heat.

Gradually add enough of the remaining sugar to form a soft paste, beating well after each addition.

Lightly dust the work surface with icing (confectioner's) sugar, then knead the icing continually until smooth, silky and no longer sticky, kneading in more sugar if necessary.

Tint with food colouring if desired, then use immediately for covering a cake and for making small decorations.

Makes 875g (1¾lbs) fondant icing.

INGREDIENTS
60g (2oz/4 tablespoons) white vegetable fat (shortening)
30ml (2 tablespoons) lemon juice
30ml (2 tablespoons) water
750g (1½lbs/5¼ cups) icing (confectioner's) sugar, seived

Making Fondant Icing

1. Measure the water and lemon juice and add to the saucepan containing the white fat.

2. Sift 250g (8oz/2 cups) of the measured icing sugar into the saucepan containing the melted white fat, water and lemon juice.

3. Bring the sugar syrup to the boil.

4. Gradually add the remaining sieved icing sugar.

5. Stir well after each addition of icing sugar.

6. Beat the fondant icing until smooth.

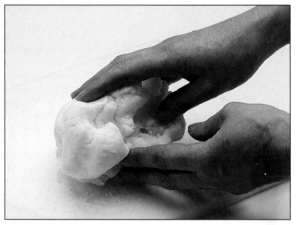

7. Quickly knead the fondant icing on a lightly icing-sugared surface.

Gelatine Icing

An easy-to-make sugarpaste, which handles well being very pliable yet not sticky. Ideal for covering cakes, or tint and use as a modelling paste. It sets hard enough to support a tiered cake, but also cuts easily.

Half-fill a saucepan with water and bring to the boil, then remove from the heat. Place the gelatine and water in a heatproof bowl over the saucepan of hot water. Stir occasionally until the gelatine has dissolved. Add the liquid glucose and glycerine and stir until liquid and warm. Remove the bowl from the saucepan.

Stir the sugar into the gelatine mixture using a wooden spoon. As the mixture begins to bind together, knead into a ball.

Dust work surface lightly with icing (confectioner's) sugar and knead icing until white, smooth and free from cracks. Store in a plastic bag, or wrap in cling film.

Makes 875g (1¾lb) gelatine paste.

INGREDIENTS
15g (½oz/2 envelopes) powdered gelatine
45ml (3 tablespoons) water
45ml (3 tablespoons) liquid glucose
15ml (1 tablespoon) glycerine
few drops of vanilla or almond essence (extract), optional
750g (1½lb/5¼ cups) icing (confectioner's) sugar, sieved

Quick Sugarpaste

This is a quick and easy icing to make. Once it is made, it can be tinted and used to ice all types of cakes. It is soft and pliable enough for moulding all types of sugar decorations. It dries firmly, but not hard enough to support another cake.

Place the egg white and liquid glucose in a clean bowl. Add the sugar and mix together with a wooden spoon. Knead together with the fingers until the mixture forms a ball. Dust work surface lightly with icing sugar and knead until smooth and free from cracks.

Wrap the icing completely in cling film or store in a polythene bag with all the air excluded.

Use white, or tint with food colourings for covering cakes and moulding decorations. On drying it sets firm, but not hard and brittle. If the icing is too soft and sticky to handle, knead in some more sieved sugar until it becomes firm and pliable. If the sugarpaste dries out and becomes hard, knead in a little boiled water until soft and pliable, or cut off the dried outer edges.

Makes 625g (1¼lb) icing.

Ingredients
1 egg white
30ml (2 tablespoons) liquid glucose
500g (1lb/4 cups) icing
(confectioner's) sugar, sieved

Making Quick Sugarpaste

1. Measure the liquid glucose and add it to the bowl containing the egg white.

2. Sift the icing sugar into the bowl.

3. Stir the icing sugar, egg white and liquid glucose together.

4. The mixture beginning to bind together.

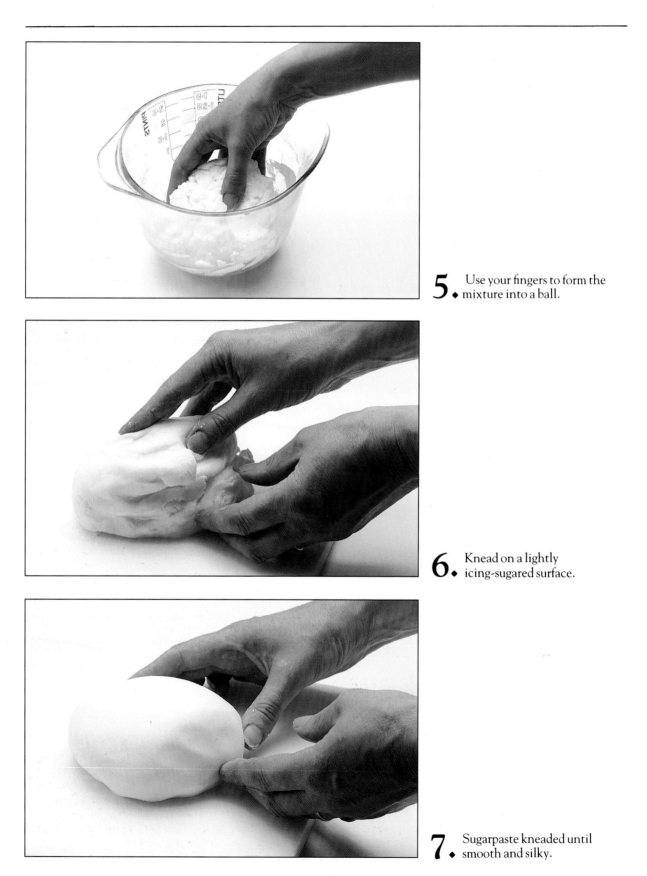

5. Use your fingers to form the mixture into a ball.

6. Knead on a lightly icing-sugared surface.

7. Sugarpaste kneaded until smooth and silky.

Covering a Cake with Sugarpaste

1. Brush the cake with sherry or cooled, boiled water to moisten the surface of the marzipan so that the sugarpaste will stick.

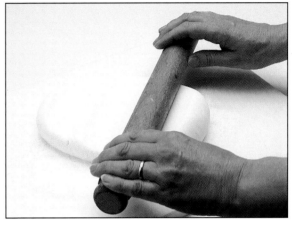

2. Roll out the sugarpaste on a lightly icing-sugared surface.

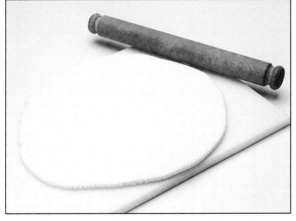

3. Sugarpaste rolled out 7.5cm (3in) larger than the top of the cake.

4. Support the sugarpaste with the rolling pin and unroll, over the top of the marzipanned cake.

Covering a Cake with Quick Sugarpaste or Gelatine Icing

Place the marzipanned cake on a turntable and brush the surface with a little sherry or spirit such as kirsch or gin, or with cooled, boiled water.

Sprinkle the work surface with sieved icing (confectioner's) sugar to prevent the icing sticking. Roll out the icing, using more sugar if necessary, to a round or square 7.5cm (3in) larger than the top of the cake.

Lift the icing carefully over the top of the cake, supported by a rolling pin, brushing off any excess sugar. Using well-cornfloured (cornstarched) hands smooth the icing over the top and then down the side of the cake so that the excess icing is at the base, removing any air bubbles between the surfaces.

Trim the excess icing off with a knife and, still with hands dusted, rub the surface in circular movements to make the icing smooth and glossy.

Knead the trimmings together and seal in cling film or a polythene bag to use for decorations.

5. The cake completely covered by the sugarpaste.

6. Gently press the sugarpaste onto the cake, starting at the top and carefully smoothing around the sides so that the excess sugarpaste is at the base of the cake on the board.

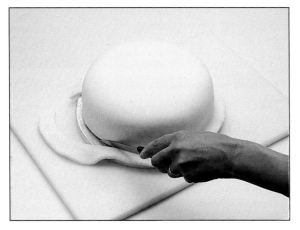

7. Use a knife to trim away the excess sugarpaste from the base of the cake.

8. The cake smoothly covered with sugarpaste, ready to decorate.

Making a Painted Sugarpaste Plaque

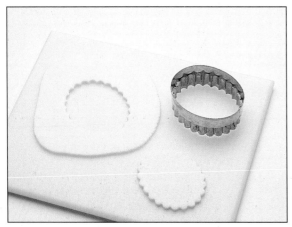

1. Use an oval or circular-shaped cutter to cut out the plaque from thinly rolled out sugarpaste.

2. Use a food colouring pen to draw the outline of the design onto the dry sugar plaque.

3. Paint the design using fine paint brushes and powdered food colourings with water.

4. The completed painted design.

5. A selection of painted sugar plaques.

Sugarpaste Quantities

Cake Sizes	13cm (5in) square 15.5cm (6in) round	15.5cm (6in) square 17.5cm (7in) round	17.5cm (7in) square 20cm (8in) round	20cm (8in) square 22.5cm (9in) round	22.5cm (9in) square 25cm (10in) round	25cm (10in) square 27.5cm (11in) round	27.5cm (11in) square 30cm (12in) round
Quick Sugar-paste or Gelatine Icing	500g (1lb)	750g (1½lb)	875g (1¾lb)	1kg (2lb)	1.25kg (2½lb)	1.5kg (3lb)	1.75kg (3½lb)

Decorating Ideas

A cake covered in sugarpaste looks so delicate and pretty that it hardly needs decorating; the soft lines and silky finish requires a dainty finishing touch.

Marbling

Sugarpaste lends itself to tinting in all shades, and a very effective way of colouring is to only partially knead the food colouring into the sugarpaste, giving a marbled effect to the icing. Another method is to use two even-sized pieces of sugarpaste, each coloured a different shade. Roll each colour into four thin rolls and place them together, alternating the colours, forming a stack. Roll out thinly to give a marbled effect and use to cover a cake, or for cutout work.

Crimping

Use the same method as marzipan crimping. Ensure the crimper is clean and dusted with cornflour (cornstarch). Only crimp on a freshly sugarpasted cake or the icing will be too rigid and may crack. Try out the design on a spare piece of sugarpaste before attempting to decorate the cake. Remember to release the crimper fully each time it is used to mark the pattern or the icing may tear.

Painted Designs

Try out this skill on a sugarpaste plaque or a runout sugar piece. If a mistake occurs, it gives you the chance to make another painted design. This form of decorating may be applied on to the surface of a royal iced or sugarpasted cake when you are confident enough to paint directly onto the surface.

Almost any design or shape can be transferred to the plaque or cake surface, either drawn freehand or traced. For festive designs, draw Christmas trees, bells, candles, holly leaves and lanterns. Other shapes could include flowers, animals, figures and simple scenes.

Use food colouring pens, available in assorted colours which are ideal for outlines and small work. Liquid, paste or powdered food colourings may be used and applied with a fine brush.

Ensure the surface on to which you are applying the design is completely dry. If you are making a sugar plaque, roll out the sugarpaste thinly and cut

1. Add food colouring to the sugarpaste using a cocktail stick. The colour can be partially kneaded in for a marbled look, or completely kneaded in for an even colour.

2. Coloured sugarpaste rolled out thinly and cut into different shapes using a variety of cocktail, alphabet and numeral cutters.

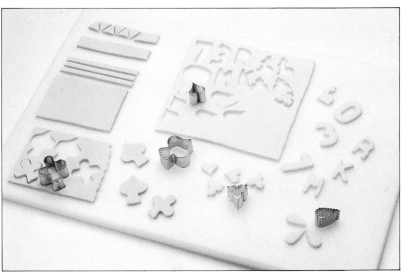

out an oval, round or square shape. Leave it until completely dry, then trace or draw a freehand design on to the surface. Using the food colouring pens or food colourings and a paint-brush, paint in the details. If you are using food colourings, choose a very fine paintbrush and place small drops of colouring onto separate pieces of greaseproof paper. Dip the brush into the chosen colour and blot the end with kitchen paper, eliminating any drops of colouring. Carefully paint the design, cleaning the brush

thoroughly between colours.

Make a border design on the cake by painting dots, lines or curves to create an attractive pattern. Always practise on a spare piece of sugarpaste before attempting the main design.

Cutouts make an instant decoration for a sugarpaste cake; simply colour the icing in the chosen colours, roll out thinly and cut out small icing shapes using aspic or cocktail cutters. Press these shapes on to the sides and top of the cake, securing with egg white if necessary.

LESSON 6

Royal Icing

Royal Icing

To produce a beautifully royal iced cake it is essential to make good royal icing, otherwise it is impossible to obtain a smooth coating. Everything must be spotless when making the icing as little bits that get into the icing will come to the surface on a flat coat.

Fresh egg whites or dried albumen may be used, both producing good results. A little lemon juice helps to strengthen the albumen in fresh egg whites, but care must be taken not to add too much as this will make the icing short, causing it to break during piping and it will be difficult to spread. Do not add glycerine to egg albumen as it does not set as hard as fresh egg white icing.

Adding the icing (confectioner's) sugar must be a gradual process, with plenty of mixing rather than beating during each addition of sugar, until the required consistency is reached.

Royal icing should be light and slightly glossy in texture, and should be capable of forming a peak with a fine point when a wooden spoon is drawn slowly out of the icing. This ensures that the icing will flow easily for piping or spread smoothly for coating, even though the consistencies may be different.

Royal icing made with too much sugar added too quickly will form a dull, heavy icing and be grainy in appearance. It will be difficult to work

with, producing bad results. As it sets it will be chalky in appearance instead of having a sparkle. It will soon become short and break when piped.

The icing must be covered to exclude all air and prevent the surface from setting. Damp cling film is a good way to seal the surface, or use an airtight container filled to the top with icing to exclude any air.

Use small quantities of icing at a time in a separate bowl from the main batch, covering with damp muslin (cheesecloth) during use. Keep the icing well scraped down; if this icing does become dry, causing hard bits, the whole batch of royal icing will not be affected.

Covering with a damp cloth is fine during short periods but if left overnight the icing will absorb all the moisture from the cloth, causing the consistency to be diluted.

If the icing is too stiff, add egg white or reconstituted egg albumen to make it softer. If the icing is too soft, gradually stir in more icing (confectioner's) sugar until the icing is of the required consistency.

Consistency

The consistency of royal icing varies for different uses. Stiff for piping, slightly softer for flat or peaked icing, and thinner for runouts.

Piping consistency: when a wooden spoon is drawn out of the icing it should form a fine, sharp point; termed stiff peak.

Flat or Peaked consistency: when the spoon is drawn out of the icing it should form a fine point which curves over at the end; termed soft peak.

Runouts consistency: soft peak to pipe the outlines, and thick cream consistency to fill in the shapes.

Glycerine

Glycerine may be added to royal icing provided that it is not made with egg albumen. Glycerine stops the icing from drying very hard so also makes cutting easier. Do not add glycerine to icing which is to be used for fine tube work, piped flowers or runouts.

Mix the glycerine to the finished icing and beat in. Add 8-10ml (1½-2 teaspoons) to each 500g (1lb/3½ cups) icing (confectioner's) sugar.

Royal Icing 1

This is a traditional icing used to cover celebration cakes. According to the consistency made, it may be used for flat icing, peaked icing or piping designs.

Place the egg whites and lemon juice into a clean bowl. Using a clean wooden spoon, stir to break up the egg whites. Add sufficient icing sugar and mix well to form the consistency of unwhipped cream. Continue mixing and adding small quantities of sugar every few minutes until the desired consistency has been reached, mixing well after each addition.

The icing should be smooth, glossy and light. Stir in the glycerine. Do not add too much sugar too quickly as this will produce a dull, heavy icing which is difficult to handle.

Allow the icing to rest before using it; cover the surface with a piece of damp cling film and seal well. Stir the icing thoroughly before use to disperse the air bubbles, then adjust the consistency if necessary.

This icing is suitable for flat or peaked icing, piping and runouts.

Makes 500g (1lb/3½ cups) royal icing.

INGREDIENTS
2 egg whites
1ml (¼ teaspoon) lemon juice
500g (1lb/3½ cups) icing
(confectioner's) sugar, sieved
5ml (1 teaspoon) glycerine

Making Royal Icing

1. Measure the lemon juice and add it to the bowl containing the egg whites.

2. Sift some of the measured icing sugar into the bowl.

3. Using a wooden spoon, stir the icing sugar into the egg whites and lemon juice.

4. Stir in sufficient icing sugar until the consistency is of thick cream, then beat well.

5. Royal icing beaten until smooth and white, after gradually adding enough icing sugar until thick.

6. Soft peak consistency of royal icing, ready to use for flat or peaked icing.

7. Sharp peak consistency of royal icing, ready for piping.

Colouring
Royal Icing

1. Add the food colouring to the royal icing a little at a time using a cocktail stick.

2. Stir the colouring into the icing until blended.

3. Evenly coloured royal icing, ready to use.

Royal Icing 2

Dried powered egg albumen may be used in place of fresh egg whites for royal icing. Simply blend the egg albumen with water and use like egg whites. Used as flat icing for tiered cakes, it sets hard enough to support the weight of the cakes.

Put the egg albumen into a clean bowl, gradually stir in the water and blend well together until the liquid is smooth and free from lumps.

Add sufficient sugar and mix well to the consistency of unwhipped cream. Continue mixing and adding small quantities of sugar every few minutes until the desired consistency has been reached, mixing well after each addition of sugar. The icing may be made in an electric mixer on a slow speed and using a whisk, not a beater.

The finished icing should be smooth, glossy and light. Do not add too much sugar too quickly as this will produce a dull, heavy icing which is difficult to handle.

Allow the icing to settle before using it; cover the surface with a piece of damp cling film and seal well. Stir the icing thoroughly before use to disperse the air bubbles, then adjust the consistency if necessary.

This icing is suitable for flat or peaked icing, piping and runouts. Use double-strength dried egg albumen for runouts so that they will set hard enought to remove from the paper.

Makes 500g (1lb/3½ cups) royal icing.

INGREDIENTS
15ml (1 tablespoon)
dried egg albumen
75ml (5 tablespoons) tepid water
500g (1lb/3½ cups) icing
(confectioner's) sugar, sieved

Flat Icing

Royal icing cannot be applied quickly. Thin layers of icing are applied to the cake in sections and time has to be allowed in between for each to dry.

Make a quantity of royal icing to soft peak consistency and cover with a clean, damp muslin (cheesecloth) to prevent drying make sure the marzipan on the cake is dry and firm, then place the board and cake on a turntable.

Spread a layer of icing about 5mm (¼in) thick evenly over the top of the cake, remove the excess icing from the edges with a small palette knife. Remove from the turntable and place on a rigid surface.

Stand directly in front of the cake with a rule or straight edge poised at the far edge of the cake. Hold the rule or straight edge comfortably in both hands and pull it towards you in one steady movement to smooth the top of the cake.

If the surface is not satisfactory, spread another thin layer of icing over the cake and repeat as above until the icing is smooth.

Remove the excess icing on the side of the cake to neaten the top edge using a small palette knife. Leave to dry for at least 4 hours, or overnight, in a warm, dry place.

Place the cake on a turntable again, spread a layer of icing 5mm (¼in) thick around the side of a round cake. Carefully remove any excess icing from the top edge.

Place a side scraper on to the side of the cake, resting on the board. Pull the side scraper with one hand while rotating the turntable with the other hand, in one continuous steady movement. The side of the cake should be completely smooth. Repeat if necessary.

Carefully pull off the scraper, which will leave a fine pull off mark on the round cake. Using a palette knife, remove the excess icing around the top of the cake. For a square cake, ice two opposite sides. Spread the icing onto one side, pull the side scraper across to smooth. Trim off excess icing and repeat on opposite sides, allowing time in between to dry.

1. Place the marzipanned cake with cake board on the turntable. The royal icing should be at soft peak consistency.

2. Use a small palette knife to spread the icing smoothly over the top of the cake to cover evenly.

3. Remove the excess icing from the top edges of the cake.

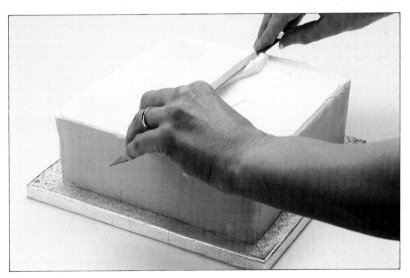

4. Steadily pull the straight edge across the top of the cake in one movement to smooth the icing.

5. Trim away the excess icing from the top edges of the cake to neaten before drying.

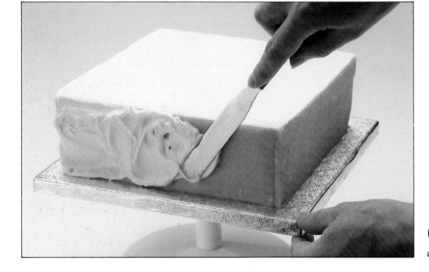

6. Use a small palette knife to smoothly spread the side of the dry cake with icing.

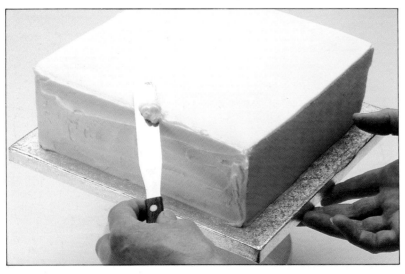

7. Remove the excess icing from the dry icing on the top edge of the cake.

8. Pull the side scraper across the side of the cake. Trim away the excess icing from the top edge and corners of the cake to neaten before drying.

9. The cake covered with one coat of royal icing. Dry before coating again.

10. Spread a thin layer of icing along one side of the cake board to cover evenly.

11. Pull the side scraper over the icing on the cake board to smooth.

Royal Icing Quantity Guide

It is difficult to estimate how much royal icing will be used to ice a cake as the quantity varies according to how the icing is applied and to the thickness of layers. The design also has to be taken into account, whether it is just piping, or runouts and sugar pieces.

The best guide to follow when icing cakes is to make up the royal icing in small batches using 1kg (2lb/7 cups) of icing (confectioner's) sugar, which is double the quantity of the recipe. Each batch of icing made is fresh and free from any impurities which may occur when large quantities are made for one cake.

The chart below is a guide for covering each cake with two or three thin layers of flat royal icing.

Cake Size	Quantity of Royal Icing
13cm (5 inch) square.	500g (1lb/3½ cups)
15.5cm (6in) round.	750g (1½lb/4¾ cups)
15cm (6in) square.	
17.5cm (7in) round.	1kg (2lb/7 cups)
17.5cm (7in) square.	
20cm (8in) round.	1.25kg (2½lb/8¾ cups)
20cm (8in) square.	
22.5cm (9in) round.	1.5kg (3lb/10½ cups)
22.5cm (9in) square.	1.75kg (3½lb/12¼ cups)
25cm (10in) round.	
25cm (10in) square.	
27.5cm (11in) round.	

Decorating

Royal icing must be the most versatile Icing; it can be smoothed on to a cake to make a perfectly flat base for decorating, or peaked and swirled to give texture to a Christmas cake. It can be piped as curves or lines from different-shaped tubes.

Peaks and Swirls

A simple way to decorate a Christmas cake is with swirls or peaks of icing with a festive centrepiece on the top. To swirl royal icing, quickly spread the top and sides of the cake as evenly as possible. Using a small palette knife, go over the surface again in circular movements to swirl the icing.

To make beautifully even peaks, the icing must be of soft peak consistency. Cover the cake evenly with icing and smooth the top and sides with a palette knife. Using a small, clean palette knife, dip one side into the icing. Starting from the top edge and working around the edge of the cake, press the palette knife onto the icing and pull sharply away to form a peak. Repeat to form about six peaks, then re-dip the palette knife into the icing and repeat to make peaks around the top edge.

Make the second row of peaks, in between the first row, about 10mm (½in) below and continue until the

side is complete. Repeat to peak the top, leaving a smooth area for decorations if necessary. If the top is to be flat, follow the step-by-step guide for flat icing the top of a cake then, when completely dry, peak the sides as above.

Purchased Decorations

Flat or smooth icing takes more time and patience, but by following the step-by-step instructions and with practice, a good standard can be achieved. Once iced smoothly, the cake may be decorated with purchased decorations to suit any occasion. Tie ribbon around the side of the cake and use sugar flowers, or coloured dragées to decorate the top. Cake decorating suppliers have a vast selection to choose from.

Painted Designs

Painting or pen designs may be applied in the same way as the sugarpaste painted designs. Damp is

the main problem as the icing absorbs moisture, causing colours to bleed. Small runout icing plaques can be made in any shape, then the design painted on with either food colourings and a fine paintbrush, or food colouring pens. Store in a warm, dry place.

Coloured Swirls

Coloured icing spread into swirls over the surface is a simple way of introducing colours on to a white royal iced cake. Spread the top and sides of a marzipanned cake with white royal icing. Smooth the top and sides with a palette knife. Tint a small quantity of royal icing; use a small palette knife, dip into the tinted icing and press on to the cake and swirl. Repeat by swirling the icing, evenly spaced, over the top and sides of the cake. Try several shades of icing or contrasting colours to give a variety of swirls on the cake.

Quick Icings & Frostings

Buttercream

A versatile filling, icing or frosting for almost any type of cake, which can be spread evenly and patterned with a knife or scraper, or piped into designs using different icing tubes. Flavour with chocolate, coffee, orange or lemon rinds.

Place the butter in a bowl and beat until pale and fluffy. Add the icing (confectioner's) sugar a little at a time, beating well after each addition. Beat in the lemon juice, vanilla essence (extract) and any other flavouring if required.

Alternatively, place all the ingredients into a food processor and blend for 30 seconds.

Makes 250g (8oz/1¾ cups)

INGREDIENTS
125g (4oz/½ cup) butter, softened
250g (8oz/1¾ cups) icing (confectioner's) sugar, sieved
10ml (2 teaspoons) lemon juice
few drops vanilla essence (extract)

VARIATIONS
15ml (1 tablespoon) cocoa blended with 15ml (1 tablespoon) of boiling water.
10ml (2 teaspoons) instant coffee blended with 5ml (1 teaspoon) of boiling water.
10ml (2 teaspoons) lemon, orange or lime rind.

Making Buttercream

1. Beat the butter with a wooden spoon until light and fluffy.

2. Sift some of the sugar into the bowl.

3. Stir the sugar into the butter, then beat well after each addition.

4. Add the lemon juice or other flavourings and beat until smooth.

5. Use a cocktail stick to add food
colouring to the buttercream.

6. Beat the food colouring
into the buttercream.

7. Buttercream evenly coloured
and ready to use.

8. Spread the buttercream on to the top of the cake using a small palette knife.

9. Cake evenly coated with buttercream before it is smoothed.

10. Smooth the buttercream using a small palette knife dipped into hot water.

American Icing

A pure white icing (frosting) made with white vegetable fat (shortening) instead of butter or margarine. It is light in texture and can be flavoured or coloured if desired. As the icing is white, tinting with food colouring is more accurate.

Place the white fat in a bowl and beat until white and fluffy. Add the icing sugar a little at a time, beating well after each addition. Beat in the vanilla essence and any other flavouring if required.

Alternatively, place all the ingredients into a food processor and blend for 30 seconds.

Makes 250g (8oz/1¾ cup)

INGREDIENTS
125g (4oz/½ cup) white vegetable fat (shortening)
250g (8oz/1¾ cups) icing (confectioner's) sugar, sieved
15ml (3 teaspoons) milk
5ml (1 teaspoon) vanilla essence (extract)

VARIATIONS
15ml (1 tablespoon) cocoa blended with 15ml (1 tablespoon) boiling water.
10ml (2 teaspoons) instant coffee blended with 5ml (1 teaspoon) of boiling water.
10ml (2 teaspoons) lemon, orange or lime rind.

Crême au Beurre

A light-textured buttercream suitable for large and small cakes, which keeps the cakes moist. It spreads or pipes well, giving a glossy finish. For best results, make and use it when required; do not chill or freeze until it has been applied to the cake.

Place the sugar and water in a saucepan. Heat gently until the sugar has dissolved, stirring occasionally. Boil rapidly for about 1 minute until the syrup reaches thread stage. Test by placing a little syrup between two teaspoons: when pulled apart, a thread of syrup should form.

Whisk the egg yolks and pour in a steady stream of syrup, whisking all the time. Continue to whisk until the mixture is thick and pale.

Beat the butter in a separate bowl until pale and fluffy; add the egg mixture a little at a time, beating or whisking gently after each addition, until all the egg mixture has been incorporated.

Add any flavourings at this stage, if required, and use at once.

Makes 250g (8oz/1¾ cup)

INGREDIENTS
90g (3oz/6 tablespoons) caster (superfine) sugar
60ml (4 tablespoons) water
2 egg yolks, beaten
155g (5oz/½ cup + 2tbsp) unsalted (sweet) butter, softened

Glacé Icing

Place the sugar into a bowl; using a wooden spoon, gradually stir in the water until the icing is the same consistency as thick cream. Tint with food colouring if desired.

INGREDIENTS
250g (8oz/1¾ cups) icing (confectioner's) sugar, sieved 30-45ml (2-3 tablespoons) boiling water

VARIATIONS
Add 10ml (2 teaspoons) cocoa to the sugar. Replace the water with any fruit juice, or strong black coffee.

Making Crême au Beurre

1. Measure the water and sugar into the saucepan.

2. Dissolve sugar in the water to form sugar solution before boiling to a syrup.

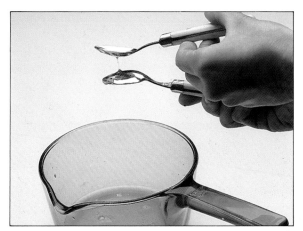

3. Test a little of the boiled sugar syrup between two teaspoons: a thread is formed when the spoons are pulled apart.

4. Pour a thin stream of sugar syrup into the beaten egg yolks.

5. Whisk well after each addition. Whisk the mixture until light and thick.

6. Beat the butter with a wooden spoon until light and fluffy.

7. Pour the egg mixture into the butter.

8. Whisk the mixture gently after each addition until light and creamy.

9. Add some grated orange rind to flavour the Crème au Beurre.

10. Use a spatula to carefully mix in the orange rind without beating.

Quick Frosting

A quickly-made icing (frosting) suitable for pouring over cakes to give a smooth, satin finish or for spreading with a knife to give a textured appearance.

Half-fill a saucepan with water and bring to the boil, then remove from the heat. Place the butter, milk and icing sugar in a heatproof bowl over a saucepan of hot water. Stir this occasionally until melted, then beat with a wooden spoon until smooth.

Use immediately to pour over a cake to coat evenly, or leave until thicker, then spread over a cake to give a textured finish.

This quantity will cover a 17.5-20cm (7-8in) square cake, or a 20-22.5cm (8-9in) round cake.

INGREDIENTS
60g (2oz/4 tablespoons) butter
45ml (3 tablespoons) milk
250g (8oz/1¾ cups) icing (confectioner's) sugar, sieved

VARIATION 1
Fruit or Coffee Frosting: replace the milk with any flavour fruit juice, or strong black coffee.

VARIATION 2
Fudge Frosting: replace 90g (3oz/¾ cup) of icing (confectioner's) sugar with dark, soft brown sugar.

VARIATION 3
Chocolate Frosting: add 15ml (1 tablespoon) of cocoa to the icing (confectioner's) sugar or 60g (2oz) of plain (semi-sweet or unsweetened) chocolate to the milk and butter.

Chocolate Fudge Icing

A rich chocolate icing (frosting) suitable for coating, filling and piping onto cakes. Use the icing immediately to give a smooth, glossy finish or leave it to thicken, then spread with a small palette knife to give a swirly textured finish.

Half-fill a saucepan with water and bring to the boil, then remove from the heat. Place the chocolate and butter in a heat-proof bowl over the saucepan of hot water. Stir this occasionally until melted.

Add the egg and stir with a wooden spoon until mixed together and well blended. Remove the bowl from the saucepan, stir in the sugar and beat until smooth.

Use immediately for pouring over a cake smoothly or leave to cool for a thicker consistency.

This quantity will cover a 17.5-20cm (7-8in) square cake, or a 20-22.5cm (8-9in) round cake.

INGREDIENTS
125g (4oz/4 squares) plain (semi-sweet or unsweetened) chocolate
60g (2oz/4 tablespoons) butter
1 egg, beaten
185g (6oz/1¼ cups) icing (confectioner's) sugar, seived

Simple Decorations

Buttercream is easy to use for decorating a cake. It can be coloured and flavoured, used as a cake covering, topping, filling and for piping. The consistency remains the same for all finishes.

Iced Top and Coated Sides

Sandwich a sponge cake together with buttercream and spread the sides to coat evenly. Press chopped nuts, coconut, chocolate strands (vermicelli) or crushed macaroons on to the side of the cake to coat evenly. Spread the top as evenly and smoothly as possible. Make a pretty edging with red and green coloured cherries cut into thin slices and arranged around the edge, or arrange with a selection of marzipan fruits or sugar flowers.

Scraper Design

A side scraper can produce a very attractive pattern when used to smooth the icing on the sides and top of a cake, or in a zig-zag movement on the top. It looks like a plastic side scraper but the edge is serrated, rather than flat.

Spread the top and sides of the cake with Crème au Beurre, buttercream, chocolate or American icing (frosting). Place the side scraper on to the side of the cake and pull across or around the side in one movement to make the pattern. Repeat to pattern the top if desired and decorate with fruit rinds cut into tiny shapes using aspic cutters, chocolate dots, nuts cherries, angelica or sugar flowers.

Finishes with Simple Icings

Lines: Buttercream lends itself to various finishes, being soft and easy to spread. Try using a small palette knife to create an attractive finishes. Spread the top and sides of a cake with buttercream, Crème au Beurre, chocolate or American icing (frosting). Using a small palette knife on the top of the cake, spread the icing backwards and forwards in a continuous movement to make a lined pattern. To create the same pattern on the sides, place the palette knife at the base of the cake and work up and down, pressing the knife into the icing (frosting) marking the same pattern. Apply a few nuts or sugar flowers to make a pretty border.

Peaks: These can also be formed in soft icing (frosting) just like royal icing peaks. Once the top and sides of a cake have been spread evenly with icing (frosting), press a small palette knife onto the icing and pull sharply away to form a peak. Ensure the icing (frosting) is not too firm or the palette knife may pull the sponge cake away with it, causing crumbs. Peak the side, working around the top of the cake and gradually down to the base, keeping the top smooth. Arrange some mimosa balls and angelica, or split almonds and crystallied violets to make a flower design.

Edible Decorations: Many ingredients can make attractive decorations. Place some cocoa or coffee on a piece of kitchen paper, then dip a skewer into the powder and press onto an iced cake to make a line. Repeat, marking lines in both directions to form a lattice design. Very fine lines of chopped nuts may be used in the same way. Melted chocolate drizzled on to the surface makes a cake look special.

Coloured Swirls: The use of coloured icing spread into swirls over the surface is a simple way of introducing colours onto a cake iced (frosted) with buttercream. Spread the top and sides of a cake with buttercream; smooth with a palette knife. Tint a small quantity of buttercream. Use a small palette knife, dip into the tinted icing (frosting) and press on to the cake and swirl. Repeat by swirling the icing (frosting), evenly spaced, over the top and sides of the cake. Try several shades of one colour icing or contrasting colours to give a variety of swirls on the cake.

Quick Icing and Frosting quantities for Buttercream, Crème au Beurre and American Icing

Cake Size	17.5cm (7in) square 17.5-20cm (7in-8in) round	20cm (8in) square 22.5cm (9in) round	22.5cm (9-10in) square 25-27.5cm (10-11in) round
Icing and Frosting Quantity	250g (8oz/1¾ cups)	375g (12oz/2⅔ cups)	500g (1lb/3½ cups)

LESSON 8

Introduction
to Piping

Basic Piping

The skill of using a piping bag is worth mastering. A purchased plastic or fabric piping bag or homemade paper one, fitted with a plain or fancy piping tube, can produce shells and scrolls, bold edgings or very fine filigree work.

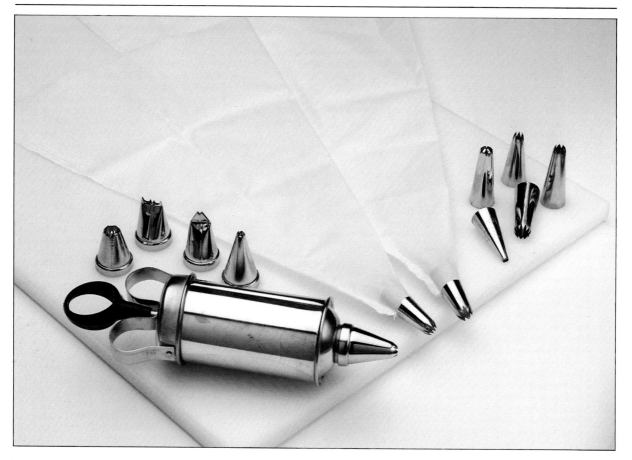

Although piping appears to be complicated, with patience, practise and a few simple guidelines, you will discover how easy it is.

Icing: Before using any piping equipment it is essential to have the icing at the correct consistency. When a wooden spoon is drawn out of royal icing, it should form a fine but sharp point. If the icing is too stiff it will be very difficult to squeeze out of the bag; if too soft the icing will be difficult to control and the piped shapes will lose their definition.

Commercial Bags: Piping bags made of a washable fabric are available from most cake specialist or kitchen shops. They are especially good to use if you are a beginner as they are easy to handle. Sizes vary from small to large and are ideal for piping cream, buttercream and icing onto gâteaux and simple sponge cakes. Plastic bags for piping are also available.

Paper Piping Bags: These can also be purchased ready-made, but that is rather expensive as they are so simple to make. The great advantage of paper piping bags is that they can be made in advance in various sizes and can be used without a piping tube, simply by snipping the end into different shapes. After use they are thrown away, or, if the icing runs out, simple transfer the tube to a new paper bag. Choose good quality greaseproof (waxed) paper for making the bags and follow the instructions below carefully.

Piping Tubes: These are available in a wide variety of shapes and sizes, metal and plastic, with or without a collar, so it is quite daunting to know which ones to choose. For beginners, it is advisable to start with a small selection, choosing perhaps two writing tubes and a small, medium and large star tube. After mastering these, build up a collection for trying out new piping designs.

Straight-sided metal tubes fit commercial bags as well as paper piping bags and give a clean, sharp result. Kept clean and stored carefully they will never need replacing and are worth the extra expense.

Some piping tubes have a collar with a screw thread at the top. This fits some commercial bags and icing syringes and has to be fitted with a screw piece. Once the bag or syringe is filled with icing, any tube with a collar may be attached so the tubes can be changed while piping. The disadvantage of these bags and tubes is that sometimes the screw is forced out of the end of the bag while piping. A collar tube is unsuitable for use with a paper piping bag.

Making a Paper Piping Bag

1. Fold the rectangle of greaseproof (waxed) paper diagonally in half so that the two triangles are equal.

2. Cut into two triangles.

3. Fold the blunt end of the triangle over into a sharp cone to the centre and hold in position.

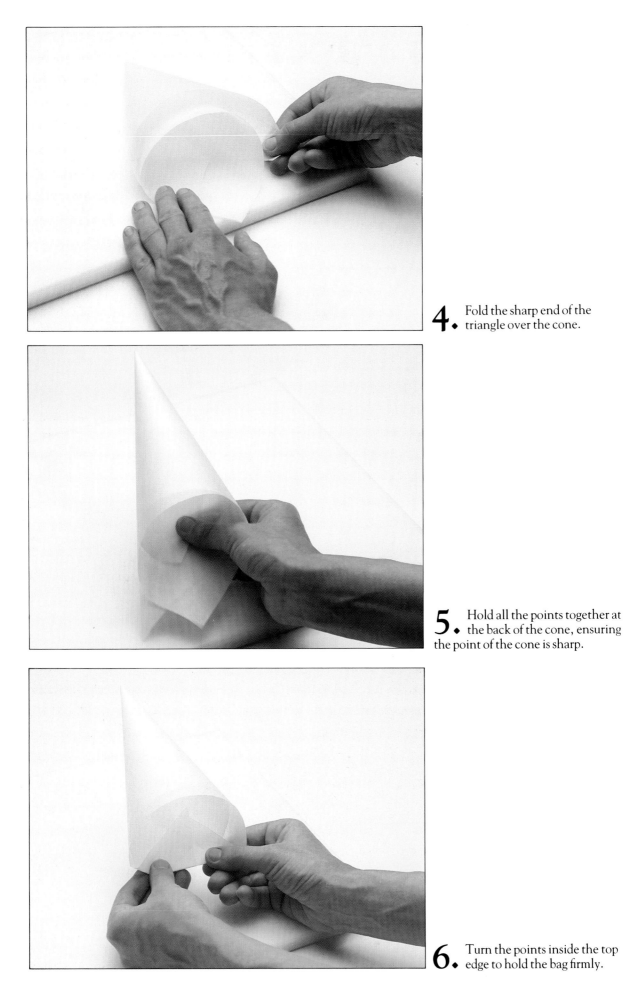

4. Fold the sharp end of the triangle over the cone.

5. Hold all the points together at the back of the cone, ensuring the point of the cone is sharp.

6. Turn the points inside the top edge to hold the bag firmly.

Trimming the Paper Piping Bag

1. Cut off the point of the bag, at an angle. Make the second cut across the pointed end of the bag to form an inverted V shape.

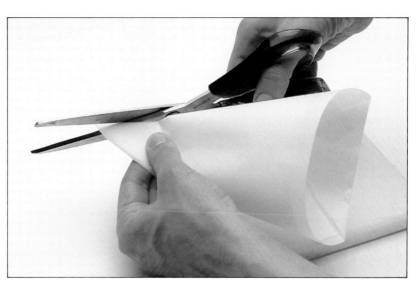

2. The open V shape at the end of the bag, ready to pipe leaves.

3. Cut the W shape at the end of the piping bag, after the point has been cut off.

Fitting a Piping Tube and Filling the Bag

1. Snip the point off the end of the piping bag.

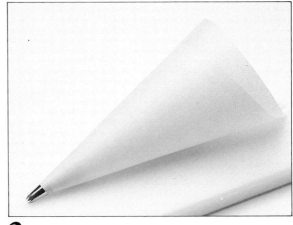

2. The bag fitted with a star tube.

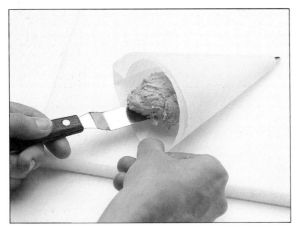

3. Use a small palette knife to place the icing in the piping bag.

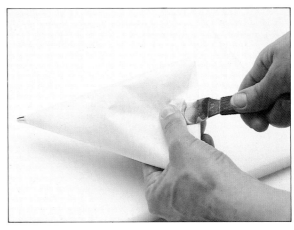

4. Press the bag over the icing and withdraw the palette knife.

5. Fold the top corners of the bag into the centre.

6. Fold down the top of the bag, ready for piping.

Simple Piping

Piping is the obvious choice when decorating a cake, but it is easy to be discouraged by complicated piping designs. Begin with these simple designs and practise until you are proficient, then you may apply these skills to decorating a cake.

Choose just a simple star tube and fit it into a greaseproof paper piping bag to pipe swirls, scrolls and shells. Tint some buttercream or royal icing of sharp peak consistency with a small amount of food colouring. Half-fill the piping bag, fold down the top and squeeze the icing to the end of the tube. Place the icing tube just onto the surface of the cake. Pipe a swirl of icing in a circular movement, stop pressing the bag and pull up sharply to break the thread. Repeat to pipe swirls around the top edge and base of the cake if desired.

To pipe a star shape from the same tube, hold the bag straight above the surface of the cake. Press the icing out to form a star on the edge of the cake, then stop pressing and pull up sharply to break the icing; repeat to make a neat border.

To pipe scrolls hold the piping bag at an angle so that the piping tube is almost on its side.
Pipe some icing on the top edge of the cake to secure the scroll. Pipe outwards in a circular movement and return the piping tube to the edge of

the cake. Stop pressing the bag and break off the icing. Repeat again, but pipe the icing inwards to the cake in a circular movement, then return the piping tube just to the edge. This is piping scrolls curving inwards and outwards. For a different design, pipe the scrolls in one direction only.

To pipe shells, hold the piping bag at an angle to the cake so that the piping tube is almost on its side. Press out some icing and secure to the surface of the cake, press gently move the tube forward, then move it slowly up, over and down almost like a rocking movement. Stop pressing and break off the icing by pulling the tube towards you. Repeat, piping the icing onto the end of the first shell to make a shell edging.

To pipe lines, fit the piping bag with a plain writing tube and fill with icing. Pipe a line of icing, securing the end to the surface of the cake. Continue to pipe the icing just above the surface of the cake, allowing the thread to fall in a straight or curved line. Stop pressing the bag and sharply break off the line of icing.

To pipe leaves, cut the end of the greaseproof paper piping bag into an

inverted V. Fill with icing and press the icing to the end of the bag. Place the end on the surface of the cake. Press out the icing to form a leaf shape, press harder to make a larger leaf then sharply break off the icing. Repeat to make a pretty border, or just to decorate flowers or to make a design.

To pipe a star border, use a greaseproof paper piping bag, trim the end into a W shape and fill with icing. Place the pointed end on the surface of the cake at an angle and pipe out a star shape. Repeat, piping the stars close together to form a border design.

To pipe basketweave, fit a paper piping bag with a ribbon or basketweave tube. Pipe a vertical line from the top of the cake to the bottom. Pipe 2cm (¾in) lines across the vertical line at intervals the width of the tube. Pipe another vertical line of icing on the edge of the horizontal lines, then pipe short lines of icing in between the spaces across the vertical line to form a basketweave. Repeat until the cake is completely covered.

Simple Piping

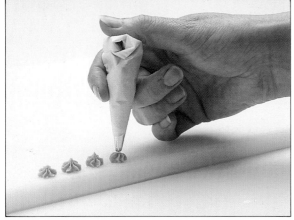

1. Hold the piping bag vertically and pipe a simple star of icing. Stop pressing the bag to stop the flow of icing and lift up sharply.

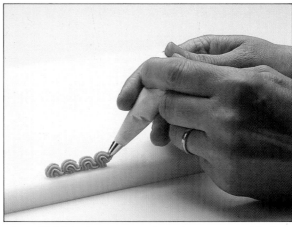

2. Hold the bag at an angle and pipe a row of shells. Stop pressing the bag to finish each shell, before piping the next one.

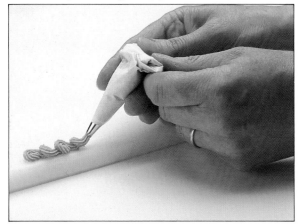

3. Hold the piping bag at an angle and pipe reverse scrolls as a border. Pipe one scroll towards the edge and the second scroll away from the edge.

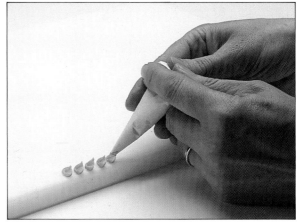

4. Use a greaseproof paper piping bag snipped into a V shape and pipe leaf shapes as a border.

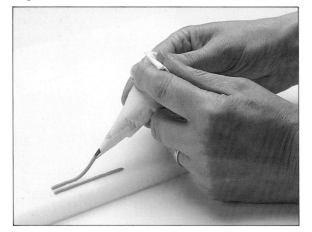

5. Use a plain writing tube to pipe lines of icing. Secure the end of the icing to the surface, then pipe allowing the thread to fall in position.

6. Pipe lines of icing; break off the thread by sharply lifting the tube upwards.

7. Using a greaseproof paper piping bag snipped into a W shape and piping a border design.

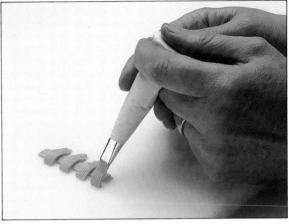

8. To pipe a basketweave, pipe a vertical line of icing, then overpipe horizontal lengths of icing at evenly spaced intervals.

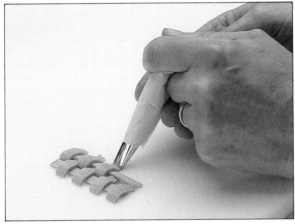

9. Pipe second vertical line of icing over the short horizontal lines, then repeat the pattern.

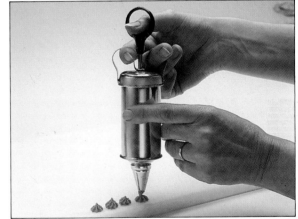

10. An icing syringe fitted with a star tube in the vertical position to pipe stars of icing.

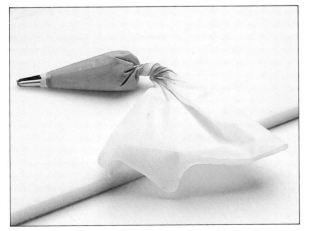

11. A purchased nylon piping bag filled with icing, fitted with a star tube.

12. Hold the nylon piping bag in an upright position and squeeze the top to pipe stars.

Simple Decorations

Once you have mastered the skills of piping, it is the most effective form of decoration on a cake. Piping can quickly transform a plain, everyday cake into something quite spectacular.

Buttercream Sponge: spread the top and sides of a 20cm (8in) round sponge cake with 250g (8oz/2 cups) of buttercream. Smooth the surface with a small palette knife dipped in hot water. Tint some buttercream with a few drops of orange food colouring and fill a nylon piping bag fitted with a small star tube. Pipe alternate inwards and outwards scrolls around the top and bottom edges of the cake. Mark 6.5cm (2½in) circle in the centre using a plain cutter and pipe scrolls around the outside of the marked circle. Pipe groups of three stars of icing at intervals around the side and top of the cake.

Basket Cake: make a quick-mix pudding basin cake (see chart on page 33) flavour 250g (8oz/2 cups) of buttercream with cocoa and spread thinly on the cake, place on a small cake board. Fit a paper piping bag with a basket or ribbon tube and fill with icing. Fold down the top and pipe a basketweave design all around the cake until completely covered. Pipe a shell edging around the base and the top edge using the same piping tube. Fold a 20cm (8in) length of foil into a narrow strip. Wrap 1.5cm (½in) wide ribbon just ovelapping around the strip of foil to cover, then secure the end with tape.

Bend to form a handle, press carefully into the top of the cake and tie a bow on the handle. Fill the centre of the basket with sugar and chocolate eggs, or sugar flowers.

Piping Techniques

Piping Techniques

When piping a celebration cake with royal icing, it is as well to practise before starting on the cake. Make sure the icing is the correct consistency. Use a piping bag fitted with a straight-sided metal tube, as this gives a clean sharp icing result.

Half-fill the bag with icing; do not be tempted to fill it to the top as it is more difficult to squeeze the icing out of a full bag. A good guide to remember is the smaller the icing tube, the less icing you require to work with.

Hold the piping bag comfortably, like a pencil, with the tube through the first two fingers and thumb. Apply the pressure at the top of the bag. Wrists and arms should be relaxed, ready to guide the tube.

Stand or sit comfortably and hold the tube just above the surface of the cake, in an upright position. Press the icing gently on the surface of the cake to form a star. Stop pressing and sharply lift the bag to break off the icing. Pipe another star next to the first one, and continue to pipe the required design.

For piping lines, the tube should be tilted at an angle and a continuous flow of icing should be maintained. Pipe the beginning of the line on to

the surface of the cake, lift the bag slightly and pipe just above the surface. Allow the line of icing to fall where required before breaking off the thread. See page 101 for instructions on making piped flowers.

Scrolls and Trellis Work

1. Hold a paper piping bag fitted with a star tube at an angle to pipe individual scrolls. Stop pressing the bag and pull off sharply to finish each scroll.

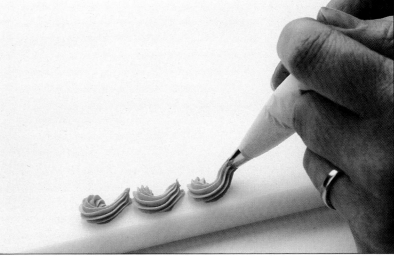

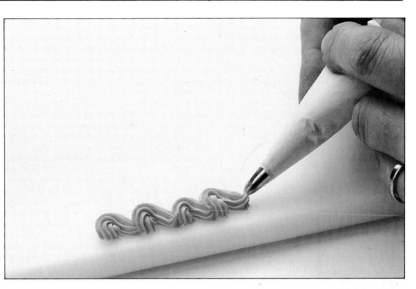

2. Pipe a line of joined-up scrolls.

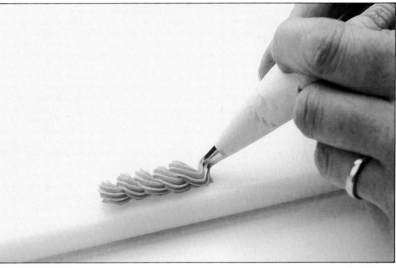

3. Hold the paper piping bag fitted with a star tube at an angle and pipe a continuous line of icing in a rope design.

4. Use a paper piping bag fitted with a plain writing tube to pipe a lattice or trellis design. Pipe evenly spaced lines of icing, allowing the thread of icing to fall straight.

5. Overpipe threads of icing in the opposite direction to form a lattice or trellis design.

Cornelli Work

1. Fill a paper piping bag with a No 0 or 00 piping tube. Hold your bag between your thumb and first finger using the bag like a pen. Draw a W and M shape with the piping tube keeping up a constant pressure. Work in an erratic pattern not in lines.

2. Completed cornelli work shown in a contrasting colour but it is equally effective worked in the same colour as the base.

Colours and Tints

The ordinary bottles of liquid colourings available in supermarkets and shops will readily tint or colour icings and frostings in the basic primary colours, and with careful blending other colours and shades can be made.

Moulded and cutout flowers and sugar pieces can now be coloured with blossom tints, or painted with lustre colours when dry. This prevents the risk of colours running into the icing when the atmosphere is damp, and also ensures that the colours will not quickly fade.

Good quality colours are available as pastes, powders and liquids. They are very concentrated and need to be added drop by drop using a cocktail stick to carefully tint the icing to a delicate colour. Remember that food colourings deepen on standing and dry a deeper colour than when first mixed. Colour icings in the daylight and leave them for at least 15 minutes to assess the colour.

If several batches of coloured icing have to be made, keep some icing in reserve to match the colour correctly. Always remember that a cake should look edible, so keep to pastel shades.

Step-by-Step Simple Flowers

Showing a variety of simply piped flowers using only a paper piping bag snipped into an inverted V.

1. Tint the icing pale mauve and press out a petal shape from the piping bag. Pipe three individual petals with the fourth petal in the centre.

2. Tint the icing pale pink and pipe 5 petals in a circle, then pipe another 3 petals in the centre of the 5 petals, and 2 more petals to finish the flowers.

3. Pipe 5 white petals in a circle. Fill a paper piping bag with yellow icing, and pipe one circle of icing in the centre, then over-pipe with another 2 circles.

4. Tint the icing pale pink and pipe 6 petals in a circle. Fill a paper piping bag with white icing, snip off the point and pipe a swirl of icing in the centre.

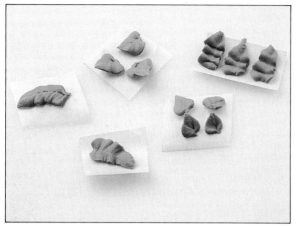

5. Tint the icing green and pipe the icing into short or long leaf shapes.

6. Tint the icing orange, hold the paper piping bag at an angle so it is almost flat with the surface. Pipe the petals flat in a circular movement, bringing the end inwards. Pipe 6 petals in a circle. Use yellow icing to pipe beads of icing in the centre.

7. Tint the icing yellow and pipe 5 petal shapes in a circle. Pipe a circle of orange icing in the centre from a paper piping bag with a tiny end snipped off.

8. Pipe 3 yellow petals in a circle, then pipe 2 more in the centre and pipe the last petal on top.

Simple Flowers Piped with a Petal Tube

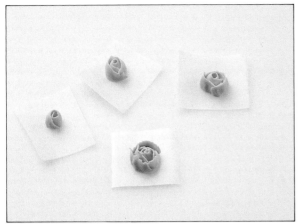

1. Using a petal tube with the thick end on the base, pipe a cone. Add more petals around the outside to the required size.

2. Pipe as for the rose bud, adding more petals as required but holding the tube flatter to create more open petals.

3. Holding the petal tube on the side so it is flat, pipe about 12 tiny petals in a circle. Using yellow icing, pipe small beads to fill the centre.

4. Holding the petal tube flat, pipe the petal shape in a circle. Pipe another 2 petals on each side. Pipe the fourth petal to join up the circle. Pipe the last petal the opposite way round in a circle. Pipe yellow threads of icing in the centre.

Simple Piped Flowers

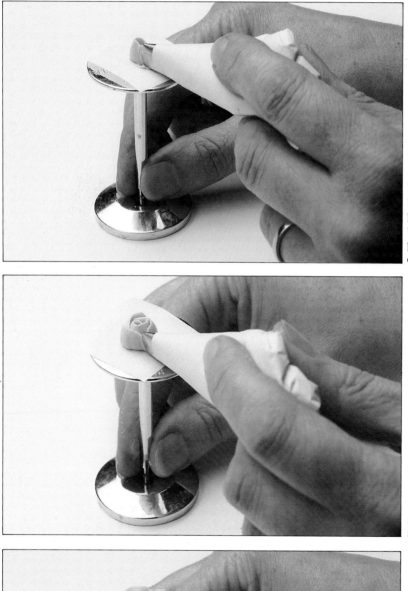

1. To pipe a rose secure a piece of greaseproof or waxed paper to the rose nail with a bead of icing. Pipe the centre using a petal tube on the paper and turning the nail at the same time to form a cone shape. Keep the piping tube upright and the thick end of the tube at the base.

2. Pipe the third petal around the centre petals turning the nail at the same time as pressing the bag.

3. Hold the piping bag at an angle to pipe the final petals. To pipe a rose bud, start with the centre cone, then pipe around more petals until the bud is the size required.

Simple Lettering on a Plaque

1. Trace the letters onto a piece of clean greaseproof or waxed paper. Place the tracing over the sugarpaste plaque and mark out each letter.

2. Using a filled paper piping bag fitted with a No 1 writing tube, pipe the outline of each letter. Stop pressing the piping bag halfway through each letter to prevent the icing piping on.

3. HAPPY BIRTHDAY piped on the plaque.

Simple Decorations

Once the cake has been marzipanned and iced, it is ready to be piped according to the design you have chosen. Always choose a simple design at first with simple piping; do not attempt too much, otherwise the result may be very disappointing.

Think carefully about the design and the colour of the cake. Cut out a paper template and transfer the design by pricking through or around the template with a pin onto the surface of the cake. Pipe the design using only one or two different piping tubes. Mark the design onto the side of the cake and repeat the piping to match the top, or tie ribbon around instead.

Add some simple sugar flowers and leaves, which may be piped in advance and stored. Most of them require just the paper piping bag trimmed to an inverted V.

Pink and White Wedding Cake: make a 25cm (10in) round and a 20cm (8in) round rich or light fruit cake or madeira cake, marzipanned and royal iced. Cut two paper circles each 5cm (2in) smaller than the top of each cake. Fold each circle in half, then fold the half circle twice more to form a cone shape. Place an upturned cup on the wide end of each cone and draw an arc shape around the outside of the cup. Using a pair of sharp scissors, cut out the arc shape to make a scallop. Open the template and place the larger size on the large cake. Mark around the template using a pin to transfer the design to the cake top.

Half-fill a bag fitted with a No 1 plain tube. Use white royal icing. Pipe a thread of icing from each point of the design. Repeat to pipe a second line 1.5cm (½in) outside the first scallopped design, then overpipe with pink icing using the same piping tube. Pipe short trailing threads of icing towards the top edge and base of the cake, keeping the thread touching the surface.

Pipe seven white beads of icing on each thread of icing nearest to the board and overpipe with pink beads. Use 16 simple pink sugar flowers and secure 8 on top of the cake with a little icing opposite each point. Secure the remaining 8 flowers to the end of each thread of icing on the side of the cake. Using a piping bag filled

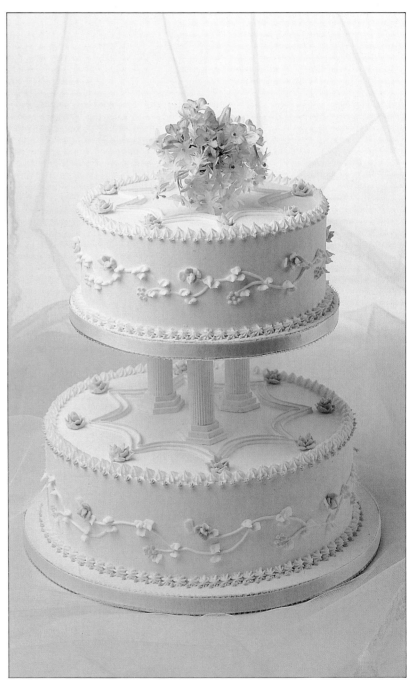

with white royal icing, snip into an inverted V and pipe leaves in groups around the side of the cake. Using a medium-sized star tube, pipe a star border around the top and bottom edges of the cake and leave to dry.

Repeat the same design on the

smaller cake. Trim the cake boards with white ribbon and support the top cake with three white cake pillars. Make an arrangement of silk flowers to go on top of the cake, secured with white marzipan or sugarpaste, or fill a small vase with silk or fresh flowers.

LESSON 10

Icing Runouts

Icing Runouts

Make simple runout shapes to decorate a variety of cakes. Choose bold shapes at first with one outline, then try some more complicated shapes. Icing consistency is very important, and do have everything ready

The consistency and texture of the royal icing must be right or the runouts will be difficult to make and handle. Use double strength dried egg albumen or egg whites with no additives such as glycerine or lemon juice. The icing should be light and glossy, not heavy and dull. When the spoon is lifted, a soft peak should form which will bend at the tip. This is the consistency required for piping the outline of the runouts. If the icing thread keeps breaking, it is because the consistency is too stiff or the icing has not been made correctly: too much sugar added too quickly and not enough mixing.

Icing to fill in the runout must be soft enough to flow with the aid of a paintbrush, just holding its shape until tapped, then becoming smooth.

Leave the icing to stand for at least 2 hours or overnight if possible, covered with damp muslin (cheesecloth), allowing any air bubbles to come to the surface. Tap the bowl several times until there are no more bubbles.

Once made, runouts can be kept successfully between layers of waxed or greaseproof paper in a box stored in a dry place. This means a quantity of runouts can be made in advance, allowing more time to flat ice and pipe the cake.

Runouts are very fragile so it is wise to choose a solid shape at first, and make more than required to allow for breakages. When you are confident about making simple, small, solid shapes, practise making finer pieces, figures and scenes. Accuracy, not

speed, is important when making runouts, so allow plenty of time.

EQUIPMENT
Good quality double sided waxed paper is best for tracing the design or shape on, and being fine it does not wrinkle as the runouts dry. If using single sided use the shiny side face up. For larger, more solid, runouts, non-stick baking parchment (paper) may be used instead. Pencil, fine paintbrush, cocktail stick, needle, paper piping bags, No 0 or piping tube. Royal icing, edible food colours, a board or tray on which to put runouts while they are being piped.

Making an Icing Runout

Royal Icing runouts are one of the most useful forms of cake decoration. They can be made in any shape or form by simply tracing over a chosen design or pattern.

Draw or trace the chosen design several times on a piece of paper, spaced well apart. Secure the paper to a flat surface with sticky tape or dots of icing. Cover the design with a piece of waxed paper and secure with four or six dots of icing.

Fit a paper piping bag with a No 0 tube and half-fill with icing to pipe the outline. Fill another paper piping bag with soft icing.

Pipe carefully around the outline with as few breaks as possible; a small runout can be piped with one continuous thread of icing. Squeeze out a little icing at an unobtrusive point of the runout and secure the icing thread. Lift the thread of icing just above the surface and squeeze the bag gently following the outline of the tracing, and allowing the thread to fall on the marked line around the shape of the runout. Stop squeezing to prevent the icing thread from running on, and join the icing at the point where it started.

Snip the pointed end off the soft icing bag and fill in the runout. Start by piping around the inside edge to keep the outline soft, otherwise it may break, and work towards the centre. Fill the shape so that the icing looks rounded and full.

Using a fine paintbrush, needle or cocktail stick, ensure the area is completely covered and the icing is smooth. Gently tap the board so that any air bubbles rise to the surface; if so, break these with a pin.

Carefully remove the waxed paper and runout from the template and leave to dry. Cover the drawing design with more waxed paper and repeat to make as many runouts and spares as required.

Leave the runouts to dry in a warm, dry place overnight until they set hard. The more quickly they dry, the glossier they will be. Carefully peel off the paper from the runout and store runouts in a box between layers of waxed paper.

Arrange runouts on the cake and secure with small dots of icing.

Christening Cake

Christening Cake:
Make a 20cm (8in) square rich or light fruit cake or Madeira cake. Marzipan and flat ice with royal icing.

Make four pairs of butterfly wings, a pair of booties, and a rattle runouts, tracing from the template and following the instructions. Make a few extra of each in case of breakages. Use pale blue icing.

When completely dry, carefully remove the runouts from the paper and half-fill a paper piping bag, fitted with a No 0 plain piping tube, with white royal icing.

Pipe tiny beads of icing all around the edge of each runout and pipe circles of beads around a centre bead of icing all over the booties to represent tiny flowers. Pipe threads of icing into bows on the booties and rattle, and pipe BABY across the centre of the rattle. Leave to dry.

Using a paper piping bag fitted with a medium-sized star tube, half-filled with white royal icing, pipe a shell border around the top edge and base of the cake. Pipe a star of icing on the back of the booties and rattle and place on the centre of the cake. Pipe a line of white icing at each corner and press the butterfly wings in position. Half-fill a paper piping bag fitted with a No 1 tube with blue icing. Pipe a thread down the centre of each butterfly, with two beads on the end. Pipe blue beads of icing in between each shell and leave to dry.
(See photograph on page 107)

Bootie Runout

1. The runout shape drawn on a piece of paper with waxed paper ready to cover the drawing.

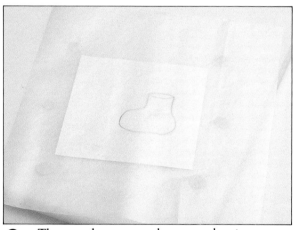

2. The waxed paper over the runout drawing held in position by beads of icing.

3. Using a number 0 plain piping tube and royal icing, pipe the outline of the runout with one continuous thread of icing.

4. Fill in the runout with pale blue royal icing starting at the edges and working inwards.

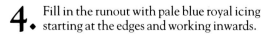

5. The runout completely filled in with royal icing.

6. Use a pin to level the surface of the icing runout.

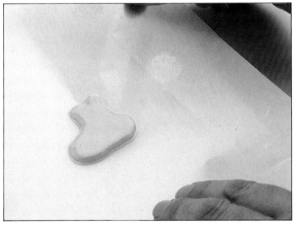

7. Gently vibrate the runout to smooth and level the icing and encourage any air bubbles to rise to the surface.

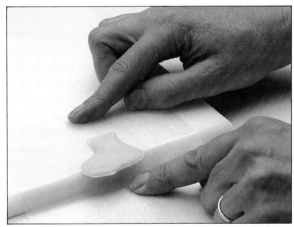

8. Carefully remove the runout from the paper by resting the runout on the edge of a board and pulling the waxed paper away from underneath.

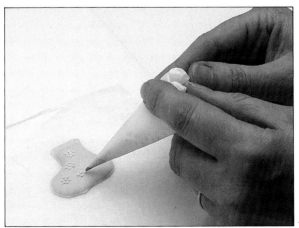

9. Using the outlining tube to pipe beads of icing on to the runout into a tiny flower pattern.

10. Pipe beads of icing around the outside edge of the runout.

Rattle Runout

1. The runout shape drawn on a piece of paper with a piece of waxed paper ready to cover the outline drawing.

2. The runout drawing covered with waxed paper and held in position by pressing on to the beads of icing ready for piping.

3. Use a number 0 plain piping tube and royal icing, pipe the outline of the runout with one continuous thread of icing.

4. The runout completely outlined with a thread of royal icing.

5. The round part of the runout filled in with pale blue royal icing and piping in the handle.

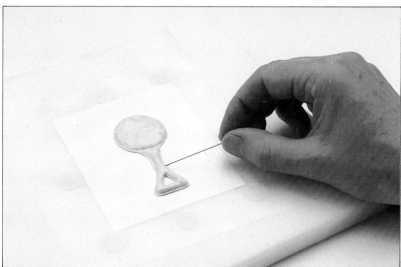

6. Use a pin to level the surface of the icing runout.

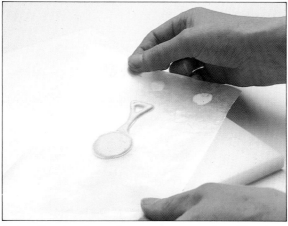

7. Gently vibrate the runout to smooth and level the icing and encourage any air bubbles to rise to the surface.

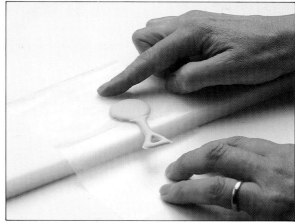

8. Carefully remove the runout from the paper by resting the runout on the edge of a board and pulling the waxed paper away from underneath.

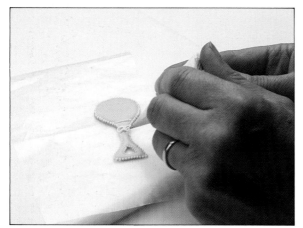

9. The runout outline piped with beads of icing from the number 0 tube. Pipe a tiny bow from one thread of icing.

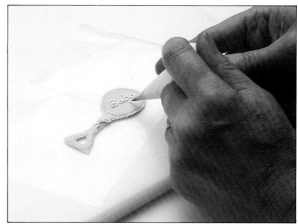

10. Pipe the word BABY in the centre of the runout.

LESSON 11

Ribbons

Ribbons in Cake Decorating

Choosing ribbons

Specialist shops and department stores offer an enormous variety of ribbons made from paper, nylon, polyester acetate and velvet. Each one has many different uses, but the type most commonly used is double-faced polyester satin with woven edges. This has an attractive sheen and will not fray. It is available in widths from 15mm to 2.5cm (⅟₁₆-1in), in over one hundred colours. Double-faced polyester satin is used for loops and bows in flower sprays, ribbon insertion and banding, and in all kinds of top and side decorations.

Nylon ribbon comes in a large range of colours and sizes, but it is really suitable only for banding boards or cakes. Nylon ribbons are unsuitable for bows and loops as they are too limp to hold a shape. To test whether a ribbon is suitable for loops, take a piece and fold it over. If it supports its weight, then it will look attractive. A ribbon that goes limp will produce flat, messy bows.

Velvet ribbon is rich looking but heavy, so it is usually used only for cake boards. Occasionally, narrow velvet ribbons are used as loops and trailers in sprays.

Paper and synthetic fabric ribbons, including filigree ribbons and metalic twine found in gift wrap departments, can also be used to great effect. Filigree ribbons are delicate in sprays, and look pretty around cake boards, particularly when combined with narrow satin ribbons.

Equipment

Ribbons in various fabrics
and widths
Fine paintbrush
Scissors
Tweezers
Craft knife with cutting blade
Craft knife with ribbon
insertion blade
Covered and uncovered
floristry wire
Florist's tape
Small piping bags with royal icing
Glass-headed pins

Ribbons are certainly the most widely used nonedible decoration in sugarcraft. As well as being used in all flower sprays and arrangements, ribbons are used to cover cake boards, band cakes, make pictures or designs on the top or side of a cake, or to decorate an entire cake, as in the Maypole Cake on page 126.

Ribbon collages

These simple, colourful designs are quick and easy to create and require no special skills. The ribbons can be positioned directly on the top or sides of a cake, or on a prepared sugarpaste plaque. Choose a simple design, such as the ones shown here, and draw it on paper. Cut different lengths of ribbon and place it on the design. Transfer the ribbons to the cake or plaque, fixing them with a little royal icing. The easiest way to do this is to paint the royal icing on the back of the ribbon with a fine paintbrush.

Make this sailboat collage with a ribbon flower made from 5mm (¼in) satin ribbon, and a sailboat cut from different widths of satin ribbon. Bands of narrow ribbon can be used to finish the collage. Add miniature bows in matching colours.

Ribbons of different textures and widths are used to make this pretty strawberry basket. To weave the basket, fix the light coloured ribbons in place, then thread the dark ribbons through them fixing with dots of icing. Add the curved handle, then fill the basket with flowers, leaves and red strawberries. Pipe tiny dots of white royal icing for the seeds.

Ribbon Insertion

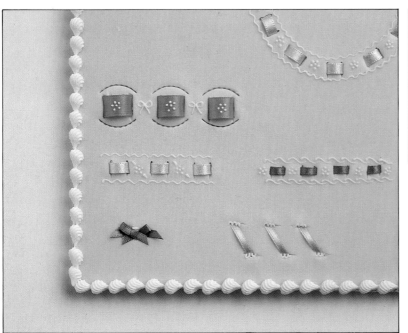

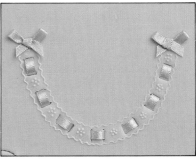

Ribbon insertion is a technique to create the effect that a single piece of ribbon has been threaded or woven through the icing. It is usually done on sugarpaste, although it can also be attractive on a marzipan-covered or royal-iced cake. The designs can be straight, diagonal or curved, and are often combined with crimper work.

The sugarpaste should be skinned, (ie.it should have dried to form a thin crust, but not be set hard). Plan the design on paper first, then use pins or a scriber to transfer it to the cake. Choose ribbon of the required width, and cut as many pieces as necessary to make the design. The pieces should be slightly longer than the spaces, leaving enough at each end to tuck in.

Use a very fine-bladed sharp knife, such as a craft knife or scalpel, to cut slits in the sugarpaste. Use the ribbon insertion blade or a pin to tuck the ribbon into the slits. It should stay in place without fixing.

Finish off the ribbon insertion with miniature bows and piped embroidery designs, if wished. If the ribbon is wide enough, tiny flowerrs can be piped on each piece.

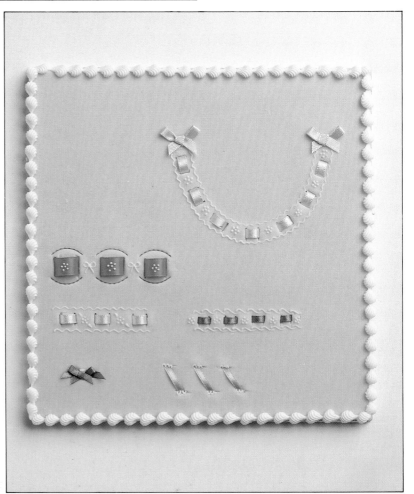

Banding Cake Boards

Any kind of ribbon can be used to cover the cake board. Choose colours which combine or contrast with the colours of the cake. It is usual to pin the ribbons onto the board, do not use glue, which may stain the ribbon, or give off toxic fumes.

1. Hold the board firmly and use a long, flat-headed pin to attach the ribbon in position.

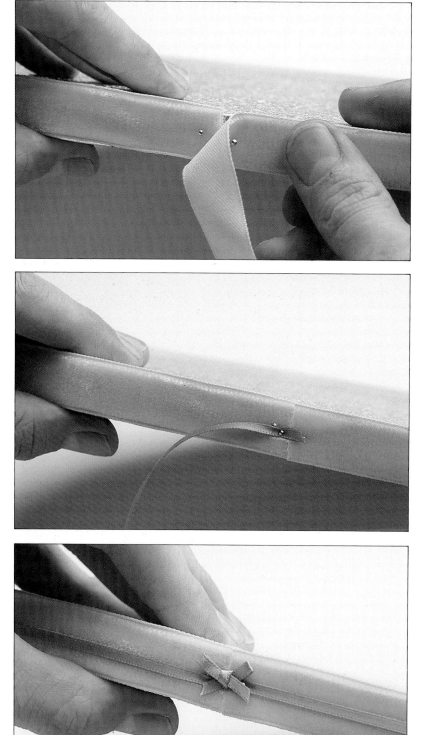

2. Stretch the ribbon tightly around the board. If the board is large it may be necessary to use more pins or dabs of royal icing to keep the ribbon from slipping. Pin in place at the join.

3. Cut the ribbon evenly. If adding a contrasting band, pin over the join and stretch the ribbon around the board as for the first one.

4. Pin the second ribbon and trim neatly. Finish off the board by pinning a small bow over the join.

Floristry Ribbon

Floristry ribbon is made from shiny paper, and it is used in commercial bouquets and in gift wrapping. It is very inexpensive, and it can be used in cake decorating to band boards, for ribbon collages, and for simple curled designs.

1. Cut the ribbon into lengths of about 60cm (24in). Hold it tightly to stop if from curling up.

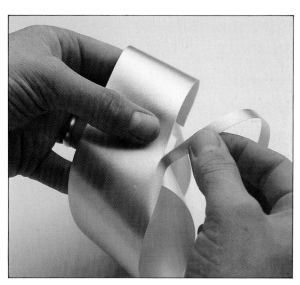

2. Hold one side of the ribbon and tear it in strips, starting at the top of the other side. It should tear evenly into about ten narrow strips.

3. To curl the ribbon, run the blade of a pair of scissors down the length. The curls could be used on the Maypole Cake.

4. The strips can be made into loops and used as fillers in fabric flower arrangements. Fasten with royal icing.

Miniature Bows

Tiny bows are used in many different ways on cakes. They can decorate the sides of a plainly iced cake, placed above frills and flounces, used in runout, embroidery and broderie anglaise designs, or placed on

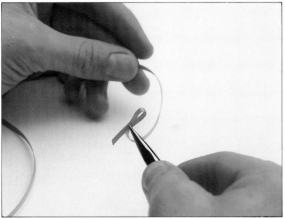

1. Hold the ribbon in one hand and make a loop with a small tail in the end. Hold the loop with the tweezers.

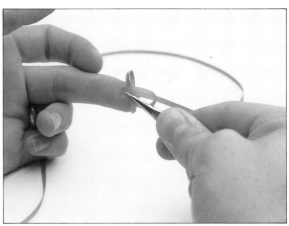

2. Take the length of ribbon around the tweezers, making a complete circle. There should be two small loops.

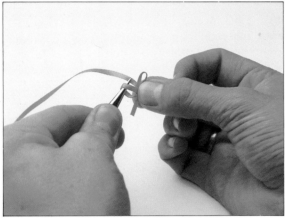

3. Hold the loops with your fingers and release the tweezers. Put the tweezers through the loop and pull through the ribbon from the other side.

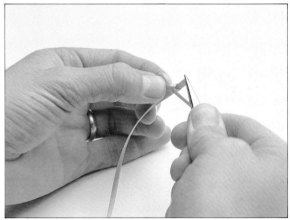

4. Use the tweezers to pull the loops tight and ensure that they are the same size.

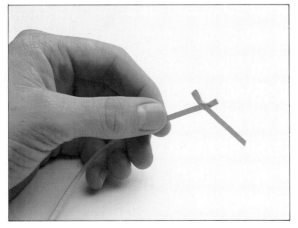

5. When the bow is tight, cut the tails evenly. Save the trimmings to use for ribbon insertion.

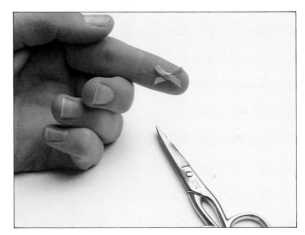

6. Finish off the bows by cutting a V in each tail, or by trimming neatly on the diagonal.

top of bells, horseshoes or other top decorations. The bows must be tied so that they will lie flat. Larger bows can be tied with your fingers, but tweezers are necessary for very tiny ones.

1. Miniature bows in an assortment of colours.

2. Two-colour miniature bows.

3. Larger bows which can be made without the use of tweezers.

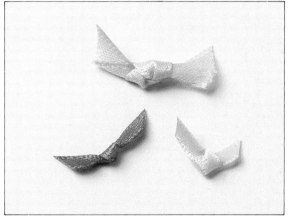

4. Make as for the double loop, but fold the ends of the ribbon and bring these up to make the tails.

5. Single loops fixed with royal icing. Decorate with tiny piped or fabric flowers.

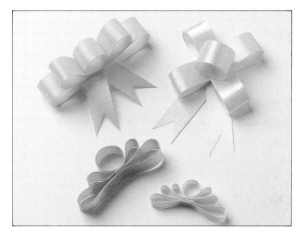

6. Ribbon loop bows. These can be made from any width of fabric or paper ribbon. Fix in position with royal icing.

Wired Ribbons

The loops and bows shown here are all for use in floral bouquets and sprays. They are all made with floristry wire, usually 28-gauge, so that they can then be wired into the

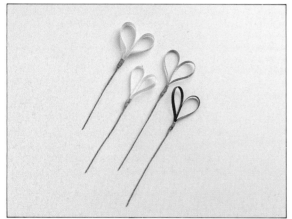

Swallow tail: Fold a piece of ribbon in half. Take a length of wire and wrap it round the fold of the ribbon several times, then bend the wire down and cover with tape. Trim the ribbon ends to points.

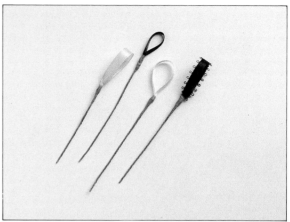

Single loop: Make a ribbon loop and wrap floristry wire tightly around the ends. Cover the join and the length of wire with tape.

Double loop: Make two ribbon loops of equal size and join with wire. Cover the join and the wire with tape.

Triple loop: Make three equal-sized ribbon loops, wrap floristry wire tightly around the joins, and cover the join and wire with tape.

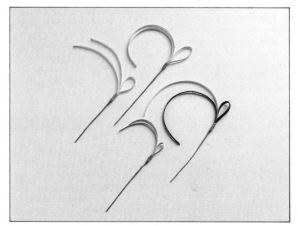

Single loop with tails: Make a ribbon loop, then bring the ends up to make two long tails, or trailers. Bind the wire tightly around the fold, then cover with wire.

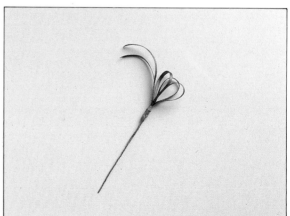

Triple loop with tails: Make as for the triple loop, but fold the ends of the ribbon and bring up to make the tails, which can be long or short, curled or straight.

sprays. For a simple and unusual decoration, place a bunch of ribbon loops in a small vase, or combine the loops with fabric flowers. Never place the wires directly into the cake.

Figure-of-eight: Take a length of ribbon in one hand and bring it round your hand so that it lies flat. Make three more loops, changing direction each time. Bind with wire where the points of the loops meet. Trim the ends of the ribbon.

Wired bows: Fold a length of ribbon into three equal pieces, then wrap a piece of wire around the centre. Trim the ends to make a bow shape.

Double wired bows: These can be made with several loops. Fold the ribbon as for the single bow as many times as required, wire in the centre and trim the ends.

Maypole Cake

Use the ribbon-making techniques you have mastered to make this delightful Maypole Cake. Although the design is very simple, it is effective and appealing.

If the cake has not already been marzipaned on a board, centre the cake on the board. Evenly spread the top with the green icing, then use the flat side of the palette knife to bring up tiny peaks to look like grass. Place the cake on a turntable and evenly spread the sides of the cake with white icing, then pull on icing comb evenly around the sides to make the wavy lines. Spread the board with green icing as for the top. Cover the piece of dowelling with ribbons, fix them with dabs of royal icing, and insert the pole into the centre of the cake before the icing sets. Fill a small bag with a No 3 tube with white icing. Pip dots of icing around the top and base of the cake and quickly attach the sugarpaste flowers. Position some flowers around the base of the pole. Pipe green leaves above and below the flowers with a No 67 tube or snipped paper piping bag. Make six bows and attach around the sides of the cake. Cut each ribbon in half and fasten to the top fo the Maypole with a pin. Pin a miniature bow at the top. Cover the cake board with the three ribbon bands and pin in place.

EQUIPMENT
30cm (12in) round cake board
20cm (8in) piece of wooden dowelling, ribbon to cover the dowelling
2m (2yd) 5mm (¼in) ribbon, in each of pink, peach and lemon
1m (1yd) 5mm (¼in) ribbon in each of dark pink, yellow and mauve for covering the board.
flat-headed pins
Pallette knife
Icing comb
Piping tube No 3
Leaf tube No 67

Time
2 hours

INGREDIENTS
20cm (8in) round fruit cake, covered with marzipan
or
20cm (8in) round, firm sponge cake, sandwiched with jam and lightly covered with buttercream
450g (1lb) pale green royal icing
450g (1lb) white royal icing
approximately 100 sugarpaste plunger-cutter flowers in pale pink, dark pink and lemon.

VARIATION
The sides of the cake can be covered with ribbon bands to match the streamers, instead of the rings of flowers.

LESSON 12

Designing a Cake

Designing a Cake

The design of a cake is most important. When decorating a cake you should have a mental picture of what the cake will look like when it is finished.

The design of the cake begins before you even bake the cake and is broken down into several main areas.

Shape and Design

Nowadays there are so many different shaped cake tins available that it is sometimes a difficult decision to make to decide on the shape. Often at this stage you will have to sit down with a sketch pad and draw various cake shapes, then work out the basic design. If a spray of flowers is the focal point, decide on the shape of the spray. This may give an idea of the shape of cake it will suit. For a runout motif, see what shape it suggests.

These are all important factors, as a cake should look evenly balanced with not too many bare areas. Sometimes if you are commissioned to decorate a cake you will be given some idea of colour, shape or design. This gives a base upon which to plan your design and makes the overall design a lot easier to work out. If no instructions are given, try and find out favourite colours, flowers, hobbies and pastimes of the person the cake is for. This can spark off the imagination and may provide a theme for the cake design.

Once the shape has been decided upon think about the size. This again

is very important, especially when designing a wedding cake. It would be silly to make a 30cm (12in) birthday cake if only 15-20 portions were required, as a 20cm (8in) cake would be more than enough. The other extreme would be a 13, 18, 23cm (5, 7, 9in) wedding cake made if 450 portions were required. With a wedding cake it is traditional to keep the top tier for the first anniversary or the christening of the first child. This means that enough portions should be got out of the bottom tier/s. An additional cutting cake can also be made. This is a cake iced but not decorated.

Base Colour and Covering Medium

The colour of the base of the cake has to be a well thought out decision, as it can dramatically alter the finished effect of the cake. There are two main choices of covering medium: royal icing or sugarpaste. Both give different effects. Royal icing, with its sharp precise angles, gives a more formal effect and sugarpaste, with its soft rounded edges giving a more feminine effect. A few years ago all wedding cakes were covered in white; nowadays white cakes have taken second place to pastel shades. The covering looks more attractive if it is a pale colour, but not too pale as very pale pastels look washed out or dirty, and do not make too dark, as it will look too harsh once decorated. Remember most colours dry slightly darker, so take this into consideration when colouring the icing.

Main Design

Once the cake is covered you can then move onto the main decoration. Designs can be copied straight out of a book, if you find it difficult to design, or look through your books and take different parts from different cakes. For example, you may like an embroidery design from one cake and a spray of flowers from another, and so on.

If you are putting runout collars on a cake you will have to design these. If you are putting on frills or lace you will have to make templates to ensure correct positioning.

The overall design of the cake can be made up of lots of ideas, favourite colours, flowers, hobbies, designs taken from wedding stationary, the wedding dress or veil, a christening robe, etc. Inspiration can also be taken from nature. Often on a country walk you will see something that could work well in icing.

It is better to under-decorate and it is not necessary to use all the skills and techniques you have learnt on one cake. Your skill as a decorator will improve if you try new designs all the time rather than sticking to one or two favourite designs. Although you will become quicker if your repeat a design over and over again, you will also become stale and get little satisfaction from your cakes. There is nothing nicer than to design and decorate a cake then to stand back and think you created the whole thing from your mind and hands. Many cake designs, especially patterns for runouts, collars and plaques involve the use of geometry because accuracy is of vital importance.

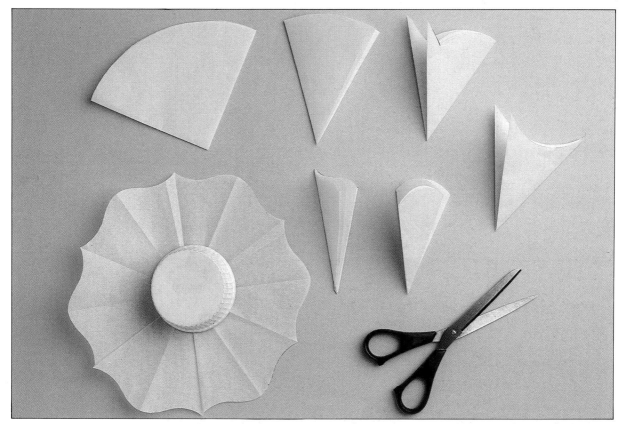

Drawing Geometric Templates

Here a 10cm (4in) circle drawn with compasses, shows the radius. This is the straight line drawn from the centre point to disect any point on the outer line. This line is known as the circumference.

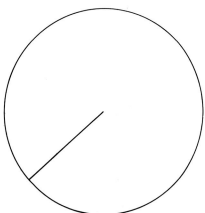

The same circle showing the diameter. This line crosses from one side of the circle to the other at any angle, but should go through the centre point.

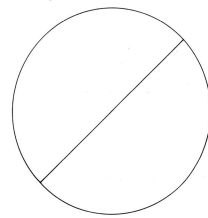

The radius of a circle disects the circumference into six equal parts.

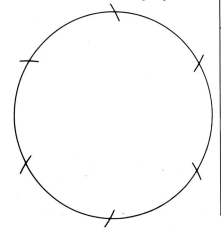

Hold the compass from the centre to the outer edge, mark the edge and then place the needle on the mark and mark in front where it crosses again. Continue all the way around until you have six marks on the circumference.

Here the six points have been joined with six straight lines to make a perfect hexagon. This principle is ideal for drawing hexagonal plaques and boards.

The circle with its six marks can also be used to make a triangle by only using three of the six points.

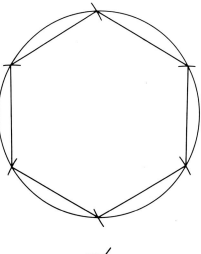

Portions from a Cake
The chart gives a rough idea of how many portions you would get out of a particular size cake. The calculations have been based on catering portions. Some caterers will cut 2.5cm (1in) squares, others 1cm x 5cm (½in x 2in) slices. It is always better to over estimate the number of portions required.

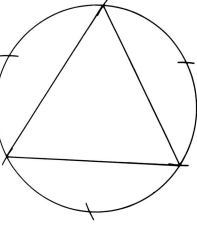

Portions

Round	Portions	Square	Portions
13cm (5in)	14	13cm (5in)	16
15cm (6in)	22	15cm (6in)	27
18cm (7in)	30	18cm (7in)	40
20cm (8in)	40	20cm (8in)	54
23cm (9in)	54	23cm (9in)	70
25cm (10in)	68	25cm (10in)	90
27.5cm (11in)	86	27.5cm (11in)	112
30cm (12in)	100	30cm (12in)	134

At a glance Wedding Cake Portions)		(Portions for Total Cake)	
		Round	Square
3-Tier Small 13, 18, 23cm (5, 7, 9in)		98	126
3-Tier Large 15, 20, 25cm (6, 8, 10in)		130	171
2-Tier Standard 18 and 25cm (7 and 10in)		98	130

Note
You can also make an additional cutting cake if more portions are required. The other shapes such as heart, hexagonal, octagonal and petal will give approximately the same portions as a round cake of the same size.

The design sketch for the blue birthday cake featured at the beginning of this chapter, showing top and side elevation.

Americans excel at pressure piping, with beautiful cakes decorated completely in pressure piping. Flowers piped flat on flowers nails are popular. Gum paste (pastillage) is used for cake ornaments, figures and boxes for candies.

Australia

The Australian style of work has now become very popular worldwide, with many people taking courses in the types of techniques used in Australia.

Australians cover cakes with sugarpaste, never with royal icing which is only used for piping. They excel in fine piping techniques, such as embroidery, lace and extension work. A decorator may spend weeks on one lace extension border around a cake. Sugar flowers are also popular. The warm climate produces exotic flowers and cakes often feature the Australian wild flowers.

South Africa

The warm climate in South Africa produces beautiful flowers, and sugar flowers feature in the cake decorating. The flowers are almost always the main focal point of a cake. The basic cake is usually quite simply decorated to show off the beautiful, imaginative sprays of flowers.

Another South African technique which is now used all over the world is the Garrett frill. This original idea came from Elaine Garrett of Cape Town, although there are now many adaptations of the basic principle.

Filigree work is another technique used in South Africa, cobweb-fine pieces in the form of wings and top ornaments are often added to the cakes.

The World of Cakes

Designs vary throughout the world due to national decorating styles and techniques. A few years ago this was very apparent, as each country had its own style of work, but now with books on techniques available everywhere, cake decorating has become international.

America

Americans rarely use fruit cakes and are famous for their sponge-type cakes which they use for celebrations, covered with frostings in every conceivable colour and flavour. A lot of English cake decorators frown on Americans' choice of colours but forget that colours can be used with more imagination. Colour has a lot to do with the climate. Most weddings and celebrations throughout the world are held outside, and with the sun shining, bright colours seem much more appropriate.

The range of American tubes is vast, with tubes to pipe every imaginable design and shape.

England

The English are famous for their royal icing techniques which first became popular in Victorian times. However, English decorators have now incorporated styles from Australia and South Africa, and the English style is now quite international.

Designs for runouts, collars and plaques are first cut from paper templates

Create simple side designs by cutting interesting shapes along the flat edge of icing scrapers. These are particularly effective on buttercream cakes.

Side designs may combine a geometric shape and piped ornamentation.

Scroll designs

Scrolls are a common feature in cake design, they are simple to pipe once the basic scroll shape has been mastered.

Cake Boards

Designing
Cake Boards

The board the cake sits on is as important as the cake itself. As with the design of a cake, the choice of board starts at the initial stages of planning. Originally, only round and square boards were available, then came heart-shaped and hexagonal boards and more recently manufacturers have started producing boards to match every tin shape. You can also make your own boards for an unusual cake. The picture below shows a variety of cake pillars used for assembling tiered cakes to complete your design.

Shape and Size

The board that you choose does not always have to be the same shape as the cake, for instance, a round cake can look attractive on a petal-shaped board. It all depends on the effect that you want to achieve. Most of the unusual cake boards come in three or four sizes to match the size of the tins. This is fine for most designs, however, if you are planning runout collars you may find that the collar will extend beyond the board. In this case, it is preferable to make the board yourself.

The basic guideline for the size of board is that the board should be 5cm (2in) larger than the cake. The bottom tier of a wedding cake or any cake with a collar should have a board 7.5cm (3in) larger. On wedding cakes it is important not to overshadow the cakes, so the chosen board should not be larger than the cake on that is on the tier below.

Some manufacturers still make boards to the imperial standard of a half inch. Metric boards are slightly

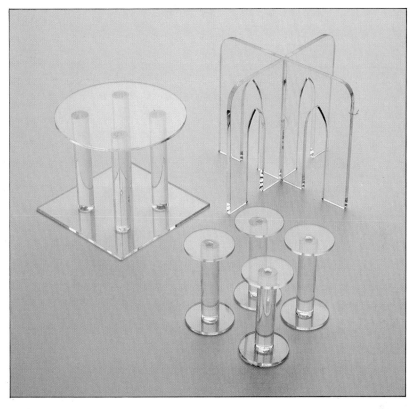

thicker at 2cm. When making a tiered cake, be sure to use boards of the same thickness throughout. If the boards are to be trimmed with ribbon bands, these should also be of the same thickness.

Fruit cakes should always go on 2cm (½in) thick drum cake boards or wooden boards to take the weight of the cake. The other boards, known as double-thick and single-thick cards are only suitable for sponge or novelty cakes.

Jigsaw Boards

Unusual and substantial cake boards may be cut with a jig-saw and made to your own design from 2cm (½in) thick wood or wood-vaneered chipboard. These may then be left plain for some novelty designs decorating the sides with ribbon, or they may be covered to complement the iced cake. The templates at the end of this chapter provide many design ideas.

Covering Cake Boards

You can cover purchased or made boards with various papers and fabrics to create a special look for each cake. For instance, at Christmas it is attractive to cover the board with red foil or coloured wrapping paper for a seasonal look.

Use laundry starch or cornflour (cornstarch) to stick the paper or foil to the boards. Place a little powdered starch or cornflour (cornstarch) in a small saucepan, add a little water and mix into a smooth paste, thin the paste with a little more water. Bring

to the boil then add more water to dilute the glue which at this stage should be quite runny. Use immediately; if the glue cools and thickens, reheat as the glue sticks better when hot. A rubber-based glue is suitable for sticking fabrics.

Covering the Board

Using the board as a template, outline the shape onto the back of the covering paper using a pencil. Draw the outline again this time adding a 5cm (2in) border. Cut out both shapes. Brush hot glue over the top surface of the board, turn the board upsidedown and position centrally on the larger piece of paper. Spread some glue over the edges of the board and a little on the underside. Pull the excess paper over the sides smoothing as you work. On a square board work opposite side together. Make sure the paper is completely stuck down then spread some more glue over the underside of the board. Stick the small piece of paper over the bottom. Sometimes small lumps and air bubbles will be visible but, just like with wallpaper, these should disappear on drying.

Covering the Board with Royal Icing

When coating a cake or even a dummy in royal icing it is usual to coat the board as well. The board will require at least two coats of icing, to achieve a smooth finish and to prevent the icing from splintering.

Covering the Board with Sugarpaste

To cover a board in sugarpaste, follow the principles for making sugarpaste plaques. The board is covered at the same time as the cake and both are left to dry for two to three days. If the cake is placed on the soft paste you are liable to damage the board covering when trying to centre the cake on the board.

Royal Iced Board

1. The cake has received two coats of icing and is thoroughly dried. Now move onto the board. Using royal icing and a palette knife pat the icing onto the board. With the side of the knife, continue all the way around the board.

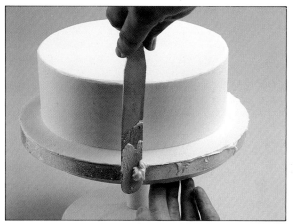

2. Hold the palette knife flat on the surface of the board and rotate the cake starting and finishing at the seam at the back of the cake.

3. Holding the knife at right angles to the board, rotate the cake to remove excess icing.

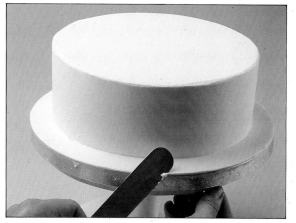

4. Rotate the cake again, this time holding the knife at a slight angle to remove the sharp edge from the board coating. On certain designs the edge of the board is relied upon for supporting the hands and an angled edge tends to splinter easily.

Sugarpasted Board

1. Roll out the sugarpaste in the required colour to 5mm (⅛in) thick. Lift up and drape across the board.

2. Cut off the excess paste using a palatte knife, taking care to keep the edge straight.

3. The finished board covered with sugarpaste is left to dry thoroughly before the sugarpasted cake is positioned.

The following templates provide the patterns for the jigsaw boards illustrated in this chapter. Many of the patterns represent half the completed board, the remainder are shown whole. Size up or down as required.

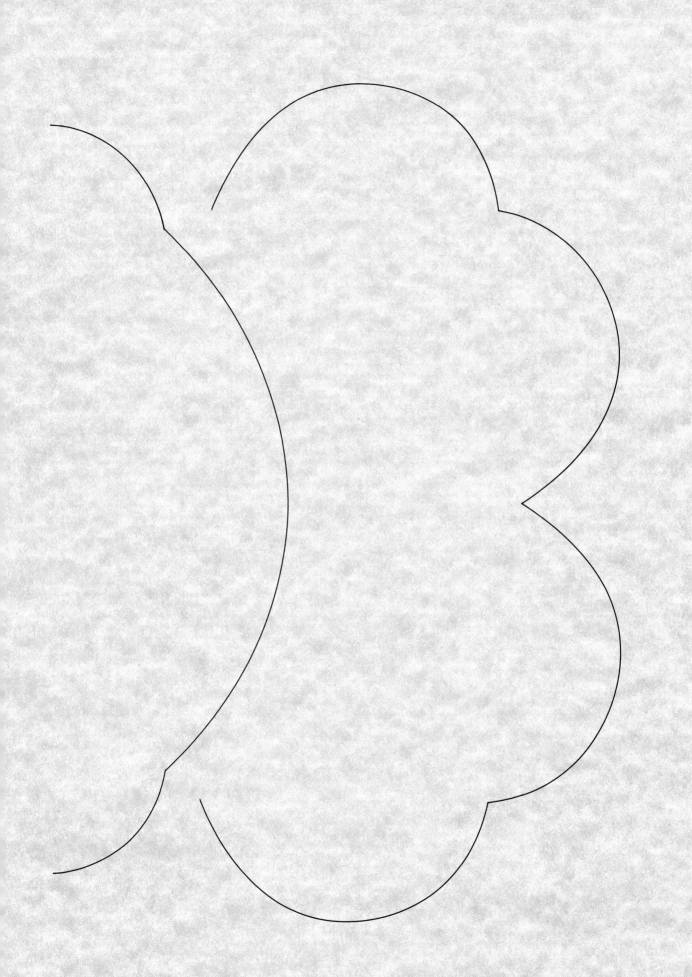

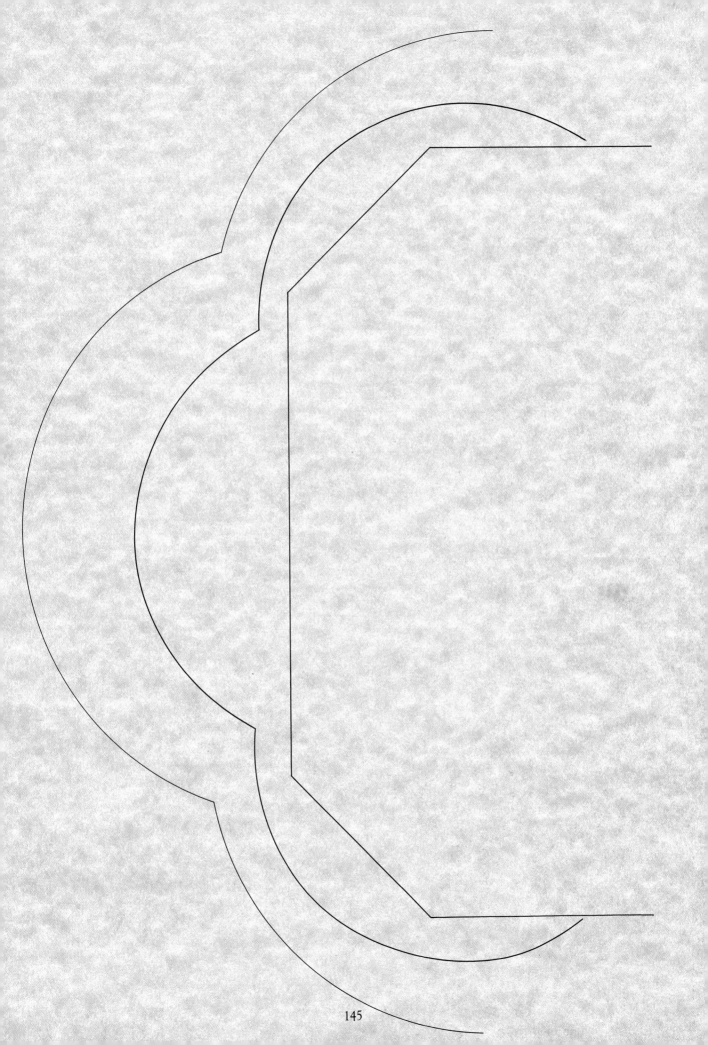

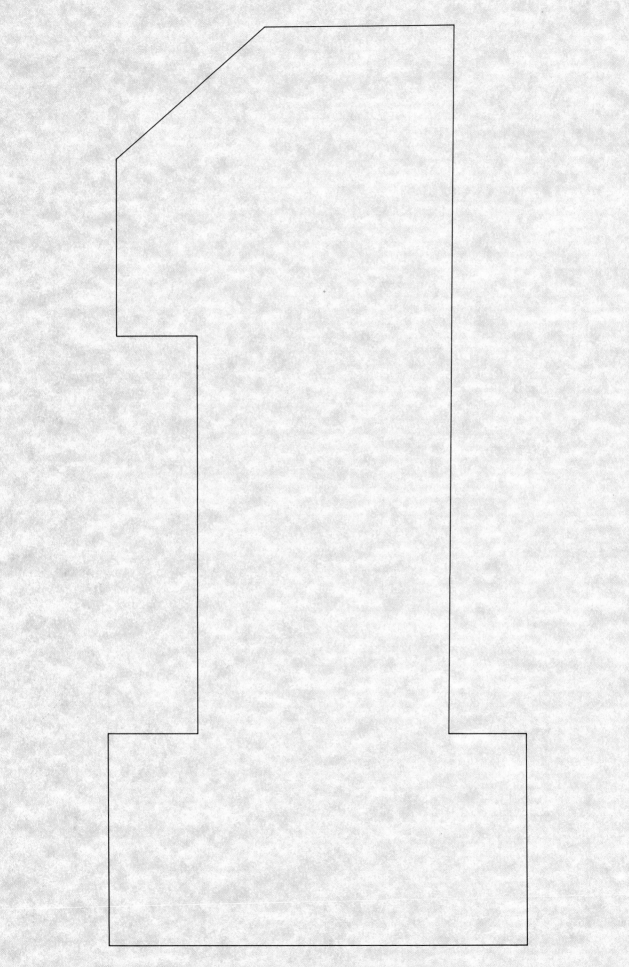

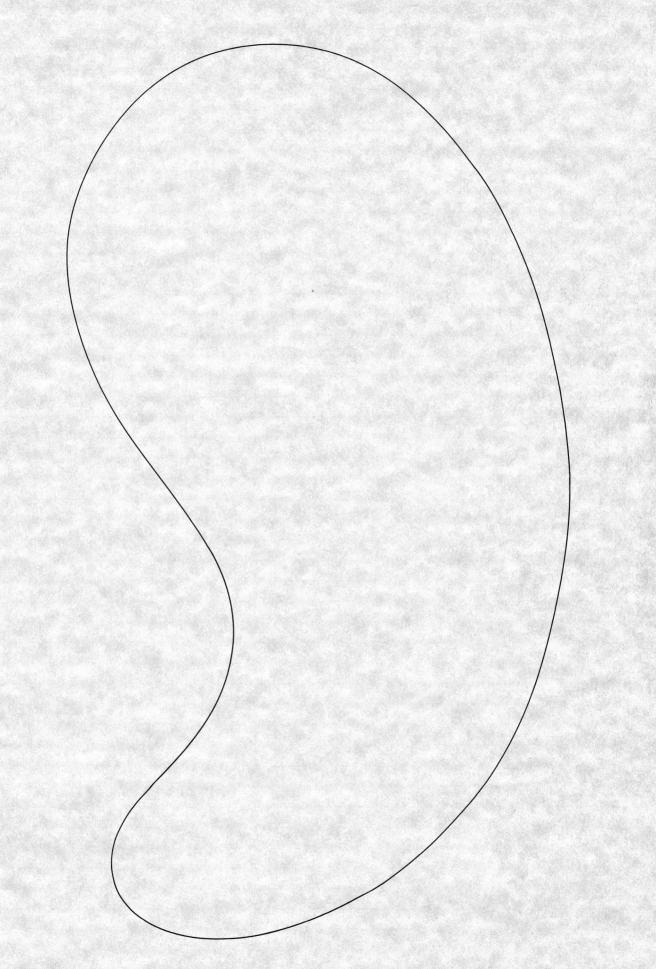

148

LESSON 14

Sugar Moulding

Sugar Moulding

Sugar moulding is a very enjoyable part of cake decoration – it is very easy and someone with no experience in cake decoration can produce very attractive pieces.

The principle is no different from a child filling a bucket at the seaside with damp sand then turning it out to produce the shape of the bucket. For sugar moulding the two ingredients are water and caster (superfine) sugar. A teaspoon, small spatula, cranked palette knife, food colouring and waxed paper will also be needed.

INGREDIENTS
450g (1lb) caster (superfine) sugar
20-30ml (4-6 teaspoons) cold water

If making coloured objects, add food colour to the water before mixing with the sugar.

Place the sugar into a bowl and slowly add the water. Mix through with a spatula. When all the water has been added the mixture should be the consistency of damp sand. Keep the sugar mixture covered with a damp cloth to stop it crusting in the bowl.

Have clean, dry moulds ready. For solid items, pack the mould with sugar using a teaspoon. After two or three teaspoonsful have been put in, pack sugar tightly with the back of a spoon to ensure no gaps or cavities will appear on the finished item. Spoon in more sugar and continue until the mould is full. Using the cranked palette knife, run over the surface of the mould to remove excess sugar and make a level base.

Take a piece of waxed paper slightly larger than the mould. Place over base and carefully flip over holding both waxed paper and mould.

Place on a flat surface to dry. Gently tap the mould and lift. The sugar shape should come away from the mould. If it does not, tap until it comes free. Leave a day to dry out completely before decorating or sticking together.

For hollow objects, fill as for solid objects and turn out on waxed paper. Leave them to form a crust on the surface, then place back into the mould. Use a spoon to remove the damp sugar from the centre, leaving a crystallized translucent shell. The length of time that the shape has to be left before scooping out depends on the size of the piece and the temperature of the room. Once dried the point of a sharp knife should not be able to penetrate into the hard surface.

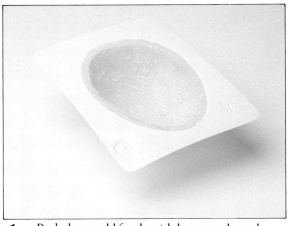

1. Pack the mould firmly with lemon-coloured sugar and use a palette knife to level the base.

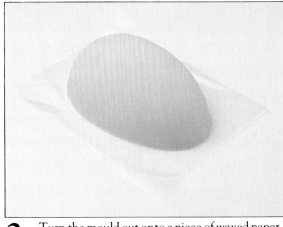

2. Turn the mould out onto a piece of waxed paper and set aside until a crust of dried sugar has formed on the surface.

3. Return the egg to the mould and scoop out the damp sugar in the centre of the egg. Turn the egg out of the mould once more and leave until completely dry. Make 2.

4. When dry, trim the rims of the egg shells with a piped garland using a No 6 tube. Decorate the top of the egg with purchased silk flowers and leaves.

5. Stick the base of the second egg shell onto a cake board and trim with a frill. When completely dry, fill with chocolates.

6. When completely dry the egg can be assembled.

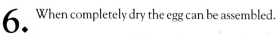

Easter Egg

This hollow standard sized egg was moulded in lemon sugar. Fill with mini chocolate eggs, then stick the halves together. Finish with purchased sugar flowers. Pipe a green shell edge with a No1 tube.

Panorama Egg

Mould a hollow lemon egg. Cut off half of one part using a piece of thin wire. Place a piece of waxed paper over cut end so it does not dry out. Leave to form a hard, thin shell, then scoop out the damp sugar remaining in the centre. The bottom half has a small fabric chick placed in it, with some piped grass and mauve forget-me-nots. Stick the lid in position with a little lemon royal icing, pipe a small shell around the side and over the cut edge. Finish with tiny piped flowers in the corners.

Any type of scene can be put into a panorama egg and they can be made in different sizes using the egg moulds available.

Mini Eggs

These solid sugar eggs would be ideal to fill a larger egg. To serve as after dinner mints, add oil of peppermint to the sugar before filling the moulds. Once moulded, turn out and stick the two halves together with a little royal icing. Decoration has been piped on in various colours using No1 tubes.

Sugar Bells

1. Pack a sugar mould tightly with white sugar, turn out and set aside until a crust of dried sugar has formed on the surface.

2. Hollow-out the centre of the bell.

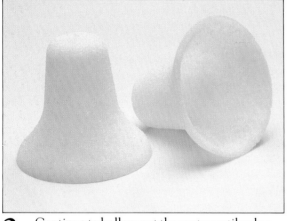

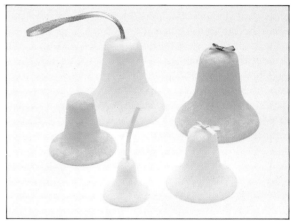

3. Continue to hollow-out the centre until only a thin shell remains.

4. The shells can be made in white sugar, food colouring may be added to the water to create coloured sugar bells.

Holly Plaque

Mould sugar holly leaves and the bell. Leave to dry. Pipe a 15cm (6in) circle onto a plaque or directly onto the cake surface. Using a No1 tube in a bag filled with green royal icing, pipe some spruce and stick the sugar holly in position. Once dry, outline the holly leaves with royal icing. Placing a double figure-of-eight bow at the top of the wreath. Paint the bell with gold food colouring, stick on to the wreath and position a gold stamen into the bell to represent the clanger. Pipe red berries with No1 tube.

Posy Bowls

Mould, dry and hollow out posy bowls, using commercial moulds. These are suitable for use at a dinner party to serve after-dinner mints or chocolates, sugar cubes. If wished, make them in colours to match the table setting. For weddings sugared almonds could be put into these sugar bowls and for children's parties fill with sweets (candies).

Sugar Cubes

Sugar cubes in pretty shapes look festive for a special tea or dinner party. The sugar can be coloured or designs can be piped or stencilled on the surface.

Shell

Mould two halves of a shell using a chocolate mould or a clean scallop shell. Leave to dry slightly and scoop out. Dry. Fill in one half with ribbon loops and flowers. Here silk flowers have been used, but sugar ones could have been chosen. Pipe a line of icing along the back and stick the top half in position. If necessary, support the lid open until the icing dries.

Pink Heart Box

This heart box was made using a chocolate mould. Pack pale pink sugar into the base and lid. Turn out and leave until surface is dry. Scoop out damp sugar and leave pieces to dry completely. The lid has some stems and leaves piped with a No2 tube with green royal icing. Position blossoms with pink royal icing stamens.

Snowman

Mould two halves of a snowman using a chocolate mould. When dry stick the two halves together with royal icing. Plait (braid) some red cord for a scarf or use red marzipan or sugarpaste. Pipe eyes, nose and mouth in black royal icing with a No1 piping tube.

Sugar Mice

These sugar mice are moulded in a commercial mould. While in mould, push in a piece of string for the tail. Turn out and dry. For a child's party sugar mice can be made in a variety of different colours.

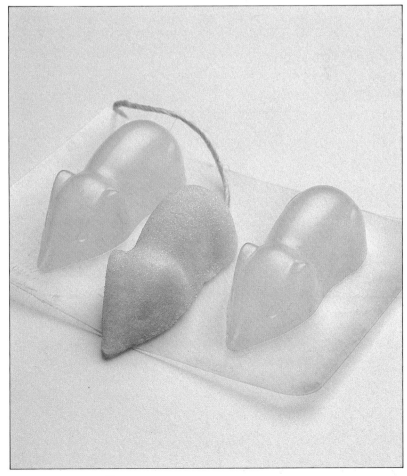

Spring Chocolate Box

This brown chocolate box was moulded in a plastic corsage box. Fill the mould in usual way, and hollow out both pieces. Leave to dry. On the top half pipe some stems and leaves and place silk flowers onto the stems. Pipe a dropped line around both sides with dots above. A suitable inscription could be written on the box if desired.

After-Dinner Mints

The after-dinner mints shown here have been moulded in chocolate moulds. Add oil of peppermint to the sugar mixture before packing in the moulds. Once moulded and dried pipe on designs using royal icing. Here a small petal nozzle and No2 tube have been used to make various flowers and patterns.

LESSON 15

Frills &
Flounces

Frills and Flounces

Frills and flounces, which are made in the same way, add pretty, side decorations to sugarpasted or royal iced cakes. Frills can be wide or narrow, white or coloured, single or layered, and in many different combinations.

To make frills or flounces, all that is needed is a cutter, a sharp knife, nonstick worksurface, rolling pin, and cocktail sticks. The most popular frill cutter is the Garrett frill, named after cake decorator Elaine Garrett, who introduced the idea. However, any round cutter, whether fluted or straight, can be used.

To make a frill, roll out sugarpaste until it is almost translucent. Plain sugar can be used, but the frills will hold their shape better if gum tragacanth is added in the proportion of 5ml (1 teaspoon) to 250g (8oz) sugarpaste. Cut out the shape using a cutter. Cut the circle, then gently frill with a cocktail stick, taking care not to stretch or tear the paste. Attach to a sugarpasted cake with a little egg white or water, or by crimping if the coating is fresh. Attach to a royal-iced cake with a thin line of icing.

Frills and flounces can also be used to decorate the top of a cake, on plaques, and to add clothes to modelled figures. Frills and flounces can also be used to make simple flowers, such as carnations.

Small Flower Plaque

This little plaque made from a Garrett frill cutter would be suitable for any type of cake. A small runout, painting or spray of flowers could be put on the plaque with an inscription. If you feel unhappy about writing straight on to the cake surface writing on a plaque is safer, if you do make a mistake you can always make another plaque, but a drastic mistake on to a cake can result in taking off all the icing and re-coating it.

Garrett Frill

Roll out some sugarpaste, cut out with a Garrett frill cutter without the fixed centre. Use a cocktail stick to frill the edge; dry. This plaque was painted with a simple freehand design using food colours. The edge was also dusted with petal dust to give a contrast to the cake surface.

Garrett Frill

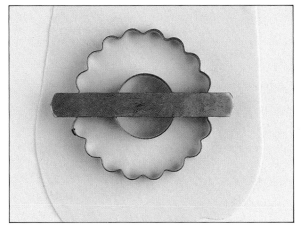

1. Roll out the sugar paste on a lightly cornfloured (cornstarched) surface until it is almost translucent. Cut the shape using a Garrett frill or serrated cutter and the hole using a smaller plain cutter if you are not using a set centre frill cutter. Take care to centre the hole.

2. Carefully frilling the edges of the circle using a cocktail stick by rolling the cocktail stick along the edge of the paste moving all the time to stop it from sticking.

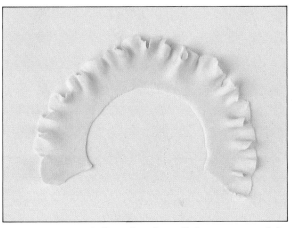

3. Continue frilling the edges all the way around the shape. Cut the ring open with a sharp knife.

4. The frill may then be gently eased open and is ready to be attached to the cake.

Plain Frill

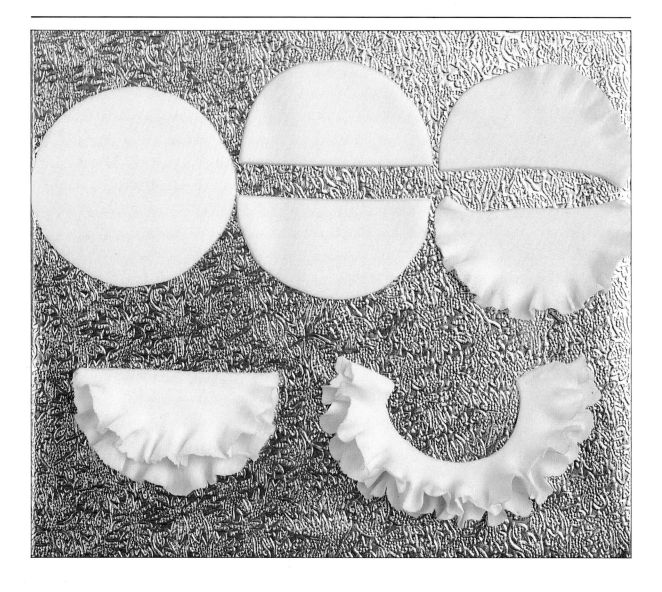

1. Roll out some paste, and cut out using a plain pastry cutter.

2. Cut the circle in half.

3. Frill each half, carefully using a cocktail stick.

4. Lay one half on top of each other, as for a scalloped frill, sticking together with a little egg white. When dry dust the edge with petal dust.

Attaching the Frill

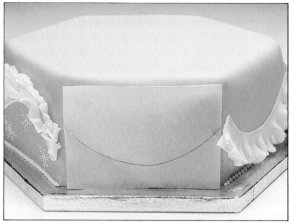

1. Make a paper template to indicate the curve of the frill, attach to the cake securely with pins.

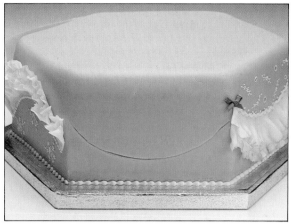

2. Using a scriber or needle scribe the curve-line on the cake.

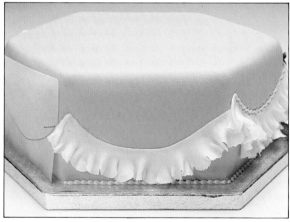

3. Attach the frill to the cake using a little egg-white or water.

4. The second frill is attached with a crimper. Pipe tiny dots in contrasting colour following the crimped line.

5. Allow to dry thoroughly then dust the edge of the frill with petal dust.

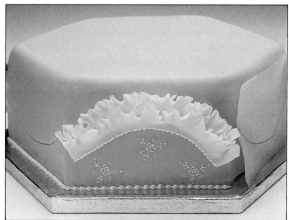

6. To create a different effect, the frill may be attached with the curve in the opposite direction.

Cutout Frills

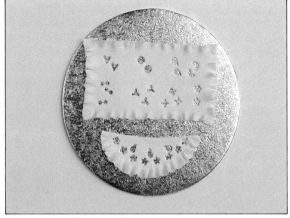

1. Make plaques as described above and press-out the shapes from the paste before crimping.

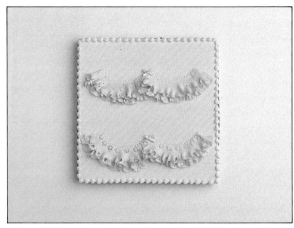

2. If the cutouts are to be on the frilled edges, the shapes should be cut from the paste before the circle is frilled.

Layered Frills

Scalloped frills may be attached in several layers to achieve a variety of different effects.

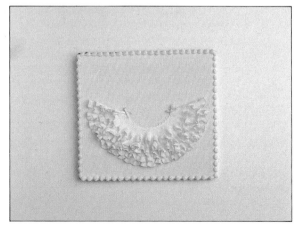

1. Four layers of frill are shown, each dusted with petal dust and finished with piped royal icing.

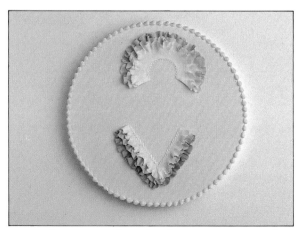

2. The paste is coloured with various amounts of colouring to achieve a graduated effect. The graduated effect is offset by a contrasting frill. The frill is shaped into a 'v' as an alternative to the curve.

Straight Frills

This plaque shows straight frills as an alternative to
scalloped frills

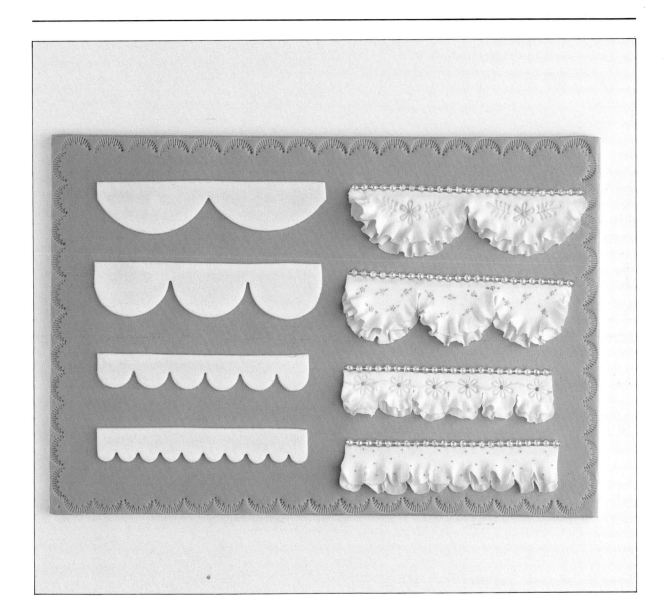

1. This shows a double frill. The top layer is
embossed with a daisy and leaf design. When dry,
dust the bottom edge. Pearls have been placed on the
top edge.

2. The frill shown here has forget-me-nots and
leaves painted with food colouring. Once dry dust
the edge.

3. Another double-layered frill with embossed
daisies along its length. Paint in the stems and
centres of the daisies.

4. This narrow double frill has tiny piped dots all
over the surface.

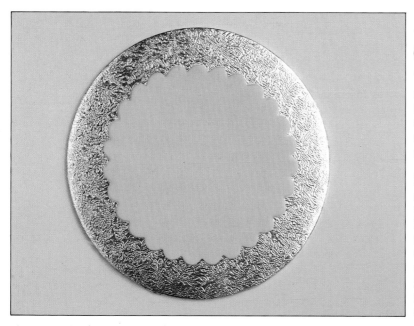

Pastry Cutter Carnation

These quick little carnations are made with sugarpaste. They can be made white and dusted with petal dust or, as shown, in a pastel shade and then dusted with additional petal dust to give a natural effect.

The carnation sizes can be altered by using different sized cutters: the smaller the cutter the smaller the finished flower will be. In damp or humid conditions a little gum tragacanth should be kneaded into the paste. Use approximately 2.5ml (½ teaspoon) to 250g (8oz) of paste. Leave half an hour before using. Keep in a polythene bag to prevent it from drying out.

1. Roll out the paste on a lightly cornfloured (corn-starched) surface. Using a serrated pastry cutter cut out the shape. The paste should be thin to ensure good frilling.

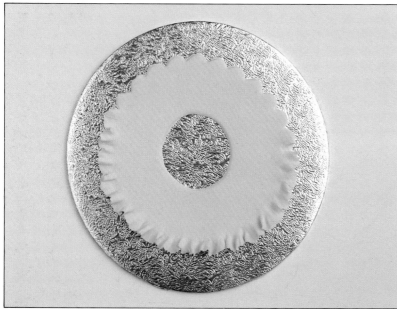

2. Cut a hole in the centre using a small round cutter. Using a cocktail stick dipped in a little cornflour, start frilling the edges only.

3. Continue frilling the edges all the way around, then cut open the ring with a sharp knife.

4. Gently use your fingers to pleat the straight side and shape into a straight edge. Do not worry if bottom cracks, as it will be trimmed off afterwards.

5. Brush some egg white along the strip from the bottom to where the frill starts. Starting at the left-hand end, roll up. The first 5cm (2in) should be rolled tightly to ensure a good centre and overall shape.

6. Continue rolling, making sure the overlap is stuck round, then use scissors to cut off the excess paste. Place the carnation into a small artist's pallet until it is dry.

Frilled Leaves

1. Colour some sugarpaste green. Roll out thinly on a lightly cornfloured (corn-starched) surface.

2. Using a cocktail cutter or a cardboard template, cut out the leaf shape.

3. Using a cocktail stick start frilling the edge.

4. Continue frilling all the way around the edge of the leaf.

5. Place on a piece of foam rubber. Mark the veins on the leaf with a cocktail stick.

6. To finish off the leaf mark the central vein and leave to dry. The leaves can be placed over formers or crumpled up tissue so they dry in a natural, individual form.

Frilled Plaques

1. Cut out some white paste using two sizes of plain pastry cutters. Completely frill both circles.

2. Brush a little egg white into the centre of the large round. Stick the smaller one on top of the larger one. Using the thicker end of the pastry cutter mark a ring as a guideline to pipe around. Dry for 2 to 3 hours.

3. Brush a little petal dust on the edge. Match the frill, if using on a cake. Using lemon icing and a No1 tube, pipe a small shell around the marked circle. Pipe '16', or another inscription. Finish off with a miniature bowl.

Sweet Sixteen Cake

Marzipan a 20cm (8in) oval fruit cake. Cover with lemon sugarpaste and transfer onto a 25cm (10in) oval board. Dry for 2 days.

Using a scriber or needle, scribe a line onto the cake surface. This makes attaching a frill easier as you have a guideline to follow for keeping a straight line. Start the line two-thirds of the way along on the left-hand side, bring the line up at a fairly steep angle, go along the top edge, down the other side and round to meet at the board. Pipe a lemon shell around the base using a No2 tube. Attach a white double frill. Pipe a scalloped line above it with a No1 tube, then put a line of narrow ribbon insertion above the frill. Pipe a dot of icing in between each piece of ribbon.

Make ten leaves and four carnations. Place three leaves and one carnation for the bottom spray, sticking in position with royal icing. The top spray is assembled out of seven leaves and three carnations.

Make a frilled plaque and position.

Dust the frill around the cake. This should always be dry before you dust it as if it is soft you will squash it. A violet/mauve petal dust was used with a little additional lilac lustre colour to give a slight sheen. Using a number three or four brush that should be dry, dust the frill from the outside to get a density of colour on the edge of frills.

Additional designs suitable for use on frilled plaques.

Runout Borders & Collars

Runout Collars

Runout work is an important feature of Royal icing. It is very popular in competition work because of the intricate designs that can be achieved. There are two main types of runout collars, simple collars and sectional collars.

The sectional pieces do not have to be designed each time, as you design them once to fit say a 20cm (8in) square then each time you coat a 20cm (8in) square cake these pieces will fit. Each full collar must be individually designed because every time you marzipan and ice a cake it will vary slightly in size. You have to be a little bit of a mathematician as well as a cake decorator to draw the collars to fit accurately.

In addition to your normal cake decorating you will need drawing paper, compass set, pencil, ruler, fine paintbrushes and a good quality waxed paper.

Icing

Icing made with pure albumum powder is the best type of icing to use for runout collars as boosted albumum substitute is not really strong enough. Softening the icing as necessary by

adding cold water a little at a time to the piping consistency of royal icing. Leave to stand for at least an hour before using to enable the icing to settle and the air bubbles to surface.

Unfortunately there is no hard and fast rule as to how much water to add to the royal icing because different consistencies are used for different types of runout. As a general guideline, lift a little icing up on a spoon and let it run back into the bowl, its trail should disappear on a count of 8 to 10. If the trail does not disappear, add some more water to the icing. If the trail disappears after 3 or 4 seconds, add some more royal icing. After doing a few runout collars and borders you will get to know the correct consistency for each individual collar.

Attaching Collars
When the collars are dry, remove from the waxed paper using a fine cranked palette knife. Another method is to bring the collar to the edge of the table top and pull the waxed paper down at right angles,

carefully going around until the collar is removed. Pipe a line with a No2 tube in the same colour as the base icing and put the collar on the cake, making sure it is evenly positioned.

Borders
There are three ways of attaching a collar or border, to the cake board. The first is to make the border and let it dry, then slide it over the top and down the side of the cake. However, if the sides are not perfectly straight or if the board coating is slightly uneven the collar may break. The easiest method is to do a runout directly on to the board using a pattern. Make a

single cut in the paper pattern, open it up and place it around the cake. Join the cut ends and pipe a line slightly outside the template; allow to dry for a few minutes, then remove the pattern. Flood the area from the line to the edge of the cake with icing. Alternatively, pipe a freehand line on the board and then flood.

The final method has to be done in a fairly dark room. Place a desk lamp about 30cm (12in) above the cake and shine onto the centre. This has to be done after the top collar has been positioned. The collar will cast a shadow on the cake board and all you have to do is to pipe a line along the edge of the shadow on the board.

Making a Collar

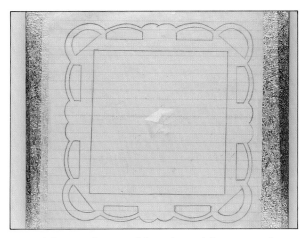

1. Measure the top of the cake and draw a template of the collar design on a piece of paper. Attach securely to a glass or board surface. Secure a piece of waxed paper over the design.

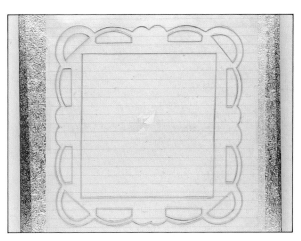

2. Pipe a line of royal icing over the pencil lines on the template.

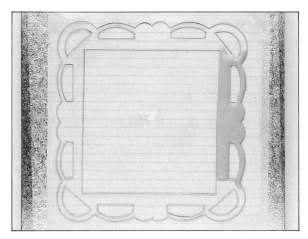

3. Flood the collar section by section working quickly but neatly.

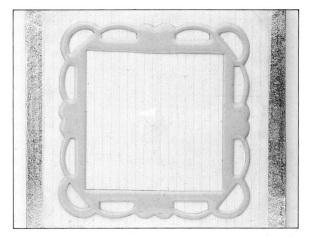

4. Continue flooding until the collar is completely filled. Dry thoroughly overnight.

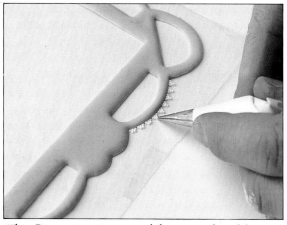

5. Pipe petit point around the outer edge of the dried collar.

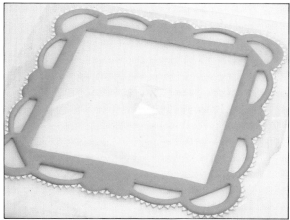

6. Continue piping until the collar is completed. Dry thoroughly.

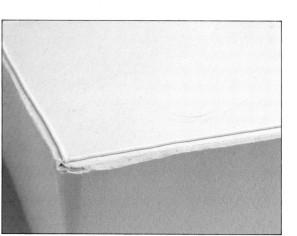

7. Pipe a solid line of icing around the top of the cake upon which to fix the collar.

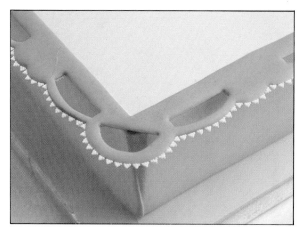

8. Remove the collar carefully from the waxed paper using a fine cranked palatte knife. Position the collar on the cake.

Pink Collar

When the runout icing on this collar is quite dry, dry pipe some stems and leaves with a No0 tube and then attach some blossom made with an ejector. Just before cutting the blossom, pipe a small dot of icing to mark where each one will go. Once positioned pipe a small dot of pink icing in the centre of each flower to represent the stamen. Pipe the edging using a No0 tube.

White Holly Collar

This solid white collar has holly leaf embroidery piped all over the surface usng a No00 tube and green icing. Use red icing and No0 tube to pipe the berries. A half-diamond edging is piped using the No0 red tube, pipe small dots on the points.

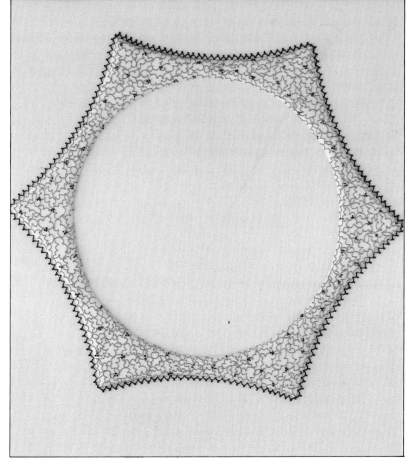

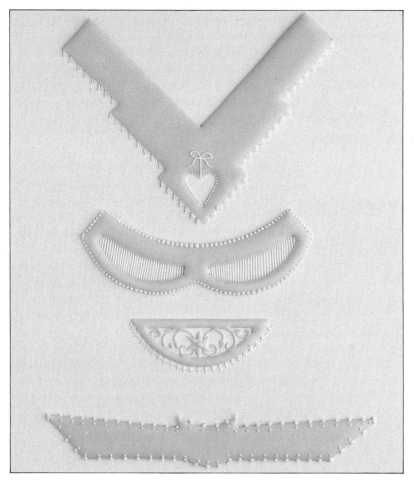

Collar Sections

A pink corner section suitable for a square cake. Pipe 3:2:1 petit point lace edging with No0 tube and a dot beading around the heart.

Dry the lilac sectional runout, then turn over and pipe fine lines with No0 tube across the two gaps. Let these dry and turn the collar over. Pipe beading around the edge.

A small pink sectional runout with flowers and stems piped with a No1 tube before the edge is flooded.

A plain lilac runout section suitable for the top edge of a square cake. Pipe a scalloped rope with a No1 tube.

This sectional collar was made in lilac royal icing. The S and C scroll pattern has been piped using a No1 tube.

This corner section is suitable for a square cake. The solid band of lemon runout is then filigree piped using a No1 tube. The outer line has been piped using green royal icing and a No0 tube.

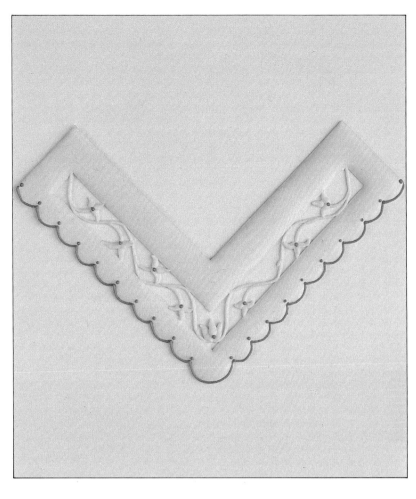

The lilac sectional collar was decorated with a daisy and leaf design piped with a No1 tube.

Open Collar with Hearts

Make a plain runout collar from the template and four hearts. The collar shown here is in lemon and the hearts in white. Once the collar is dry, pipe cornelli work in the four sections with a No0 tube. Pipe a beaded edging on the hearts. When dry, remove from the waxed paper and stick on the collars with small dots of royal icing. Pipe 3:2:1 edging around the edge of the collar.

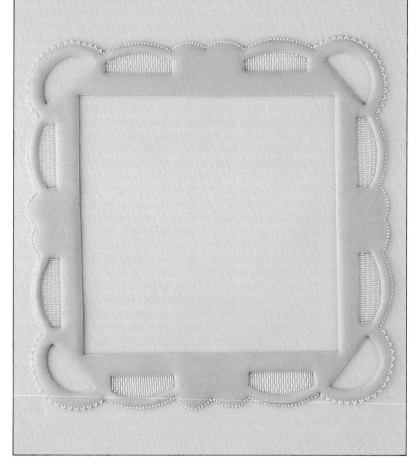

Lilac Collar

This collar with dainty line work has been flooded in lilac. When dry, pipe lines with a No0 tube. Allow to dry, turn over and pipe tiny dots on the lines, alternating the dots to give an attractive finish. Pipe pearly edging along the sides and finish with 2:1 petit point lace.

Lemon Collar

This yellow hexagonal collar has a flower and leaf cutout. The collar inside line was piped, then the flower and leaf design. Once dry, pipe scalloped line with a No0 tube, then pipe a small shell from the centre of the scallop outwards. The plaque has some fine lines piped on to show how to finish off the inside edge.

Peach Collar

This solid peach runout, has white cornelli work piped all over it using a No0 tube. Add petit point 3:2:1 lace around the edge in a darker shade of peach.

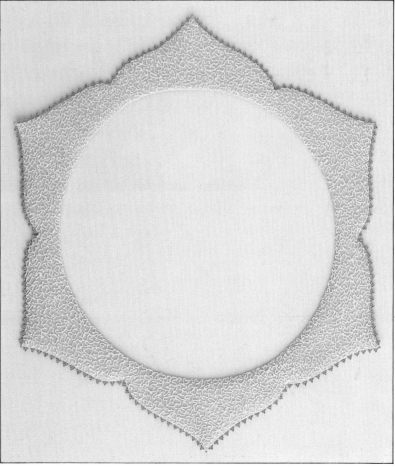

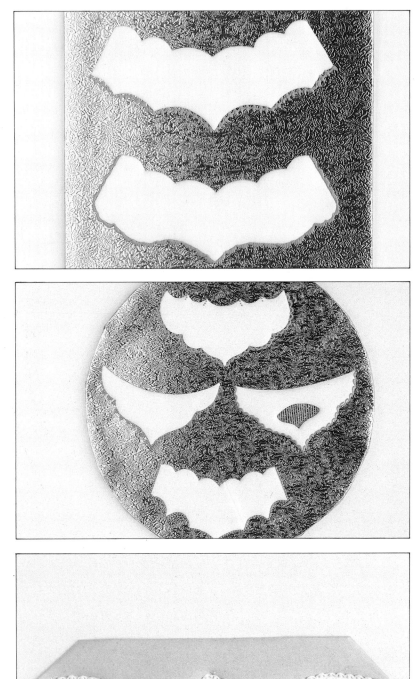

These two sectional runout pieces are suitable for use on a circular or oval cake. The edging has been worked in peach royal icing using a No0 tube.

Three solid sectional pieces and one with cutout trellis work. The edging has been worked in peach using a No0 tube.

This solid pink sectional runout was designed to sit along the edge of a square cake. The piped edging was worked in white using a No0 tube.

Christmas Collar

This collar sits on the top surface of the cake, instead of on the edge. This type of collar would be suitable if you were not satisfied with the coating on your cake, as it would cover up any imperfections. All the decoration is in the collar, the only thing that is added is the inscription. Flood the collar in white, then dry for 30 minutes. Flood the candle with red. Leave to dry, then flood in a mixture of orange and red runout for the flame, followed by softened red for the wax. The holly is outlined and then flooded in green; dry, then add red berries. Pipe edging using a paper piping-bag with 'v' cut for the leaf shape. Pipe small leaves around the edge, then pipe on the red berries using a No1 tube. Dry for 24 hours.

181

Templates for runout collars and sections. These may be sized up or down to fit the required cake.

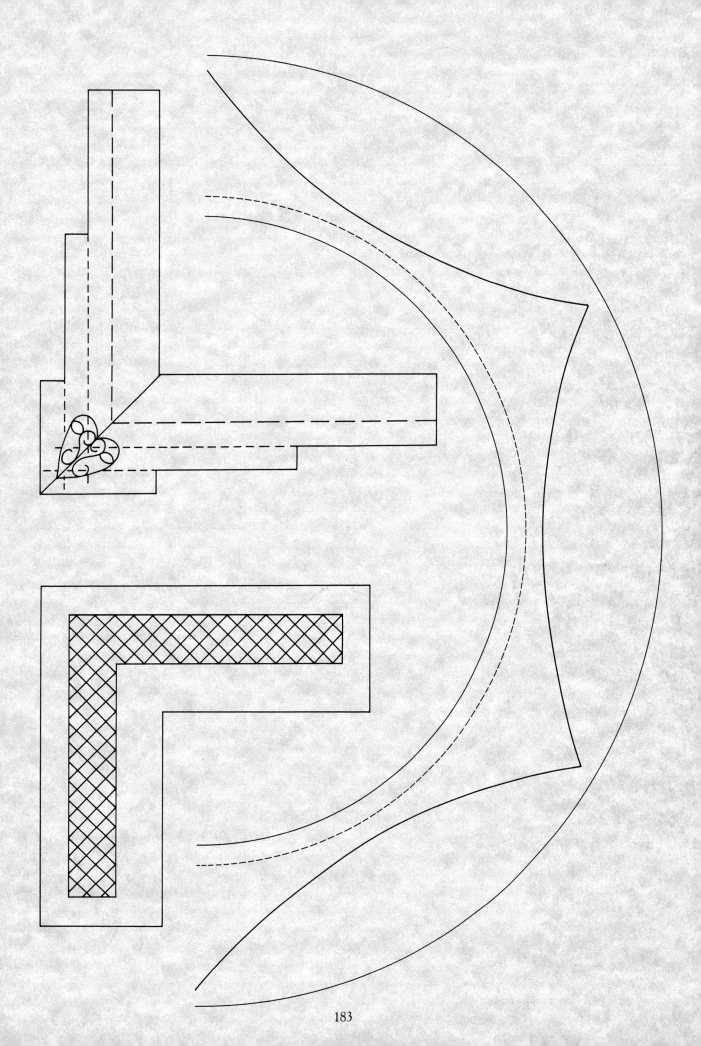

Templates for runout collars and sections.

Piped Top & Side Designs

Piped Top and Side Designs

The top and side designs piped on a cake can be as simple or as elaborate as your time and skill allow. Sugarpasted, royal-iced and buttercreamed cakes can all be decorated in this way, although it is best to stick to simple designs if working in buttercream.

Ideas for piped top and side designs can be found everywhere. Use the designs in this book, picture books, greetings cards, pattern books, magazines, etc. A nice idea for a child's birthday cake is to copy one of the child's own drawings in icing.

An experienced cake decorator should be able to pipe the designs on a cake freehand. If you are not confident enough to do this, trace the design and lightly scribe it onto the cake. When tracing side designs,

allow for any curves in a round, oval or heart-shaped cake. Remember to size up or size down the basic design if piping on a tiered wedding cake.

For accuracy when piping elaborate or geometric designs, plan the work on graph paper first, then transfer to the cake top and sides. For all designs, have all the bags of coloured icing fitted with tubes before you begin, so that you can work quickly. It is not always necessary to dry one colour before piping the next, particularly

when working in royal icing.

Pipe top designs with the cake flat, as though you were painting or drawing on paper. For the side designs, you may find it easier to tilt the cake, either on a tilting turntable or by placing something under it while you work.

Practice the design on a cake board or on the worksurface before piping on the cake. Mistakes can not always be rectified, as coloured icing will stain the cake surface.

The only necessary equipment is a number of paper piping bags and an assortment of tubes. For more elaborate designs, tracing paper, pencil, scribe and graph paper will be useful.

Halloween Plaque

This simple design would be suitable for a Halloween Cake. Scribe the pattern on the plaque from the template. Fill a small bag fitted with a No1 tube with black royal icing and pipe the witch, but not the hand and face profile. Pipe the 'Halloween' inscription freehand in black. The face and hand are piped in white and the moon in yellow. The bats are also piped freehand. Pipe a white edging with a No42 tube, then pipe a yellow and black scalloped line inside the outer shell.

Bird Table Plaque

This white plaque shows a design which may be piped freehand or by copying the template. All the work has been piped using a No1 tube. The bird table is brown, the grass, stems and leaves in green and the flowers in mauve and blue. The pulled shell has been piped with a No7 tube.

Butterfly Plaque

This wedgwood blue plaque shows a design suitable for a small cake. With the exception of the butterfly, it is all worked freehand, although you could scribe some guidelines on to the cake. The stems, leaves, flowers and words were all piped with a No1 tube. Pipe the butterfly wings with a No0 tube, and dry flat on waxed paper. Once dry, pipe a body using a No1 tube, directly onto the cake surface, stick the wings into position and support until dry with two pieces of folded paper or foam. Two stamens are used for the antenna. This design could be piped in any colour combination. Pipe the edging in a herringbone pattern with a No2 tube.

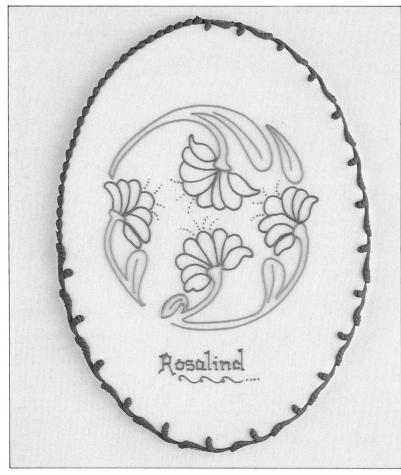

Oval Plaque

This simple line work design has pink flowers and green leaves, both piped with a No1 tube. The inscription in the same shade of pink is worked with a No0 tube. The edging features a quarter section of shells and three-quarter small S and C scrolls piped with a No2 tube.

Plaque with Silk Flowers

This quick and effective decoration is suitable for a single tier celebration cake. A spray of yellow silk flowers and ribbon loops has been used, but sugar flowers could be used in place of the silk ones. Five figure-of-eight bows were used, made and arranged with the flowers using a small piece of sugarpaste to secure. Pipe a little embroidery using a No0 tube. A suitable inscription can be piped on the plaque. Pipe the edge with a No42 tube in a scalloped rope design. A smaller No1 scalloped rope line sits inside the boarder edging.

Swan Plaque

This square design is made with a paper template. Cut a circle of greaseproof (waxed) paper, and fold into eight equal sections. Draw on one segment, and then fold up and cut to make the pattern. Place the pattern on the plaque and scribe a line along the edge. Remove the pattern and pipe a small shell with a No1 tube; cornelli the outer section with a No0 tube. The centre of the design has forget-me-nots piped all over the surface, leaving a small area for an inscription. The feature decoration is a runout sugar swan with ribbon loops and small pink fabric roses.

Wedgwood Plaque

This Wedgwood blue plaque has a runout waterlily with a pressure-piped cherub in the centre. Pipe the cherub on both sides. A cutout ejector blossom is attached to the cherub's foot. The outer part of the plaque features Wedgwood-style piped embroidery of fruit, vases, wheat, grapes and flowers using a No1 tube.

Oak Leaf Plaque

The plaque shown has a very simple but effective runout design. Make a pattern from the template, scribe on the surface and outline the leaves in green with a No1 tube. Using runout icing in the same shade, flood in the leaves. The acorns are done in the same way, using brown icing. An inscription can be piped in the centre. Pipe the edge with a No5 tube in a running scroll pattern.

Honeysuckle Plaque

The use of stencils in combination with piping and runouts is shown here. Place the honeysuckle stencil on the plaque surface. Mix white and yellow icing on the table and spread a little over the back of the stencil. By using white and yellow mixed you will get a more natural effect. Pipe the stems directly on the plaque, outline the leaf shapes and flood with some softened icing. Pipe a filigree butterfly flat on waxed paper. When dry, carefully remove the wings and stick into a body that has been piped directly on the plaque. Arrange two stamens for antenna. Pipe the pulled shell edge with a No6 tube.
(See photograph on page 185)

Figure 1 Plaque

Draw the outline of the figure 1 on tracing paper. Scribe onto the surface of the plaque or cake. Outline number using a No1 tube and flood. Leave to dry. The rabbit on the swing can be painted free-hand, as shown, or the design can be incorported or made as part of the runout design. The rabbit here was painted in food colouring diluted with clear spirit. The 'today' was piped directly onto the surface. Use a No5 tube for the shell edging.

Small Wedding Cake

Cover a 20cm (8in) round cake with white royal icing and place on a 25cm (10in) board.

Runout one large heart and four smaller hearts, pipe some small doves and bells. When the runouts are dried, pipe a picot edge around each one. Eject a small blossom straight onto the smaller one, sticking on with a little dot of icing. Pipe some stems and leaves and two initials. Here an N and S have been piped with No0 tube. Let the initials dry, then paint with silver. The larger heart has three blossoms in a spray with some leaves. Pipe an inscription with a No0 tube and paint with silver when dry.

Make a greaseproof (waxed) paper circle the size of the top of the cake. Fold in half, and in half again to get quarters, unfold and place on top of the cake. Mark a dot on the cake where each of the four fold lines meet the top edge. Using a No0 tube and a ruler, mark a dot 2.5cm (1in) each side of the centre dot and 2.5cm (1in) in from the centre dot. Scrape off the centre dot and you should be left with three dots, two on the edge and one 2.5cm (1in) from the edge. Repeat to make four groups of three dots.

Using a No1 tube, join the dot 2.5cm (1in) from the edge to the two dots on the edge. Tilt the cake and pipe a dropped line from one to the other. Using the No0 tube, cornelli the inside area. Pipe a scalloped line along the two top sides and around the dropped line. Repeat on the other three sections.

Stick the large heart into the centre of the cake. Stick the small hearts under the cornelli sections and pipe a set of S and C scrolls with reverse S and C scrolls in each of the four areas with a No42 tube. Pipe a shell border with the No42 tube. A pair of tiny flying doves are piped underneath the scrolls. Pipe a dropped line under the scrolls, with a scalloped line below. A pair of miniature bells sit under the point where the two C scrolls meet.

Using lilac icing pipe a dot with a No1 tube in the centre of each of the flowers. Pipe a scalloped rope around the shells.

Pipe the first lines of the trellis on the scrolls with the No1 tube. The first stage are vertical lines piped at an angle starting from the end of the C scroll. Bring across to meet the S scroll. Repeat on both sides of the scrolls and on all four sets. Let dry for 10 minutes.

Pipe the horizontal lines on the scrolls following the shape and then pipe a white roped line with the No1 tube on top. Finish with a miniature bow on each of the points where the C scrolls meet.

Pipe clangers for the bells and pipe some dots down the side of the cake. Finish off by placing a matching ribbon around the board.
(See photograph on page 186)

Templates for the plaques
illustrated in this chapter.

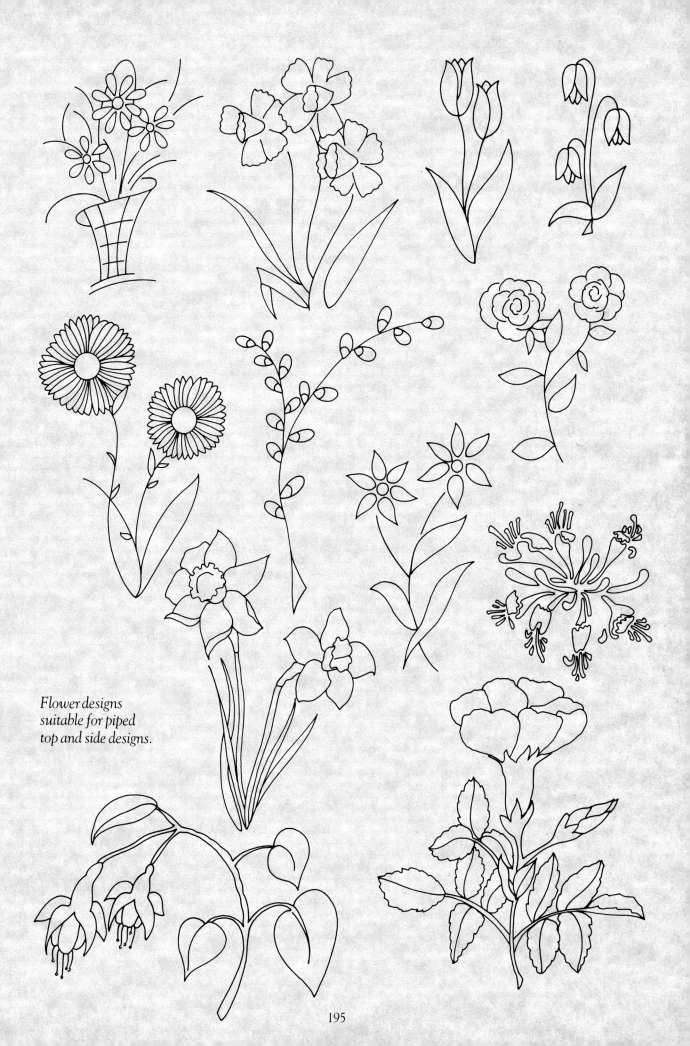

Flower designs
suitable for piped
top and side designs.

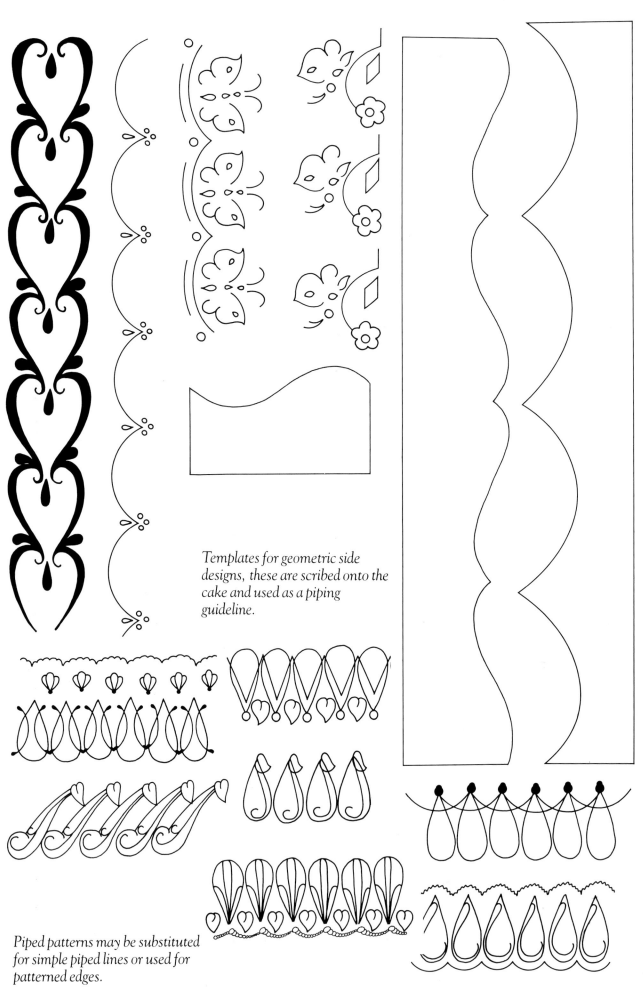

Templates for geometric side designs, these are scribed onto the cake and used as a piping guideline.

Piped patterns may be substituted for simple piped lines or used for patterned edges.

Lettering

Lettering

The most common problem is that many people have not developed a distinctive style. Many types of lettering are shown in this book, but the direct-piped basic lettering on page 214 is a good one to master.

Initially you will have no particular lettering style and although when designing and decorating a cake you will have a pre-conceived idea of what it will look like once decorated and usually it will match your expectations. However, the lettering may be a disappointment because the free-hand lettering style was not well executed. Sometimes it can be too flowing, too curly, going uphill, going downhill and sometimes cramped in areas to small to fit.

It is, therefore, necessary to develop a style of lettering to use for all general work. Once you find one that suits you, study it in depth, draw it out and place in a wipe-clean plastic

Lettering is very important, and if badly executed it can ruin an otherwise attractive cake. People often express a wish to write well on cakes but as with all piping techniques, lettering takes a lot of practice to perfect. If only making one or two inscribed cakes a year, you will not get sufficient experience to write confidently.

folder. Using a No1 tube, practise going over the shapes of the letters again and again. Try writing a letter in the chosen style; while chatting on the telephone doodle on the telephone pad. All of these things help you to learn the lettering style inside and out, and eventually you will know each letter. With your first few cakes you will need the script for reference, but as you become more experienced you will be able to write freehand.

Start off practising on a piece of glass or board so you can clean off and start again. Start with the common day-to-day inscriptions such as Happy Birthday, Congratulations, Anniversary. Learn to use letter-number association, which sounds complicated but is very easy. Associate letters with a familiar inscription which has the same number of letters. For example Love and Nick both have four letters. Once you have practised basic inscriptions, you will know how much room Love will take, and because Nick will be the same size, you know how much room to allocate on the cake surface. By using letter-number association you will always get perfect spacing and never run out of room.

If the total number of individual letters is less than a basic inscription, you should, with a little experience, realize that a name is one letter shorter than Birthday. Start half-way along the B, if writing directly underneath, so the final letter finishes half-way under the Y.

Once letter-number spacing is mastered, you will never have any problems with spacing or running out of room to pipe an inscription. Similarly consistency with the height of letters also comes with practice.

Freehand lettering is most commonly used on cakes, but runout, pressure-piped, direct-piped runout styles can be used on special cakes.

Freestyle Lettering

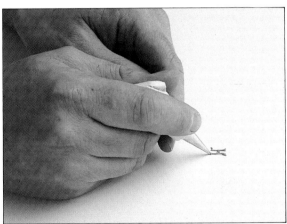

1. Have all your equipment ready before you begin.

2. Place a small amount of icing in the bag and begin writing using firm but even pressure.

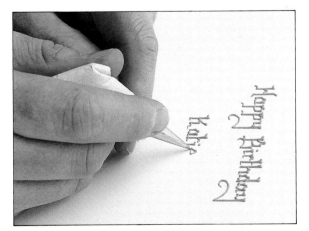

3. Take care to get the spacing even and ensure that all the tops and tails are of equal height.

4. Words on the second line should be spaced centrally below the first line.

Runout Lettering 1

This method is worked directly onto
the cake.

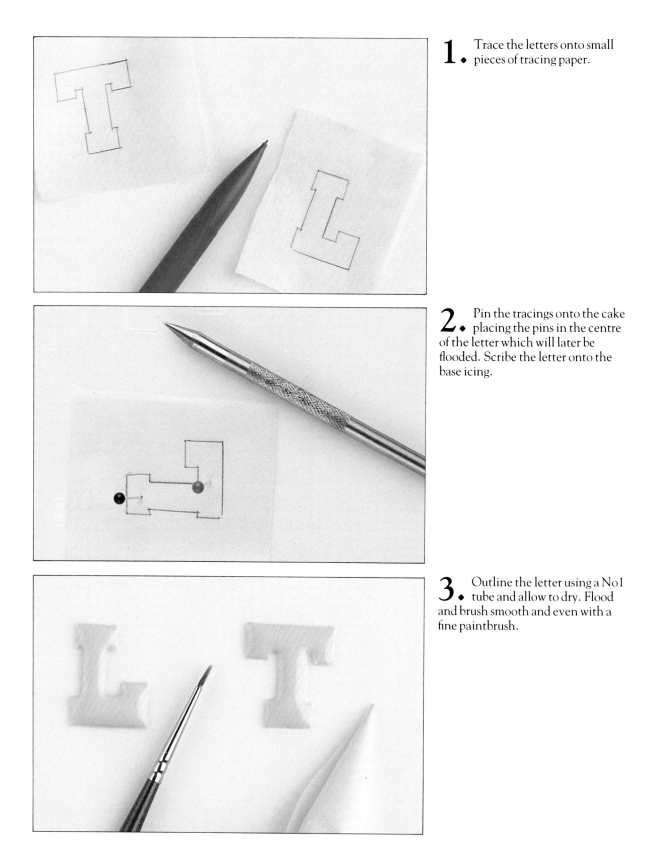

1. Trace the letters onto small
pieces of tracing paper.

2. Pin the tracings onto the cake
placing the pins in the centre
of the letter which will later be
flooded. Scribe the letter onto the
base icing.

3. Outline the letter using a No1
tube and allow to dry. Flood
and brush smooth and even with a
fine paintbrush.

Runout Lettering 2

This method is worked on waxed
paper and then transferred to the cake
when dry.

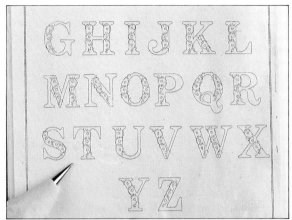

1. Place the chosen lettering in a plastic file. Secure small pieces of waxed paper over the letters to be traced and iced.

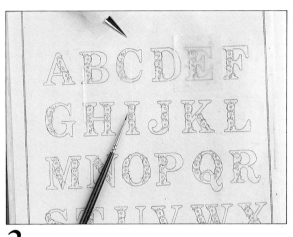

2. Outline the letter using a No1 tube.

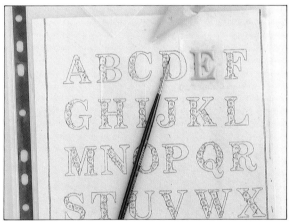

3. Flood the letter brushing it smooth and even with a fine paintbrush.

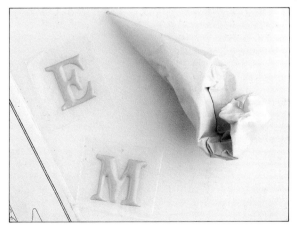

4. The letters should be completely dry before transferring to the cake.

5. Peel the letters off the waxed paper and attach to the cake using small dots of icing.

Monograms

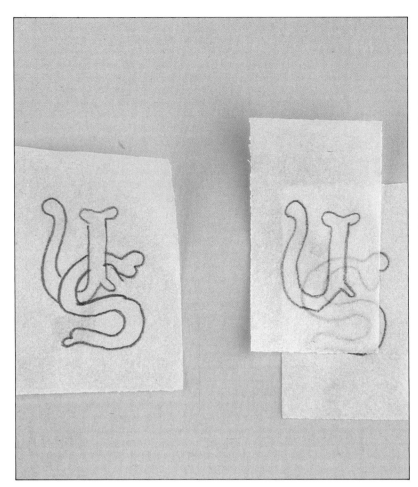

1. The two letters that have to be made into a monogram. Trace each one on a separate piece of tracing or greaseproof paper.

2. Move the letters about until you can overlap them with minimum crossovers. If too much of one letter is covered up, it is hard to read the finished monogram.

3. Once you are happy with the positioning, pin the papers together or place a piece of sticky tape over them to stop them moving.

4. Make a tracing of the completed monogram.

5. Scribe onto the plaque or cake surface using a scriber or hat pin.

6. Outline with ordinary consistency icing using a No0 or 1 tube, depending on the size of the letters – here a No1 was used.

7. The partly completed monogram. The N has been flooded. Let dry for about 30 minutes, then flood the S. It is important to dry one letter first because if you flood both letters at the same time they merge into each other and definition is lost. Monograms can be flooded in the same colours, different colours or shades of the same colour.

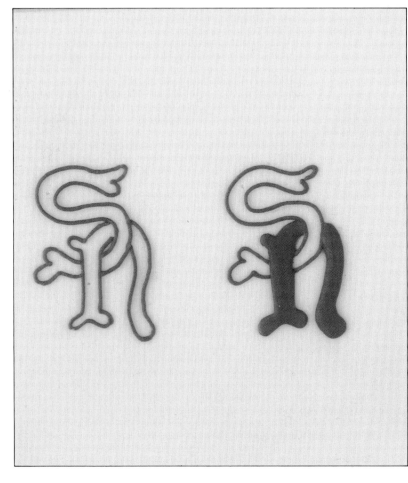

Christmas Plaques

These plaques show different types of script for Christmas cakes, but the styles could be adapted to other suit other types of inscription.

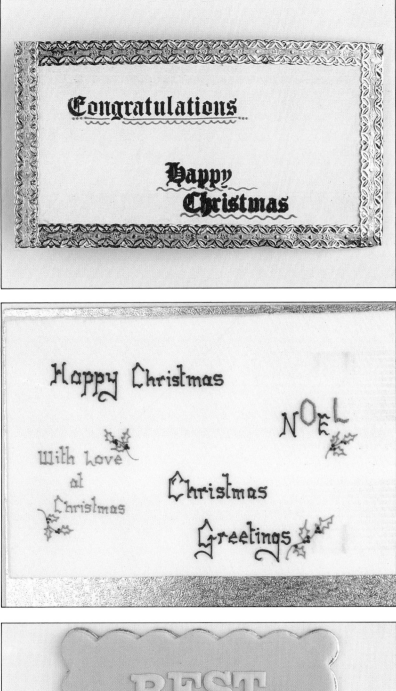

Best Wishes Mother

This simple runout lettering on a square plaque shows how block and decorative lettering styles can be used together. The Best Wishes is a normal block runout lettering style and the Mother is in large runout Old English script, with half of the M in yellow and half in white for contrast.

Lily of the Valley Script

The attractive lily of the valley lettering shown is adapted from an embroidery book.

1. Trace the basic line of the letter onto the tracing paper. Do not worry about the finer detail as this is added freehand. This design can be adapted for monograms which look pretty on the side of a wedding cake.

2. Scribe the letter onto the plaque or cake surface.

3. Pipe the basic line in green icing using a No1 piping tube.

4. Working from your pattern, fill in all the fine detail. The flowers are piped in a No0 tube and the leaves in a No1.

5. The finished name Claire with the lace is piped on freehand.

Floral Lettering

The examples show how to use embroidery techniques for lettering. The name Emily is in block runouts from the alphabet given. Pipe each letter required onto waxed paper, dry then stick to the cake surface. Pipe a rambling rose design up the letters, as shown, with a No0 tube with green icing. The rose buds are small shells piped in red, then pipe on tiny calyxes using the green piping tube.

Emma has a flooded first letter and the rest of the name is piped freehand.

Katy and Sarah have been piped the same way as Emma, but have been decorated in slightly different ways.

The Best Wishes has the B and W directly flooded onto the plaque and the rest piped freehand. The letters have been decorated with tiny piped daffodils.

Pressure-piped Gothic Lettering

1. Cover the lettering with plastic. Secure pieces of waxed paper over the letters to be traced.

2. Using a No 1 tube and white icing, pipe over the outline of the letter.

3. Pressure pipe in the denser parts of the letter as you work. Continue until all the letters are copied. Allow to dry.

4. Lettering can be guilded using silver or gold powder mixed with clear alcohol or use non-toxic gold or silver paint. Dry thoroughly before transferring to the cake.

Gilded Letters

The runout letters are made in white and when dry painted gold or silver. Gold and silver comes in powder and liquid form. The powder has to be mixed with clear alcohol (gin, vodka, etc). Use the liquid in accordance with manufacturer's instructions.

The inscription shows a combination of pressure-piping on waxed paper. When dry stick on to cake surface and gild with a small paintbrush. The other lettering styles are piped with white icing directly onto the plaque and gilded when completely dry.

Direct piped Lettering

This plaque shows various inscriptions, all piped directly onto the surface with a No1 or 0 tube.

Blue Plaque

This simple plaque has a direct piped inscription and a decorative scroll piped with a No0 tube. The spray of flowers has piped royal icing leaves.

Painted Mimosa Plaque

Paint the mimosa leaves and stalks directly onto the plaque or cake, then pipe the 'Happy Birthday' inscription. The numbers are flooded in yellow and white. When dry, stick these on the plaque and finish off by piping 'today' freehand.

Pink Plaque

This plaque shows lettering piped in a circle with a No0 tube. When finished pipe tiny daisies in the centre. Alternatively, a posy of sugar or silk flowers could go into the centre, or make a runout design.

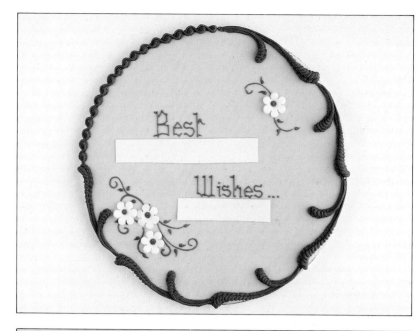

Round Plaque with Scroll Border

This plaque shows one technique for ensuring that lettering is straight. Cut thin strips of card or stiff paper and place on the cake or plaque surface. This gives a guideline to follow so you pipe in a straight line. Pipe shell and scroll edging with a No43 tube.

Dotted Lettering

This plaque shows different styles of lettering and numerals piped in dots. The name Cloe has a piped outline which is filled in with dots. The '18' and '21' and 'Best Wishes' are all piped directly onto the surface using a No. 1 tube.

The pressure-piped scroll lettering is piped in a No1 tube onto waxed paper. When dry the letters can be guilded in gold or silver or, as shown, with lustre colour mixed with clear spirit (gin, vodka, etc) and then painted over the surface. Leave to dry on the waxed paper, remove and stick on the surface with a little royal icing. A No5 tube was used for the shell edging to complete the plaque.

Monogram Plaque

This plaque shows three styles of monogram: runout, piped and painted. The R and J monogram is a runout. Trace the monogram onto tracing paper. Scribe onto the plaque or cake surface; outline with a No1 tube and flood in the monogram as shown in blue and yellow. Flood the back letter, leave to dry, then flood the second letter.

The piped monogram is started in the same way as the first, but it is not flooded for definition. Pipe using a contrasting colour to that used for the base of the cake.

The third monogram is painted. Draw monogram on tracing paper; scribe onto the surface. Paint with food colouring or with lustre colour.

Writing in a Circle

Writing in a circle looks good on a round cake. A posy or runout design could be placed in the centre of the circle. Pipe lettering before adding the centre decoration.

Place a round thin cake board on top of the cake. Make sure the board is large enough so that the centre decoration will fit. Decide on how much space the lettering will take up, then start piping. The tails of the Ps, Ys, and Gs are piped after the board is removed. Continue until the inscription is finished, remove the board and pipe any tails. Place the centre decoration in position.

Baby Plaque

This design would be suitable for a birth congratulations cake or christening cake. The main letters are direct-flooded runouts. Scribe the pattern on to the cake or plaque surface. Paint in the background using food colour mixed with clear spirit (gin, vodka, etc). Paint the stems of the foliage, the leaves and the cupids. Outline the B and W with No0 tube and flood in with pale pink royal icing. Leave to dry. Flood in the pillow and baby's head and paint in the blanket. The birds are pressure piped. Leave to dry, then position as shown. Paint the features on the baby's face. Use a small ejector to eject white blossom onto the plaque. Pipe the dots of pink icing into the centre of each blossom.

Pink Plaque

This plaque shows how to use plastic embossing script. Push the plastic piece into the paste covering of the cake or plaque within 15 minutes of coating, before a surface crust forms. Push into the paste in a straight movement – do not move about or you will get a distorted impression. Once pushed in, pull out straight to get a clean finish. When the impression is made you can leave it, or overpipe or outline the letters when the paste is dry.

Commercial Scripts

This plaque shows a few of the many types of silver and gold plastic scripts and numerals available. These can be used on cakes or plaques. If you do not feel confident to write on a cake or are short of time these are an acceptable alternative.

Easter Plaque

This plaque would be suitable for an Easter cake, or the idea could be used for a child's name. Add pressure-piped animals or runout figures. The six letters are runouts. Leave to dry. Stick on to the cake surface with a little royal icing. Paint some grass along the base of the letters; pressure pipe the rabbits, as required, and then eject some mini-ejector blossom onto the grass.

Easter Cake

Pressure-piped Rabbits

1. Pipe a bulb for the head.

2. Pipe the body. This is a large shell piped from the bottom upwards.

3. The ears and top part of the legs are piped on both using shell shapes.

4. Pipe in the feet, arms and the whiskers with a No0 tube. The body is textured with a fine paint-brush, either while piping or when the rabbit is finished. These rabbits can also be piped in miniature.

Easter Cake

Cover a 20cm (8in) square cake with pale lemon royal icing. Place on a 27.5cm (11in) square board.

Make a pattern for the large letter E by tracing onto tracing or greaseproof paper. Scribe the E on the cake surface. Outline with a dark yellow in a small bag fitted with a No1 tube, then flood with the same shade of runout icing.

Using a small cranked palette knife, smooth some green royal icing around the board. Place small mounds of sugarpaste on the sides of the cake, touching the board. Spread green royal icing over these, then, gently pat the surface with a piece of foam rubber. Dust blue petal dust around the side to make the sky.

Pressure-pipe some rabbits on the side. With a No1 tube in a small bag filled with green royal icing, pipe grass and flower stems, leaves around the edge. Eject some small ejector blossoms on the sides.

When the E is dry, dust some blue around it and paint a small butterfly. Pipe some stems with a No1 tube, using a small petal tube, pipe some daffodils directly onto the stems. Pipe in some leaves by cutting a V into the end of a bag. Spread some icing along the base of the E, then pipe the rest of the inscription with a No1 tube and pipe a pressure-piped rabbit.

Pipe a shell edging around the top edge to finish the cake.

The following scripts, figures, monograms and common words represent a good selection of lettering styles. Use in conjunction with the instructions in this chapter.

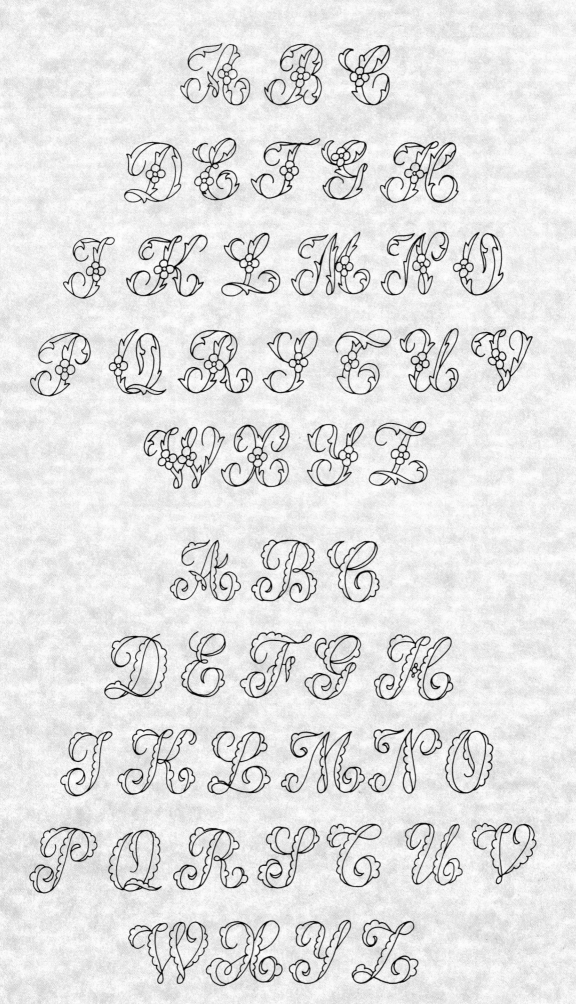

ABCDEF
GHIJKL
MNOPQ
RSTUV
WXYZ

Mother   Kate

Anniverzary

Father

ABCDEFGH
IJKLMNOP
QRSTUVW
XYZ

1234567890

1234567890

1234567890

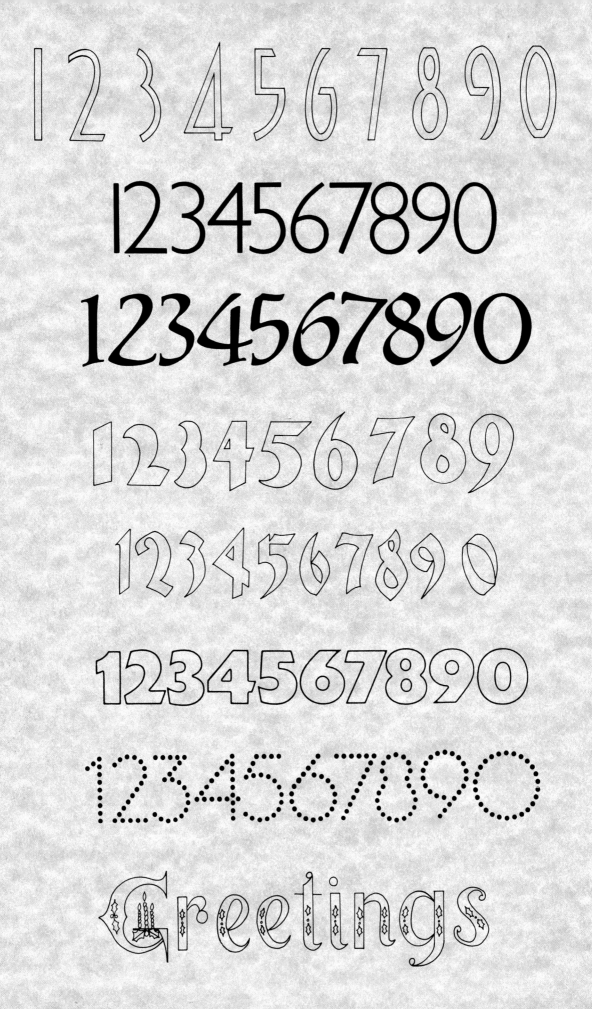

BEST WISHES

Best Wishes

Greetings

Greetings

GREETINGS

GREETINGS

Congratulations

Congratulations

Congratulations

Congratulations

Congratulations

Greetings

Greetings

Greetings

Greetings

Congratulations

G G

Claire

On your 21st

Easter

Congratulations
on your Ruby
Wedding

To My Valentine

21years

18

25

25

21

Congratulations
50
Golden years

50

224

LESSON 19

Tulle

Tulle Work

Tulle piped with royal icing offers an interesting medium to the cake decorator, as the most delicate designs and flowers can be made.

Tulle comes in silk, cotton and synthetic fibres. Silk and cotton tulle are very expensive and difficult to obtain, so a synthetic tulle is a popular choice. For most work you will need the finest tulle available, which is bridal or veiling tulle available from a fabric or wedding shop in white, ivory and, occasionally, pastel colours.

You can dye the tulle with a fabric dye or food colouring. Soak the tulle in paste or liquid food colouring diluted with boiling water; (it is also possible to dye ribbons to match using this method). Once the tulle has been left to soak for 2-3 hours, lift out of solution and pat on a kitchen towel, then leave to dry. You will only get pale colours with food colour. If more vibrant colours are required, use a fabric dye and follow the manufacturer's instructions for use.

Tulle may also be coloured with petal dust, but again this is only suitable for very soft pastels.

Old bridal veils may sometimes be bought from second-hand shops for very little money and once washed, offer a cheaper alternative to buying new fabric.

Techniques

There are two basic styles for tulle work. The first uses flat cut-out pieces for such things as petals and leaves. The basic principle is to cut out the shape and, if drying flat, put it onto waxed paper or a lightly greased surface. The design is then piped freehand or by following a pattern placed under the waxed paper. Dry, remove and assemble or attach to cake surface. For curved pieces, attach the tulle on waxed paper to curve before piping, or place tulle over a greased surface.

If complicated designs are being piped and you need a pattern, pipe flat over the pattern and then place over a curved surface to dry. Work quickly, as the object must be wet when placed over the curve to prevent cracking. The second technique is for making tulle items such as christening robes, handkerchiefs, frills, etc. These are

sewn or folded, and then royal icing embroidery is piped on them. Work on a piece of foam if necessary. For objects like the robe, embroider the back, dry, then turn over and pipe the front last.

Frills

To make tulle frills, cut a strip of tulle two-and-a-half to three times the circumference of the cake. The depth will depend on the design. Once cut, fold up again and again until the piece is 2.5 to 5cm (1 to 2in). Cut one or two scallops. When the tulle is unfolded, the scallop edge is repeated along the length of the strip. Using a needle and thread, sew a running stitch along the other straight edge. When completed, tie thread around cake then stick the tulle down using a No1 tube with royal icing to match the shade of the covering. Make sure

the frills are even all the way around before sticking down. Place a ribbon over the join. Tulle frills can be left plain or embroidered.

Tulle Extension Work

As a simpler and much quicker alternative to piped extension work you can do tulle extension work. First of all decide on the shape; the work here is in a triangular pattern.

226

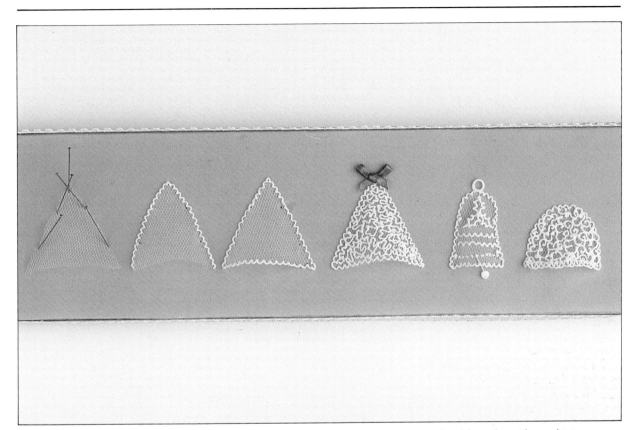

Bells and Oval Shapes

Cut out the tulle and pin onto the side of the cake. You will have to make a pattern so you know where to place each piece of tulle, either touching or slightly apart. Pipe a scalloped line along the edges, the icing should be right on the edge of the tulle so part of it touches the cake surface. Allow to dry. Pipe cornelli work all over the tulle and a scalloped line along the base. Finish off with a dropped line along the edge and place a tiny bow over the point.

Cut bell shapes, pipe in the same way as for triangular pieces. Pipe a clanger coming out of the bottom. The half oval also looks attractive on a shallow cake.

Narrow lilac frill

Cut a 2.5cm (1in) wide strip of tulle three times the circumference of the cake. Cut a scalloped edge, using a needle and thread put a running stitch along the straight edge of the strip. Gather, then stick around the side of the cake with royal icing. When dry, stick some pink and lilac ribbon above the frill, finishing off with a small bow in each colour. The embroidery on the tulle is piped with a No0 tube. Tiny dots are piped around the tulle and a scalloped line around the edge.

Wide Lilac Frills

This frill is approximately 5cm (2in) wide. Cut inverted scallops at regular intervals along the edge. Put a running stitch into the straight edge, gather and stick around the side of the cake. Embroider with tiny forget-me-nots and a scalloped line using a No0 tube. Finish off by sticking wide cotton lace above the tulle frill.

Butterfly

Cut out a pair of tulle butterfly wings using the template. Place the wings on a small piece of waxed paper. Pipe the design with a No0 tube and white icing. The design can be piped freehand or place a pattern under the template. Be sure the scalloped line on the edge has no gaps in it, or the wing may collapse. Dry the wings.

Pipe the body, using a No2 piping tube, directly on the cake surface or on a piece of waxed paper. Place the wings in the wet icing at once. Use a piece of foam or folded paper under each wing so that they dry at the angle you require.

Tiger Lily Petals

Cut out six orange petals for each lily using the template given. Lightly grease a former and stick the petals down over the former using a small dot of icing at each end. Using a No 1 tube, pipe a scalloped line up both sides. Pipe three lines from the base up to approximately one-third of the length of the petal. Pipe in brown dots for the spots on the petals. Continue on all six petals.

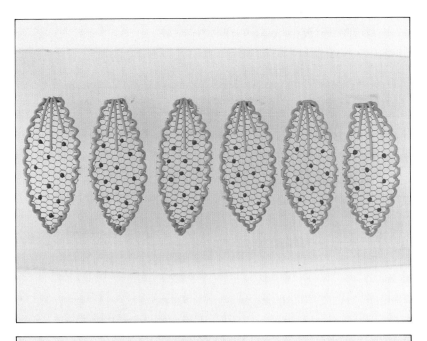

Tiger Lily Leaf

Cut out green tulle using the template. Place on a former and pipe a scalloped line along both edges. Pipe a straight line down the centre to support the leaf. Dry then reassemble around the tiger lilies. Assemble the tiger lily directly onto the cake surface or onto waxed paper. Pipe a bulb of orange royal icing and position the three base petals in a triangle. The next three petals are placed on top to fill in the three gaps left. Place six half-length stamens and one three-quarter-length stamen in the centre. Use large lily stamens brushed with brown royal icing over the ends.

Tulle Booties

These tulle booties have been piped in white on white tulle, but pastel tulle or icing could be used. The tiny bows could be in pink, blue or lemon.

A nice idea for using these is instead of a birth congratulations card. Put a pair of booties on a small plaque with a suitable inscription and give as a three-dimensional card, which could be placed in the nursery under a small glass dome. The booties look attractive on a christening cake.

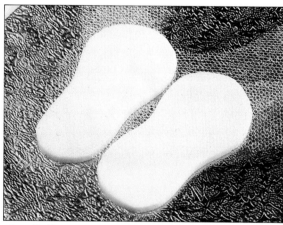

1. Roll out some sugarpaste or flower paste to approximately 3mm (¹⁄₁₀in) thick. Using the template given, cut out two soles with a scalpel or modelling knife. Turn one piece over so you have a pair of booties. Cut two tulle pieces for the tops.

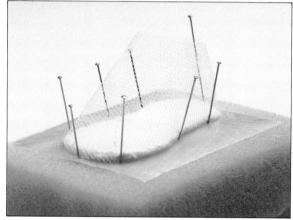

2. Place the soles on separate pieces of waxed paper and place on foam rubber. Using, a piping bag with No1 tube start at the back and stick the tulle edge to the sole. Use pins to help the tulle stick to the icing. Place the pins against the sole, but not into the paste. Thread a pin down the back of the tulle to hold together the heal end.

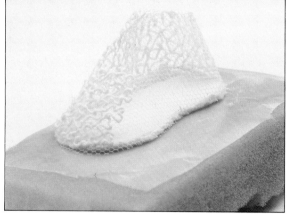

3. When the icing has dried, remove the pins by gently twisting each one. Use a No0 tube to cornelli all over the surface of the tulle.

4. Still keeping the bootie on the waxed paper, pipe a tiny shell around the base with the No0 tube. Finish with a miniature bow on each bootie.

Using white tulle, cut out the bodice using the template and cut a rectangle 40 x 12 cm (16 x 5″) for the skirt. Scallop one long edge of the rectangle and using a needle and thread, sew a line of running stitch close to the other edge. Pull the thread to gather up the tulle then sew the skirt to the bodice.

Attach blue, pink or lemon ribbon around the seam. A bow with long tails is sewn on the back and a tiny bow is sewn on the front.

Turn the robe over, place on foam rubber and start the embroidery. Use a No0 tube. Pipe scalloped lines around the bodice, with a row of bulbs to represent buttons. The main embroidery on the skirt is a rose and leaf pattern. When the flower embroidery is finished, pipe a scalloped line following the line of the hem. Tiny bows are piped on top of each one of the scallops. Leave to dry for about 30 minutes then turn over, place back on the foam, and embroider the front to match the back, except for the buttons. Leave to dry before placing on a cake.

Tulle Sprays

Tulle gives a soft effect when used in flower sprays. It softens harsh colours and flowers and fills in gaps in sprays or spaces around larger flat flowers like orchids and lilies. Choice of tulle is very important; use a very soft tulle like cotton or bridal tulle (veiling) so it folds into soft pleats. The coarser grade tulle will look very rigid and slightly harsh in sprays.

Making Tulle Sprays

1. Cut out a rectangle of tulle. The larger the rectangle the larger and longer the finished spray will be. An average size would be 7x12cm (3x5in).

2. Using your thumb and fingers, gather up the centre of the tulle along its length and hold in the the centre. Place a piece of 28-gauge wire over the centre. The wire should be approximately 15cm (6in) long.

3. Pull up both halves of the wire and twist firmly to secure. Trim off any excess tulle by pulling the sides back up and cutting with scissors. Pull out into a nice rounded shape.

Tulle and Pearl Sprays

These tulle sprays have pearls included in them and offer an alternative to plain tulle. Ribbons, feathers and silk flowers can also be wired in with tulle.

Handkerchief

Handkerchiefs look pretty in pastel colours with white piping. Tuck into a spray of flowers or place on top of a cake. Cut a square of tulle, fold into quarters and cut a large scalloped edge along both sides of the square. Open out and then fold in half diagonally, then fold the two sides under to get the shape shown. Pin together in several places. Embroider with a No0 tube. Pipe an oval cameo with an initial in the centre and daisy embroidery around the cameo. A line is then piped around the edge. Leave to dry before removing pins.

Heart

Cut out a tulle heart using the pattern given. Place on a piece of waxed paper and pipe a freehand embroidery design with a No1 tube. Similarly, a name could be piped or a runout attached. Use No5 tube to pipe a shell outline. When dry this heart can be used for the top of a cake. Make smaller hearts for the sides.

233

Posy Frill

This spray of fabric flowers in white, pink and green has been edged with a tulle posy frill.

Cut a strip of tulle 10cm (4in) wide and 40cm (16in) long. Fold in half and put a running stitch on the fold with a needle and thread. Fold in eight and cut a scalloped edge on the open side. Gather up the tulle and tie around the base of the flowers. Wrap a piece of fine wire around the posy to secure in place. With white royal icing and a No1 piping tube, pipe tiny dots all over the surface.

Briar Rose

Cut out five tulle petals for each rose from the template given. Place each petal on cupped foam as shown, pushing a pin into the centre of the tulle to cup it. Using a No1 tube, pipe a line around the tulle petals. Leave to dry. Once dry dust a little pink dusting powder at the base of each petal. Carefully pull out the pins using tweezers or fine-ended pliars.

Assemble the petals into a ring of icing piped on waxed paper or directly onto the cake surface. Support each petal with sponge pieces. Pipe some dots of bright yellow into the centre and place some yellow stamens into the wet icing. Leave to dry.

Rose Leaves

Cut out green tulle leaves.
Grease the surface of a former;
stick the broad end of the leaf
down. Using a No0 tube outline
the leaf shape. Never go over the
edge of the tulle. Pipe in the veins.
Dry, then attach to rose.

Bow Plaque

This plaque shows the steps for
making a tulle bow. Cut out the bow
pieces; two tails and one centre piece.
All the work is piped with a No0 tube.
Stick pieces into a bulb of royal icing,
folding one of each of the ends into
the centre. Pipe a scalloped line and
dots on the side pieces. Fold over the
two outer points and stick these into
the centre. Continue the piping onto
the top of the bow. Place the first tail
in position, piping a line around the
edge and dots to match the bow.
Place the second tail in position and
then fold the central piece into the
centre to finish off the tulle bow.

235

Loop bow

Cut out a loop of red tulle using the template. For the Christmas Cake featured you will need nine loops. Place a dot of icing onto waxed paper. Place one end of the tulle on the dot of icing. Pipe a scalloped line along both sides of the stuck-down end. Fold over the other side of tulle and stick on top of the first dot of icing. Continue piping the scalloped line on the top piece. Leave to dry.

Tails

Make one pair. Cut out tulle using the pattern. Pipe a scalloped line along the edge of piece. Reverse the other to make a pair and pipe as before.

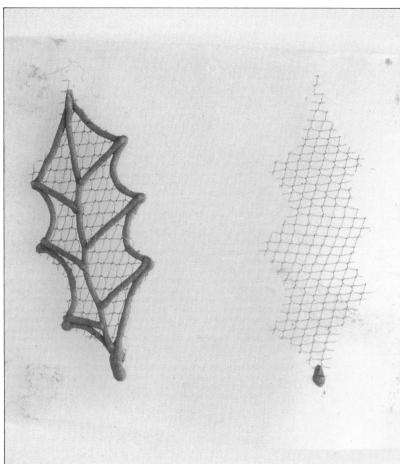

Holly Leaves

Cut out some green tulle following the holly leaf template. Pipe green outline and veins onto each leaf.

Ivy Leaves

Cut out the ivy leaves from green tulle using the template. Place on a curved surface. Pipe an outline and veins onto the leaves. Dry before use. These leaves look attractive with tulle flowers.

Christmas Rose

Cut out five petals for each rose from white tulle, using the template given. Place petals on waxed paper. Pipe an irregular straight line over the tulle to give a more natural effect to the petals. Dry the petals. When dry, pipe a circle of white royal icing, using a No1 tube, on another piece of waxed paper. Use a No0 tube to pipe bright yellow dots in the centre. While still soft position tiny yellow stamens with tweezers. When the flower is dry, dust a little moss green petal dust into the centre.

Tulle Christmas Cake

Prepare a petal-shaped board, covered in red velvet with white cotton lace around the edge. Bake a 15cm (6in) round cake, marzipan and cover in white sugarpaste. When covered place on a 15cm (6in) circle of waxed paper.

Place the cake with its circle of waxed paper onto the board. Paper stops the fruit cake from coming into direct contact with the velvet on the board.

Pipe a shell around the base using a No42 piping tube. Use a 10cm (4in) board or cutter to mark a circle on the cake top for a guideline for the wreath.

Assemble the wreath. You will need approximately thirty tulle holly leaves, five christmas roses, nine bow loops and two tails. Use green royal icing to stick tulle pieces to the cake. Leave a 40mm (1½in) gap for the bow, which is assembled last. Stick five loops into a central bulb of icing, then place three more loops on top, and then one in the centre. To finish, position the tails into the bow to trail down the wreath. Pipe the holly berries in red.

Make a strip of tulle two-and-a-half times the circumference of the cake and approximately 6.5cm (2½in) wide and cut one side with a scalloped edge. Using a needle and thread, make a running stitch along the straight edge, and tie the tulle around the cake. Stick on using a No1 tube with white royal icing. You can use pins to hold tulle in position, but make sure that you remove them once icing is dry. Place a picot edge ribbon above the tulle, covering up the join. Embroider the tulle frill with tiny dots piped with a No1 tube and using green royal icing. To finish the frill pipe a scalloped line around the edge using a No0 tube and white icing. A suitable inscription could be written in the centre of the wreath, if liked.

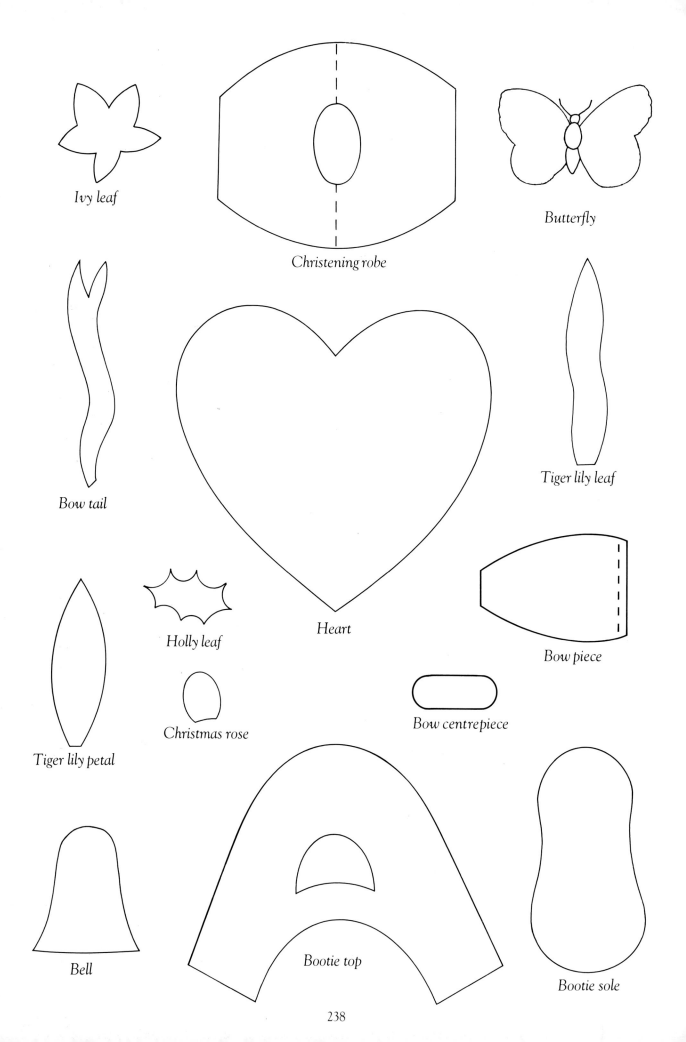

Ivy leaf

Christening robe

Butterfly

Bow tail

Tiger lily leaf

Heart

Holly leaf

Bow piece

Tiger lily petal

Christmas rose

Bow centrepiece

Bell

Bootie top

Bootie sole

238

LESSON 20

Modelling

Modelling

Marzipan and sugarpaste can be used to model all sorts of shapes and figures to decorate cakes. Figure modelling is easy once the basic shapes have been learned, and even children can quickly create interesting and attractive models.

Use white marzipan for modelling, as it takes colour well. Home-made marzipan can be used, but commercial paste tends to be less sticky. Sugarpaste is easy to model and will roll without cracking, but because it is very soft, only simple, small figures can be made. If making more complicated figures, such as the clown, add gum tragacanth to make the paste stronger and more pliable. Use 5ml (1 teaspoon) for 250g (8oz) sugarpaste, knead thoroughly, then place in a plastic bag and rest for 2 hours before using.

When assembling figures, glue pieces together with a little egg white or with melted chocolate. Do not use cocktail sticks or wires on figures for children's cakes or party favours.

Equipment

Only a minimal amount of equipment is necessary for modelling, and often household tools can be adapted if special tools are unavailable. Most useful are a nonstick work surface and rolling pin; sharp kitchen knife; and a ball modelling tool. A crochet hook can be used instead of a ball tool.

Other modelling tools are available from cake decorating shops or from craft shops. Many tools used by potters are useful for marzipan modelling, as the techniques are quite similar.

All of the marzipan and sugarpaste figures are made using the some basic shapes. Practice each shape before trying out the figures. It is useful to measure out each piece so that you learn to recognise a 15g (½oz) ball, cone, etc, as this will help you to keep the pieces for each figure in proportion.

1. To make a ball, roll the marzipan between the lower part of the palms of your hands.

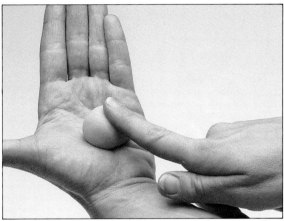

2. A butterbean shape is created when you place a ball in the palm of your hand and gently roll it with the index finger of your other hand.

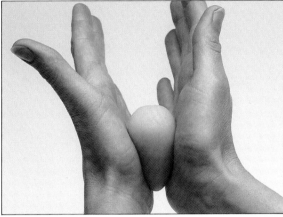

3. Form a cone by placing the ball at the base of your palms and move your hands backwards and forwards until the cone is smooth.

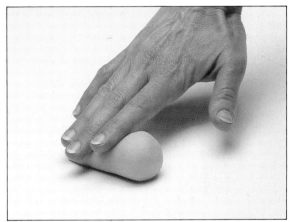

4. To make a elongated cone, place the cone on the work surface and roll the pointed end gently backwards and forwards.

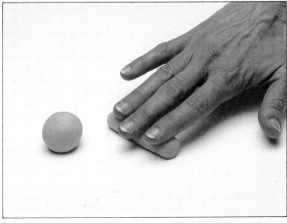

5. To make a sausage shape, place the ball on the work surface and gently roll out, using two or three fingers.

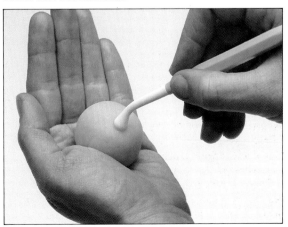

6. Use a ball tool or something similar to make indentations for eye sockets. Hold the ball of marzipan in one hand and gently press in the ball tool.

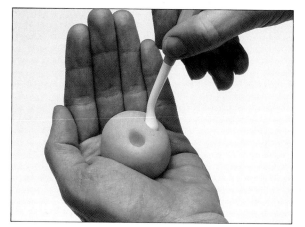

7. Pull the handle of the ball tool upwards and pull away quickly.

8. When making pieces for arms or legs, always make a ball first and then cut in half or in quarters to ensure even-sized pieces.

Sheep

Make a 4g (1/8oz) ball of black marzipan and cut in half. Make 15g (1/2oz) cone of white marzipan, with a slightly flattened end. Take one of the black pieces, roll into a ball and cut into four. Roll each one into a ball for the legs. Take the second black piece, save a little for the ears, then roll the rest into a cone and flatten to make head shape. Cut mouth using a modelling knife and make nostrils using a cocktail stick. Stick the four legs in position and place the head on the body. Using a small ball tool, make the eye cavities. Mould two small triangular ears and position. Using the clay gun, or a fine sieve or garlic crusher, with white marzipan make the fur. Attach all over the body. Pipe in the eyes using a No1 tube with white icing and let dry, then paint in black pupils.

Cat

This sweet little cat could be made in many colour combinations.

Make a 15g (½oz) ball. Cut into two pieces, one slightly larger than the other. Roll both pieces into balls, place the larger on the bottom for the body and the smaller one on top for the head. Press an oval of white sugarpaste on the front. Mould two upper and two lower legs and position. Mark the pads on the paws. Mould two small ovals and press on face for the cheeks. Mark a hole and use a half-scoop tool to mark the mouth. The nose is a pale pink ball; position and mark nostrils using a cocktail stick. Mark two indentations for the eyes using a ball tool. Place two triangular pieces for the ears; indent. Place some pink in each ear. Attach a long thin sausage tail. Place some white stamen cotton into the cheeks for whiskers. Pipe eyes with a No1 tube and, when dry, paint black with food colouring mixed with a little confectioner's varnish for the two pupils.

243

Mouse

This delightful little mouse can be used on many types of cakes and could be made larger is wished.

Make an 8g (¼oz) brown marzipan cone shape with quite a tapered end, then bend the end over for the head. Make two indentations for the ears, mould and attach the ears. Make two indentations for the eyes. Attach a pink rose. Place three pieces of stamen cotton on each side for the whiskers. Cut a small ball in half and mould two arms. For the apron, roll out some white paste, cut out a small circle, cut off the top, then frill the edges using a cocktail stick. Stick on with egg white. Cut a small rectangle of paste, place above the frilled piece for the top of the apron. Roll two thin white sausages and place one around the neck and one around the body. Trim off excess. Make a bow out of a thin sausage of paste and stick on back. Position a small pocket and add a little pink marzipan handkerchief. Attach arms. Finish off by piping in the eyes. When dry paint in pupils. Make a tiny basket filled with miniature apples or flowers to go over one arm.

Goose

Make a 15g (½oz) ball. Mark into quarters and cut out a quarter section. Make the three-quarter piece into a cone shape. Elongate the thin end into the neck. Make a bulb for the head. Squash the rounded end and cut into four. Curl over to give the effect of tail feathers. Make two eye indentations using a small ball tool and with the same tool make an indentation for the beak. Taking the remaining quarter section, cut in half, and put one piece back in the pack. The remaining piece is cut into two. Roll each piece into a ball and squash for the wings. Mark the feathers and attach wings to the body. Mould a yellow piece for the beak and attach. Make two orange pieces for the feet; mark the webbing with a cocktail stick. Attach.

Chicken

Make a 15g (½ oz) orange-brown marzipan cone. Elongate the neck. Make a bulb for the head. Flatten the other end for the tail. Cut the tail feathers with small scissors, then roll around the paintbrush to curl. Use a half-scoop modelling tool to mark the feathers all over, except on the head. Make a small ball of orange-brown paste and cut in half for wings. Thin each piece between your fingers and attach to the body. Use the scoop tool to mark the feathers and help join the wings to the body. Make a small piece of red marzipan and mould the cockscomb and gisard and place into position. Place two small pieces on either side of the face and flatten. Make the beak from yellow paste. Make indentations for eyes. Pipe the eyes using white icing. When dry paint in black pupils. The feet are cut from a thin sausage and attached. Mould two or three eggs. Dust yellow on the breast of the chicken.

Pig

Make a 22g (¾oz) pink cone. Drag the narrow end across the work surface to flatten for the snout, turn and pull the nose up. Cut the mouth with a small sharp knife and mark the two nostrils using a ball tool. Make a ball of paste and cut into four. Mould each one into a ball and position for the legs. Make indentations for the eyes and ears in the front and indent the back for the tail. Mould and position. Mould the tail and place into the cavity. Pipe in the whites of eyes using a No1 tube, and paint the brown pupils when dry.

Goat and Cow

These are made in the same way, although the faces are a little different. Pull up one end for the neck and make a bulb for the head. Pull them up and out. The back is pinched slightly to give a ridge. Mould the tail by pulling a piece from the back end of the sausage. Make two indentations each side for the legs to sit in. Squash in thin sausages of white marzipan for markings. Cut mouth, make two ears and two eye sockets. Make some indentations down front. Make small gruff to go under the goat's chin. Place a piece of white above the tail. Make four sausages for legs. The back ones are only two-thirds full length as they sit under the body. Pipe the whites of the eyes with a No1 tube; paint black pupils in when dry.

247

Farmer

Trousers: Make a 15g (½oz) blue sausage. Cut in half two-thirds of the way up to represent the legs. Mould to make rounded. Make a small cavity in each of the ends for the shoes to sit in.

Shoes: Make a small brown ball. Cut in half and mould into shoe shapes. Make two little pegs to hold shoes to trousers. Stick together and lay down on foam to dry.

Head: Make a flesh-coloured ball with a slight piece moulded down for the neck. Mould a nose and place into identations. Use a half-scoop tool to mark the mouth. The eye cavities are made using a small ball tool.

Shirt: Make a 15g (½oz) cone shape.

Cap and crook: Mould a long thin sausage for the crook. The cap is a flattened ball with a small piece on the front for the peak. Mark the lines on top with a small knife.

Arms and shirt top: Cut a ball in half and mould into a sausage. Using a ball tool, make an indentation into each end of the sausage and place cone-shaped arm in each.

Assembling: Stick trousers and top together. Make waistcoat out of green marzipan by rolling and then cutting out the shape. A brown belt is put around his waist. Make a cavity for his neck to sit in and place his head in position. Paint hair using food colouring and then put on cap. Tie a red scarf around neck. Dust cheeks pink and paint in lips. Pipe in white of eyes with a No1 tube, then paint in his pupils using a fine paintbrush. Mould 2 tiny ears and place one either side of his head.

Farmyard Birthday Cake

Marzipan and royal ice a 20cm (8in) square cake. The first two coats are white. Coat the sides only with two further coats in blue icing. Dry thoroughly.

Scribe a line along the four sides using a scriber and ruler. Place the ruler against the side with one edge resting on the board and scribe a line along the top edge. Using green food colour diluted with clear spirit (gin, vodka), paint grass around the edge.

Pipe four fence pieces onto waxed paper following the template. Use brown icing without glycerine and No2 piping tube. Leave to dry. Using a small cranked palette knife, spread green icing on the board and over the edge then pat with a piece of foam to give a stippled effect. Leave to dry. Tilt each side in turn and position the fence pieces. Dry. Using white icing and a No1 tube, pipe the clouds, then use foam or a paint brush to fluff them up. Pipe grass up fence using a No0 tube. Add small ejector blossoms for the flowers. Pipe birds in the sky.

Top assembly

Make four fence pieces following the template. Spread some green icing on to the top of the cake leaving a small white area for the inscription. Remove the four dry fence panels, and stick the first along the back of the cake with a line of green icing. The second piece goes along the right-hand side of the cake, the third along the front and the fourth is attached at the join of the first, but left open, as shown. Pipe some brown icing with a No1 tube around tops to look like rope. Place the sheep in the pen and the farmer in position. Pipe the inscription in the white area and pipe a border along top edges. If liked, position other marzipan animals around the board.

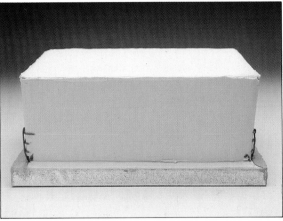

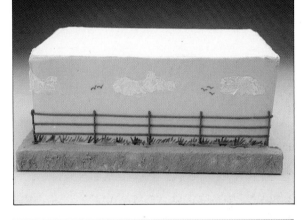

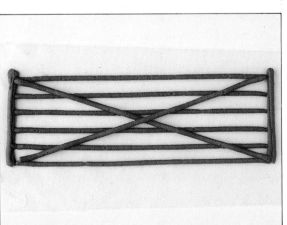

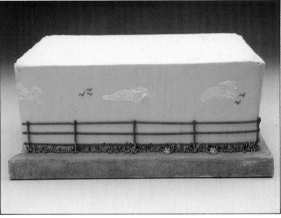

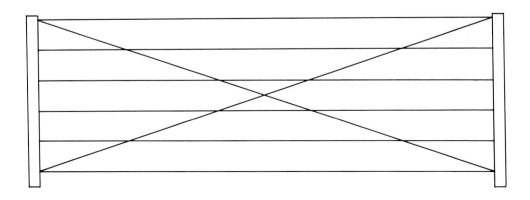

Sugarpaste and Marzipan Roses

The roses can be made in any size from sugarpaste or marzipan. The principle is the same. If you are using sugarpaste, knead in a little white fat (shortening). You can leave the rose at any of the first three stages, making it into a bud, medium or a larger rose. The size of the cone and ball of paste for the petals will determine the size of the finished rose.

1. Mould a cone of paste.

2. Take a piece of paste, roll into a ball and then place between a folded piece of polythene.

3. Thin out the petal edges. Remove from polythene and wrap around the cone, enclosing the cone completely. Waist in cone to establish shape.

4. Place two more petals, made in the same way around the cone.

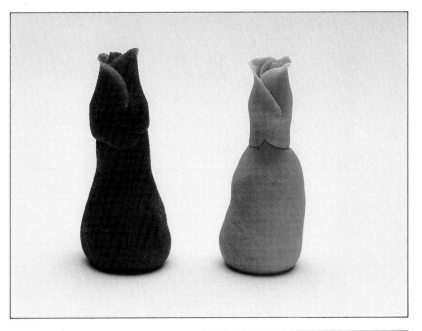

5. The third row has three petals, making a total of six petals.

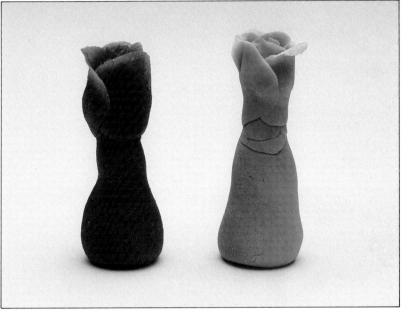

6. The full finished rose with its outer four petals has a total of ten petals.

Marzipan Blossom

These blossoms, which can be any colour, are based on the same principle as flower paste pulled flowers. Make a small cone of marzipan. Place on a wooden dowel by pushing the broad end of the cone onto the point of the stick. Carefully cut five petals with a modelling knife. Open up each petal by placing your finger down the centre. Squash, pinch and pull each petal. Continue until each petal has been pulled, giving a rounded petal shape.

Bend a piece of wire and place on waxed paper. Roll out some marzipan and cut out blossom using a large ejector cutter. Pipe dots of icing along the wire at regular intervals and place the blossoms onto the wire. Pipe a dot in the centre. Let dry for 24 hours, then use in a spray.

For three-dimensional blossom, make small Mexican hats, place ejector blossom over the cone and cut out the blossom. Make a small hook on a piece of wire and push down throat of flower. Pipe a stamen in the centre using a No1 tube. Dry before using in a spray.

Sugarpaste Clown

This little clown would be suitable for a child's birthday cake and could be made in any colour combination.

1. Make a 22g (¾oz) blue sugarpaste ball. Make a 15g (½oz) flesh-coloured ball.

2. Mould the blue piece into a cone and then stick the flesh ball on top for the head using a little egg white. Make an indentation either side of the body for the legs to sit in.

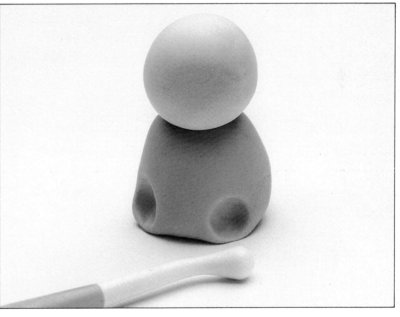

3. Make a blue ball, cut in half and mould the two legs. Position using a little egg white. Use a small ball tool to make a little cavity in the end of each foot for the pompom to sit in. Use a ball tool to make a cavity for the nose and a half-scoop tool to mark the mouth on the face.

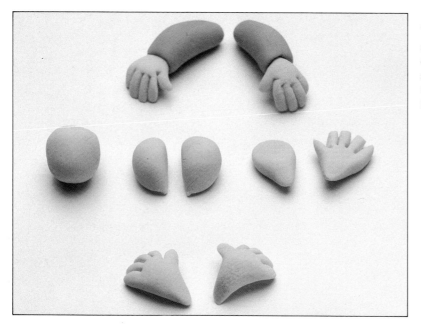

4. Make a small ball of paste; cut in half. Mould two sausages and place a ball tool in one end of each sausage. Make a hand for each arm; remember the thumb is always at the top of the hand. Place the hands in the ends of the sausage arms.

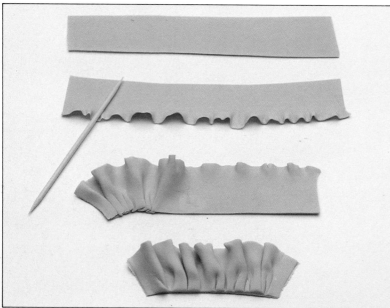

5. The frills here are blue, but on the finished clown they are white. Roll out some paste and cut a strip. Frill one edge with a cocktail stick, then turn over. The other edge is pleated between your thumb and first finger. Turn back over and stick onto clown.

To finish off the clown, put frills around the neck, base of body, ankles and wrist. Mould two small red balls of paste for the pompoms on the shoes. Use the clay gun for the yellow hair. Mould a blue hat with red pompoms. Paint the cheeks and features on face. Place two pompoms on the front for buttons. Pipe or paint red dots on all the frills.

BOOK TWO

LESSON PLANS

LESSON 1

Decorating with Chocolate

Decorating with Chocolate

As a decorative media, chocolate is not only attractive, but is a great favourite of young and old alike.

Chocolate marries well with most other flavours and colours, and may be used in combination with fresh cream, buttercream, crème pâtissière, marzipan and fondant. Decorating with chocolate can range from very simple grated shavings to more complicated piped trellis shapes. Melted chocolate can also be beaten into buttercream and crème pâtissière and used as a filling for gateaux, or stirred into fondant for coating or piping.

INGREDIENTS
Chocolate buttons, chips or block chocolate may be used, preferably plain (semisweet or bitter) as this gives the best contrast to buttercream.
Chocolate-flavoured blocks can be used for much of this work.
Icing sugar
Liquid glucose

EQUIPMENT
Double boiler or saucepan and china or glass basin
Wooden spoon
Palette knife
Greaseproof (waxed paper)
Cheese grater
Sharp pointed knife
Star piping tube
Pencil
Compass
Rolling pin
Paint scraper or butter pat roller
Cutters – round, fluted
Rose leaves

262

Simple Chocolate Decorations

Take a cheese grater and using the large hole, grate a block of chocolate until you have enough for your requirement.

Melting Chocolate

Melt some chocolate, either buttons or finely chopped block, in the following manner: put a saucepan of water on the stove to heat. Allow it to become very hot but not boiling. Place your chocolate chips either into the top of the double boiler or in a glass or china bowl. Remove the pan of hot water from the heat and stand the bowl of chocolate over the pan. Stir gently with a wooden spoon until the chocolate has completely melted.

Piping Chocolate

Put some melted chocolate into a small cup and add some water, drop by drop, until your chocolate thickens to the consistency of buttercream. Stand the cup in hot water to keep the chocolate soft, because at this stage it will harden up very quickly. Put some of the piping chocolate into a greaseproof (waxed) paper piping bag. It will depend on what you are piping whether you have a tube or not. For much chocolate piping a tube is not necessary and simply seems to assist the hardening process more quickly. A star tube however is needed if a shell border is to be piped.

Moulding Chocolate Roses

Roses and other simple flowers may be made as follows: mix equal quantities of melted chocolate with liquid glucose. Blend well together in a bowl with the aid of a wooden spoon. Turn out onto a clean work surface and knead briskly with the heel of the hand. It will feel a little like plasticine at this stage. Wrap in tin foil or cling film (plastic wrap) and use as soon as possible, to give a really high gloss to the rose petals.

Making Cutout Shapes

Take an uncreased sheet of greaseproof (waxed) paper and pour some chocolate into the middle of it, making sure you have plenty of space all round. Quickly pick up each corner of the paper nearest you and lift it away from you. Then pick up the two edges of paper farthest away and roll the chocolate towards you. Repeat this process by turning the paper round and lifting the opposite sides. This spreads the chocolate out into a thin, even sheet, with no marks or indentations which you would get by using a palette knife. The last stage is to flap the paper up and down a few times to make sure there are no air bubbles. This thinly spread chocolate will soon dry and many interesting shapes can then be cut either with a knife, or with a shaped cutter.

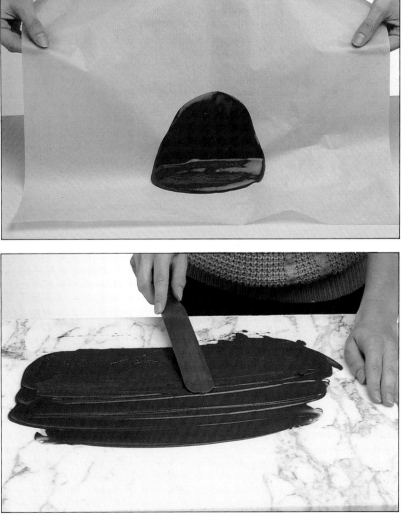

Chocolate Rolls or Cigars and Curls
A marble slab is best for this process, however if unavailable, use a spotlessly clean plastic work surface instead. Pour some liquid chocolate onto the clean surface and very quickly spread it thinly backwards and forwards with a palette knife, increasing the area of the chocolate. Continue this until the chocolate starts to dry, and the palette knife leaves a mark. For rolls, take a 15cm (6in) blade fillet knife or any other thin-bladed sharp knife. Grasp the handle of the knife in your right

hand and place your left hand over it to add more pressure. Holding the blade nearly flat on top of the chocolate, draw it towards you. The chocolate will then curl into long thin cigar shapes. The longer the downward pull, the thicker the cigar.

Curls are made by preparing the chocolate in the same manner as for cigars , but the tool used is a 2.5-4cm (1-1½in) paint scraper. This time you push the scraper away from you, holding it in a more upright position than the knife. A butter curling tool

can also be used, but the curls will have a ridged effect.

Curved Leaves
These can be made by attaching greaseproof (waxed) paper to a rolling pin and with a little melted chocolate piping directly onto the curved surface. Piping chocolate must be used as ordinary melted chocolate would drop off the paper.

Coloured Chocolate

Anyone who has been in Paris at Easter-time will have seen some of the wonderful displays of coloured chocolate birds and animals. The technique of colouring chocolate is simple, it may then be used decoratively in place of ordinary chocolate.

Colouring chocolate is not difficult, and the technique once mastered opens the gate to a whole new range of ideas.

INGREDIENTS
White chocolate
Powdered food colouring
Liquid glucose
Glycerine-based food colouring

EQUIPMENT
Saucepan
Glass or china bowl
Wooden spoon
Greaseproof (waxed) paper
Small palette knife
Small plastic cups
Small ladle or soup spoon
Cutter and moulds, if required

Heat a saucepan about one-third full of water until hot, but not boiling. Chop chocolate into small pieces and place in a bowl. Stand the bowl over the pan of water and gently stir with a wooden spoon until the chocolate has melted. The white chocolate will not be as runny as melted dark chocolate as it melts at a lower temperature, about 44°C (110°F).

White chocolate may be quite granular even when properly melted. Smooth chocolate may be obtained by standing a second bowl in hot water and pouring the chocolate into this through a very fine metal sieve. Take care to wipe the bottom of the first bowl after it has been lifted from the water as any drops of water falling into the melted chocolate will cause it to thicken and spoil. For this reason, do not use water-based liquid colouring.

Ladle a little chocolate into a plastic cup and add a little powdered colouring. Mix thoroughly until the chocolate is evenly blended. Place the coloured chocolate back into the bowl of melted chocolate and mix until the desired shade is reached.

1. Ladle the chocolate into a plastic cup.

2. Add the colouring a little at a time.

3. Stir to mix, adding more colour as required.

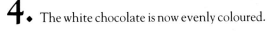

4. The white chocolate is now evenly coloured.

When making a variety of colours it is necessary to make each individually; however, colours can often be mixed to avoid the lengthy process of repetition. Moulding chocolate may be treated likewise.

Pale pink – can be turned into dark blue, purple, green and grey.

Lemon – can be turned into orange, peach, green and brown.

Always keep the chocolate standing in hot water to keep it liquid as white chocolate sets very quickly. If you are working with several colours simultaneously, stand the cups in a roasting tin half full of hot water.

Cutouts
Ladle the chocolate onto a sheet of greaseproof (waxed) paper and spread quickly with a palette knife. You must work fast as white chocolate sets quickly. Pick up the edges of the paper and flap them up and down to remove air bubbles and knife marks. Leave until the chocolate is just set before cutting out shapes. For the best results work with small quantities of chocolate and repeat the process as necessary.

Suggested Cutouts
Plaques: round or oval, fluted or plain.
Geometric shapes: squares, diamonds, circles and half moons.
Flowers: use blossom cutters in various sizes and leaves.
Figure cutters: use the cutter of your choice, such as Father Christmas, fir trees, rabbits, mice.

Cutout variations
Chocolate cutouts may be piped with detail either by using royal icing or with coloured, milk or plain (sweet or semi-sweet) chocolate. One cutter may be superimposed upon another, for instance, a flower can be made with a dark centre attached to a paler outside; or a series of different coloured plaques may be combined. Cutouts may also be dusted with petal dust to achieve a shaded effect which is particularly attractive on flowers, leaves and butterflies. Leftover pieces of coloured chocolate may be broken into small pieces and finely chopped with a sharp knife. They may then be used like hundreds and thousands on the tops and sides of cakes. Store in an airtight container.

Moulding Chocolate
Moulding chocolate is used to make flowers, leaves and small animals. Colour the chocolate before adding the glucose using either powder or paste colours. Equal quantities of liquid glucose and chocolate are then mixed together and kneaded as described above.

EQUIPMENT
Savoy bag
Large star tube
30cm (12in) silver cake board
Palette knife
Turntable
Cheese grater
7-10cm (3-4in) open circular cutter
2-4cm (1-1½in) circular cutter
Greaseproof (waxed) paper
Bowl
Saucepan

Gateau with Chocolate Disks

Sandwich sponges together with jam of choice and buttercream. Pipe in cream rather than spread it as this stops it sliding about on jam and gives depth to the sponge. Use a large star tube and savoy bag. Place sponge on a 30cm (12in) silver straw board.

Coat sponge all over with the buttercream, starting with the top until an even surface is achieved. Neaten edge with flat side of palette knife. Coat sides of gateau. This operation is much easier if you have a turntable. Divide sponge into equal portions.

Grate about 250g (8oz) of the chocolate and hold the sponge in one hand, with your hand flat on the bottom and pick up grated chocolate in the other hand. Bring together by tilting slightly and pressing chocolate onto sides of cake until evenly coated all round. Put back on cake board. Take the large circular cutter and place in the middle of gateau. Thickly sprinkle remaining grated chocolate covering the whole of the inside area of cutter. Gently remove cutter.

Cut some thin strips of paper 6m (¼in) and lay on top of the shavings. Dust thickly with icing (confectioner's) sugar. Carefully lift off paper. You will be left with an attractive striped effect.

Prepare some melted chocolate on a sheet of greaseproof (waxed) paper and with a small plain round cutter 2.5-3cm (1-1½in), cut out 12 circles of chocolate into each marked section of your gateau; pipe a whirl of buttercream on outside edge. Take a circle of chocolate and press lightly into buttercream whirl. Pick back off and turn over. Press plain side of circle back into whirl. The best results are achieved in a cool kitchen and the whirl and buttercream imprint are best made one at a time rather than all at once, as the first one will probably have dried too much to make a pattern on the chocolate.

Circles of chocolate for gateau with chocolate disk as seen on page 12, also showing chocolate cigars for rose gateau as seen on page 18.

INGREDIENTS

2x25cm (10in) whisked sponge cakes
500g (1lb/2½ cups) vanilla-flavoured buttercream
Strawberry or raspberry jam (jelly)
175g (12oz) plain (semisweet) chocolate
Icing (confectioner's) sugar

VARIATIONS

Liqueur-flavoured Gateau: Whisked sponges absorb liqueur-flavoured syrups very well without disintegrating. Pour evenly over cake bases before coating.

SYRUP

INGREDIENTS

600ml (1 pint) water
500g (1lb) granulated sugar
Juice and zest of two lemons and one orange
12 coriander seeds
Cinnamon stick
Bay leaf

Rose Gateau

Method

Melt the white and plain (semisweet) chocolate in two separate bowls over pans of hot, not boiling water. Meanwhile, sandwich together the sponge cakes using about one-third of the buttercream. Use the remaining buttercream to cover the top and sides of the cake. Draw the comb scraper around the sides, neaten the edges, then smooth the top of the cake using a palette knife.

Ladle a little melted white chocolate onto some greaseproof (waxed) paper, flatten with a palette knife and flap the paper up and down to smooth and level. As soon as it is just set, cut out a small oval shape. Return remaining chocolate to the bowl. Following the procedure above, cut out a larger oval plaque in pink.

Colour the remaining pink chocolate to a darker shade of pink then add an equal quantity of liquid

glucose, mix with a wooden spoon, then turn out onto a clean surface and knead well. Cover with cling film (plastic wrap) and leave for about 15 minutes before making roses. When the roses are complete, colour the remaining moulding chocolate green for the leaves. Flatten a walnut-sized knob of chocolate between the thumb and forefinger, place on a flat surface and stamp out a rose leaf using the cutter. Mark veins on leaves with a sharp knife. Refrigerate leaves if they are too soft to handle.

Make about two dozen chocolate rolls from the plain (semisweet) chocolate. Fasten the small white plaque to the larger pink one and arrange the roses and leaves on top. Lift with palette knife onto the centre of the cake. Mark the cake into four and arrange chocolate rolls. Cut very thin strips of paper and arrange on the rolls

equidistant apart. Gently sieve the icing (confectioner's) sugar over the top, carefully remove paper strips. Place chocolate rose leaves in the corner of the rolls.

This gateau is not suitable for refrigeration, as if exposed to alternate cold and warm air, condensation will form on the chocolate causing the flowers to droop and become sticky; the icing (confectioner's) sugar would also dissolve.

INGREDIENTS

2x25cm (10in) whisked sponge cakes
125g (4oz/1 cup) raspberry jam (jelly)
500g (1lb/2½ cups) vanilla-flavoured buttercream
250g (8oz) white chocolate
60g (2oz) liquid glucose
Pink powdered colouring
Christmas green paste colouring
250g (8oz) plain (semisweet) chocolate
Icing (confectioner's) sugar

EQUIPMENT
28cm (11in) cake board
Turntable
Palette knife
Comb-edge scraper
Greaseproof (waxed) paper
14x12cm (5½x4in) oval cutter
8x5cm (3½x2in) oval cutter
Thin-bladed sharp knife
Scissors
Fine sieve or icing (confectioner's) sugar Dredger
Rose leaf cutter
2 saucepans
2 glass or china bowls
2 wooden spoons

VARIATIONS
Pipe the recipient's name or the occasion, on the plaque or use sugar flowers. Tiny marzipan fruits could be arranged in a little mound while dark chocolate medallions attached to the white surface can look quite stunning.

Coffee Gateau

INGREDIENTS

2x25cm (10in) coffee sponge bases
Apricot jam (jelly)
500g (1lb/2½ cups) coffee
buttercream
500g (1lb) dark (semisweet)
chocolate
1 walnut
12 angelica diamonds

EQUIPMENT

Greaseproof (waxed) paper
30cm (12in) cake board
Pencil
Compass
Palette knife
Small sharp knife
Piping bag
Large star tube
Comb scraper
Turntable

Spread apricot jam (jelly) on base of sponge. Pipe with coffee buttercream; smooth and flatten. Cover top of gateau fairly thickly with coffee buttercream. Smooth round with palette knife, then using a comb scraper, draw round sides of cake as if coating with royal icing. Place on cake board and mark top of cake into 12 equal sections.

Melt the chocolate. Draw a 25cm (10in) circle on a sheet of greaseproof (waxed) paper and, with the aid of a compass, divide it into 12 sections. On another sheet of greaseproof (waxed) paper pour some more chocolate and spread out thinly, allow to dry. Cut out six 3.5cm (1½in) squares of chocolate. Cut each one diagonally, giving 12 triangles. Stick these all round the base of the gateau by pressing slightly onto combed side, take back off, reverse and put plain side to edge of cake. The striped effect of coffee buttercream on dark chocolate is most attractive.

Take a little melted chocolate and pour into a small cup. Add a few drops of water until it has reached piping consistency. Put into a paper piping

bag; cut off end of bag leaving a hole about the size of a No 2 plain piping tube. Pipe a fairly thick line round every other segment of your drawing. Repeat the process, but in every other segment, or do them one at a time. Put some more piping chocolate into another bag and pipe in between the chocolate frame in a squiggly pattern, making sure the chocolate touches the edges of frame and that the lines touch each other, (see detailed photograph). These pieces dry quite quickly. As they do so, ease off paper with a palette knife or by taking the paper to edge of table and gradually peeling off. As you complete each piece put to one side. On each segment of the gateau pipe a line of buttercream with 1cm (½in) plain tube from near centre to outside edge, pipe another on top 5cm (2in) along outside edge and a third on top of that about 2.5cm (1in) long. With the

aid of a palette knife, lift up segments and prop each one against the line of cream until you have covered the top of the cake. Pipe a whirl of buttercream in the centre and decorate with a walnut and twelve angelica diamonds.

Small piped decoration that can be used on gateaux or fancies.

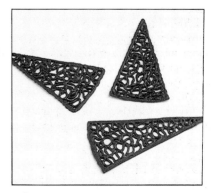

Strawberry Chocolate Gateau

INGREDIENTS

25cm (10in) whisked sponge bases
Strawberry jam (jelly)
Small jar redcurrant jelly
250g (8oz) melted chocolate
125g (4oz) strawberries plus 12 even
sized strawberries
600ml (1pt/2½ cups) whipping
cream
60g (2oz/¼ cup) caster (superfine)
sugar
Icing (confectioner's) sugar
Kirsch

Method

Take two 25cm (10in) sponge bases and spread one with strawberry jam. Wash, hull and quarter about 125g (4oz) fresh strawberries. Place in a bowl and sprinkle with a little sugar and a few drops of kirsch if required. Whisk the cream to piping consistency and fold one-third of the cream into the strawberries. Spread onto jam and place the other sponge on top.

Spread remaining cream on top and side of gateau. Mark into 12 portions. Pour melted chocolate onto a sheet of greaseproof (waxed) paper. Proceed as for cutout shapes. Press grated chocolate round bottom edge of cake.

When set, place the 25cm (10in) sponge tin (pan) on the chocolate and cut round the tin using a sharp knife to produce a large chocolate circle. Using a long bladed knife cut circle into 12 even triangles. Melt some redcurrant jelly in a small saucepan adding just a little water to thin slightly. Wash and dry 12 even sized strawberries leaving on the green culots. Hold the culots and dip the strawberries into the jelly. Put onto greaseproof (waxed) paper to set. Place strawberries, thin edge to centre. Ease six chocolate segments off the paper and thickly dust with icing (confectioner's) sugar.

EQUIPMENT

30cm (12in) cake board
Greaseproof (waxed) paper
Palette knife
Turntable
Whisk
Bowl
Saucepan
Icing (confectioners) sugar dredger
25cm (10in) cake tin (pan)
Sharp knife

Moulded Roses

To use this modelling paste and achieve the best results, allow to rest in a warm room for about an hour after making. When making the petals use only walnut-sized pieces at a time. Do not worry if it feels very greasy to the touch, this is because the warmth of the hand melts the cocoa butter in the chocolate. Mould a piece of the paste about the size of a little finger nail into a pear shape. Stand upright fat side down. Take a small piece of paste and roll between palms into a sausage shape. With thumb and forefinger of left hand, flatten out top piece of sausage. Hold the remainder with thumb and forefinger of right hand. Lay flattened edge in the palm of the hand with the tail pointing to outside edge of hand. With the thick end of a double ball tool, gently thin outside edge of petal. Hold petal with thumb and forefinger of left hand and with thumb and forefinger of right hand nip off surplus piece of sausage. The petals will be floppy, so lay flat on surface to set.

Make two petals about as big as thumb nail. Pick up centre-piece and lay on petal two-thirds to the left of it. Wrap left edge petal over centre. Take second petal and lay inside the first petal bringing round to overlap outside first petal. With thumb gently roll back outside edge of petals. The build up of the petals is as follows, tucking one inside the other until you have completed the sequence.

Bud – pear shape + 2 petals
Half rose – pear shape + 2 petals + 3 petals
Full rose – pear shape + 2 petals + 3 petals + 5 petals
Make each layer of petals slightly larger as they extend outwards.

Suggested shapes for chocolate cutouts and piped decorations

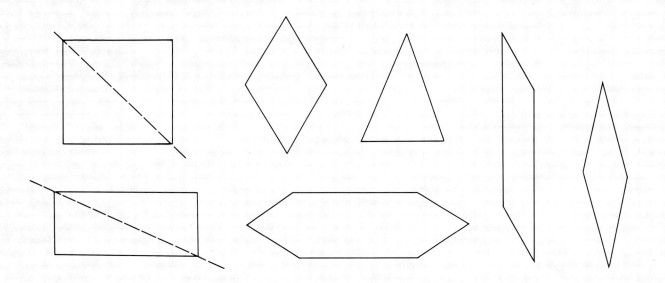

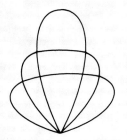

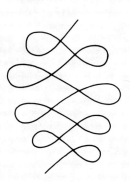

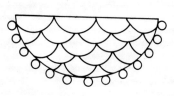

Templates for designs illustrated in this lesson

LESSON 2

Chocolate Eggs & Figures

Chocolate Easter Eggs

Making your own Easter eggs and chocolate moulded figures can be great fun. As well as gifts for the family, they can be given as presents to friends and children.

To be sure of success there are certain basic principles which have to be followed. Working with chocolate is not difficult providing you know the rules.

Rule 1: Buy the best quality moulding chocolate; chocolate-flavoured cake covering will not do.

Rule 2: Never overheat chocolate.

Rule 3: Never allow water or steam to get into the chocolate.

INGREDIENTS
Chocolate buttons (chips) or block chocolate either milk (sweet), plain (semisweet) or white
Icing (confectioner's) sugar
Egg white
Food colouring for eggs, decorated with piped sugar flowers
Ribbons for eggs and rabbits.

EQUIPMENT
Easter egg mould
Animal or figure moulds
Double saucepan or saucepan and china or glass basin
Wooden spoon
Small ladle
Greaseproof (waxed) paper
Piping tubes
Small sharp knife
Tissue paper

Purchasing Materials
Most sugarcraft shops will stock all you need to make your eggs or moulded figures, and some hardware shops and supermarkets also sell moulds. Expensive plexi-glass moulds may also be hired or ordered specially. Many supermarkets as well as specialist shops now sell moulding chocolate, your local baker may also be able to sell it to you. Health stores will sell carob.

Method
Check that your Easter egg mould is spotlessly clean and dry. The moulds are bought in halves and can be either smooth surfaced or a crazy paving pattern. When you are satisfied they are dry, take a clean, soft cloth and polish the inside. Put some water in the saucepan or bottom of the double boiler and place on the heat until very hot, but not boiling.

Half fill basin or top of double boiler with chocolate. If you have bought block chocolate cut it into small pieces before putting it into the basin. Stand basin of chocolate in the water. Stir gently with wooden spoon until chocolate has melted. It should be at a temperature of about 44°C

(110°F). Maximum workable temperature for plain (semisweet) chocolate is 49°C (120°F), it is not possible to work with chocolate that has been overheated. White and milk (sweet) chocolate should be used at a slightly lower temperature 42°C (105°F). If you do not have a thermometer, crook your little finger and touch the chocolate with the flat side. The chocolate should feel just warm (the correct heat).

Cut out some rectangles of greaseproof (waxed) paper slightly larger than the mould.

Pick up the Easter egg mould, holding the rounded part in the palm of your hand, and ladle in some chocolate until it is about one third full. Gently tilt the mould in all

directions until the chocolate has covered the whole of the egg-shaped area. Hold the mould over the basin and turn it upside-down, allowing the surplus chocolate to drip out. Still upside-down, place the mould onto the cut rectangle of paper. Leave to dry. This takes about ten minutes.

If the water in the saucepan has cooled considerably, take out the basin of chocolate and pop the pan back on the stove and reheat water.

Check the inside of egg is dry by peeling off the paper. If dry, the chocolate should look dull. If you have a little ridge of chocolate inside the egg, shave it off with a sharp knife and put surplus back in basin. Refill the egg with liquid chocolate, repeating the same swilling and

emptying motion as before. Replace on greaseproof (waxed) paper.

Put the egg half or halves into the refrigerator. Look at the egg after 15 or 20 minutes. If the surface through the mould has taken on an overall silvery-grey colour, the egg is ready to be unmoulded. Remove from fridge and peel off the paper. Lay mould flat side down on paper. Hold each side of the flat edge of mould and gently pull sideways. The egg should then just drop out. Trim edges of the egg with a sharp knife.

To assemble, take a piece of tissue paper, fold it in half lengthwise, in half again and twist round into a rope shape, bring both ends together and tuck one around the other until you have formed a ring of tissue paper

with a hole in the middle. Chocolate should be handled as little as possible as it marks very easily. Lift the bottom half of the egg and place it hollow side up in your tissue paper nest.

If you wish to fill the egg with chocolates it is best to put some paper shavings into the bottom half of egg, as these will cushion the weight and stop the egg from breaking. So at this stage fill the lower half of egg with shavings, tucking them in neatly, and place in your chocolates.

Remove top half of egg from mould, using the same method as before. Gently holding egg, dip edges into melted chocolate and place over the bottom egg. This will seal the two halves together. Your egg is now ready to be decorated.

Moulded Easter Eggs

1. Ladle melted chocolate into the egg mould until it is about one-third full.

2. Gently tilt the mould in all directions until the surface is completely covered.

3. Turn the mould upside-down and allow surplus chocolate to drip into the basin.

4. Place the mould on greaseproof (waxed) paper and refrigerate until set. Repeat steps 1–3.

5. The chocolate looks silvery when it is set, carefully unmould and trim the surplus chocolate from the edges of the mould using a sharp knife.

6. Diminishing sized eggs combined to create the Russian doll effect.

Decorating Eggs

Chocolate Decoration

Put a little melted chocolate in a small cup and add a few drops of water until it thickens to piping consistency. Put a small star tube into a piping bag. Scrape in chocolate and pipe shells round the join between the two halves. This looks very attractive if you have a milk chocolate egg and you pipe the shells in dark chocolate, and vice versa.

Two Chocolate Egg

An attractive variation to single flavour Chocolate is to combine milk (sweet) with plain (semisweet) in the following manner: melt two basins of chocolate, one milk and one plain as in the method previously explained. Take some plain chocolate and put into a small cup. Thicken slightly with a few drops of water. Put into a piping bag without a tube. Cut off the end of bag, leaving a small hole. Pipe in a cornelli design all over the inside surface of the mould. Ladle in two coats of milk chocolate as previously described.

When stuck together pipe round the joins with dark chocolate. Decorate with chocolate roses and leaves.

Royal Iced Decoration

Make up some royal icing. Tint to a colour of your choice. Put into a piping bag with a small star tube and pipe a shell border round the join between the two eggs.

The egg can be decorated with piped sugar flowers and leaves; bows; artificial flowers and fern; moulded chocolate roses and rose leaves; and particularly attractive is the piping of the recipient's name on the egg.

Clear cellophane boxes can be bought at most florists. The egg can be laid on coloured tissue paper and the box tied with a ribbon. Equally, proper Easter egg boxes are now available at most sugarcraft shops.

Half Egg with Chicken

Take a half Easter egg and secure with melted chocolate upright on a cutout circle of chocolate about 6mm (¼in) thick. Pipe dot border of chocolate round circular base and attach a Garrett frill and bow around the outer edge of the egg. Fill base with miniature eggs and secure a small fluffy chicken sitting on top of eggs. Pipe the child's name on the flat base of chocolate, if desired.

Slimmer's Egg

Buy a ballon. Blow it up to about 10cm (4in) in diameter. Mark a line round half the balloon with pen. Lightly oil surface of balloon with vegetable oil and place thin end up, slightly angled, in a ring of tissue paper. Holding tied neck of balloon with one hand, pipe a border following the marked line.

Fill another piping bag with slightly stiffened chocolate. Do not use a tube, but cut off bag to make a hole approximately the size of a No2 plain piping tube. Pipe squiggles all over surface between shell piping, covering area well but leaving enough small spaces so that the finished effect is lacy. Allow to dry at room temperature. Pop the balloon, which will leave you with a lacy looking half Easter egg shape.

Secure the half onto an oval shaped base of chocolate. Place in base of egg, a single rose made from modelling chocolate, then arrange smaller roses, leaves and buds on the oval base.

Chocolate Moulded Figures

As a change from Easter eggs small children love the Easter bunnies, ducks and other figures. In addition, many attractive moulds for Christmas figures to hang on the tree can now be purchased. Small moulded chocolate figures or space rockets can be an added extra to a child's birthday party as a take home gift. These smaller figures need about 30-60g (1-2oz) of chocolate and therefore are fairly inexpensive.

There are two main types of mould on the market: the half moulds where two sides are stuck together, as with the eggs, these are usually made in a soft, easy-care transparent plastic; or there are more expensive rigid plastic moulds, where the figure comes out all in one piece. These rigid moulds are in two halves which clip together and range from 5cm (2in) figures to ones several feet high.

EQUIPMENT
Moulds
Double boiler or saucepan and basin
Glass or china bowl
Wooden spoon
Ladle
Greaseproof (waxed) paper
Small, sharp knife
Good quality block or button (chip)
moulding chocolate
Ribbons

Chocolate Figures

The method of preparing the chocolate is fully explained in the Easter egg section. Exactly the same method should be followed for figure moulding, paying particular attention to the heating of the chocolate at all times.

The figure moulds are full of indentations, far more so than the Easter egg moulds, therefore special care must be taken to ensure each crevice is thoroughly clean and dry before use. Should the chocolate stick never try to gouge it out with a sharp knife or use a rough surfaced pad. Always wash mould in warm, soapy water, rinse with clean, warm water and dry thoroughly. Then polish mould with a soft, clean cloth.

Prepare chocolate. Cut squares or rectangles of greaseproof (waxed) paper larger than the base or flat side of mould. Half figures are made in exactly the same way as Easter eggs, swilling round the chocolate to cover all areas of the mould. However, because there are so many indentations it might be necessary to give the mould a sharp tap on the table to make sure all the cracks and crevices have been thoroughly coated. Reverse mould over basin and allow any surplus chocolate to drip back in. Place flat side down onto paper and allow to dry.

When dry, repeat the process with a second coating of chocolate; put back onto greaseproof (waxed) paper. Put into fridge until the silvery grey appearance on the outside of the mould tells you that the chocolate is dry and has contracted away from the mould. Remove from fridge and turn out. Any surplus chocolate extending beyond the figure line can be carefully cut away with a small, sharp knife. The two halves of the figure can then be cemented together as previously mentioned for joining Easter eggs.

Bows can be tied round the necks of figures where appropriate, perhaps a different colour for each child, or with Christmas angels for example they can be tied with gold and silver thread and hung on the Christmas tree. Given as small gifts for unexpected visitors they should create an excellent impression.

Rigid Plastic Figures

These moulds are quite costly but produce excellent results, making figures somewhat larger than the half moulds. The finished product requires less handling than the halves, and they are so well made that every detail of the figure stands out sharply. The moulds are tough and rigid and should last a lifetime. The average mould has between four and five strong metal clips to hold the two sides together. An 18cm (7in) high bunny takes about 75g (2½oz) of chocolate.

Method

Check that the mould is spotlessly clean and dry, paying particular attention to the ears, nose and tail or similar indentations with other moulds. Polish well. Clip together. Prepare chocolate. Cut out square of greaseproof (waxed) paper larger than base of figure.

Hold mould upside down, and ladle in chocolate, half filling mould. Tap sharply to get rid of any air bubbles which might be trapped. With a tilting action towards you, gently roll the mould round and round. Bring the chocolate evenly towards the base of the mould. It is best to do this holding it over the basin, so that surplus chocolate will drip straight into the basin. When the chocolate has stopped dripping, look down through the mould, holding it to the light. If you can see daylight anywhere this means the chocolate was slightly too warm and slid off the surface. Recoat with more chocolate.

Stand mould upright on paper and leave until dry. Recoat the inside of mould. There is no need to tap this time, but roll chocolate down to the base in the same manner as before. Drain over basin. When the chocolate has stopped dripping, place on a square of greaseproof (waxed) paper and put into fridge. Leave in fridge for 20 to 30 minutes until the mould has taken on a silvery-grey appearance. Remove from fridge.

Take off clips. Slide the point of a sharp knife or thumb nail between the join of the two halves of mould. One half of the mould should just come away. Lay the figure, exposed chocolate side down, hold each side of the mould with fingers pulling sideways, and at the same time press down on mould with thumbs. This should release the figure. Handle as little as possible. Stand upright, and place on bow around the neck where suitable.

Making Rigid Plastic Figures

1. Ladle the chocolate into the mould, roll round until the entire figure is thoroughly coated with chocolate.

2. Drain the excess chocolate from the mould into the basin.

3. Stand on paper and chill until set and silvery-grey.

4. To unmould, remove the clips from the side of the mould by pressing firmly with the thumbs.

5. Pull the mould apart gently

Decorative Ideas

With rabbits particularly or with the angels, melt a little white chocolate and pipe into ear and tail, or wing cavities. Then proceed with a double coating of chocolate.

Milk and plain (sweet and semisweet) chocolate can be used together to highlight any feature in the mould of your choice. Rabbits of varying sizes can be made and placed on a cake top covered in green marzipan that has been pushed through a sieve to resemble grass.

LESSON 3

Marzipan Figure Modelling

Marzipan Figures

Making your own marzipan figures is great fun and with a little practice excellent results can be achieved.

Marzipan is made from ground almonds and caster (superfine) sugar plus egg white and sometimes liquid glucose. Because of the high percentage of oil in the almonds, working with the paste under certain conditions means it becomes rather oily. It is best not to make figures in damp humid weather if it can be avoided. The paste becomes very soft and sticky, difficult to handle and the figures will droop. However, a little dry icing (confectioner's) sugar worked into the paste will help to stiffen it up.

For figure modelling the white marzipan is most appropriate because it is easy to colour, and some animals, such as the panda, require white marzipan. Good quality white marzipan is on sale in most supermarkets these days. Sugarcraft shops always have a plentiful supply. If making your own, it is best to use icing sugar with the ground almonds as this will produce a smoother textured paste with which to work.

Always work with clean utensils, hands and work surfaces and wash hands frequently as they will become sticky. Always dry hands thoroughly as damp hands will make the paste tacky. Use icing sugar to keep hands and table surface dry. Never use flour as this will cause fermentation, cornflour causes cracking and leaves white patches in coloured paste and caster sugar is too granular.

Paste can be coloured with either dust or paste colours. It is not wise to use liquid food colourings as they make the marzipan sticky, particularly if a strong or dark colour is required.

The marzipan figures will dry off very well at normal room temperature, but keep away from strong sunlight which will soften the paste causing the figures to wilt. Never put completed figures into plastic boxes, covered tins or shut away in kitchen cupboards as this will also cause the marzipan to soften and the figures to disintegrate. It takes a very long time for the figure to go rock hard, at least six months, after which time it does not taste very good.

There are many recipes for making your own marzipan, a selection of which have been given in book 1. However, the rule of thumb is twice the amount of icing sugar to ground almonds and 60g (2oz) egg white to 500g (1lb) dry ingredients. For the real perfectionist, a professional recipe used by the experts is:
400g (14oz) raw marzipan
50g (2½oz) liquid glucose
300g (10oz/2½ cups) icing (confectioner's) sugar

Marzipan should be stored in a sealed plastic bag to keep it pliable and to stop a crust from forming. If you do have a crust, cut it off with a sharp knife and check that no fermentation has taken place by smelling it. Re-knead before use.

Never try to knead in bits of hard crust, as they will not soften and simply make figure moulding impossible.

EQUIPMENT
Food colouring, powder or paste
Royal icing for piping eyes and small details
Cocktail sticks
Small rolling pin
Small scissors
Egg white
Marzipan modelling tools
Stamens with the ends cut off for whiskers

284

Prehistoric Range

These are a great favourite with small children, who simply love eating the monsters.

Each of the figures weighs approximately 60g (2oz). Over that weight and they tend to become ungainly. Average height is 5cm (2in) and overall length 7.5cm (3in). Some figures are fashioned from one piece of marzipan, others comprise of as many as ten separate pieces.

<table>
<tr><td>

INGREDIENTS
60g (2oz) marzipan per figure
Royal icing
Egg white
Dust or paste food colouring
Dry icing (confectioner's) sugar

</td><td>

EQUIPMENT
Piping bags
Scissors
Small sharp knife
Cocktail sticks
Paintbrush.

</td></tr>
</table>

Brontosaurus

Colour 60g (2oz) marzipan a dark, coffee brown colour. Roll between palms of hands to a pear shape. Press lightly on work surface, dusted with icing (confectioner's) sugar to flatten bottom. Pull out tail from sharp end of pear shape. Flatten and round off.

Holding the body in one hand, start to pull out neck from far end of body. When it is about 5cm (2in) long, bend over 2cm (¾in) to form the head.

Push a cocktail stick down the length of the neck to support it. With the back of a small knife, cut a slit in the lower part of the head for the mouth. Pinch out feet from the main body, the front ones being well forward. Flatten and mark claws with the back of knife. Mark the body all over with the tip of a sharp knife to give the skin a textured look. Pipe in eyes, use a large dot of white and a smaller dot of chocolate. The placing of the chocolate dot will determine the expression on the face.

NOTE: Any small child eating this animal must be warned of the cocktail stick in the neck.

Tyrannosaurus

Colour 60g (2oz) marzipan green.
Divide into two. Roll one piece into an
elongated pear shape. Bend the thinner
end to lift up, while holding fatter end
pressed down on work surface until the
piece will stand upright by itself with
the tail flicking up slightly. With the
scissors make two cuts near top of fattest
part, keeping tail to the back. Flatten
the cut pieces with thumb and
forefinger to form the paws. Divide the
remaining paste in half. Take one piece
and roll into a ball. Gradually square off
ball stroking one side downwards for
front of head. This will also elongate it
slightly at the same time. Cut slit in
head for mouth and attach to body with
egg white. Cut two thin strips out of the
almond for teeth and stick each side of
mouth. Divide the remaining paste in
two and roll into sausages about 2.5cm
(1in) long. Form into reverse S shape
and flatten one end to represent paws.
Stick legs either side of body with egg
white. Take a No3 plain piping tube
and gently poke all over body. Pipe in
eyes.

Stegosaurus

Colour a piece of marzipan the size of a thumb nail a light, coffee colour. Roll out with a rolling pin until about 5.5cm (2½in) long and 12mm (½in) wide. With a round fluted cutter, cut frill. With a sharp knife trim off in a curve following line of scallops making it thinner at each end. With remaining spare piece cut out the horn for the tail.

Between palms of hands roll marzipan into a ball, and with outside edges of hand gently roll each end of ball to give it a double ended pear shape. Pull out and flatten one end for the tail. Pull out other end but keep more rounded for the head. Cut slit for mouth with the back of a knife.

Pull out feet by pinching marzipan between finger and thumb. Mark claws. Paint a little egg white down the spine of the animal and attach the scalloped piece. Attach the horn with a dot of egg white. Pipe eyes as for brontosaurus.

Dimetrodon

Colour 60g (2oz) marzipan with edible plum dusting powder. Break off about one-eighth of the paste. Roll this out thinly and cut out a half moon shape about 5.5cm (2½in). Mark with back of knife. Divide remainder into four balls. Elongate slightly, flatten one end and mark in claws.

With rest of the paste roll into a flat cigar shape. Pull out tail. The head is rather like that of a tortoise, so when pulling keep it rounded rather than flat or pointed. With the back of a knife gently press the area between head and body to give a distinct division. Mark body all over by gently pressing sharp side of knife to make very shallow cuts. Cut slit for mouth. Attach feet and thin frill on back with egg white. Pipe in eyes as for brontosaurus.

Wild Animals

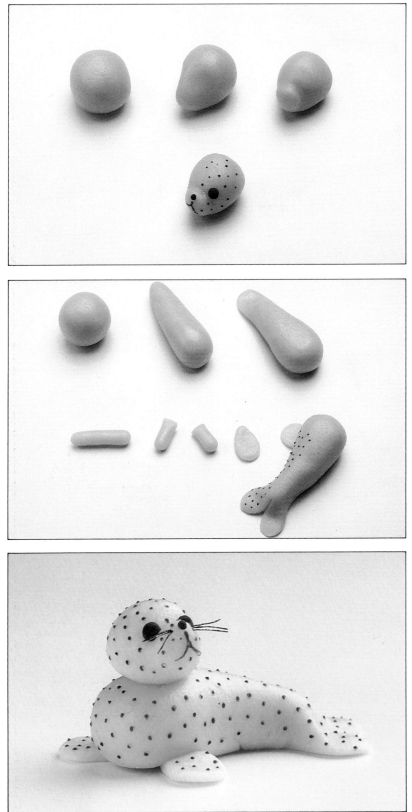

Baby Seal

Divide white paste into four. Take two small finger nail sized pieces of white paste. Roll into sausages 18mm (¾in) long and flatten out to 12mm (½in) wide for flippers. Mark paws with a sharp knife.

Roll three-quarters of the marzipan into a long pear. Taper end then flatten out. Snip end and flatten each half with thumb and forefinger to represent tail. Fasten flippers with egg white each side of front of body. Roll the remaining marzipan into a ball, pinch out centre to a point. With forefinger flatten the point and push back into the head to make the little rounded nose. Stick on head with nose in line with front right flipper. Put some chocolate icing in a bag with a No0 tube. Pipe tiny dots all over seal.

Pipe in nose and mouth. To give the seal an endearing look, pipe large eyes in chocolate only. Affix three black stamens each side of the nose to represent whiskers.

Whale

Colour tiny piece of paste pink. Make two balls, flattened out about 6mm (¼in) across. Colour three-quarters of remaining paste black. Pinch off enough to make three fins. Two side fins are small sausages 2.5cm (1in) long flattened to 6mm (¼in) wide. Back fin is shaped slightly thicker at base and fractionally curved with a rounded tip. Start with 12mm (½in) long sausage shape. The main body of black is moulded like a cigar, the tail pulled out and then flattened. Make a central snip with scissors then flatten. Bend upwards. Flatten underside of body by pressing onto work surface. With forefinger, flatten front end of nose and bend upwards slightly.

Roll white paste like a cigar. Taper one end and flatten for mouth. Flatten part that is to be fitted onto the black upper part of body. Pinch up two pieces either side and pull slightly forward. Fasten two pieces of body with egg white, pressing and moulding together, keeping mouth well open. Stick in pink tongue. Secure side fins pointing slightly backward, then top fin in lower middle of back. Pipe in eyes. If the tail will not stay curved up, support for several hours to secure.

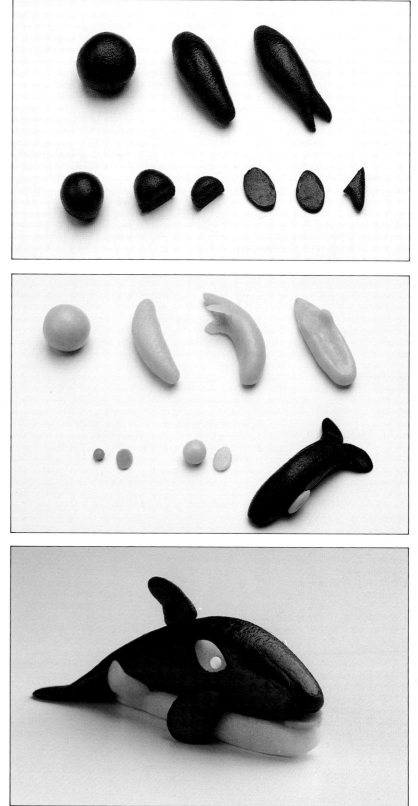

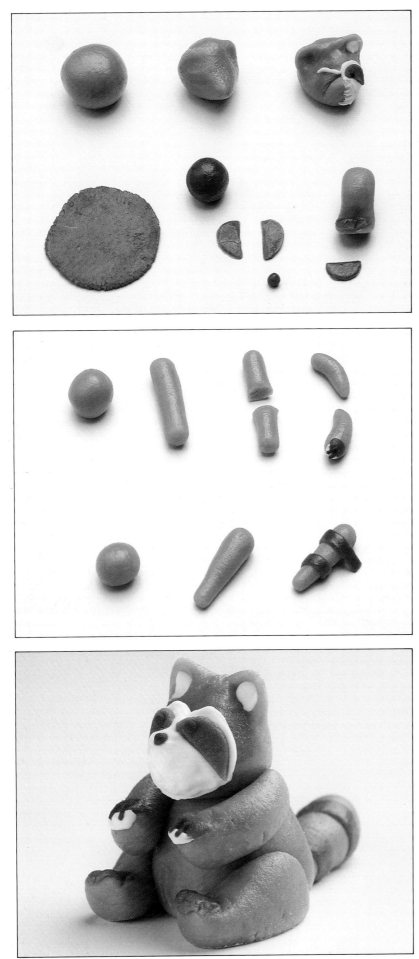

Raccoon

Colour 60g (2oz) marzipan light brown. Pinch off a little ball about the size of a small finger nail and colour it dark brown. These are for the two stripes round the tail, paws on feet and patches on face. Roll out very thinly, cut two strips 6mm x 2.5cm (¼ x 1 in) for tail; two pear drops for the face (can be done with aspic cutter), and 6mm (¼in) circle for feet. Cut circle in half and flatten out slightly.

Take two-thirds of the remaining paste and roll into ball for the body, press onto surface lightly until it will stand on its own. With a sharp knife make two downward cuts 12mm (½in) in from each side of ball halfway down the body. Pull out to form legs, press ends flat to represent paws. With remaining one-third of paste, nip off about one-quarter and divide in half. With one half roll into a sausage, making it thinner at one end for the tail. To assemble, fasten dark brown stripes of marzipan round tail. Tuck under back of body securing with egg white. Attach head, arms and brown pieces on paws with egg white. With the other half roll into a sausage about 5cm (2in) long. Cut in half. Flatten one end of each small piece for paws. With remaining paste, roll into a ball and with thumb and forefinger gently pull out into a pointed shape from centre of ball to represent nose. Pinch out ears and hollow slightly with ball tool. Put some white icing into a bag and pipe on a face. Smooth over with a very slightly damp paintbrush. Attach pear drop shapes onto wet icing. Ease into position with a cocktail stick. Pipe a little white icing in ear cavity, tips of arm, paws and eyes. Finish by piping brown nose, claws and eye centres.

Squirrel

Colour 60g (2oz) marzipan a reddish brown colour. Divide in half. Roll one half into a pear shape, press onto surface flat side down and lean slightly forward. Divide rest of paste into three pieces. Roll one-third into a sausage 5cm (2in) long for the tail making it fatter at one end. With a small, sharp pair of scissors make little cuts pointing upwards all over the tail. With another third, fashion face, making it rather pointed, and flatten either side of point to represent the fat cheeks. Pinch up ears and hollow with small ball tool. With remaining marzipan, take about a quarter to make two little sausages for arms and two larger sausages for legs. Bend the larger sausages into a reverse S shape for legs. Flatten one end of each for paws. To assemble, tuck tail under body and prop up with foam until set. Fasten all remaining pieces in position with egg white. Pipe in eyes and a little cross in chocolate icing to represent nose.

Panda

Colour one-third of the marzipan black. For the arms take half of the black paste and roll into a sausage about 6cm (2½in) long. Bend round into a half moon. Pinch off two small pieces of black paste about the size of a little finger nail. Form into balls and flatten out for ears. With a ball tool, hollow out the centre. Take another tiny piece of black, flatten out and cut two tiny pear drops for facial markings. Reserve a minute piece of the remaining black for the nose then divide the rest in half. Roll into fat sausages 18mm (¾in) long. Curve inwards slightly, pinch up ends and flatten for feet. Divide the white paste into two, one slightly larger than the other. Take a tiny piece off the smaller ball, roll into a ball, stick black nose on.

Roll white body into a ball. Press base flat. Roll head into a round shape. Stick on nose. Make two indentations with back of knife under black piece pointing downwards at an angle. Either side of nose fasten pear drops, thicker end uppermost. Stick on ears. Fasten arms with egg white onto top of body and attach legs either side, with the inside curve of the legs tucking round body. Stick head into position securely.

Woodland Scene

Put 60g (2oz) vanilla buttercream to one side, colour the remainder brown using chocolate or food-colouring. Coat board with one-third of brown buttercream. Unroll the white swiss (jelly) roll and wrap it round the chocolate one. Stand upright on board towards back. Cut the other swiss roll at an angle and stick with buttercream, pointed side down to side of main roll. Unwrap any remaining swiss roll and wrap round base of upright log, to give a thick looking base. Spread brown buttercream thickly all over log and branch, leaving a flat surface. Fork upwards to make the surface look like bark. Spread the 60g (2oz) vanilla buttercream onto the flat surface of log. Pipe tree rings in chocolate icing.

Take 500g (1lb) marzipan and colour it green. Press small pieces at a time through a wire mesh sieve to resemble grass. Slice off with sharp knife and place all over board and round tree trunk. Use the remaining marzipan to make the animals

125g (4oz) light brown for raccoon x 2
125g (4oz) red for toadstools x 4
125g (4oz) red brown for squirrel x 2
15g (½oz) grey for mouse
15g (½oz) pink for flowers
250g (8oz) dark brown for small log and rabbits
some white dots for toadstools.

Small Log

Take 60g (2oz) marzipan coloured dark brown. Roll into a sausage shape about 10cm (4in) long. Hollow out ends with the tip of a sharp knife. Score with the knife all over log to look like bark.

Toadstools

For the stalk, make a fat sausage shape thicker at one end. Stand firmly on surface to flatten end. The cap is made from a ball of paste flattened on one side with the edges pulled thinner with finger and thumb. Attach the two pieces with egg white. The white paste for the spots is rolled out and cut out with the knob end of a pen, attach with egg white.

Ivy

Pipe ivy stems at random round the log, then stamp out leaves from some green sugarpaste with a small ivy leaf cutter. Attach to the stems around cake.

Flowers

Roll out pink paste thinly and cut out with tiny blossom spring cutter. Arrange in clumps on grass in between the animals.

INGREDIENTS

500g (1lb) vanilla buttercream
3 swiss (jelly) rolls,
chocolate and white
1.2kg (2½lb) marzipan
Royal icing
125g (4oz) green sugarpaste

EQUIPMENT

Piping bags
Small ivy leaf cutter
30cm (12in) cake board
Sharp knife
Scissors
Tiny blossom cutter with spring

Human Figures

Figure modelling is an enjoyable, but time consuming activity. Although appreciated by children as decorations for cakes, these figures would also make excellent showpieces for exhibitions and competitions.

These nursery characters represent two methods of figure modelling. Marzipan is a heavy material to work with and, ideally, the figures should be kept small to prevent the marzipan bending and breaking. The girl figure is 15cm (6in) high and is supported by a wooden dowel which is hidden beneath her skirt. Figures with two legs are much more unstable and should generally be smaller, the gnomes are about 8cm (3½in) and are supported by a cocktail stick, inserted through the body and part of the head. Do not forget to warn children that these figures contain supports and should not be eaten.

Gnomes

Head
Colour 15g (½oz) marzipan to a flesh tone. Roll into a ball and elongate slightly to form jowls, indent eyes with a ball tool. Take two tiny balls of flesh-coloured paste and flatten into a triangle for the hands, mark in fingers with a sharp knife. Colour a minute piece dark pink for the nose.

Colour 8g (¼oz) marzipan brown, mould into two pear shapes and, with a ball tool, hollow out the fat end to stand the legs into. Ease up sides slightly. Colour a small ball of marzipan black for the belt, roll into a long sausage. Divide the remaining paste into three and colour brightly for the trousers, jacket and cap.

Trousers
Roll into a rectangular ball and make a cut in the middle of one short side, ease two pieces apart and round off for the legs. Flatten the base of each leg and stand into the shoes securing with a little egg white.

Jacket
Roll into a rectangular ball and with finger and thumb hollow into a bell shape, cut a small V in the centre. Fasten with egg white onto the trousers. Push a cocktail stick through the body leaving 12mm (½in) protruding to attach the head. Roll out two small sausages for the arms and mould into shape. Attach to the body at the shoulder and stick on the hands.

Finishing
Make an elongated pear shape and hollow out until it is large enough to fit onto the head. Leave pointing upwards or bend as desired. Stick the cap onto the head and attach the head to the body. Stick the nose in place. Make a small triangle and elongate for the beard. Pipe white icing for the eyes and brush white icing onto the beard. Paint in features when the icing has dried. Stick belt around the waist and pipe in the buckle.

INGREDIENTS

125g (4oz) marzipan
Food colouring
Royal icing
Cocktail stick

Girl

Head and Body
Dust the plaster head moulds with a little cornflour (cornstarch) and press flesh-coloured marzipan into each half, trim any surplus marzipan level with the mould. Unmould and stick the two halves together with a little egg white, smooth the join with thumbs. With about seven-eighths of the remaining flesh-coloured marzipan, mould into a body shape emphasizing the waist. Insert dowel through the centre of the moulded piece.

Skirt
Roll the blue marzipan thinly and cut out a circle, the radius should equal the body length from the waist to the base. Cut a hole in the centre of the skirt and position securing around the waist with egg white. Arrange the flounces.

Arms

Fold the wire pieces in half and twist all strands together. Cut off two lengths for the arms in proportion to the body. Make two sausages from the remaining flesh-coloured marzipan and mould around the wire leaving about 6mm (¼in) exposed at one end, bend into shape. Flatten the other end for the hands and score the fingers with a knife. For the sleeves, roll two pieces of red marzipan into fingernail-size balls. Flatten slightly, make four indentations in the rounded edges and attach to the surplus wire on the arms. Pipe white royal icing into the indentations.

Hair

Divide the black marzipan in half. Roll one half into a ball, hollow out with the thumbs to form a cap large enough to fit over the head for the hair. Elongate the back of the hair and stick into position. Mark a parting with a knife. Roll out a tiny piece of red for the ribbon and bow and attach.

Bodice

Roll out a rectangle with the remaining black paste, the width should be half the circumference of the bust and the length should be twice the length from the neck to the waist. Cut a hole for the neck section and fashion the front into a V shape. Ease over the body and smooth the side joins. Attach sleeves, arms and head. Paint in face.

INGREDIENTS

165g (5½oz) marzipan
Royal icing
Egg white
Food colouring

Colour marzipan as follows:
90g (3oz) marzipan flesh colour
45g (1½oz) blue
15g (½oz) black
15g (½oz) red

EQUIPMENT

13cm (5in) piece of dowel
Plaster face mould
2 pieces of 24-gauge covered wire
No 00 paintbrush
Small rolling pin
Sharp knife

Pastillage & Sugar Miniatures

Figure Modelling

Pre-formed moulds are readily available and will produce competent figures but the poses and sizes available are restricted. Far more original and lifelike results can be attained by building up the figure freely with the use of an armature (wire support).

If the figure or animal is to be dressed, the body itself can be a fairly rough shape as it will be hidden and the areas that will be visible such as the arms and head can be modelled in greater detail. One important point to remember is that the addition of clothes will enlarge the figure so that the body needs to be thinner and needs to be thoroughly dry before clothing is added otherwise cracking will occur.

Proportions are very important when modelling human figures. The head should measure one-sixth of the body size. When modelling a child, this proportion is different. The head is much larger and will roughly measure a quarter of the body size. When the arms are held at the side of the body, the fingers should reach mid-thigh. Many people tend to make the arms far too short and this will spoil the balance of the figure. Ask someone to pose if possible so that a natural position can be achieved.

The Face
This is the most important area as it tends to be the focal point of the figure and the whole effect can be spoiled if, for instance, a flower fairy, Goldilocks or baby has a cracked or lined face with a crooked nose. A mould can be made from plaster using a doll's head cut in half. The head then can be formed by pushing a small ball of paste into the mould so that the features are formed on one side and the back part of the ball forms the back of the head.

When painting on the features, the eyes should focus on an area within the modelled scene, so that they don't appear vacant or staring. Paint the iris (the coloured area of the eye). When dry, paint the black pupil and again, when dry, highlight with a dot of white. This should bring some life to the eyes. Blush the cheeks with dusting powder, lightly add freckles, if desired, with minute dots of paprika paste colour. Paint lips also with paprika, not bright red or bright pink.

Hair can be piped with royal icing or it can be made by pushing soft paste through a garlic press or a potter's clay gun. It could also be rolled with the fingers into fine strands. It can be applied to form tight curls or, by using the gun, plaits or ringlets.

Modelling Animals
When modelling animals, try to work from photographs, real life or illustrations so that the pose is correct and most important, the colour and markings of the fur and formation of paws and features are correct and a realistic likeness is achieved. The body shape and pose are important if it is to bear any resemblance to that particular creature even if an animal is to be dressed or is a fantasy animal.

Cards, Caskets and Moulded Decorations
Again, moulds can be used to produce bells, caskets, slippers and any other basic shape, but it is far more rewarding to produce something that is truly original. Look for more unusual moulds, for example a flower pot, doll's shoes, aspic dishes. Templates can be cut and made for cards, caskets and houses for a more personal result.

Paste
For the rough body shapes or anything that will be hidden with royal icing or clothes, use gelatine paste. For finer detailed work, clothes, faces, hands, for instance, use fine flower paste or modelling paste.

Breakages
It is advisable to make spares if any item is particularly fragile, for example cards and caskets, in case of breakages because of time involved in the drying process.

Use of Wire and Plaster Moulds
A warning must be given if wire, plaster moulds or cocktail sticks have been used to support the modelling in case it is eaten by a child.

Pastillage Cards

Pastillage Cards

It is important to dry the pieces on a completely flat surface, lightly dusted with cornflour (cornstarch). Roll some paste out thinly. Cut the card shape on the surface on which it is to be dried. Do not attempt to lift and transfer the piece after any cutout shapes have been removed, as this could distort the overall shape. Cut the card shape with a very sharp knife. Use a single rocking movement, do not drag the knife as this will stretch and distort the paste. Cut in from the corners, not out to the corners. When drying turn the pieces so that they will dry flat and will not warp.

Heart-shaped Card

Cut out card pieces as above. Use a biscuit cutter to remove the heart shape from the front card. Cut a heart shape in paste, medium thickness, place on inside face. Smooth the edge with fingers and modelling tool to give a padded effect. Paint a monogram on the inside of the raised heart. Pipe an edge with royal icing around the padded heart on the inside and also round the cutout heart edge.

Confirmation Card

Cut out window on front face. Form base of candlestick by cutting out shape quite thickly and indenting with a modelling tool and rounding edges to give a three dimensional look. Build up the top of the candlestick and make an indentation large enough for the candle to be placed inside. Make two thin sausage shapes, tapering at one end for the candle, insert black stamen cotton for wick. Support with foam until set so that the candle will stand away from the card.

Cut out chrysanthemum leaves. Place around edge of book area. Cut out the cover of the book and indent the spine. Place on a thick rectangle of sugarpaste for pages of book. Round the edges at the centre of the book. Cut out a single page from a thin piece of paste. Turn up edges and support with the fine slivers of foam until dry. Add writing with NoOO brush. Dust the surface of the pages with cream powder and gold sparkle. Add chrysanthemums. Position a thin piece of paste for the ribbon bookmark.

On the inside face, paint the church window using paste colours. Use clear, pastel colours. Write the verse with a fine, non-toxic pen.

To Assemble Cards

Pipe a snailstrail along inside edge of inner card. Place the two cards together. Support until dry. Pipe another decorative edging on spine of the card to strengthen.

Bramble Mice

Mother Mouse

Make a rough shape for the body using gelatine paste. Allow to dry thoroughly. Colour flower paste blue. Roll out paste quite finely. Using the pattern, cut out the bodice and attach to body. Cut out the skirt. Fold and drape pleats, mostly at the back of the skirt and place around the body. Place the seams at the front of the figure so that they will be hidden by the apron. Make a bustle from a thick piece of paste. Place at the back of the figure and attach to the skirt.

Head

Make a small cone, indent eyes, nostrils and mouth, paint in facial markings. Make mop cap by rolling a small ball of paste, indent with large ball tool, pinch edge around indentation and place on the mouse's head. Make ears with pinky grey paste, first make a small ball, flatten and indent with a ball tool. Pinch together the base of the ear and attach to the hat. Use a cocktail stick and frill a long narrow piece of paste and attach to the edge of the cap. Roll two small balls of black paste and place into eye sockets. Texture the surface of the paste with a scalpel to look like fur. Cut out apron skirt and frill edge, apply to dress. Cut out apron bib, attach to body (try to hide the waist seam). Make two ribbon ties and a bow, attach to back of apron. Paint a pattern on the dress with a fine paintbrush.

Arms

Make a long sausage shape in pinky grey colour paste. Flatten one end to form a spade shape. Cut four long, thin fingers. Pinch and round ends of fingers. Place paw on foam and indent with a ball tool to curl fingers. Thin out the wrist, shape arm. Place in a curved position and leave to dry. When dry, wrap the sleeve paste around the arm. Attach to the body with royal icing, support until dry.

The Egg Cradle

Roll out a piece of paste of medium thickness, dust a small egg with cornflour (cornstarch). Drape the paste over the egg. Smooth the paste carefully downwards so that the paste follows the shape of the egg. Cut the jagged points with a scalpel, remove paste from the egg and lightly smooth edges. Replace paste onto the egg until dry. When dry, place a sugarpaste mattress inside the egg so that the baby mouse will be upwards

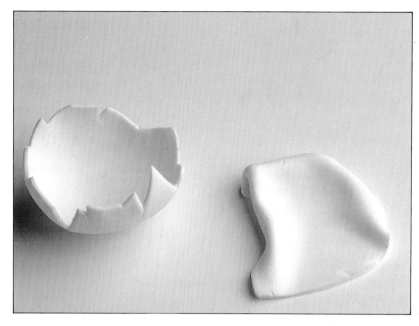

when placed inside and become more visible. Make a pillow out of a roughly square piece of sugarpaste. Pinch the corners to give a natural look. Frill a thin, narrow piece of flower-paste to form lace edging. Make a small head as for mother mouse. Make a rough conical shape for the body from sugarpaste. Roll out a thin piece of paste for blanket. Fold and tuck in the edges. When dry, dust yellow and paint on a flowered pattern with a fine brush. Dust egg blue, add on brown markings with a fairly dry paintbrush using brown paste colour.

Prepare plaque by colouring gelatine crystals with green dusting colour. Cover area with gum arabic or egg white, sprinkle on crystals. Tip away excess. Make blackberry leaves, (see page 219),arrange in a spray. Attach to the plaque with royal icing along with the egg and mother mouse.

Baby Wrapped in Quilt

Head
Make baby's head by pushing a large ball of skin-coloured paste into a plaster mould (made from cutting a small doll's head in half and making the impression). Place on a cocktail stick to dry.

Body
Make a large cone, bend the cone slightly backwards and exaggerate abdomen. Create a curve between the back and bottom using forefinger. Make an indentation with a large ball tool where head, arms and legs are to be placed.

Hands and Arms
Tap one end of a sausage and flatten to form a spade shape. Cut out a small 'V' for the thumb then cut fingers. Separate each finger, smooth and round tips. Place onto a piece of foam and curve fingers by drawing a ball

tool over them towards the palm, indent palm with ball tool. Form wrist, elbow and upper arm by rolling paste with fingers. Place in a natural pose to dry.

Legs
Taper one end of a sausage and flatten to form a spade shape as for arms. Make 4 cuts for toes, round ends. Form heel and ankle using thumb and forefinger. Shape knee and thigh. Indent bottom of foot to create arch. Place in a natural position and dry.

To Assemble
Attach head to body, and legs to torso. Make a nappy by rolling a piece of white paste to medium thickness and wrap around body. Texture nappy by pinching paste with fine pointed tweezers to create a towelling-like effect. Attach arms.

Pipe on hair using royal icing. Paint facial features and dust cheeks.

Quilt
Position baby on a tissue paper template and practise wrapping baby in tissue until satisfied with folds, shape and lay the quilt so that when the baby is wrapped in the actual paste it can be handled as little as possible as over handling and re-wrapping will cause the paste to crack and tear. When satisfied, mark on template the position of the baby's bottom. When the quilt is completely dry, paint in the patchwork pattern with a fine brush using clear paste colours. If working with more than one colour on each pattern, allow each colour to dry thoroughly or streaking will occur. Keep the brush as dry as possible, over-wetting of the paste will cause it to disintegrate.

Koala in Tree

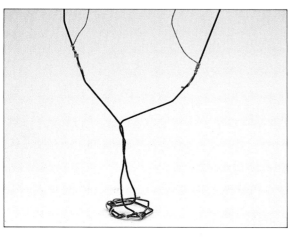

Make a wire support for the tree using heavy-gauge wire. Make two circular bases, wrap together with a finer-gauge wire, twist wire together to form a trunk. Divide into a fork shape. Add finer-gauge wire near the top of the tree for smaller branches. Colour gelatine paste brown. Build up the trunk with pieces of paste pushed into the wire, becoming thinner where the branches fork, leave to dry. Pipe royal icing over the shape and brush with a dry brush to create a textured finish.

Koala
Make a greyish brown-coloured paste. Make a conical shape for the body. Tilt to one side slightly. Make a round shape for the face. Pinch out the nose until it protrudes, pinch together slightly to narrow. The face tends to be fairly flat and the eyes are quite far apart and quite small. Indent eyes with a small modelling tool. Make ears as for mouse but attach sideways into the head.

Attach head to the front of the cone, not the top. Smooth edges together with a modelling tool. Fix to tree at this stage with royal icing while the koala is still fairly moveable so that the branch indents the front of the koala and it fits snugly into the fork of the tree. It will then appear to be clinging to the tree and not simply placed on it.

Arms and Legs
The thumb on the paw is fairly high up so make the first cut higher than usual. Make three further cuts for the other four digits. The wrist and arm are quite thick so only shape the wrist slightly. Repeat for the back legs but leave larger pieces of paste for the haunches. Attach limbs to koala so that it appears to be clinging to the tree itself.

Texture fur with royal icing and a dry brush. Make some eucalyptus leaves and attach to hand. Pipe in black eyes, glaze nose and when dry, glaze eyes.

Skunk

Head and Body

Make a cone shape, uptilt snout. Indent eyes with a small ball tool. Make a large flattened sausage for the body. Cut a large insertion and divide for legs. Smooth and round each leg. Insert a long wooden skewer into body to support it while dressing. Insert half a cocktail stick into each ankle, allow to dry thoroughly.

Clothes

Make a normal frill for each ankle. Thinly roll out pink paste and using the pattern, cut out the skirt, smooth with large ball tool and thin all cut edges. Slightly frill bottom hem of skirt with ball tool. Wrap around the body. Place the seam at the front of the figure where it will be hidden by the apron. Smooth seam with finger to hide join as much as possible. Cut apron skirt in white paste and attach over the pink skirt with the opening at the back of the figure. Cut back and front bodice shapes and attach to the body. Indent with No1 tube and pipe bottom edge of bodice and around neck for a fine lace effect. Make two arms from black paste as for mouse. When dry, wrap sleeve around arm. Cut away excess paste on the inside at the top of the arm.

Boots

Using black paste, make a sausage shape, bend for the ankle. Flatten bottom of boot, form a heel by moulding with forefinger. Glue and push onto cocktail stick.

Tail

With white gelatine paste, make a tail. Roll a sausage long enough to place up inside the skirt. One end should be fairly narrow, it should be thicker in the middle with a thick end to attach to the body. Support each end with foam to lift while drying.

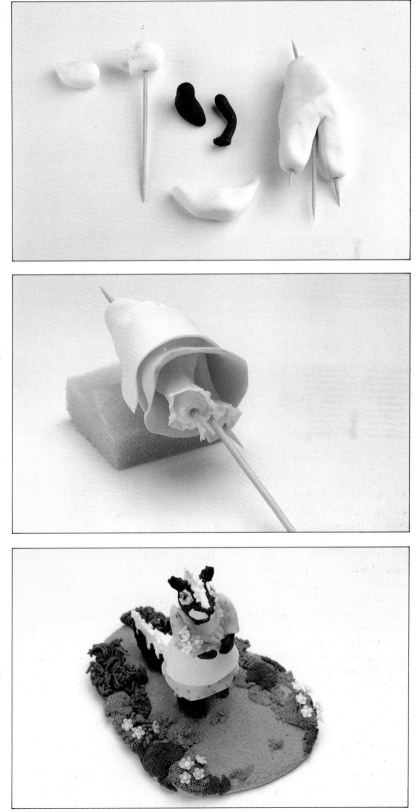

Teddy Birthday Plaque

Make rounded cone shape for body and insert cocktail sticks where head, arms and legs will be positioned. Texture body by pinching the paste with fine pointed tweezers. Make the head quite large in proportion to the rest of the body. Make a tall pinch one side of the ball to form snout, indent eyes with ball tool. Make ears as for mouse, and attach to head, texture as before.

Legs and Arms

Make a large cone for each arm, pull out pointed end and flatten to form paw. Shape wrist by rolling fingers, texture and place in a curved position to dry. For each leg, make a large cone, flatten and pull out as for arm to form foot, bend at the knee and leave a large piece of paste for haunch; texture. Note: Place both arms and legs onto body before drying so that the cocktail sticks inserted into torso will form a hole in the limbs. Support with foam when drying then attach to body with royal icing. Attach head.

Honey Pot

Make a flattened barrel shape. Roll a fine sausage. Join ends to form a ring. Place on top of barrel. Make a label from finely rolled white paste cut into a rectangle when dry, paint in 'HONEY'.

Wrapping Paper

Roll out a piece of blue paste quite finely. Roll out a piece of white paste to the same thickness. Place one piece of paste over the other and roll together to form one piece of paste. Cut some small shapes using a plunger cutter and place on blue paste, these could be in a contrasting colour. Roll again to form one piece of paste. Cut into a square shape, roll up and lift or bend down corners to give a natural effect, support

until dry. Make a small birthday card by cutting a rectangular shape in white paste, fold in half and leave to dry. Paint message inside and design on front of card.

Bee

Make two balls of paste one yellow and one black. Slice each ball into sections. Reassemble to form a ball of alternative colours. Make a ball for the head, insert two stamens for antennae. Roll black paste finely into strands, bend to form legs. When dry, attach to body with royal icing.

Wings

Use a small rose petal cutter. Cut two wings, dry. Paint veins; dust with gold sparkle. Wings can either be attached to the body with royal icing when both are dry or the dry wings can be inserted into the body while the paste is still soft.

Clown Jack-in-the-box

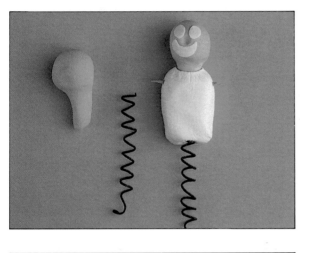

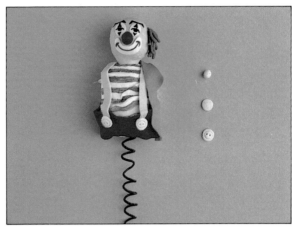

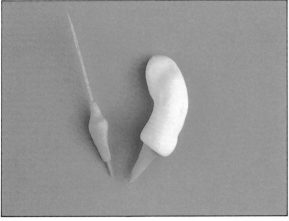

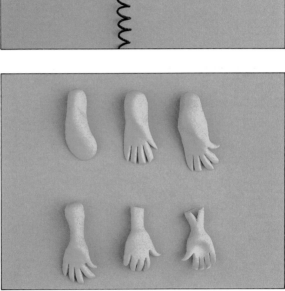

To Assemble
Make ribbons and place into plaque.
Place wrapping paper on top of ribbons.
Place honey jar on paper. Fill pot with
honey-coloured icing made to runout
consistency, allow to drip down the side
of the jar and onto the paper. Position
teddy, bee and card.

Clown Jack-in-the-box

Spring
Make a spring by wrapping a heavy
gauge wire around a round pencil,
remove and screw into body shape.
Push a perspex tube up through the
spring and push into the body, dry.

Face
Make a ball of skin-coloured paste. Roll
to form neck, roll and push finger into
paste to form a chin.

Cut out two white ovals for the eyes
and curved half moon for the mouth.
Indent with a ball tool for nose. Paint
on features with black and red paint,
add a red ball of paste to nose
indentation. Glaze nose with gum
arabic glue or confectioner's glaze.

Clothes
Make a fairly rough body. Using pattern
cut out T-shirt. Place on the body,
create creases and folds in the paste.
When dry, paint on the stripes. Cut a
long strip of red paste, wrap around the
waist area for the trousers. To create a
baggy effect, pull down and stretch edge
with finger and thumb. Cut two thin
strips for braces. Make two buttons by
rolling two small balls of cream paste,
flatten and indent a circle with a large
icing tube, make two holes to create a
shank with a large needle.
Cut out jacket-fronts. Smooth cut

edge with a large ball tool. Shape
bottom edge to create a natural effect.
Cut out back of jacket and glue in
place. Cut two lapels. Ball to slightly
frill cut edge. Roll and form lapels,
again to create a natural effect.

Heads and Arms
Make a long sausage for the arm, bend
and leave to dry. To make a wrist
shape, make a cone of skin-coloured
paste, push a cocktail stick into the
paste and taper the end; leave to dry.
Push the wrist shape into the arm, leave
to dry.

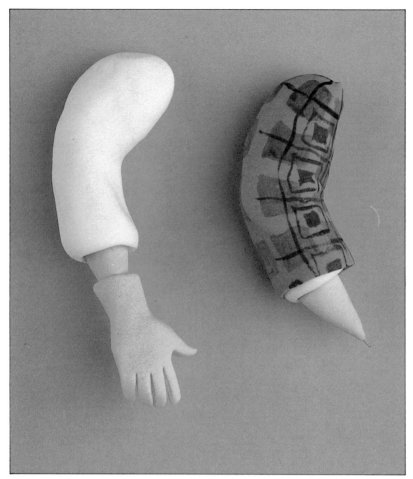

Glove

Make a hand as for the baby. Extend the wrist to push a piece of dowelling the end of the glove and open up the paste. Cut a V section from the cuff. Roll edge to thin, push onto wrist shape. Before covering the arm with a sleeve, decide on the position of the arms so that the sleeve seam is placed where it will be less visible, either on underside or inside the arm. Paint the check pattern on the jacket. Make hair by pushing some soft paste through a clay gun or a garlic press, attach to head.

Bow Tie

Roll out some green paste, make small balls of red paste and push these into green paste, re-roll paste and cut out the shape using the pattern. Pull the tie ends towards the middle and glue. Wrap a small strip of paste around centre of bow. Glue in place at the neck.

Box

Roll out pale yellow paste to medium thickness, using template cut five squares. When dry, paint a design, letter or number on each square. If numbers are chosen, the age of the child could be on the front of the box.

To Assemble

Pipe royal icing on edges of square, butt edges together. Support until dry. Assemble three sides. Push clown on perspex rod into cake. Place three box sides around clown, attach fourth side and lid. Make beach ball from gelatine paste and paint when dry. Make a small rag doll or teddy, prop against ball. Attach ribbons to cake in colours to match clown.

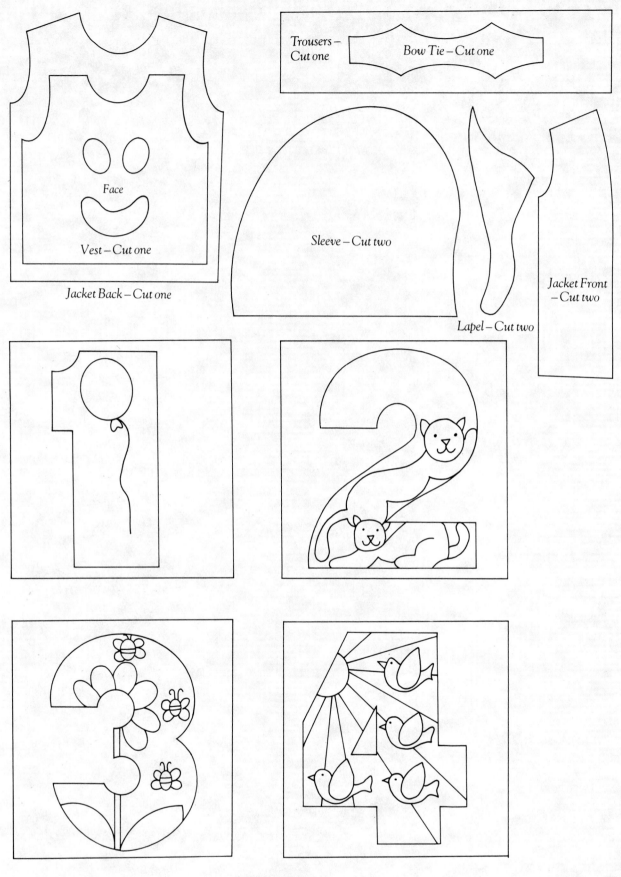

Trousers – Cut one

Bow Tie – Cut one

Face

Vest – Cut one

Jacket Back – Cut one

Sleeve – Cut two

Lapel – Cut two

Jacket Front – Cut two

Jack in the Box

Bramble

Apron Rib – Cut one

Dress Bodice – Cut one

Apron Bow – Cut one

Sleeve – Cut two

Apron Skirt – Cut one

Skirt – Cut one

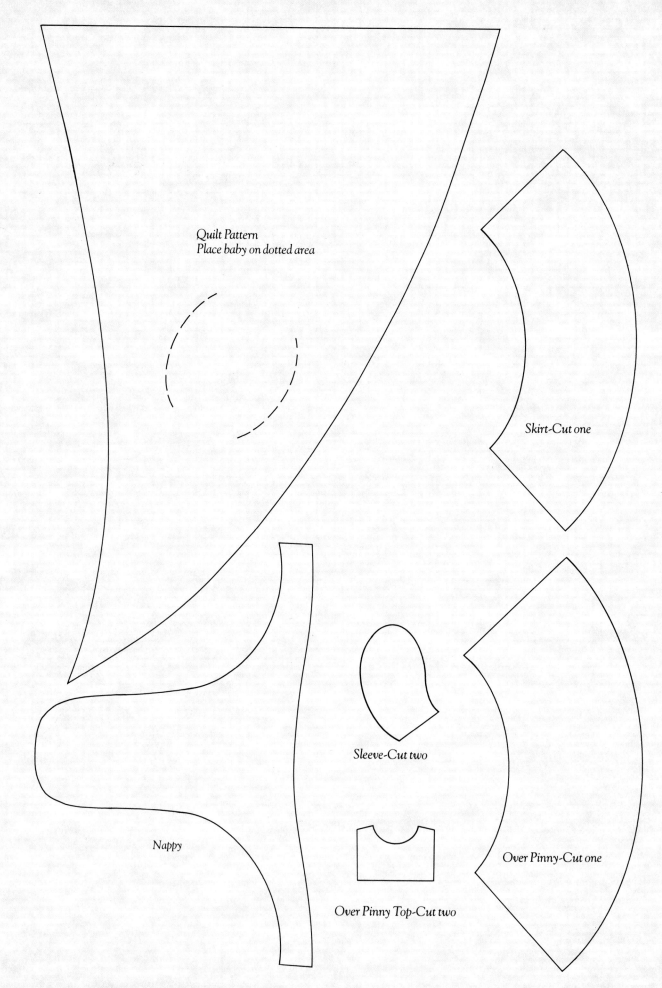

Quilt Pattern
Place baby on dotted area

Skirt-Cut one

Sleeve-Cut two

Nappy

Over Pinny-Cut one

Over Pinny Top-Cut two

Tube Embroidery & Broderie Anglaise

Iced Embroidery

Embroidery designs of all kinds are very easily adapted for use as cake decorations. This involves piping the individual 'stitches' with a fine icing tube using fairly soft icing.

Embroidery refers to both large complex designs using several colours and also to the fine lacy embroidery motifs commonly used for side decoration which are generally piped in one colour. This method allows the decorator endless scope as it can be effectively used for a variety of designs including symmetrical patterns, floral, figures, crests and lettering.

Once you have practised the stitches, any embroidery pattern can be used as a guide. Fabrics, wall coverings and even some china will give many lovely designs which may inspire you to create patterns.

Before starting a design, mix up all the colours and shades of icing which you will be needing. Put a small amount of all the colours in piping bags with a No 0 tube. Use small bags and do not more than half fill them, this allows you more freedom of movement and is more accurate as you will be working closer to the design.

Start working the design beginning with the background, working towards the front. Complete one section at a time, changing the shade where necessary before starting another part of the design. For

example, a petal may be pale at the tip darkening towards the base, therefore, the pale tip should be piped first. While this is still wet, change to a darker colour and carry on piping all in one operation. This will produce a smooth result and the shades will blend well. A fine, slightly damp brush should be drawn through the stitches if they look uneven and any little peaks should be flattened while still wet. If some parts need special emphasis, they may be built up slightly by using extra pressure.

Marking out the Design

Pricking
Trace the design onto tracing paper. Place this on the cake or plaque and carefully prick the outline with a pin. Do not mark too many details as this will be confusing and these small features can easily be copied when the design is almost finished. This method is not suitable for hard surfaces.

Pencil Tracing
The usual method of tracing is to turn over the design, re-draw on the back with a sugarcraft pen, or with non-toxic pastel pencil, place this side on the surface to be decorated and trace again over the outline. This leaves the fine lines of the pattern on the surface. Do not use very heavy lines as these will be difficult to conceal and could smudge. Small pieces of outline embroidery which are mainly used to decorate the sides of a cake or scattered around a large decoration to give a softening effect are usually done freehand with a No0 or 00 tube. The focal points of the design may be pricked out with a pin, this will ensure that the side motifs look uniform even though there may be some slight variations. The icing nozzle should gently scrape the surface as the icing is squeezed out using an even pressure and should be held rather like a pen. Fresh soft icing which has been well beaten should be used, this should flow easily without needing too much pressure.

Embroidery Stitches

1. Long and Short Stitch
Is used to fill a large shape with an arrangement of stitches blended to create a smooth surface. Pipe a fine outline. First row ,make long and short stitches. Second and successive rows, the stitches are all the same length. The last rows need tidying up so another row of long and short will fill the spaces left. The direction of stitches should follow the lines of the design.

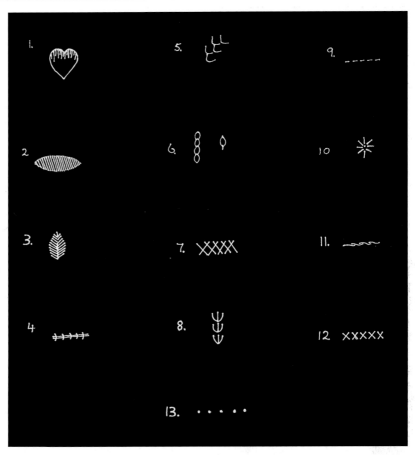

2. Satin Stitch
These are straight stitches, worked together to form a band or shape and are used for small or narrow shapes.

3. Fishbone Stitch
Made up of lines piped diagonally towards the centre and repeated the other side in reverse direction. Useful for leaves or feathers.

4. Couching
One or more threads are laid down and stitched into position. This can be used where a very bold outline is required. This stitch is used by embroiderers when they are using metallic threads like gold or silver and would be appropriate in oriental designs.

5. Feather Stitch
Pipe a U shape with the next one starting below and to the centre of the first stitch.

6. Chain Stitch
A row of chains makes an interesting outline and can be used for stems. A long chain stitch worked singly is known as a lazy-daisy stitch and is used for small flower petals.

7. Herringbone Stitch
A series of diagonal lines overlapping at the top and the base.

8. Fern Stitch
A simple arrangement of three stitches worked at angles to each other. Useful for grasses or leaf veins.

9. Running Stitch
Short straight stitches with a gap between them. Useful for outlining or for filling shapes when a very light effect is required.

10. Star Stitch
Straight stitches radiating from a central point.

11. Stem Stitch
Used for stems and outlines.

12. Cross Stitch
The traditional stitch for samplers. Used for outlines, fillings and borders.

13. French Knots
Pipe a tiny bulb of icing. Used for stamens or decorative fillings.

Tube Embroidery

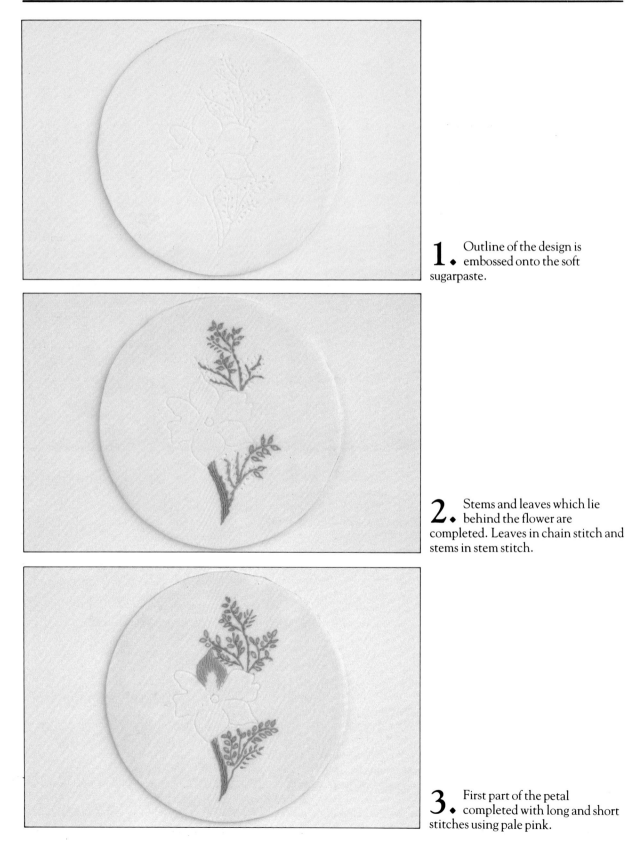

1. Outline of the design is embossed onto the soft sugarpaste.

2. Stems and leaves which lie behind the flower are completed. Leaves in chain stitch and stems in stem stitch.

3. First part of the petal completed with long and short stitches using pale pink.

4. Centre of the petal completed in darker colour and blended at the change-over point. Complete petals at the back first.

5. Design is completed by adding the petals which appear to be in front. The centre is piped in black satin stitch and stamens around the edge are French Knots.

Harebells worked in long and short stitch.

Crewel work lilies.

Pansies worked in long and short stitch.

Crewel work floral plaque.

Broderie Anglaise

This is also known as eyelet, Madeira or Swiss work. Designs usually consist of simple floral motifs as the round and oval holes lend themselves so well to floral formations. Work on fresh soft sugarpaste.

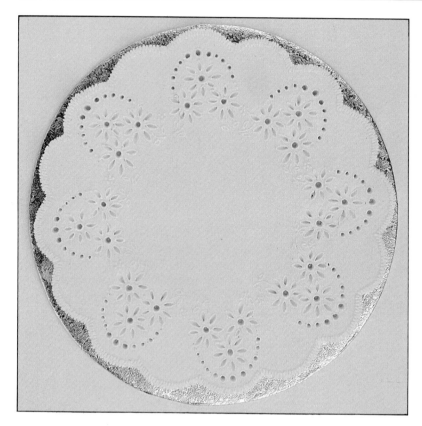

Prick out focal points with a pin. Take care when pricking designs not to lean hand on the surface of the paste as this will spoil a good finish. Round holes are made by holding a paintbrush handle or knitting needle (pin) at right angles to the cake and pressing gently into the paste.

Oval holes are made by holding the same tool at 45°, this will make an elongated hole. Pipe around all holes with a No 0 tube. To give a perfectly round circle, outline half the hole in a clockwise direction then pipe the other half in reverse direction. Neaten the take-off point with a damp brush if necessary. Traditional broderie anglaise has a scalloped edge which is sewn with buttonhole stitch. This effect can be achieved by piping a small open zig-zag.

1. Design pricked out through the pattern with a pin.

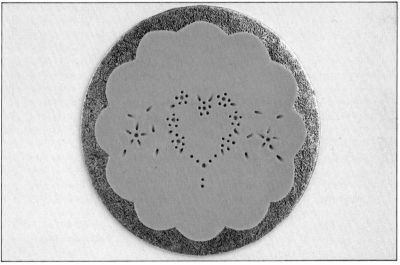

2. Holes are made with paintbrush handle.

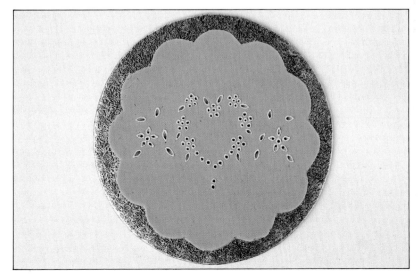

3. All holes are outlined with a No 0 icing tube.

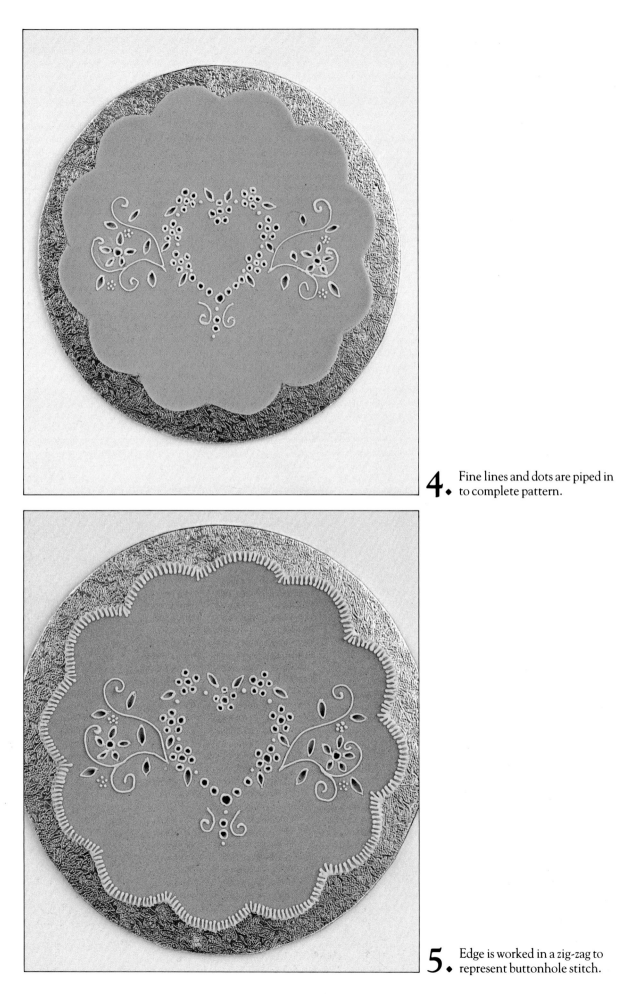

4. Fine lines and dots are piped in to complete pattern.

5. Edge is worked in a zig-zag to represent buttonhole stitch.

Lazy Daisy Cake

Coat a 28cm (11in) round board with coloured sugarpaste. Cut a scalloped template from a 28cm (11in) circle by folding into 16 sections and cutting about 1cm (½in) away from the edge of the pattern to form a curve.

Roll out white sugarpaste quite thinly. Cut scalloped shape and carefully lift onto the board. Mark the main holes for broderie anglaise using pattern as a guide. This process should be completed before the cake is placed on the board as it will be easier to make the holes.

Cover the cake with coloured sugarpaste. Gently lift into the centre of the board and secure with icing. Make a small scalloped shape for the top using same method as before, the finished shape should be about 2.5cm (1in) smaller than the diameter of the cake and should also have 16 scallops.

Mark out the pattern and make the main holes. By pressing right through to the coloured paste, the deeper colour will show through enough to make a better contrast. Care should be taken not to press into the cake itself as this will cause a dark stain to gradually seep through to the surface.

Outline all the holes on the board and the top of the cake and pipe in fine embroidery. Edge stitch scallops using zig-zag lines. Make a template for side decoration, using a strip of paper to fit the side of the cake. Cut shape from the guide. Attach to the cake and mark out the pattern. With cake tilted away from you, pipe the curved lines. Pipe daisy decoration. Pipe snailstrail around the base of the cake. Attach bands of ribbon around base and make small bows using two colours of ribbon together. Add top decoration of flowers or an ornament to suit the occasion.

319

Templates for designs illustrated in this lesson

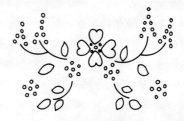

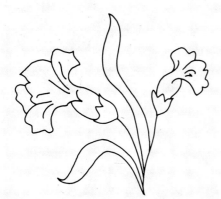
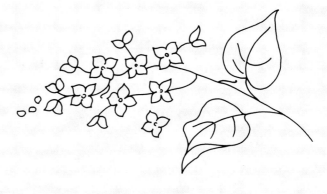

Templates for designs used in this lesson

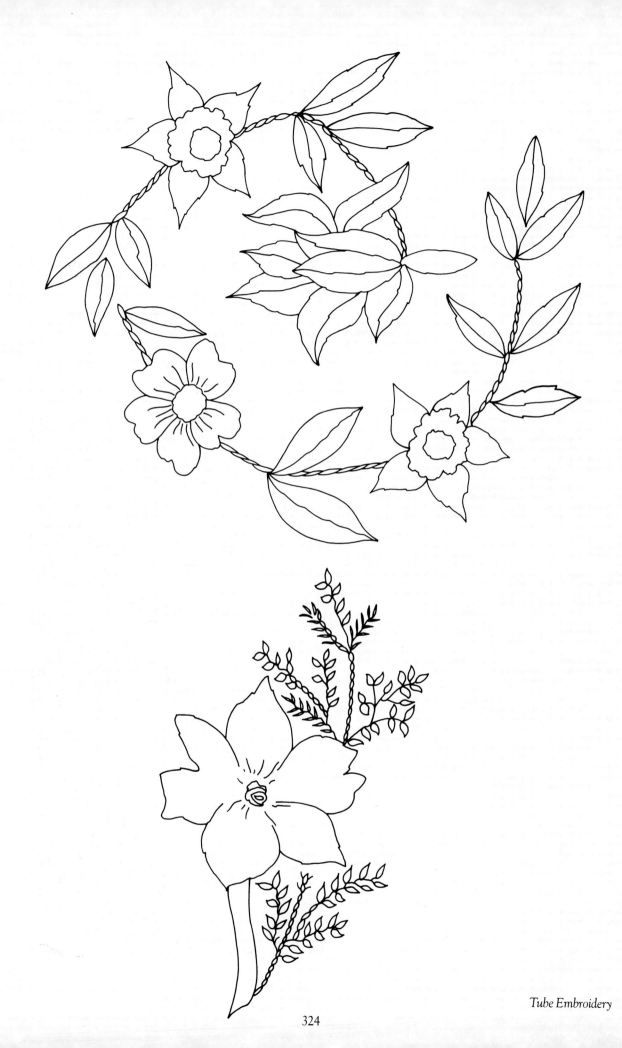

Tube Embroidery

LESSON 6

Brush Embroidery

Brush Embroidery

This is a versatile technique whereby the decorator can produce attractive designs quite simply and quickly. If a little more time is taken for highlighting and shading the design, the same method can be employed to create a beautiful, delicate finish.

A white design on a white background which would be most suitable for a wedding cake makes a very elegant decoration and brush embroidery would be a good technique for reproducing the design of the bridal lace. Although the pattern is not very clearly defined it will show up quite well by contrast of light and shade.

A more dramatic effect will be achieved by piping a white design on a dark background, or a dark brown design on a cream background. In this case the pattern is defined by varying the density of the icing and brushing in the direction of the natural veining of petals and leaves. However, the most beautiful designs are those in which several complementary colours are used and delicately highlighted with diluted food colouring after the icing has completely dried.

Transfer of Design

On soft, fresh sugarpaste it is best to emboss the design by placing the pattern under a piece of perspex or glass which should be larger than the top of the cake so that the surface will not be marked by the edge of the perspex. If glass is used it should be bound with strong tape to prevent cuts.

Outline the design by piping on top of the perspex with a No 0 or 1 tube and white icing made without glycerine. Do not pipe in small details as these can be added later. Allow to dry thoroughly. This method will produce a reverse image and if this is undesirable, the design should be turned over and re-traced on the back before placing under the perspex.

Pencil Transfer

This method, which seems to be popular, should be very carefully worked, as a mistake will result in a dark line in the wrong place which may be very difficult to conceal.

Trace over the pattern with tracing paper and a medium hard pencil to give a clear, sharp line. Turn over tracing paper and re-trace the pattern with a non-toxic pencil or pastel. Place this side on the cake and using a smooth tip such as a ball point, lightly trace on to the cake.

This method is useful where the design of the top continues over the side of the cake. The icing should be allowed to harden for a few days before tracing to avoid making pit marks.

Pricking

This is only suitable for very simple designs or freehand work where it is only necessary to mark positions of small decorations, as the result may not be clearly enough defined for accuracy. It is not a very successful method for use on hard icing.

Materials

A No1 tube is used for most designs but where the work is very small and a large build-up of icing is undesirable, a No 0 should be used. Choose a good quality sable brush as this will be firm and springy and will give better results than a cheap brush with weak bristles. Use a No2 or 3 for brushing the icing and highlighting and a 2/0 or 3/0 for adding fine detail.

Use fairly soft, fresh royal icing or, if you need longer to work on the design before it dries out, add about one teaspoon of clear piping gel to every four tablespoons of icing. The gel is seldom necessary, so try working without it and then compare the results when the gel is added.

Working Brush Embroidery

When preparing to start a multi-coloured design, fill several small icing bags containing a No 0 or 1 tube with all of the colours you intend to use. As this entails using a lot of expensive tubes you can try using a firm bag without a tube and carefully snipping off the end of the bag after filling it to form a tiny hole about the size of a No1 tube. The bag must be changed as soon as the hole becomes distorted. Keep your colours quite pale as they can be emphasised where necessary by touching up when the work is finished.

Work from the outside of the design towards the centre, dealing with the background first and working on only one small section at a time. The background should be light and delicate so that it will not over-power the detail in the foreground.

The paintbrush should be damp. If it is too dry the icing will become rough and uneven. If it is too wet it will make a puddle which will spoil the surface of the cake. The brush should be held at an angle of 45° and long strokes should be used which start at the edge of the petal or leaf and continue to the base to avoid ridges.

Pipe a line around a leaf in the background then, before the icing dries, quickly pipe another line within. Using long smooth strokes, brush the icing through both lines towards the base, leaving more icing at the edge of the leaf and fading away to a thin film at the base. Where the leaf is serrated, it is more satisfactory to pipe a small blob of icing at each point within the outline instead of a continuous line. Take care to conceal transfer lines with your outline and to brush the icing in the direction of the natural veining on petals and leaves.

As you are brushing from the background towards the front, a little icing may be inadvertently brushed on to the area immediately in front of the part on which you are working. This is not important if it is only a light film of icing, as this will be covered when that section is outlined and brushed.

The flowers in a design are usually in front of the leaves and the back petals should be done first so that the front petals will be emphasised. The furled edges of a flower should be left until last and completed by piping a heavy line all around it and infilling with icing. Light brushing with a damp brush will smooth the area. Finally pipe in any stamens. Leaf veins can be defined by either brushing away the wet icing or by piping them in with a very fine tube.

Shadows and highlights should be painted in when the icing is completely dry, using as little moisture as possible. Water may be used to dilute the food colouring but care should be taken not to get the icing too wet. A spirit such as gin or vodka is preferable as this will dry immediately. Before brushing the colour onto the icing, try it out on a spare piece of icing as the wrong colour will be impossible to remove. To take away the flat look from a leaf, brush one side darker and always darken the same side to show that the light is coming from one direction. The base of a petal will be a deeper colour than the tip. Use an almost dry brush and very light strokes to obtain subtle shading.

Working Brush Embroidery

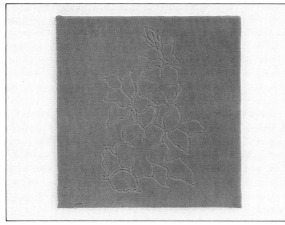

1. Mark out design by embossing or tracing.

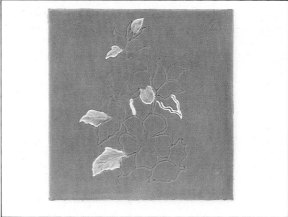

2. Outline leaves in the background. Pipe inner line, complete each section first. Brush through from tip to base with long smooth strokes using a damp brush.

3. Pipe and brush through leaves in the foreground. Pipe in calyx of bud.

4. Brush flower petals leaving furled edge.

5. Pipe furled edge of petals with heavier line, smooth with damp brush and add details.

Magnolia Cake

Cover cake with sugarpaste. Cut a template to fit the side of the cake, mark into 6 or 8 sections and cut into a scalloped shape. Mark line of scallop onto the side of the cake with a scriber. Transfer the magnolia design by embossing or tracing. Mark side motif in each scallop. Pipe fine snailstrail around the cake base.

Complete brush embroidery on top of the cake. Tilt cake away from you for side embroidery, which is easier if done at eye level.

Make flounce using a circular frill cutter. To layer the flounce at the points, cut circles into three equal sections, frill and stick by brushing the unfrilled edge with water. Stick each piece to the cake below each point at board level adjusting the frill as you go. For the second layer, cut each circle into four equal pieces and repeat the procedure, sticking each piece above the first layer. A third layer can be used, but if the top edge extends beyond the marked scallop

line, this must be carefully cut away with a scalpel.

For the top flounce, cut circle of paste and open out. Frill one edge and cut to fit the scallop. Stick to the cake, adjusting frill and neatening the top edge. Repeat all around cake, tucking in ends of the frill at the points. Finally, pipe a fine edging around top of the flounce to disguise the join.

LESSON 7

Lace

Lacing

Fine lace makes the most beautiful and delicate decoration which has always been prized for adding a touch of elegance to a garment, raising it above the ordinary level.

In recent years there has been a revival of interest in lace-making as a craft and of course, it has always been popular for wedding dresses. It follows naturally that lace work is also a very popular form of cake decoration, since the addition of finely piped lace will add delicacy to many designs. Although it is very fragile, when it is made correctly, it is quite easy to apply to the cake and transport without breakage. Small lace pieces are commonly used as an edging above a border of extension work or flounces, to add interest to a row of ribbon inserts, or to surround a picture or floral arrangement on top of a cake. Larger pieces can be placed close together around the base of a cake at an angle of 45°, taking the place of a flounce or extension work.

The icing must be very strong and you will have more success by using egg white in icing for this work.

Designing Lace

To design pieces of lace, draw the shape of one side quite roughly. Lay a piece of tracing paper over this shape and improve on it in pencil, altering the lines until you are satisfied with the shape. Fold the tracing paper in half and trace off the other side which should match perfectly.

Method of Work

Method

Tape the pattern to the flat board and stick the wax paper on top with dots of icing.

To pipe small lace pieces, take a 00 or 0 tube and a small paper bag. Put only a little icing in the bag. For lace which consists of small curves, the bag should be held rather as you would hold a pen, with the tube close to the pattern. Pipe over the design, but do not actually scrape the surface. Even pressure is very important – too much pressure will cause uneven lines, too little pressure will produce weak spots which will be easily broken. It is important that all the lines of the lace touch as any gap will make it weak. Pipe many more pieces than you need to allow for breakages. Leave to dry. To remove, slip the palette knife underneath to free it or loosen with a dry paintbrush. To attach to the cake, pipe a few dots of icing where the lace is required, gently touch the lace to the icing and position at 45°.

Care of Equipment

Fine tubes will easily become blocked even when the sugar is finely sieved so it is best to avoid wearing fluffy sweaters or to wear an overall with sleeves and to keep the icing covered at all times.

If the tube should block, put it to soak and later clean it with a small brush. Fill another bag with fresh icing. Never try to clear a tube with a pin as it could damage the end of the tube.

Storage

To store any lace which is not required, leave on the wax paper and lay flat in a box with a lid. As sugar absorbs moisture, any humidity in the air will cause the icing to soften, therefore, it must be kept in a dry cupboard or the box should contain some silica gel crystals which are available from chemists. The self-indicating variety change colour when they become damp and should be dried out in the oven.

Colouring Lace

Sometimes it is necessary to colour lace to match ribbons or flowers. If you decide to tint the icing before piping, it would be better to use liquid colouring for this purpose as most paste colours contain glycerine which will soften the icing. Another method is to pipe the lace in white and when dry and still attached to the wax paper, brush lightly with petal dust mixed with a little icing sugar.

Large Lace Pieces

These should be piped with a fine tube for a delicate effect but the outline may be piped with a No1 tube to add strengh. Another way of strengthening a large piece of lace is to turn it over by slipping an artist's palette knife underneath the icing to remove it from the wax paper, or by drawing it to the edge of a table and letting it protrude a little over the edge, at the same time gently peeling away the paper, supporting it well all the time. When the lace is turned over, pipe another line on the back of the outline and leave to dry.

Lace Piped on Net

Some of the finest needlepoint and bobbin lace in the world is embroidered or appliquéd on to a fine net base. It is possible to create a very authentic effect by piping a lace design on to a net base. This is a very practical method for making a deep lace border.

Border 1

Cut a strip of fine net deeper than the motif. Place the pattern on a board, cover with transparent plastic film and stick the net on top with dots of icing or pins if the board is suitable. The icing should be quite soft for this as it will break away from the net if it is too stiff, but it will need to be firm enough to hold its shape. Pipe the pattern as many times as the strip requires including the scalloped edge. When dry, cut the edge close to the scallops with small pointed scissors. This border has small pleats between motifs to give fullness. These should be stitched to hold in place. The net should be bent over the finger to take away the stiffness. This will enable it to flounce nicely. Pin the completed strip to the cake and pipe a neat line to secure the net to the cake. Remove pins when dry. Small pieces of lace make a pretty edge to hide the join.

Border 2

This border is piped the same way and is applied straight to the cake by piping with royal icing and attaching separately piped lace pieces over the top edge of the cake.

Floral Motif 1

Place wax or plastic film over the design and lay fine net on top. Using medium peak icing and 0 or 00 tube pipe all the outlines and fill in the solid areas. Dry for several hours. Using pointed scissors or a sharp scalpel, cut around the flower. These can be fixed to the cake using dots of icing or egg white.

Floral Motif 2

The fuchsia motif is piped and cut out as before. It is then gently bent into a curve and pinned into place on the cake, then attached with small dots of icing. The pins are removed when the icing is dry.

337

Side Decorations

Side 1

Here small lace pieces are used to accentuate a heart shape which was scribed on to the side of the cake. The spotted decoration could be replaced with a monogram or floral design.

Side 2

Larger pieces of lace attached to the top of a band of ribbon and left suspended. As they are a little heavier than the small pieces, they should be supported for a few minutes until the icing is able to hold them.

Side 3

Two rows of lace are attached to the top of a straight flounce. The top row of lace pieces are smaller than the underneath row. Small plunger flowers are an added interest.

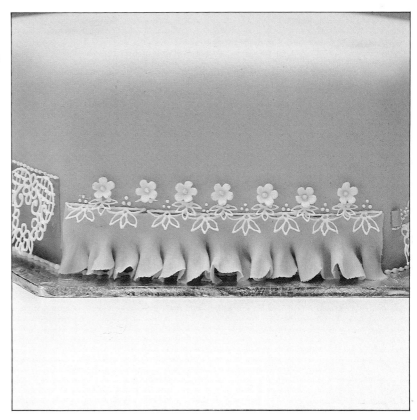

Side 4

This side decoration is based on a band of ribbon at the centre with embroidery and lace above and below.

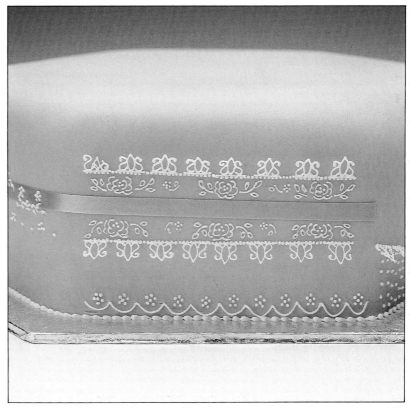

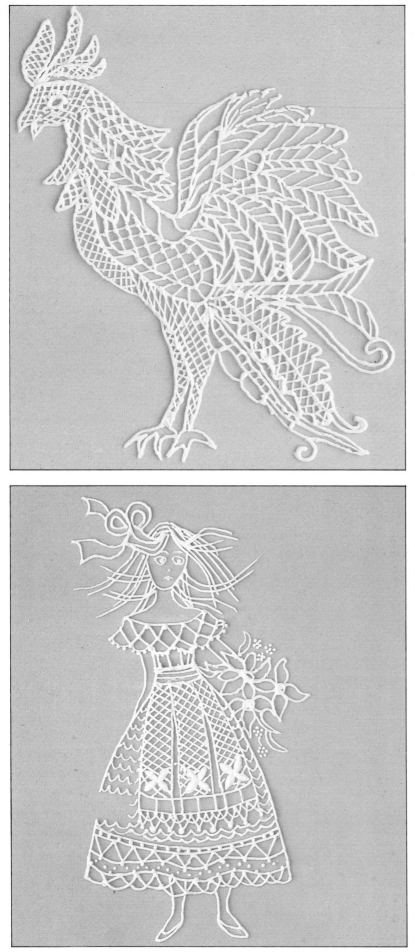

Cockerel

This was piped on plastic film which had been taped over the design. All of the open areas must be filled in as illustrated to strengthen the figure. Dry well, remove from the film by drawing to the edge of the table and easing the film away. Care must be taken to support all parts with the hand. Attach to cake top with small dots of icing.

Girl

Pipe as for the cockerel. All areas of the dress and apron must be filled in with piping. It is better to pipe the facial features and the hair directly onto the cake after the figure has been transferred into position.

340

Blue Cake with Flounce

Pipe the figure of the little girl on wax paper using the pressure-piping technique, allow to dry. If you wish to inset the figure, cover the top of the cake with a disc of sugarpaste exactly the same size as the cake. Using a cutter or a template, cut out a circle large enough to take the figure. Now cover the cake in the normal way. Ease the paste around the cut out area and make a cut in the middle to make the shaping easier. When the covering is quite smooth, drop in a disc to fit the hole. Stick the figure in position with a little royal icing. Surround the inset figure with small pieces of lace standing upright. A double flounce around the base of the cake has the same lace as an edging trim.

The butterflies are piped on wax paper using a No 0 tube. They are piped in two colours and allowed to dry. Attach to the side of the cake with small dots of icing. The antennae must be piped directly on to the cake to avoid breakage. Use a dry paintbrush to help support this delicate lace.

A small posy of miniature flowers is placed off-centre. There is also room to pipe a name if appropriate.

The cake is illustrated in full on page 84.

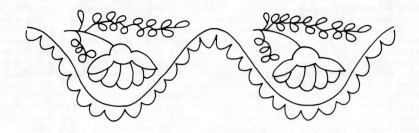

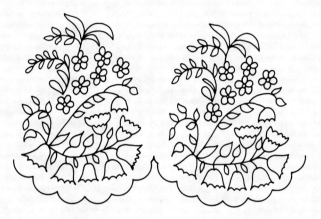

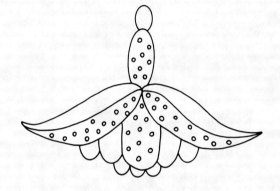

Starting with Scrolls

Starting with Half Circles

Arrangement of Petal Shapes

Variations on Hearts

Based on Oval Centre

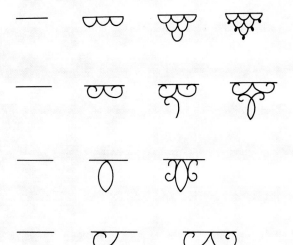

Drawing a row of lace pieces onto squared paper or graph paper so that the pieces are all the same size.

Templates for Cockerel and Girl

LESSON 8

Extension Work

Extension Work

Extension work or curtain work is a very delicate form of decoration. Simple extension work consists of a bridge which is formed by piping a series of dropped loops with subsequent rows piped exactly on top of the previous row.

The bridge supports very fine vertical lines which are piped from a straight or shaped line previously marked on the side of the cake and attached to the bridge at the base. Use a No 0 or 00 tube to achieve this fragile effect. Patience is needed to produce the neat, even finish which is essential in work of a high standard and the decorator should practise using a fine tube before attempting this work.

The extension work should be designed to complement the shape of the cake and any other decoration which is to be used. Therefore, all of the features on the cake must be planned together to make a balanced design. A narrow straight band of extension work will fit in with most cakes whatever their shape and size and will allow plenty of freedom to use lace, flower or embroidery work. An ornate section of perhaps tiered extension or overpiped extension work with a lace edging is an important feature on its own, and to show up its delicate beauty, the rest of the decoration should be simple.

If there is to be a straight band of ribbon above, the curtain work will look better if it has a straight top. If the top edge is to be shaped with points or scallops and decorated with lace, both should be worked out together to be sure that the lace is not too wide to fit small spaces. The extension work is not usually any deeper than one-third of the depth of the cake, otherwise it looks out of proportion. It is also more difficult to pipe very deep lines as the pull of gravity may cause threads to break.

Where there is to be a flower at the base of the cake or a very long spray trailing low over the side, the extension work could be designed in sections with a gap in the appropriate place or have high and low points so that the flowers could be positioned above the low point. A square or hexagonal cake is ideal for tiered extension work as this makes a very good corner design with two or three rows of extension work, one above the other at the corner tapering down to a single row in between. When

working out the design for a tiered cake, the same method is used for each cake regardless of size, the scallops will be the same width on each cake but the number will vary.

Preparation

Before commencing the extension work, check that the coating of the cake is smooth and free of blemishes right down to the board as very fine work will not hide any major faults in the covering. Check that the sides of the cake are quite straight.

It is easier to pipe curtain work when the cake board is not too large but it must be large enough to protect the bridge from accidental knocks.

Icing

Good extension work requires good quality icing which must be of the correct consistency, well beaten and free from lumps or specks which could block a fine tube. The addition of a little liquid glucose will give the icing more stretch, which is a great advantage when piping the fine vertical threads. Use 1ml (¼tsp) liquid glucose to each egg white used and stir into the finished icing. To make the icing stronger, the egg white may be left in a greasefree glass bowl for about 24 hours at room temperature. Sieve the icing sugar several times through a very fine sieve or clean nylon stocking. This is a very laborious task but well worth doing when it saves the frustration of blocked tubes. The icing should be smooth and beaten to medium peak. Experience will show what is the correct consistency, if it is too firm it will not flow easily from the tube but if too soft the drop threads will have a tendency to break.

Templates

Decide on the type of extension work to be used and make a template from greaseproof (waxed) paper the same length as the circumference or one side of the cake.

Fold this strip in half and repeat several times until the section is the right width for the base scallop,

approximately 2.5 cm (1in). The top edge of the template should now be drawn and cut into the required shape. For a straight edge, decide the depth of the extension work and cut the template in a straight line. Hold the template firmly against the side of the cake or secure with sticky tape. Mark the line for the top edge with a needle or scriber. Mark the position for the base scallops by inserting a needle at each fold in the paper. Pipe a snailstrail or row of beads around the base of the cake with a No 0 or 1 tube.

The Bridge

Put the cake on the turntable or elevate to eye level. Tilt the cake away from you and pipe dropped loops to form a bridge with a No 0 or 1 tube, using the pin marks as a guide to the high points of the scallops. These loops should not touch the board and should also be clear of the snailstrail, they should lie securely against the side of the cake. A second row of scallops is piped exactly on top of the first row and the bridge is built up in this way, drying each row thoroughly before another is piped, until approximately six rows have been piped with a No1 tube or ten rows with a No0 tube. There should be no gaps between the rows of scallops as this will make a weak bridge. If several rows are piped without drying each row, the whole bridge could sag or collapse. When the bridge is quite dry, the piping of the curtain work can be started.

Tilt the cake towards you to prevent the threads from sagging towards the cake. Commence piping straight lines by touching the tube to the marked top edge and squeezing out a thread which is then secured under the bridge. The next thread should be piped very close to the first. It is important that the spaces should not be wide enough for another thread to be fitted in between. Keep the bridge clean by wiping off any untidy ends with a damp brush. The threads must be piped straight and not leaning to either side, these should be checked every few inches and rectified if they are beginning to slope. If a tube gets blocked or the bag bursts, do not put the icing back in the bowl, discard and use fresh icing.

To finish the lower edge, one of the following methods may be used.

1. Pipe a dropped line with a fine tube, touching at the high point of the bridge and following the line of the bridge.
2. Pipe tiny loops at the base of the drop lines.
3. Pipe a row of tiny dots at the base of the drop lines following the line of the bridge. The top edge is neatened with finely piped dots or loops or lace pieces.

The Bridge

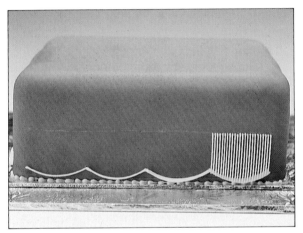

Plain extension work with a straight top.

This shows rows of bridge work piped one on top of another and the vertical lines piped from the top edge, over the bridge and secured underneath.

Bevelled extension work.

This shows each row of bridge starting in the centre with a short line, a longer line is piped on top in the next row extending the same distance each side of the first line, each row is longer until the bridge covers the whole section.

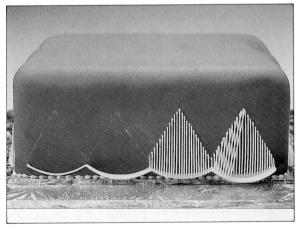

Overpiped extension.

Showing build up of the first bridge, the vertical drop lines and finally the second bridge with overpiped curtain effect.

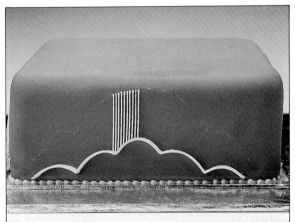

Upside-down bridge.

This is piped with the cake upside down.

Basic Extension Work

Piped with No 0 tube and finished with drop loops and lace pieces.

Extension Work with a Shaped Top

The template is made by marking the base scallops as before and cutting the large scallop at the top, the width of two base scallops. Pipe the bridge and curtain work as before and finish by piping hailspots evenly over the surface. This must be done with a very light touch or the threads will break. The top edge is finished with a fine snailstrail and the bottom with more tiny dots.

Overpiped Extension Work

The template is made as before but the top edge is cut into points, each one the same width as the base scallop. Pipe the usual way and allow to dry. The second bridge is piped exactly the same as the first and following the same lines. When all the rows are dry, the diagonal lines of the overpiping are done by tilting the cake to one side before piping in the direction the cake is leaning. Tilt the cake in the opposite direction to pipe the diagonal lines of the other side.

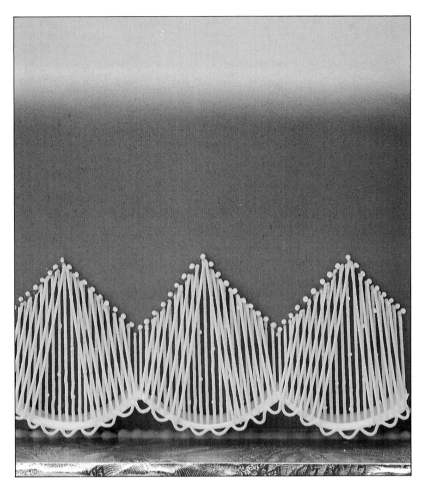

Plain Extension with Ribbon Inserts

Narrow ribbon is let in at intervals by cutting the ribbon the same length as the piped lines and attaching with a dot of icing at the top and the bottom between each scallop. The top edge is finished with drop loops hanging away from the cake.

This is achieved by tilting the cake towards you very steeply, allowing gravity to pull the loops away from the cake. When the loops are dry, pipe tiny dots on them to decorate.

Diagonal Overpiped Extension Work

This is a little more difficult and plain extension work should be perfected before attempting it.

Pipe the bridge as before and dry. Tilt the cake towards you and at the same time, put a prop underneath one side so that it is leaning sideways. This will allow the diagonal lines to hang straight. Pull out a strand of icing from the top line and attach it to a point on the bridge about 5mm (¼in) to the left or right of this point. Pipe all lines close together and evenly so that the angle remains the same all round. Dry. Remove the prop. Pipe a second bridge over the top of the first one. When this is dry, place the prop the other side of the cake then overpipe with diagonal lines in the opposite direction.

Bevelled Extension Work

The base lines for this type of extension work are straight instead of scalloped. The first line is very short and centred between the section marks. The second row is piped on top and a little longer, extending the same distance either side of the first line. Each line of the bridge is piped a little longer and the last line extends across the whole section. The finished bridge is in the shape of a crescent. The dropped lines are then piped in the normal way.

Tiered Extension Work

The illustration shows two tiers but three tiers can be used if the cake design requires it.

Mark the base scallops on the cake. At the same time mark another row of scallops at the height required. The top of the second tier is shaped to a point, but any shape may be used to suit the shape of the cake.

Pipe the first bridge and when dry pipe vertical lines all around the cake. The second bridge is made by dropping loops close to the top of the first layer of drop lines. Pipe several rows as before. Pipe drop lines from the top of the design to the bridge and finish off both bridges with dots.

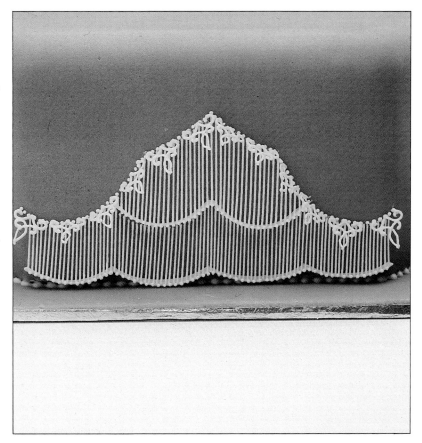

Extension Work with Arched Bridge

Mark the design using a template cut to the shape you require. To pipe the bridge, the cake must be inverted by placing a piece of perspex or a smooth board on top and turning the whole thing upside-down. The cake should be iced several days before this to allow the covering to set. Pipe the bridge in the usual way and when dry, turn the cake right-side-up and continue with the extension work.

Bells

Make a template in the shape of a bell and mark the design on the side of the cake. The bases of the bells are piped as for bevelled extension work but are slightly arched to give the appearance of a hollow bell. The cake should be turned upside-down for this part of the operation. The shape of the bell is piped by running drop lines from top to base, following the line of the bridge and this automatically forms the curve of the bell. Pipe a large bulb of icing at the base for the clanger.

Extension Work Suspended on Points

For this type of extension work, the board should first be covered with a thin layer of paste. The covered cake is placed in position and a fine snailstrail piped around the base of the cake. Using a template mark the place where the extension will touch the board, about 8mm (⅜in) away from the cake and the normal width for the scallops. Mark a straight line for the top. Turn the cake upside-down and elevate it so that the board surrounding the cake can be clearly seen. With No1 tube, pipe dropped loops from the board, suspending them from one mark to the next. Allow to dry for several hours before turning the cake upright. Leave until next day before piping the vertical lines. Pipe the fine threads from the top line and ending just below the arched loop which is standing on the board. Care should be taken not to knock these loops as they cannot be repaired unless the cake is turned upside-down again. When the drop threads are quite dry, pipe on decoration if required. Finish off the base of the drop threads with tiny dots. The top is also finished with dots, piped either side of a band of ribbon which was applied to the cake before the extension work was started.

Bird Cake

This cake has the theme of birds running right through from the bird on the branch of blossom to the lace which represents feathers, down to the filigree birds which have been incorporated into the extension work.

The bird on the top was made by piping the basic shape minus the tail feathers, using the pressure piping technique. When dry, this was turned over and the same thing was piped on the back.

Feathers

These are made from thinly rolled flower paste. To apply the feathers, start from the tail. Cut out a template from the pattern and cut the individual feathers with a sharp knife. Curl them slightly by stroking along the length with a dog bone tool, starting at the top. While the feathers are still soft, stick to the body with a little egg white. Layer the feathers as in the pattern, working up to the body. Use bits of foam to support the curl of the feathers until they are dry. The body feathers are much smaller and a daisy cutter was used to cut out a basic shape from which individual petals were cut. These were then shredded with small scissors forming a fringe which was then stuck on, overlapping the tail feathers. Complete the body by sticking rows of these feathers slightly overlapping the previous row and work towards the head. Paint the eye and the beak with a fine brush. The background blossoms were piped freehand using the brush embroidery technique to create the illusion of the bird being surrounded by blossom, disappearing into the distance.

The hawthorn blossoms were made by making a tiny calyx, attaching a wire to which cotton stamens had been taped. Petals were cut with the smallest of the miniature rose cutters and arranged around the stamens as for the dog rose.

Cut leaves from template, shape, vein and attach wire. When dry, bind flowers and leaves to form a branch. Stick the bird in position using dots of icing. Lay the branch over the bird, securing with icing. Pipe little feet on the branch.

Filigree Birds

Place wax paper over the pattern, secure with small dots of icing, pipe with a 0 tube. The central flower and the neck may be overpiped to give extra strength. Pipe more than you need as they are extremely fragile.

Extension Work

Measure the circumference of the cake and cut a strip of greaseproof (waxed) paper to fit exactly. Fold into even sections until you have the desired width for scallops. Draw the shape required for the top, planning the low points so that they are the same height as the filigree birds. Using the template, mark the design on the cake. Pipe fine snailstrail with a No0 tube. Pipe bridgework with a No0 tube as previously described.

Lace

Pipe pieces of lace in the feather design making more than you need. For a delicate effect use a No00 tube.

Pipe extension work with a No00 tube, keeping the threads very close together. When dry, pipe dots across the bridge to neaten.

Remove filigree birds very carefully from the wax. A cranked artist's palette knife is useful for this purpose. The birds have to be leaned against the low areas of the extension work and secured with tiny dots of icing. A dry paintbrush is useful to help support the birds until the icing is dry enough to hold them.

Attach lace pieces with dots of icing of the same colour. Pipe a neat row of tiny dots just above in a slightly deeper colour than the main coating.

Templates for designs used in this lesson

LESSON 9

Creating Embroidery & Lace Designs

Tube Embroidery

Embroidery and lace are of great importance in the creation of a beautiful cake which will form the centre-piece of a wedding or other important occasion.

This has become such a popular form of cake decoration that the same designs appear with monotonous regularity and, whilst still being very skilful, are no longer remarkable.

Originality is all important in making an impact and, although you may have adapted the design from another source, your interpretation in sugar will make a fresh original design for your cakes. Instead of always copying designs from cake decorating books, it is exciting to look at other sources of inspiration such as dress embroidery, wrapping paper, cards and lace wedding veils.

The following examples have been taken from some of these sources.

Bird and Floral Branch Plaque

This design was taken from a Chinese fringed stole. It is worked entirely in bands of satin stitch. The tracing was taken from a photograph and was very small. It was enlarged using the grid method then lightly traced onto the plaque using a non-toxic pencil. A larger version of this design would make a good top decoration for an embroidery enthusiast or perhaps for a man who considers sprays of flowers to be too effeminate for him.

Toadstool Plaque

The toadstool caps are worked in long and short stitch, the stems and leaves in satin stitch, the blackberries and small stones are made up of French knots, the larger stones in satin stitch, grasses in feather stitch.

The background is piped first, gradually working to the front. Toadstool caps are done in one operation, changing the shade where necessary and brushing through to even up the stitches. This tablecloth design would be suitable for the top of a cake, or, if reduced in size, would work well as a side design.

Honeysuckle Plaque

This honeysuckle design was taken from a blouse; the design was roughly traced by placing tracing paper on top of the fabric and tracing through. Using the blouse for reference, the lines were drawn over with a pen to make them clearer. The design did not need reducing or enlarging for this plaque. The embroidery was executed with satin stitch, stem stitch and French knots, using medium peak icing and No 0 tube.

Broderie Anglaise

All of the pattern examples were taken from fabrics, tablecloths, handkerchiefs, table napkins and blouse collars. A complete tracing was done, as for the honeysuckle plaque. The tracing paper was placed on the plaque which had been left to dry for a few hours but was still soft enough not to craze when the holes were made. Focal points were pricked with a pin, the pattern was then removed then the holes made with a brush handle as in Lesson 5. The design was worked as in previous step-by-step instructions. Use the same method for transferring the design to the sides and top of a cake.

This border design is simply a series of motifs joined by a curved line, embellished with leaves. This border may be adapted for any size of cake, just add more flowers to each row until you have the correct size. Try using other motifs to make your own design.

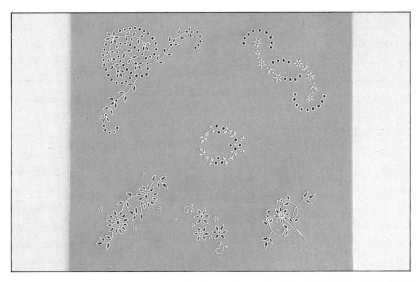

Brush Embroidery

Rose Design

Taken from wrapping paper. The individual flowers were attractive but did not form a compact design suitable for a cake so they were traced off separately and re-grouped. Method of work as described in Lesson 6.

Butterfly Plaque

Work the background first, then the flowers, finally the butterflies so they appear to be on top of the flowers.

Freesia Plaque

These are straggly flowers and difficult to group tidily but they are much loved by many people and are useful because they fit into many colour schemes, growing as they do in such a variety of colours. Team brush embroidery with a few moulded freesias arranged at the base of the cake is demonstrated here.

Enlarging or Reducing a Design

1. Trace the outline of the picture on to tracing paper then transfer the design to squared paper by inserting carbon paper or by rubbing soft pencil on to the back of the sheet. Draw a rectangle around the tracing.

2. Draw another rectangle smaller to fit the size of the design you want. Count the squares in the original grid and draw the same number of squares in the second rectangle. Carefully copy the design on to the new grid. It will help to make tiny marks on each square where the lines of the design cross it, then you can join up these lines.

Method 2
The quickest and simplest method of altering the size of the picture is by photocopying. Many of the modern machines will enlarge or reduce images and if you do not have access to photocopying facilities, some public libraries, colleges and large stores offer this service for a small fee.

Creating Lace Designs

Some wedding dresses and veils have such beautiful embroidery that the bride may wish to make it part of the theme for the wedding and as the cake is an important part of the wedding breakfast and the bride will stand near to it, the cake decorator may be asked to incorporate the embroidery into the design of the cake.

The following examples of embroidery are taken from pieces of Nottingham lace and the designs were transferred from the fabric as follows: lay a clean piece of tracing paper over the design and lightly trace the main points of the pattern, taking care not to tear the paper and risk soiling the garment with pencil.

Keeping the fabric close at hand for reference, re-trace the main lines. Draw in the fine details. Reduce or enlarge the design as necessary.

Another method of transferring the design is by photographing the material, then trace the outlines from the photograph. White lace will photograph better when taken against a dark background.

It may be necessary to simplify the design as some lace embroidery has a random effect due to the way the threads are laid down and this could make your piping look untidy.

Lace Plaques

These are piped with a No0 or No00 tube and would be suitable for the sides of a cake. You will see that the shapes have been modified in some cases to give clearer lines to pipe.

It is not usual to trace the complete lace design onto the sugarpaste surface. As this work must be very fine, there is a danger that pencil marks may show. The focal points of the design should be pricked out and the piping done freehand.

Nottingham Lace Cake

The side decoration is adapted from a piece of ecru Nottingham lace. The main features of the lace are the type of flower, the criss-cross effect of the line of the stems and the colour. The inverted V shape is a perfect place for extension work.

Cover an 20cm (8in) hexagonal cake with sugarpaste which has been tinted by kneading into it egg yellow or tartrazine-free cream paste colouring and just a trace of black to soften the colour. Mix the colour first into a small piece of paste and when thoroughly mixed, add this in small portions to the main piece of paste and knead well. If the paste has become too soft after kneading, cover and allow to rest in the refrigerator for a short time to become more manageable. As the tinting may cause the paste to dry out a little, this should be used on the day it is coloured to avoid problems of crazing. Leave the iced cake to set for at least a day before transferring the design. Trace the design onto paper. Hold the pattern against one side of the hexagon. Prick out the main points.

Pipe snailstrail around the base of the cake with No1 tube. Tilt the cake away from you and with a No0 or No00 tube, pipe the embroidery before starting the extension work. Pipe lace pieces onto wax paper or clear baking parchment. Leave to dry thoroughly. Always pipe more pieces than you will need to allow for breakages. Pipe a few dots or a fine line above the extension work in the position where you want to attach the lace, gently touch the lace to the wet icing and check that each piece is in line. Finish the lower edge with small dots or scallops. Add an arrangement of flowers to suit the colour of the cake or to match the bridal flowers.

See page 105 for illustration of completed cake.

Lace Designs

Tube Embroidery

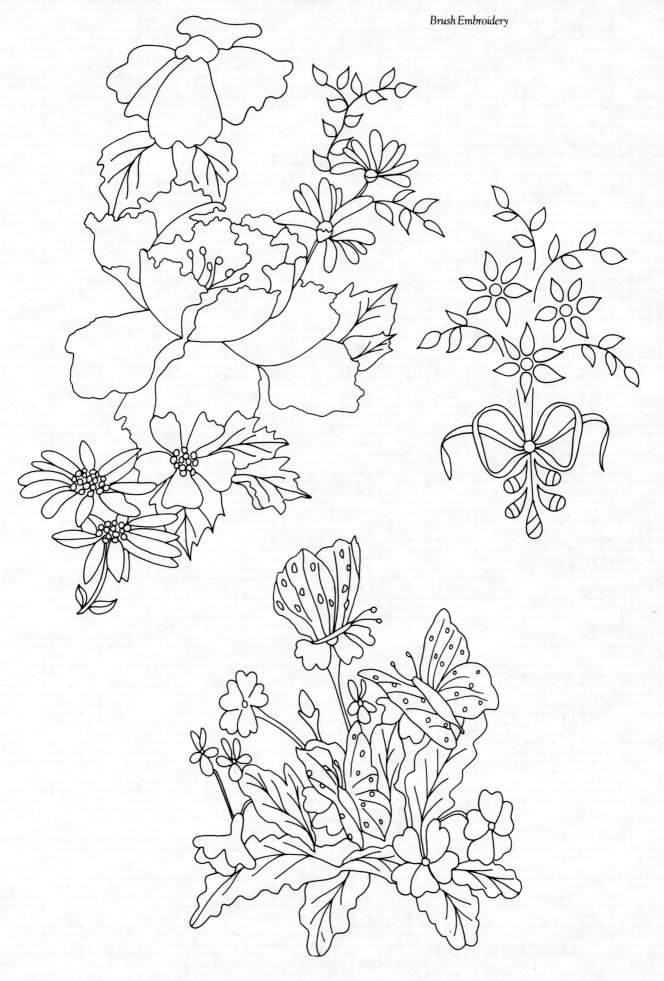

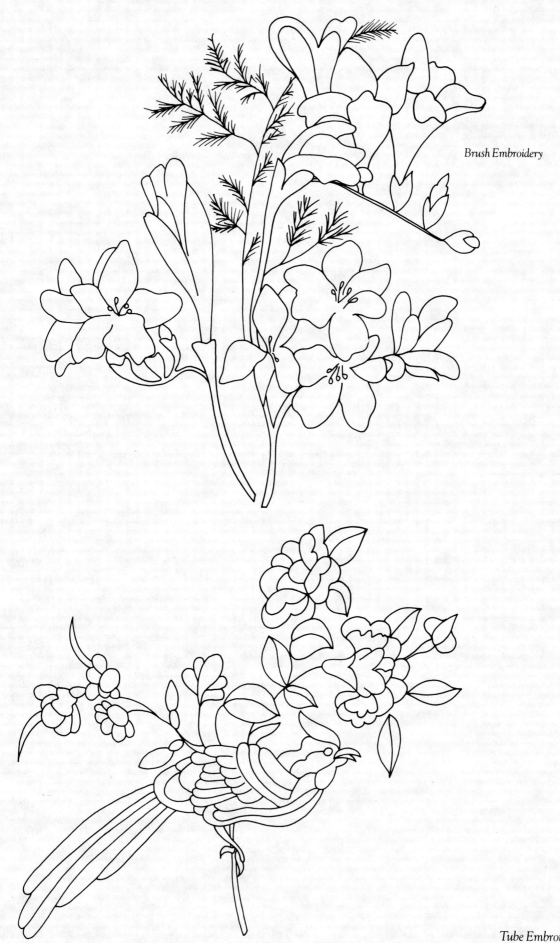

Brush Embroidery

Tube Embroidery

LESSON 10

Bas Relief & Smocking

Bas Relief

Bas Relief is a form of three-dimensional modelling in which less than half of the true depth of the figure projects from the background. Throughout history it has been widely used as a surface decoration in pottery, woodcarving and sculpture.

More recently bas relief has been adapted for use in cake decorating, as sugarpaste has shown itself to be an excellent medium for this technique. Cake covering fondant should be used in preference to modelling paste as it remains soft, thus giving a longer working period, it will also be more palatable when the cake is eaten.

The design should be transferred to the cake or plaque using one of the methods used in Lessons 5 and 6. If there is to be a background to your picture, this should be completed by hand painting, outline piping or brush embroidery before the bas relief is started.

The paste should be rolled out to about 5mm (¼in) thick or even less if the figure is very small. With a sharp pointed knife, cut out the section which is to be executed in bas relief. Moisten the underside and stick to the cake within the outline already marked. Generally the contours of a figure can be defined quite well by depressing the low lying areas or those appearing behind but if you wish to emphasise an even more raised area, a small piece of paste may be slipped underneath before the figure is stuck down, then commence the modelling. If necessary, decoration can be applied to the modelled figure by piping or by using the appliqué method.

Step-by-Step
Bas Relief

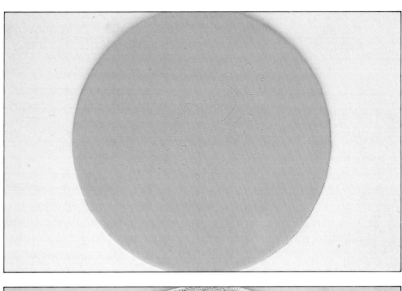

1. Design transferred to plaque with scriber. (Icing should be left to harden for a few days before attempting this method).

2. Sections of design cut out, edges neatened.

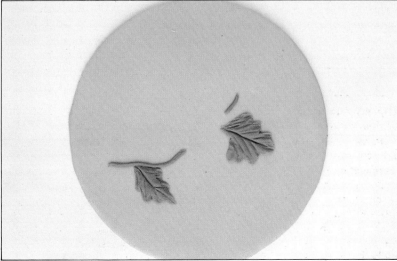

3. Parts appearing behind are worked first. Bevel edges with a divan tool and mark veins or any other definitions.

4. ◆ Add petals, bevel edges and mark petal veins.

5. ◆ Complete flower by adding the centre of the daisy and calyx. Prick the centre all over and pipe yellow dots around.

Bas Relief

Plaques

Birds

The textures of the feathers are marked with a divan tool and the rounded body is emphasised by slipping a tiny piece of paste underneath. Smooth all the edges so that they almost blend into the background.

Fish
This is an example of bas relief combined with appliqué. The weeds and fins are cut from modelling paste, shaped with a ball tool and applied to the surface before the body, which is decorated with piping and appliquéd bands of colour.

Dutch Girl
The unclothed body and face were shaped with a divan tool. Extra care was taken when smoothing the face to avoid leaving any ridges. A pretty face is difficult to attain but keep the nose and chin small, trim the edge if it spreads too much, carry on smoothing and trimming until the result is pleasing to you. Arms and hands are applied after the dress. The cap is added last and decorated with cornelli work.

Appliqué

The technique of appliqué consists of applying cut-out shapes of material to the surface of other material, one shape can be laid on top of another to build up the picture.

In textile embroidery, felts are often used because they do not fray, whereas other woven materials have to be very carefully stitched to prevent fraying. The stitches most commonly used are straight overcasting and basic buttonhole stitch which serve the dual purpose of securing the shape to the foundation and preventing the pieces from fraying. In sugarcraft there are obviously no problems with fraying so the pieces can simply be stuck to the foundation. If the effect of embroidery is desired, a mock edging stitch can be piped around the pieces to complete the figure with one of the following stitches.

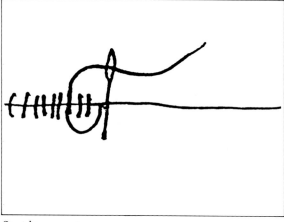

Straight overcasting

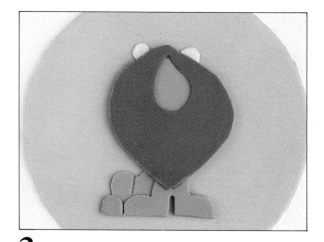

Basic buttonhole stitch

Step-by-Step Appliqué (Lion)

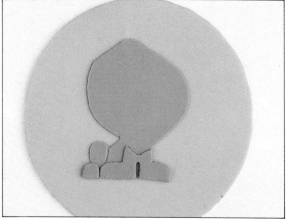

1. Body stuck to base. Legs moistened and laid in position on top.

2. Add mane and ears.

3. ♦ Add nose, eyes and muzzle.

4. ♦ Add black eyebrows, black nose and pupils of the eyes.

5. ♦ Paint black detail.

Bells

The bells are cut from sugarpaste and the flowers and ribbons are made from finely rolled flower modelling paste. Flowers are shaped by pressing into a foam pad and completed with piped stamens. Decoration on bells is piped with No 0 tube.

Bird

This is a good design for a child's cake. Any colours can be used to fit a theme. The small details are piped.

Pink and White Floral Design

This consists of various shapes cut with petal and leaf cutters and laid out to form a pattern. Some of the petals have been cupped with a ball tool to add further interest.

Smocking

Smocking is a technique traditionally applied to clothing and used for holding the fullness of the fabric in a decorative manner. Once the material is evenly gathered, a variety of stitches can be used for decoration

This method of smocking with sugarpaste is as near as possible to the conventional smocking of thin fabrics and its only function is that of decoration. It is a painstaking task as it must be neatly and evenly tucked but it forms a very attractive cake decoration.

EQUIPMENT
Cake covering fondant mixed half and half with flower modelling paste.
Cocktail sticks
Scalpel

Method
To form the basic gathers, roll out the paste very thinly on a lightly cornfloured (cornstarched) surface. Cut a straight strip about 8cm (3in) deep and twice the width of the finished panel. If you require a very long strip to go all round a cake, this will have to be made up from several panels butted together.

Place one cocktail stick under the strip of paste making sure that it is straight, the next stick is laid on top, very close to the first. Carry on alternating the sticks, pressing them close until you have the width you want. Allow to set for about fifteen minutes.

Meanwhile, cut a strip of sugarpaste to the width and depth required for the finished panel. Remove the cocktail sticks and lay the ridged strip carefully on the moistened strip of the base. Adjust the gathers with a cocktail stick if they have become disarranged.

With a ruler and scalpel, using the minimum of pressure, cut the top and bottom edges straight. Panels should be arranged on the cake as soon as they are manageable, before they are completely dry. The panel is then ready to be embroidered in a variety of stitches.

Some of the traditional stitches pull and distort the tucks. If you wish to get this effect, plan the design and gently pull the tucks into shape before drying.

Step-by-Step Smocking

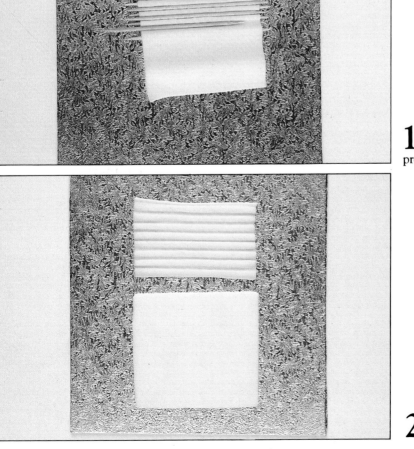

1. Cocktail sticks placed alternately on top and underneath paste, pressed together to form folds.

2. Gathered strip of paste ready to be stuck onto base.

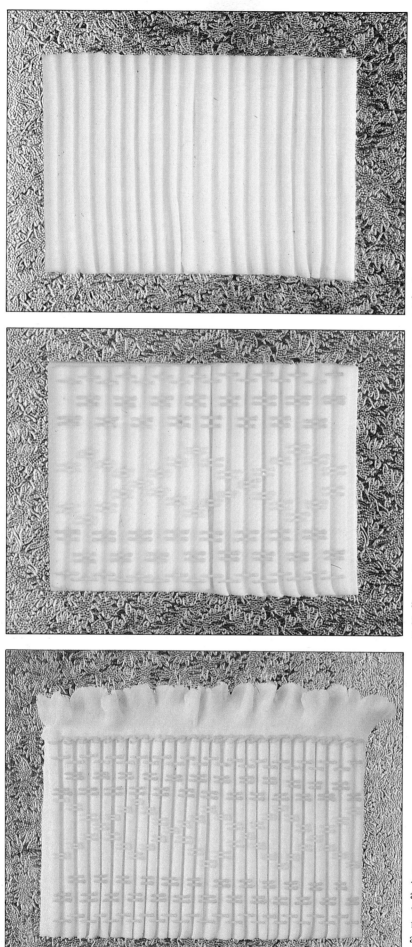

3. Gathers are stuck to the base and the top and bottom edge has been trimmed.

4. Smocking completed in a traditional design showing outline and trellis stitch. These stitches do not cause distortion so gathers have been allowed to remain straight.

5. The usual edge for smocking is a frill as this is naturally formed at the end of a band of smocking where the fullness of the material is released. Here a frill has been made and attached to the smocking. The join is overpiped with a smocking stitch.

Stitches shown on Plaques

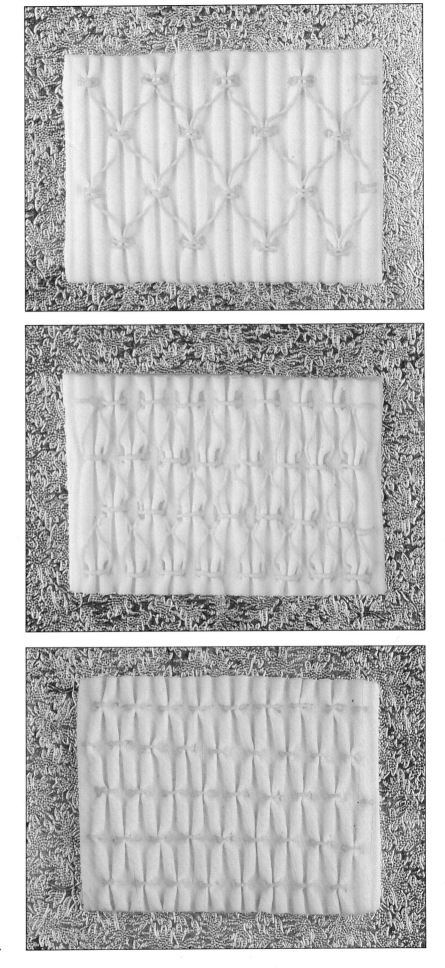

1. Vandyke Stitch.

2. Honeycomb Stitch.

3. Surface Honeycomb Stitch.

Bird Cake

This cake combines the techniques of bas relief and appliqué. The design was traced and transferred to the top of the cake.

The branch was piped first with No2 tube. The birds were cut from white sugarpaste, fixed in place and modelled by the bas relief method.

Any type of blossom cutter may be used for the flowers as long as it is large enough to be in scale with the rest of the picture. No attempt has been made to make the flowers realistic, the aim is to achieve an overall decorative effect. The flowers have been shaped by pushing them into a pad of foam and allowing them to set before sticking with a little royal icing. The birds were coloured by brushing lightly with black and blue blossom tint mixed together with cornflour (cornstarch) and wing and tail tips painted with diluted brown colouring. All the leaves were shaded with a darker green mixed with gum arabic liquid to give depth.

The base of the cake has a straight single flounce. Ivy leaves were attached in an irregular line and the stems piped in to finish.

For illustration of the finished cake see page 115.

Appliqué

Body

Mane

Eyebrows

Muzzle

Nose

Foot

Legs

Ears

Eyes

Templates for designs illustrated in this lesson

Templates for designs illustrated in this lesson

LESSON 11

Filigree

Filigree

Filigree is a most useful form of decoration, which can be used to produce extremely intricate patterns. It can be used in its own right as a covering over a coated cake surface, or used to make a variety of models and decorations.

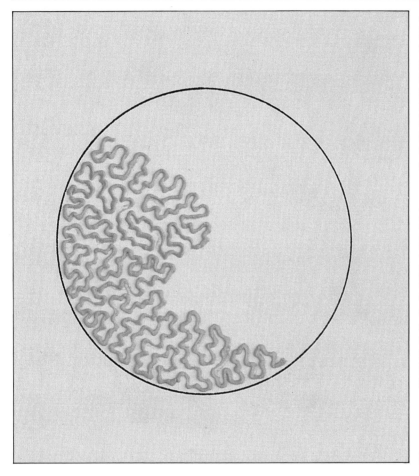

Filigree as its name suggests, should be fine, delicate and lace like. For this reason, filigree is normally executed using fine writing tubes No1, No0 and No00.

Use freshly made royal icing that has not been overbeaten, air bubbles can be a nuisance when piping with such fine tubes. Smooth the icing out using a palette knife on a clean flat surface, this will ensure the icing is lump-free. For shaped or formed filigree pieces, a pinch of cream of tartar in the icing will make a more solid finished item. If you intend to pipe filigree over shapes to be removed when dry, lightly grease the mould with a light white fat. The finished item can then be warmed gently to soften the grease and ensure an easy release.

Try to avoid making lace and filigree work on a damp, rainy day or in a steamy kitchen, the icing is so fine and fragile that any trace of moisture or humidity will hinder your work and delay the drying time of the icing. Remember also to take care to store the finished items in a dry place otherwise the filigree will collapse.

Probably the most difficult part of filigree work is removing the finished pieces from the waxed paper, so always make plenty of spares.

Piping Filigree

An easy exercise to begin with is to draw out a shape such as a circle or a square onto thin card or a used cake board. Practise piping filigree using the outline as an edge to work to. Use coloured royal icing that will show up well and aid your practice. Use normal consistency royal icing and a fine writing tube such as a No1 or No0. Hold the tube lightly against the surface to be decorated and apply pressure as for general piping work, then as you pipe, move the bag and tube from side to side and up and down to create a continual line of irregular shapes based on the letters 'm' and 'w' in a continuous string. Ideally when finished you should not be able to see the beginning and end of your piped line.

Buttercream Filigree

Do not think of filigree as decoration produced with royal icing only. Buttercream is an ideal medium for piping filigree. The easiest way to apply buttercream filigree to a buttercream coated cake is to first chill the coated cake. This chilling will create a firmer surface on which to pipe. The cream used for piping can be warmed slightly in a bowl over warm water, this will help towards piping smoother lines. Use a No1 tube.

Using Templates

Now cut out a simple template such as a crescent shape, use this for further practice. Templates can be very useful on actual cakes when piping filigree patterns, you can experiment with them on cake tops and sides to produce many interesting effects.

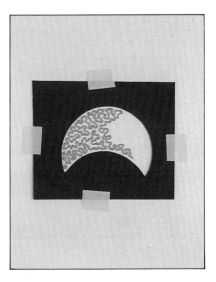

Coffee Gateau

Coat a prepared cake in coffee-coloured and flavoured buttercream. The cake could be layered with coffee buttercream flavoured with a coffee-based liqueur such as Tia Maria. Comb scrape the sides of the cake, and decorate the base with plain shells piped in chocolate buttercream. Rest a strip of waxed paper onto the top of the chilled cream surface and pipe a straight line against it, remove the waxed paper. Use chocolate buttercream or piping chocolate (melted chocolate thickened with a few drops of cold water). Pipe the filigree in one half of the cake. Decorate the other half with small chocolate drops, made by piping melted chocolate onto waxed paper. A sugarpaste inscription plaque and some piped linework complete the gateau.

Strawberry Cake

Prepare the cake by layering with strawberry-flavoured buttercream. Coat the cake in pink-coloured, strawberry-flavoured cream. Comb scrape the sides and chill the cake. Mark the cake top into four sections using the back of a knife. Place a food cutter in the centre of the cake and sprinkle some sieved jap biscuit crumb or fine nibbed nuts into the shape of the cutter, remove the cutter carefully. Next pipe straight lines of white buttercream using a 6mm (¼in) plain piping tube. The lines should start at the edge of the centre dressing and come out to the edge of the cake. Pipe filigree in the four sections, using pink buttercream. Now pipe a wavy line on the white buttercream lines using piping chocolate. Finish the top edge and the base with pink buttercream shells piped with a No44 tube. Model four strawberries from marzipan and mount them on discs of chocolate, piped onto waxed paper. Position the strawberry decorations on the cake.

Filigree with Tulle

Filigree can be used to good effect when piped directly onto tulle. The tulle is so fine it becomes hardly noticeable against the piped filigree, but does help to keep the filigree together for shapes and formed filigree that would otherwise collapse.

Filigree Casket

Using the templates provided at the end of the lesson, cut out the necessary shapes from tulle. The easy way to do this is to make a tracing of the shapes and place this over the tulle, then cut through the pattern and the tulle at the same time. Pin the tulle quite taut over a drawing of the shapes using long, glass-headed pins. A cake board is ideal for pressing pins into.

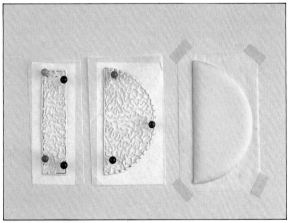

1. Pipe filigree over the tulle with yellow royal icing and a No1 tube. Edge all shapes with straight piped lines, and edge the curves with a tiny shell still using a No1 tube. Also make the semi-circle section, outline the shape with a No1 tube and flood in with yellow run-icing.

2. Secure the longest of the two straight pieces onto a curved former to dry, a ring of plastic rainwater piping is ideal.

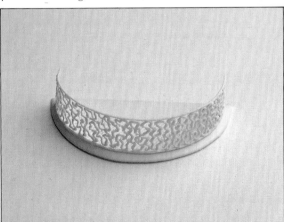

3. When all the parts are dry, assemble them as shown, sticking together with royal icing. Small pieces of polystyrene may be required to support the sides until dry.

4. Make an arrangement of small sugar flowers and attach these inside the casket. You could use piped, royal-iced flowers as shown or cutter-type flowers made from paste. Attach two lids as shown, leaving a space between each. Edge the casket with a picot dot edging piped in yellow icing using a No0 tube.

Mother's Day Cake

A delightful cake for Mother's Day. Bake a shallow cake to give this modern appearance. Coat the cake in cream-coloured royal icing and edge with lilac-coloured shells using a No44 tube. Chocolate-coloured icing is used to edge the shells on the cake top and to pipe a filigree edge around the coated base board. Position the filigree casket on the cake top and pipe the inscription using chocolate-coloured icing and a No1 tube. A narrow cream-coloured ribbon and bow complete the cake.

Engagement Cake

Coat a cake in white royal icing and edge with a shell border top and base using a No44 tube. Edge the shells with a fine rope using a No1 tube with lilac-coloured icing from the top edge and pink for the base. Pipe filigree to cover the coated cake board using a No0 tube and lilac-coloured icing. Use a strip of greaseproof (waxed) paper marked off in equal sections around the cake side. Pipe a bulb of white icing at each marker, remove the paper template. Using a No1 tube and lilac icing, pipe loops from each dot, allow to dry. Now pipe a deeper loop from each dot, this time using pink-coloured icing. Attach the filigree ring casket and complete the cake with a directly piped inscription.

Engagement Ring Casket

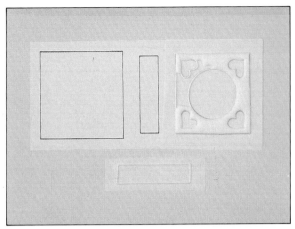

1. Prepare the runout sections of the casket using the templates provided. Outline in white using a No1 tube, flood with white run-icing, allow to dry.

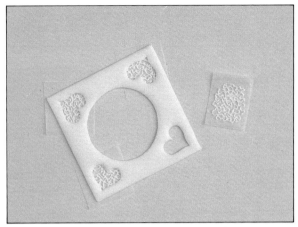

2. Pipe small squares of filigree then place runout section over them, lining up with heart-shaped cutout section, repeat in all sections.

3. Roll out some sugarpaste or flower paste. Cover half a table tennis ball with paste, allow to dry, then pipe pink filigree all over dome using a No0 tube.

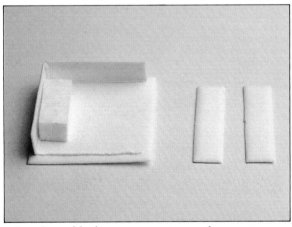

4. Assemble the runout sections as shown using small pieces of polystyrene to support until dry.

5. Pipe pink filigree over the assembled dry casket using a No0 tube. Roll out some pink sugarpaste approx. 10mm (½in) thick and cut out a disc as shown. Pipe a small bulb of icing into the base of the casket and position the sugarpaste disc. While the sugarpaste disc is still soft, insert a toy engagement ring at an angle as shown.

6. Attach the domed lid to the casket with royal icing and support with a small piece of foam sponge until set. Decorate the casket edges and the dome with a picot dot edging. A piped flower on the dome completes the casket.

Filigree Cradle

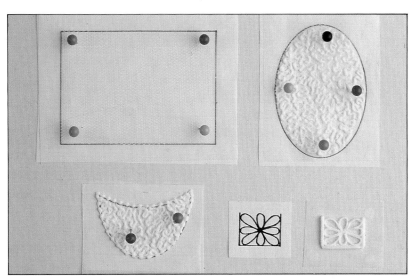

1. Using the same method as described for the tulle casket, make the necessary pieces for the cradle as shown using the templates provided.

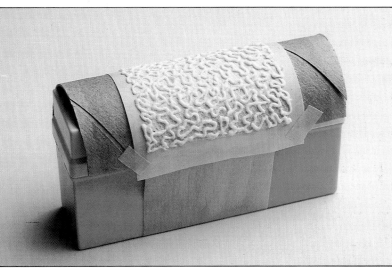

2. Shape the base of the cradle over a curved former. The picture shows a cardboard tube taped to a photographic slide box.

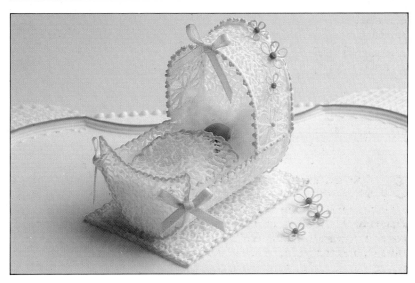

3. Assemble the sections of the cradle as shown, edging the filigree with a tiny pink-coloured icing shell. Line the inside of the cradle with cotton wool and place on a small ball of flesh-coloured marzipan or sugarpaste for the baby's head. Rest the filigree cover over the baby. A few bows can also be attached.

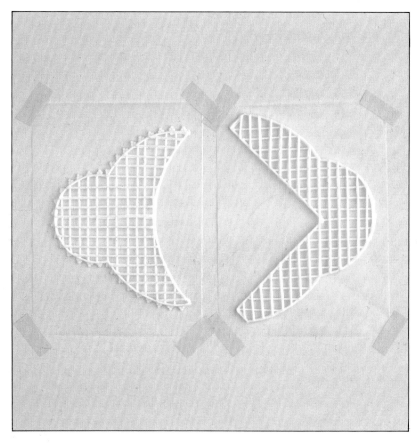

Filigree Christening Cake

Collars can also be produced using the filigree or netting type method of piping. Here we see top and base collars used in conjunction with the filigree cradle. This gives the cake a very delicate appearance.

Using the templates provided trace out the designs and secure to a work board. Cover the design with waxed paper and pipe trellis or netting as shown. Start by piping the outline shape of the collar and then fill in with the netting. Edge the top collars with a picot dot edging as shown. Using the drawing provided, cut out a template to assist in piping the linework design.

Filigree Wedding Cake

Make the trellis pieces first. Trace the drawing provided and secure to your work board. Cover the design with waxed paper and pipe the outline first using a No1 tube and white royal icing. Next pipe in the trellis and flower pattern. Overpipe the trellis and flower to strengthen the piece when attached to the cake, the flower is overpiped in orange-coloured icing with a darker centre bulb. You will need 24 pieces for the three tier cake, six for each tier and six for the top ornament. When the pieces are dry, turn them over and overpipe them in white icing. This makes them more stable and looks better when the piece is viewed from both sides.

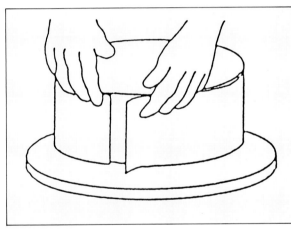

1. Cut a length of drawing paper to fit around the coated cake, the paper strip should be the height of the cake side.

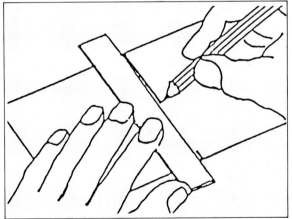

2. With paper strip flat, measure length of paper. Divide into six equal sections. Mark measured sections on each side of paper, then draw a line across.

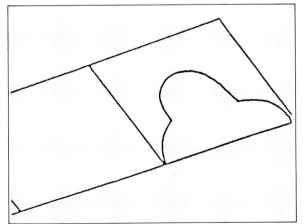

3. Make a tracing of the linework shape from the appropriate drawing and repeat the design in each of the six sections.

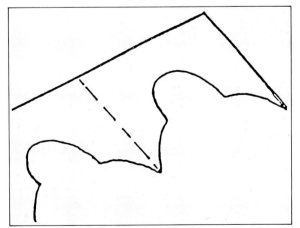

4. Carefully cut the shapes to produce the template as shown. Secure to the cake with masking tape and commence piping the linework.

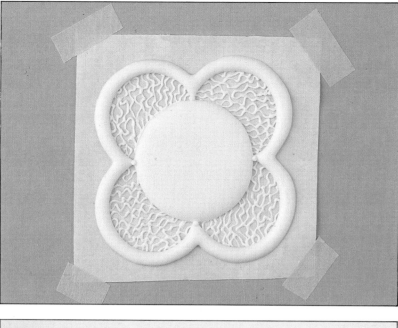

5. A runout disc is also required for the top ornament base.

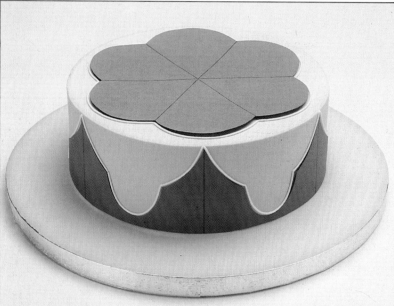

6. Prepare templates from the drawings provided as shown and secure them to the cake with masking tape. Pipe lines on the cake top and side as shown using a No2 tube and white royal icing.

7. Remove the trellis pieces from the waxed paper and attach to the cake sides. A small silk, paste or piped flower and ribbon arrangement is attached to the cake with royal icing in each of the six side panels. For the cake top ornament, attach six trellis pieces together on a round runout disc, and insert a flower in each space between the pieces.

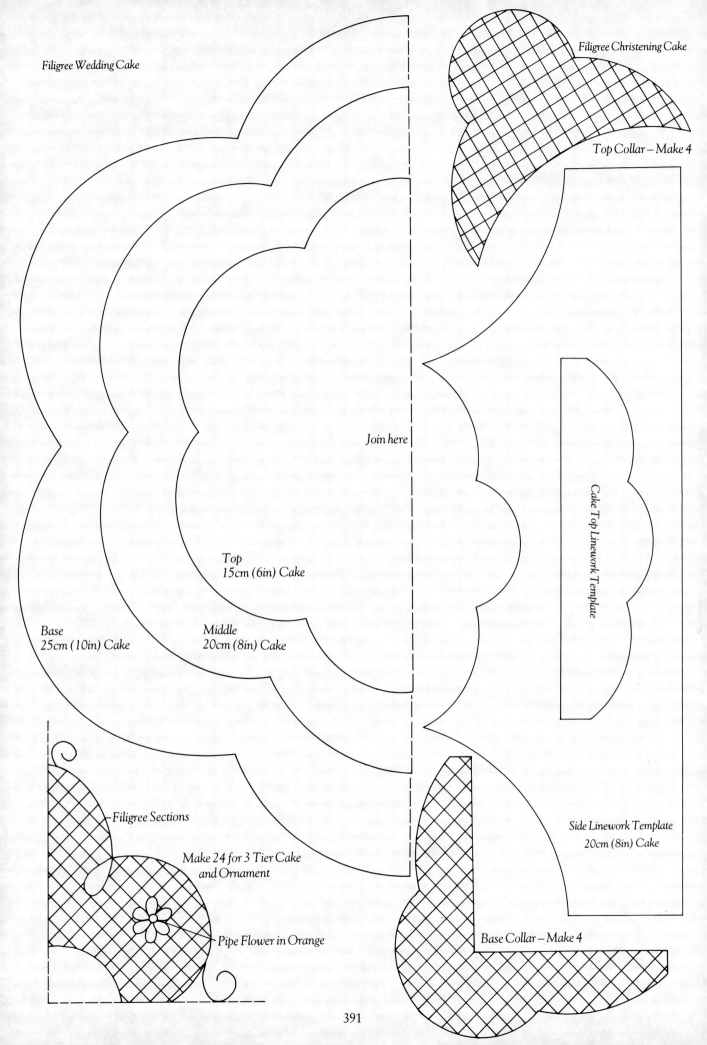

Filigree Wedding Cake

Filigree Christening Cake

Top Collar – Make 4

Join here

Cake Top Linework Template

Top
15cm (6in) Cake

Base
25cm (10in) Cake

Middle
20cm (8in) Cake

Filigree Sections

Make 24 for 3 Tier Cake
and Ornament

Pipe Flower in Orange

Side Linework Template
20cm (8in) Cake

Base Collar – Make 4

391

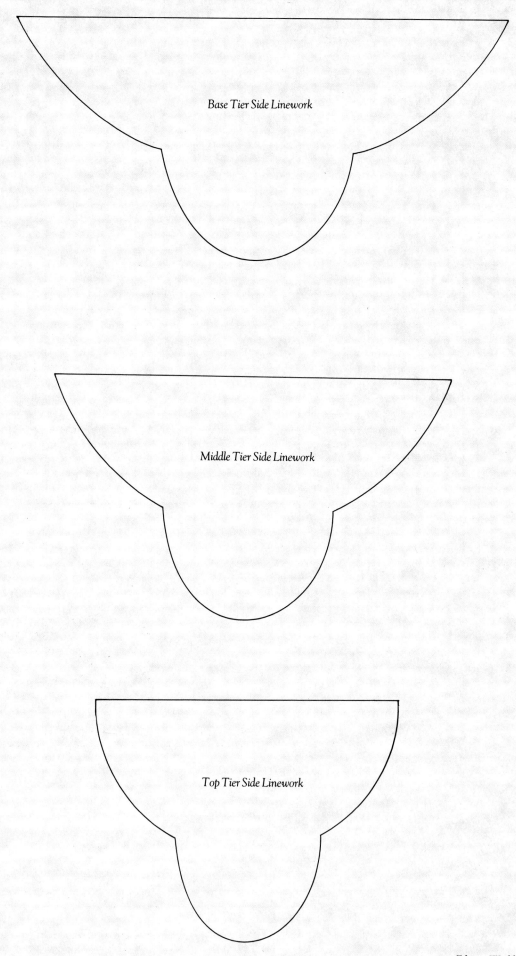

Base Tier Side Linework

Middle Tier Side Linework

Top Tier Side Linework

Filigree Wedding Cake

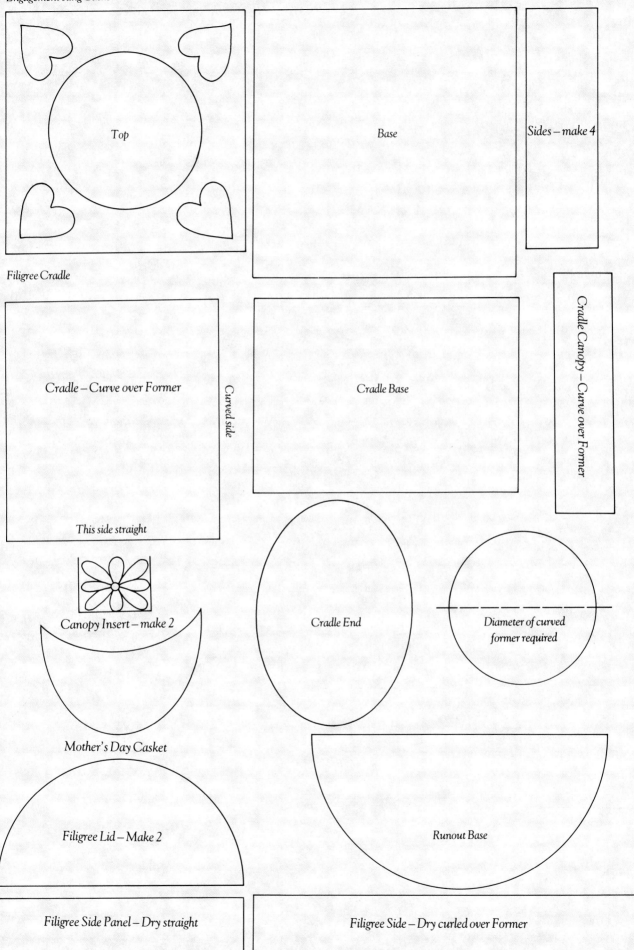

Engagement Ring Casket

Top

Base

Sides – make 4

Filigree Cradle

Cradle – Curve over Former

This side straight

Curved side

Cradle Base

Cradle Canopy – Curve over Former

Canopy Insert – make 2

Cradle End

Diameter of curved former required

Mother's Day Casket

Filigree Lid – Make 2

Runout Base

Filigree Side Panel – Dry straight

Filigree Side – Dry curled over Former

Top

Middle

Base

Advanced Figure Piping

Advanced Figure Piping

Figure piping is one of the most frequently executed and certainly one of the most fascinating aspects of sugarcraft. Scope for the use of figure piping is endless, and is seen featured on cakes for every and any occasion.

Figure piping is particularly useful for original motif cakes, when few, if any of the available standard range of decorations are suitable. A figure to depict an occasion or celebration can more often than not be found and used as a centrepiece or as part of a scene or visual theme decoration. For years now, the art of figure piping has been used to adorn celebration cakes both commercially and by the enthusiastic competitor and exhibitor. Nearly every sugarcraft competition features classes with cakes requiring or being suitable to

incorporate a piped figure of some kind, particularly so in birthday and Christmas cake classes.

Every sugarcraft artist can use figure piping in their cake decoration, from the novice to the more experienced decorator. Each time you produce a figure you will no doubt become more experienced and adventurous, eventually making the most challenging and intricate designs and allowing your imagination to develop new and wonderful ideas for figures.

There are two main types of figure

piping – pressure-piped and freehand runout. The two styles may be used separately or they can be used together to good advantage; pressure-piped figure piping is probably not used as much nowadays, except commercially for simple, quick-to-pipe figures to give a hand-made appearance and personal finish to decorated cakes. The most popular freehand piped figures used today are the love birds seen on runout collars and on side panels of wedding cakes. Such work is also ideal for children's birthday cakes.

Pressure-piped Figures

The technique for pressure-piped figure piping differs totally from that used for runout figure piping. Use fresh, well beaten royal icing, not too stiff but able to retain its shape when forced through the piping bag onto waxed paper or the surface medium of your coated cake. A fresh, light icing is preferred, as it will respond easily to the pressure put on it by your hand on the piping bag. This consistency of icing will produce bold shapes without the need for outlines, and can therefore be quickly built-up to form half-relief and full-relief figures. The main technique involved with free-hand figure piping is the amount of pressure used to control the flow of icing from the piping bag onto the waxed paper or cake surface. Three-quarters fill your piping bag with icing and neatly fold over the top of the bag to retain the contents and prevent seepage of the icing. The choice of piping tube will depend upon the size of the figure to be piped and the amount of fine detail required.

The following photographs and instructions show various figures piped in stages for you to follow. Once you have mastered these, it should be possible for you to develop other variations of your choice.

Birds

Birds are a popular feature on wedding cakes. They are easy to make either in full- or half-relief.

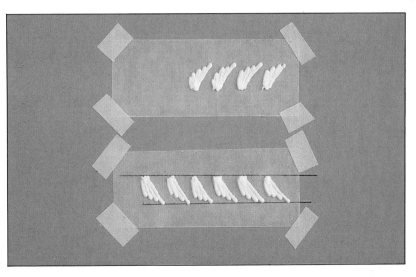

Half-relief Birds

1. Using a No1 tube, pipe left and right wings onto waxed paper as shown. Use a side-to-side movement when piping to build up the required shape. A couple of pencil lines drawn on paper beneath the waxed paper will help to achieve a consistent size. Allow the piped wings to dry.

2. Build up the body of the bird. This can be done directly on the cake surface or the birds can be piped onto waxed paper and allowed to dry before using as required. Pipe the wing first, using the same method as described previously. Next pipe a bulbous body using a No2 tube, taper the bulb as shown. Pipe on the tail feathers using a No1 tube. Now pipe a bulb for the head, then add a beak using a No1 tube. Finally insert a prepared, dry wing into the still soft body and position as required. Using the same method, but reversing the shapes, you can produce birds facing each other.

Stork

The stork is an ideal motif to make for birth or christening cakes. The bow-tie colours are used to reflect the sex of the baby.

The stork is piped in much the same manner described for the swan, using a No3 tube for the neck and body. The wings are piped using a No2 tube. Pipe the beak with orange-coloured icing using a No1 tube and the legs in a coffee-orange colour again using a No1 tube. A bow-tie may be piped on waxed paper and attached to the stork. The template provided will make piping the stork easier for you – simply trace into position on the cake surface or plaque. When proficient, the template will not be required.

The stork is a favourite motif for christening cakes.

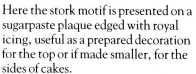

Here the stork motif is presented on a sugarpaste plaque edged with royal icing, useful as a prepared decoration for the top or if made smaller, for the sides of cakes.

Duck Birthday Cake

Here we see figure piping put to use as part of the decoration of a royal iced cake. The cake is coated in cream-coloured icing, and dried. Make a scalloped template from cartridge paper and position as shown on the cake side, secure the template with masking tape. Apply blue-coloured royal icing to the cake side exposed below the template and coat smooth using a palette knife or side scraper. Remove the template and coat the cake board with the same coloured icing. Pipe shell borders in cream-coloured icing using tube No 44. Edge the scalloped water frieze and the shell borders with blue icing. Using a No1 tube and chocolate-coloured icing, pipe dots on the top border shells, a wavy line on the cake board and the inscription. Attach prepared piped ducks to the cake side with royal icing. The candle holders are made by cutting sugarpaste with a petal cutter and forming in curved fruit trays or clean polystyrene egg boxes. Allow the holders to dry then attach them to the cake and position a candle in each.

Duck

Use an orange-yellow icing and a No2 tube and pipe the head, neck and front of the body in one operation, using various pressures on the piping bag to create the required shape. Next pipe a pear-shaped body as shown. Pipe the same shape again, smaller to form the wing.

Finally pipe on the beak with bright orange icing. A chocolate or black eye completes the duck.

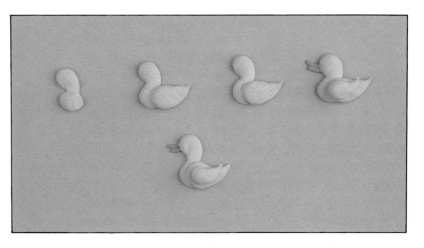

Runout Figure Piping

This second form of figure piping is used extensively nowadays by almost every sugarcraft artist. It is frequently seen in several classes of competitive sugarcraft, and can be suited to any occasion providing plenty of scope for new and original ideas.

Runout piped figures are normally produced on waxed paper to be peeled off when dry, the figure is then placed directly onto the prepared cake surface or onto an icing or sugarpaste plaque. This does not mean that every figure has to be made flat. Figures can also be made to take the curved shape of a round cake side, by producing and drying the runout on a curved former of the same diameter (or curve) as the cake on which it is to be attached.

A few things need to be considered before actual production of the figure can commence.

Selection of Motif
Suitable figures and animals for possible use as runouts can be found in most children's annuals, on greeting cards and on gift-wrapping paper. Before such figures could be used commercially, full permission would have to be obtained from the copyright owner. If on the other hand you prefer to be more creative, you could use various ideas and put them together to create your own original figure or motif. The main point to remember at this stage is to choose a figure that you can execute reasonably well, do not select a really intricate design if your piping and runout skills are limited. It is far better to choose a simpler figure that you know will be easy to reproduce.

The Correct Figure Size
Having selected the figure or animal of your choice the next stage is to ensure that it will comfortably fit in the space allocated for it on your cake. Sometimes you may have figures that you have used previously for another cake and wish to reduce or enlarge for further use. Or it may be that you have seen a figure you want to use but it does not fit on your cake. See lesson 9 (page 109) for details on methods of enlarging and reducing designs.

An alternative method to those already suggested would be to invest in a pantograph. This implement is usually plastic and consists of a painter which is used to follow the outline of the original drawing, while on the other end a pencil transfers the reduced or enlarged image. Again this may not be economically practical, the investment will obviously depend on the amount of design work you intend to undertake.

Interpreting Designs
The basic idea of a runout figure is that an outline is piped and the various sections of the figure separated. Into each section, run-icing is piped either in white, to be painted when dry, or in appropriate colours, again which can be painted with further detail. The figures may vary in one of four ways, according to the filling in and finishing techniques.

The types of figure piping are: semi-relief, outline, wafer-thin and full-relief

Teddy Christening Cake

The pink semi-relief teddy is used here as an attractive figure decoration for this royal iced cake. First make several runout sections for the borders. Using the template provided, outline in white royal icing using a No1 tube and then flood in with white run-icing. The side design is made by piping lines of white royal icing onto waxed paper, the same length as the depth of the cake side. When the lines are dry, a pink wavy line is piped on using a No1 tube. Attach the prepared lines to the side of a pink coated cake. Next attach the prepared runout sections to the top edge and base board. Attach small blossom flowers, made with a cutter and piped with a tiny centre bulb. Pipe linework around the inside edge of the top runout sections, and to follow the base border. Runout lettering completes the cake.

Semi-relief

This type of figure piping is the simplest
form that includes flood work, it is
basically an outline with sections,
flooded in and allowed to dry. For all
runout figure work you need to start
with a tracing of your design, copied
onto cartridge paper and then placed
flat on your surface. Cover the design
with a suitably sized piece of waxed
paper and secure it to the board with
masking tape.

In the first example shown the rabbit
figure is outlined in a deep orange-
colour and flooded with a lighter orange
run-icing. The eyes are flooded in with
white run-icing. When dry, paint on
the mouth and ear detail with brown
food colouring and a fine paintbrush.
The nose and buttons are piped on with
coloured royal icing.

The pink teddy bear figure is produced
in the same way with a separate runout
bow-tie attached to the dried figure.

Outline Figures

A simple but very effective way of
introducing figures onto your cakes.
Outline figures are piped directly onto
the cake surface of royal icing,
sugarpaste or fondant. Trace the figure
required onto the prepared cake
surface, use the jolly Jack-in-the-box
figure to experiment with. Prepare
piping bags of royal icing in the required
colours all with a No1, 0 or 00 tubes
depending upon the fineness or detail
involved. Using the prepared tubes,
pipe the outlines of the figures in each
of the appropriate colours.

Wafer Thin

This is a very modern method of figure piping which is now very popular. The aim is to achieve a really thin runout figure, the thinness being determined by the tube being used, in most cases a No1 tube.

Prepare the drawing and cover with waxed paper as before. Outline the design with brown royal icing using a No1 tube, use a compound colour to achieve a rich brown without diluting the icing consistency. Allow the outline to dry a little and then flood in each area with the appropriate colour of run-icing. Extra detail can be painted on when the figure is dry if required.

Full-relief

Full-relief figure piping is started in the same manner as semi-relief piping, by outlining a shape on waxed paper. With this method, however, each section is piped in a different manner to achieve a more detailed figure with definite modelling and roundness to parts of the figure. Some parts, such as those farthest away, for instance, the main part of the body on the teddy, are flooded in flat. The arms, legs and ears are flooded in a more bulbous fashion to produce the necessary roundness. As a basic rule for flooding procedure, flood in the parts that appear farthest away, then build up the flood work, allowing sections to dry before flooding adjacent sections. The final parts of the flood work should be those that appear nearest to you.

A simple method to make the flood work sequence easier is to number the parts of the body on the drawings before flooding as shown. In this way you can then flood all parts marked '1', allow them to dry then flood parts marked '2' and so on until the figure is completed.

Full-relief figure piping sequence for teddy bear motif, using one colour of icing only.

Combination Work

If you runout the figure in a single colour of icing as for the teddy bear, you can paint on extra fine detail and shading once the figure has dried, using edible food colours with a fine paintbrush. Here we see a finish sometimes referred to as built-up figure piping. This is the use of extra runout or piped sections added to a basic figure to form a built-up motif, for instance, the runout ribbon and bow and the piped flower and stem.

Teddy Birthday Cake

An attractive hexagonal-shaped cake decorated with pale blue and white royal icing. The runout collars are made using the template provided, outlining in a No1 tube. The board linework is piped using a card template prepared from the collar design. Complete the cake with a runout teddy figure and directly piped inscription.

Flower Girl

This very attractive little figure is useful for many occasional cakes. The figure is based on full-relief figure piping, this time flooding in with appropriately coloured run-icing. These types of figures can be runout onto waxed paper and completed before attaching to the cake. When you become more proficient at figure piping you could execute the work directly onto the royal iced or sugarpaste surface.

Notice how the build-up of the dress has been completed in stages, to allow individual sections to dry before flooding adjacent sections.

The finished figure painted with edible food colouring and built-up in the form of a bunch of piped flowers and stems.

Rabbit Low-Relief Figure

Teddy Low-Relief Figure

Top Border Runout Pieces for Pink Christening Cake

Base Border Runout Pieces

Jack in the box

Girl Figure

Flooding Sequence For Full-Relief Piping

Santa Wafer Thin Figure

Stork

Bow Tie

Swan

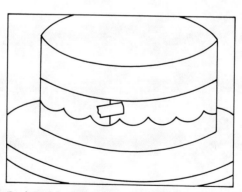

Duck Birthday Cake

Water Wave Template secured to cake side ready

for application of blue icing.

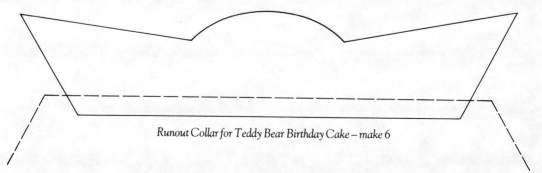

Runout Collar for Teddy Bear Birthday Cake – make 6

Advanced & Freestanding Runouts

Crown Ornament

Having now mastered basic and intermediate runout work, and gained an understanding of the characteristics and possibilities of this work, more advanced runout work may now be tackled.

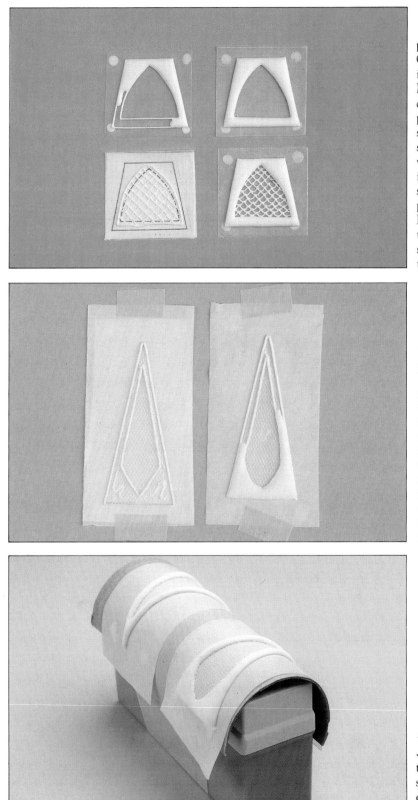

1. Using the drawings provided, trace them onto cartridge paper and secure to your work-board. Outline using a No1 tube and white icing and flood with white run-icing. Make six runout pieces and allow to dry. Using the same template again, place waxed paper over and pipe a scalloped net filigree pattern as shown using a No1 tube, outline the work with the same tube and immediately place a prepared runout section onto the net work and gently press to attach the two together. Repeat on all six sections and allow to dry. Also make a runout hexagon shape using the drawing provided, this will form the base of the crown.

2. For the points of the crown, cut out shapes from tulle. Trace the drawing provided onto paper and place onto six thicknesses of tulle, cut through the template and the tulle at the same time. Using a drawing of the full template, place a piece of waxed paper over and secure with masking tape. Secure a tulle shape with a few dots of royal icing, then continue as for conventional runout work. Outline in white using a No1 tube and flood in with white run-icing.

3. Place the shapes onto curved formers made from cardboard tubes as shown. Allow the runout shapes to dry, then pipe a tiny shell edging on the inside edge near the tulle.

4. Assemble the six side runout sections and base as shown, attach with royal icing. Use small blocks of polystyrene to support the pieces until fully dry.

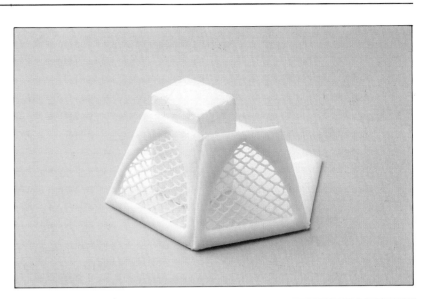

5. Once the base formation is dry, the points of the crown can be attached, again using royal icing. Blocks of polystyrene each of the same height are used to support the points until dry. Pipe a tiny shell using a No1 tube as shown around the joins and edges.

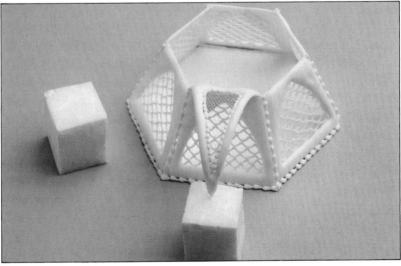

6. An arrangement of artificial, silk, paste or piped flowers is then placed inside the crown, the crown is then positioned and attached on the wedding cake top as required.

Double Collars

Double collars provide an interesting and refreshing change to the conventional single collar. Ensure your drawing and piping is accurate for double collar work, as any inaccuracies are exaggerated.

Use the drawing provided to try a double collar. Your own designs can easily be adapted to make double collars, by drawing in a second outline, a small distance from the original outline. To emphasise the double collar, outline and flood in the under collar with a slightly darker colour than that of the top collar.

Pink Celebration Cake

A very detailed cake top design requiring the use of double base boards to balance the overall effect. Note the double collars with filigree overlays.

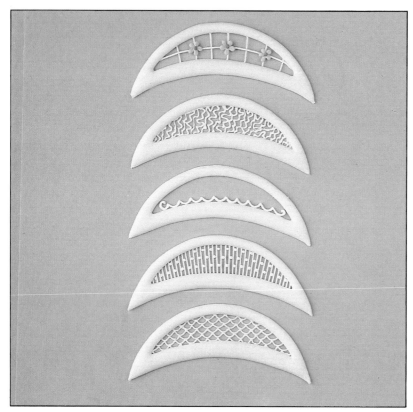

Runout Collar Fillers

The photograph shows five variations on the basic collar section used on the Pink Celebration Cake. This is another example of creative sugarcraft, making one basic idea work for you with several options on decorative finishes. The templates are at the end of the lesson.

1. Piped criss-cross lines decorated with a piped flower.

2. Piped filigree using a No0 or No1 tube.

3. Scallop edging piped using a No1 tube then overpiped.

4. Line and dot. Using a No1 tube pipe the lines first and then pipe in the dots.

5. Scalloped net filigree piped using a No1 tube.

Runout Church

The runout church is ideal for a Christmas cake decoration or made in white icing and left unpainted would make an unusual ornament for a winter wedding.

1. Make templates for all the sections of the church, then outline and flood in all shapes to make runout pieces. Notice how the clock face is flooded with icing to make painting detail easier.

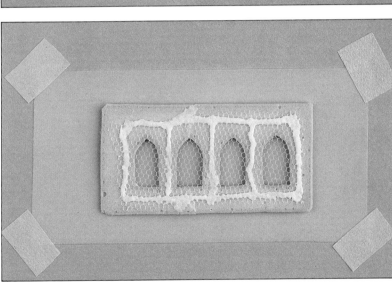

2. When the runout pieces are dry, attach pieces of tulle cut to size on the back of each window. For stained glass windows the tulle can be painted with food colouring.

3. Using edible food colouring, paint the brickwork detail on all the church walls and the two visible roof sections. Outline the window frames with brown royal icing and a No0 tube.

4. Assemble the church, using royal icing and supporting the sections with polystyrene blocks until dry.

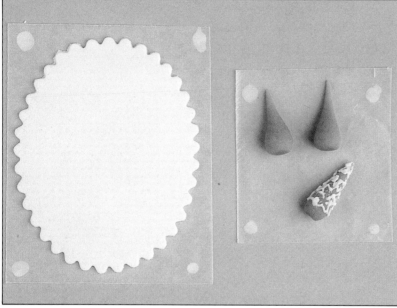

5. Prepare a sugarpaste plaque in an oval shape. A fluted edge looks attractive as shown, use a large oval food cutter or make a template from card. Brush the plaque with softened royal icing, leaving a section clear for the inscription.

Model a few small trees from green marzipan. Make cone shapes from the marzipan and snip them with small scissors to make branches. Brush with icing to represent snow.

Attach the church and brush a little softened icing on to represent snow. While the icing is still soft sprinkle with granulated sugar to give a frosty effect.

Anniversary Cake Ornament

1. Make two runout shapes as shown, using the drawings provided.

2. Make the runout numerals. Outline the numerals with white royal icing, allow to dry. Paint the outlines with silver food colour. Flood in the numerals with white run-icing. This technique creates attractive figures with silver edges and white centres.

Assemble the ornament using the floating collar technique.

3. Floating Collar Anniversary Ornament.

Floating Collar Anniversary Cake

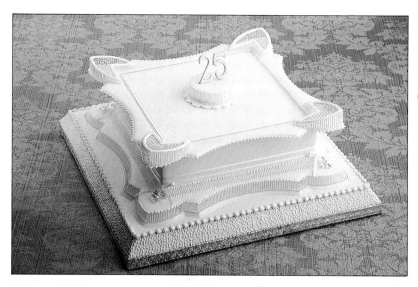

1. Make the top and base collar using the drawings provided. Coat the cake in white royal icing. The cake is presented on a double cake board. Coat the cake and board in the conventional manner, then attach the cake and board to a second board 2.5cm (1in) larger than the first board. Fill the space between the boards and smooth flat at an angle from the board to the other using a side scraper or palette knife.

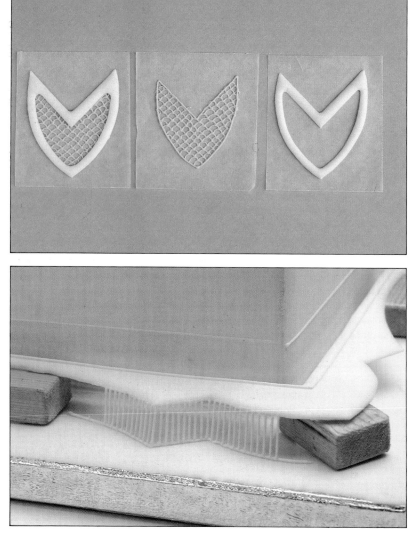

2. Make four runout overlays and then pipe blue filigree onto waxed paper as shown. Place the dry runout section over the filigree and attach with a gentle pressure.

3. Place about eight wooden blocks of even size (smooth edges and corners with sandpaper to ensure easy release of blocks) around the cake board then place the base collar over the cake and rest on the blocks. Pipe a line using a No1 tube on the cake board directly beneath the collar edge, follow the shape exactly. This can be done before placing the base collar on, using a template as a guide. Now pipe lines from the base board up to the collar edge as shown at regular intervals, use a No1 or No0 tube. Pipe at intervals around the base, allow these first lines to take the weight of the runout collar. The blocks can then be removed and line piping completed.

This stunning 25th Anniversary cake uses many sugarcraft techniques, the main feature being the floating collars.

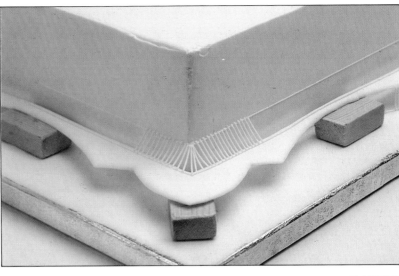

4. Using a ruler resting along the cake side, scratch a straight line onto the cake side using a No1 tube. Pipe a straight line along the inside edge of the base collar. Allow these lines to dry, then pipe lines from the side line down onto the collar as shown, again at regular intervals using a No1 or No0 tube. Finish with a tiny piped shell along the straight lines. Attach the top collar.

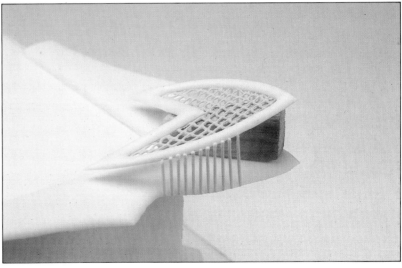

5. Using prepared blocks of wood, shaped at an angle, place a block on each corner of the top collar. Then position the prepared shield shaped runout overlay pieces on the wooden blocks. Again pipe a few lines on each side to support the overlay, then remove the blocks and continue the line piping.

6. Pipe a tiny picot dot edging around the edge of the top collar. Then pipe 3,2,1, linework around the inside edge of the top collar and following the outside edge of the base linework shape. An arrangement of ribbons, bows and flowers at each corner completes the cake.

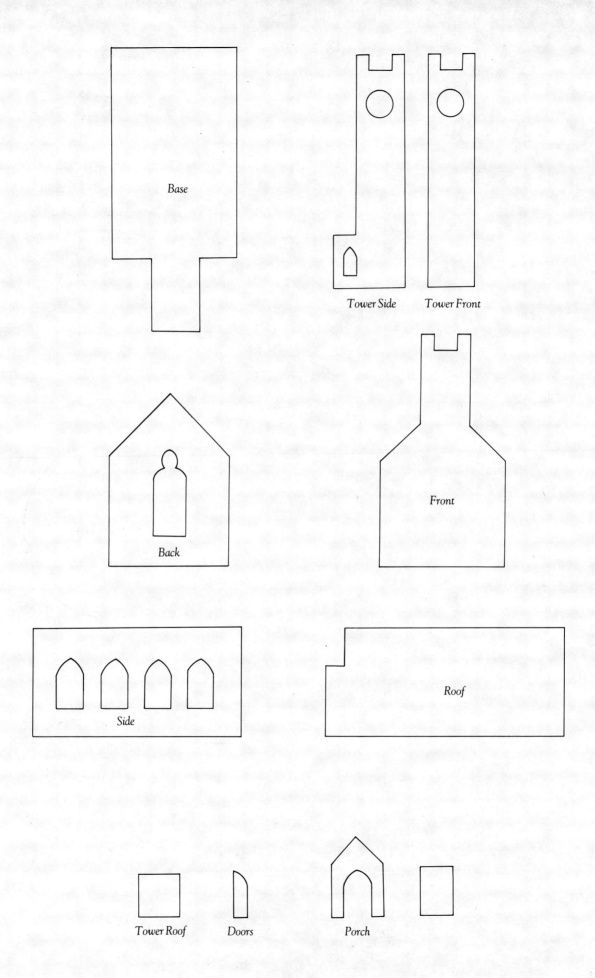

Base

Tower Side   Tower Front

Back

Front

Side

Roof

Tower Roof   Doors   Porch

Template for Runout Church

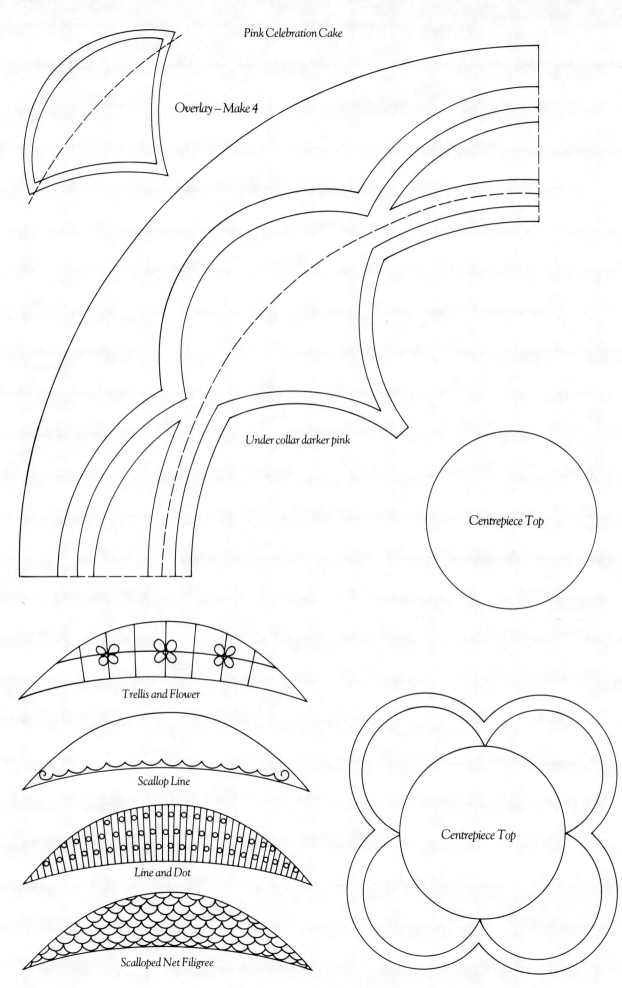

Pink Celebration Cake

Overlay – Make 4

Under collar darker pink

Centrepiece Top

Trellis and Flower

Scallop Line

Line and Dot

Scalloped Net Filigree

Centrepiece Top

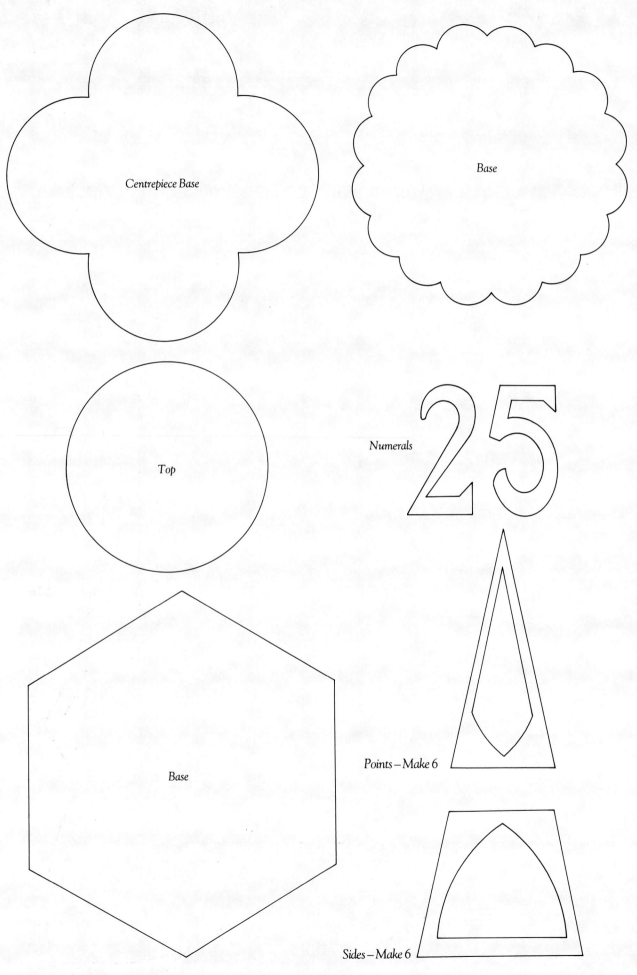

Centrepiece Base

Base

Top

Numerals

Base

Points—Make 6

Sides—Make 6

418

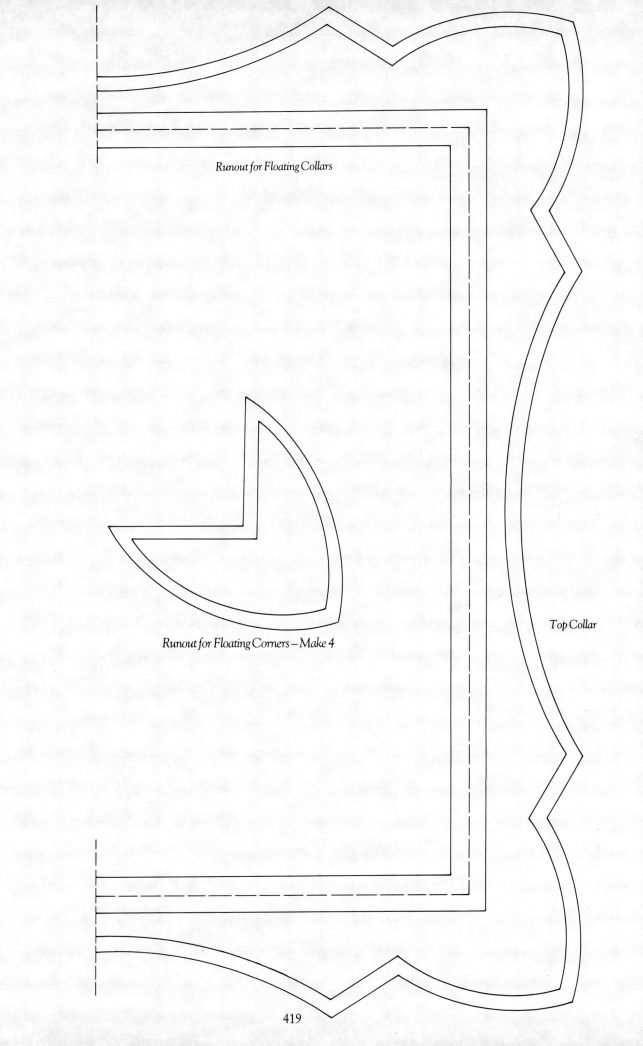

Runout for Floating Collars

Runout for Floating Corners – Make 4

Top Collar

419

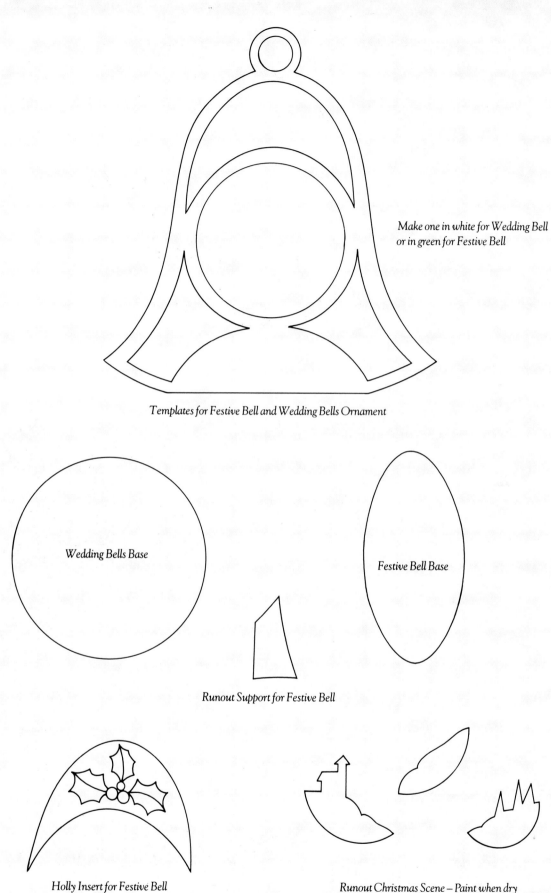

Make one in white for Wedding Bell or in green for Festive Bell

Templates for Festive Bell and Wedding Bells Ornament

Wedding Bells Base

Festive Bell Base

Runout Support for Festive Bell

Holly Insert for Festive Bell

Runout Christmas Scene – Paint when dry

LESSON 14

Introduction to Sugar Flowers

Equipment

Sugar flowers give the finishing touch to any celebration or wedding cake whether arranged in a very simple form or in an advanced spray.

Equipment
The equipment used for making sugar flowers is quite specialized and is in addition to the basic cake decorating equipment. A sewing, fishing or craft box is ideal for storing this equipment as you will collect a great number of small items such as stamens and cutters which are best kept together.

Anger tool
Use for opening the throats of flowers.

Confectioner's glaze
This is a special liquid which gives a shine to leaves and flowers.

Cutters
There is a vast selection of petal and leaf cutters available.

Dresden pewter tool
This is useful for creating special effects, such as getting the right tilt to the large petal of a pansy.

Floral tape
Use this for covering wires and for assembling sprays.

Foam rubber
Many decorators work over a large square of thick foam rubber so that if a flower gets dropped it does not shatter. Smaller pieces of foam are needed for ejecting cutter flowers, for lifting and shaping petals and for protection while transporting finished sprays.

Glass-headed pins
These have a variety of uses in cake decorating. In flower modelling, they can be used like ball tools for small petals.

Leaf formers
Rubber veiners designed for the pottery industry make realistic sugar leaves.

Pliers
Use small long-nosed pliers for bending wire and electrical pliers for stripping wire.

Polystyrene block
Use this for holding the flowers before they are wired into sprays.

Ribbed tool
Use for finger flowers.

Ribbons
All sugar flower sprays contain ribbons. Very narrow ones are best for this, and for ribbon insertion and banding. Wider ribbons can be used to cover cake boards.

Stamens
These come in many different shapes, sizes and colours.

Tape shredder
This is useful for cutting the floral tape into narrow strips.

Tweezers
Fine-pointed crank-ended craft tweezers are best for delicate work.

Wire cutters
Use for cutting the florists' wire, or keep a pair of floristry scissors specially for the job.

Wires
A selection of covered florist wire in different gauges is needed. Use fine wire for small flowers and heavier gauge for large flowers. Fine rose wire or fuse wire is useful for wiring together sprays.

Flower Paste

All of the moulded flowers in this book have been made using this recipe for flower paste. However, there are many variations on this recipe, so experiment to find one which suits you. Remember that flower paste is affected by climate, and if you live in a very humid place, then you may need to add more cornflour (cornstarch) and reduce the amount of icing sugar.

    425g (14oz/3½ cups) icing
    (confectioner's) sugar, sifted
    60g (2oz/¼ cup) cornflour
    (cornstarch)
    15ml (3 teaspoons) gum tragacanth
    or
    10ml (2 teaspoons) gum tragacanth
    and 10ml (2 teaspoons) carboxy
    methyl cellulose
    25ml (5 teaspoons) cold water
    10ml (2 teaspoons) powdered
    gelatine
    15ml (3 teaspoons) white fat
    (shortening)
    10ml (2 teaspoons) liquid glucose
    white of one large egg, string
    removed

Sift together the sugar and cornflour (cornstarch) in the bowl of a heavy-duty mixer. Sprinkle over the gum tragacanth, or the gum tragacanth and carboxy methyl cellulose. Place the mixer bowl over a large pan of boiling water. Cover the top with a dry cloth, and then with a plate or cake board.

Put the water in a small glass bowl and sprinkle the powdered gelatine over it. Leave to sponge.

Half fill a small saucepan with water and place over a low heat. Bring to just below the boiling point. Place the bowl of sponged gelatine over the pan and stir in the liquid glucose and the white fat. Stir until the fat is melted.

When the icing sugar feels warm, take the bowl off the pan of boiling water, dry the bottom and place on the mixer. Remove the beater from the other pan, dry and assemble the mixer. Add the gelatine solution and the egg white to the sugar. Cover the bowl with a cloth, and turn the mixer to the slowest speed. Mix until all the ingredients are combined and the paste is a dull beige colour.

Turn the mixer to maximum and beat until the paste is white and stringy. This will take 5-10 minutes. Remove the paste from the bowl and place in a clean plastic bag. Place the bag in an airtight container and refrigerate for at least 24 hours before using. If planning to store the paste for a few weeks, put it in four or five small bags and open one at a time.

To use the paste, cut off a small piece, add a smear of white fat and dip into some egg white before working. The warmth of your hands will bring the paste to a workable, elastic consistency. Remember that the paste dries out very quickly, so keep it covered at all times and never cut off more than a very small piece. Certain colours, particularly reds and violets, may change the consistency, so it may be necessary to add more white fat and egg white.

Quick Flower Paste

This paste is easier to make, but the flowers will not be as delicate.
    225g (8oz) commercial sugarpaste
    5ml (1 teaspoon) gum tragacanth
    white fat (shortening)
Knead the sugarpaste and gum tragacanth together, adding a small amount of white fat to get an elastic consistency. Store and use as for the previous recipe.

Hints and Tips

Flower paste and modelling paste are affected by the warmth of your hands. A cake decorator with very warm hands would need to use a slightly firmer paste than someone with cold hands.

Always colour pastes with paste food colourings, not liquid ones, which will change the consistency of the modelling pastes. Add the colour using the end of a cocktail stick.

After colouring flower paste or sugarpaste, put it in a plastic bag and return it to the refrigerator for a few minutes. Kneading in the colour will make the paste warm and stringy, and it will be difficult to work with.

Many colours, particularly yellows and reds, will deepen on standing, so colour the paste a shade lighter than the desired finished colour.

An alternative method of colouring flowers is to make them all white, cream or a pale shade then petal dust to the desired shade when dry.

Petal dust is a powdered food colouring based on cornflour (cornstarch), which can be mixed in with the petal dust in small quantities to obtain a lighter shade.

Flower paste should be rolled as thinly as possible so that the petals will be translucent and natural looking. Paste can be rolled out on a thin film of white fat (shortening) or on a light dusting of cornflour (cornstarch). Experiment to find which one works best for you.

When doing double frilling as in an orchid throat or carnation, the paste should be slightly thicker than usual or it will not frill successfully.

If using cornflour (cornstarch) to dust the work surface, place it in a square of butter muslin (cheesecloth) tied in a bag, or use a pepper pot for a miniature flour dredger.

Making Sugar Flowers

Take a small piece of paste, colour it if required with paste food colouring, work a little white vegetable fat and egg white into the paste until it is elastic and pliable, and work until the paste is warm as cold paste is extremely difficult to shape. Roll out the paste using a special small board and pin. Sprinkle the board with a light coating of cornflour (cornstarch) to prevent the paste from sticking, but avoid using excessive amounts or the paste will dry out and crack.

1. Start rolling the paste on a light dusting of cornflour (cornstarch). Check that it is translucent, if you cannot see through the paste it is too thick and requires further rolling.

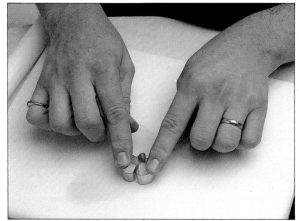

2. Place your cutter on the surface of the paste and with your fingers evenly over the cutter press down to cut out the shape.

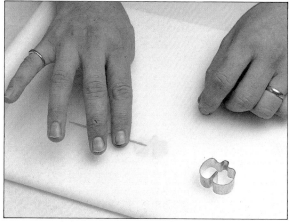

3. To soften petals for flowers such as a sweet pea, use a cocktail stick and gently roll over the edge of the petal in a gentle motion. This is a very different principle from frilling as for the carnation.

4. Cup the petals on a piece of soft, sponge rubber using a dog bone or ball tool. The more pressure you apply the more cupped the petal will become.

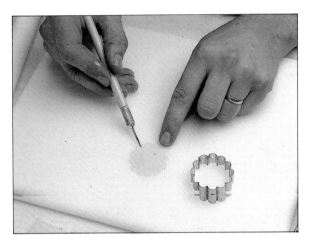

5. Petals and foliage will sometimes have to be veined. The tool shown is made specially for this purpose but a cocktail stick or porcupine quill could be used instead. As with cupping, veining has to be done on sponge. Do not put too much pressure on the petal or tool, but use a gentle stroking movement along the length of the petal or leaf.

6. On most flowers, especially pulled flowers, cutting plays an important part in the shape of the flower. Although a small kitchen knife can be used, better results will be achieved with a modelling or craft knife. For instance, small cuts put along the edge of the carnation petal prior to frilling.

7. Many flowers have to be frilled. Use a wooden cocktail stick and frill the outer edges of the petal with a firm rolling movement in a back and forward direction, take care to keep the paste moving all the time to ensure that it does not stick.

8. Stick petals and attach to each other with fresh egg white using a small clean paintbrush, but do not leave this in the egg white when it is not needed or you will apply too much to the surface of the paste. The petal here is being brushed with egg white prior to folding onto the wire of the carnation.

Making Foliage or Individually Wired Petals

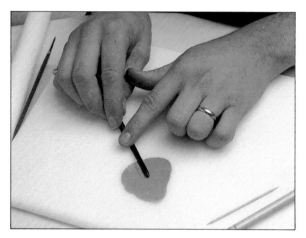

1. Take a piece of paste, squash between your thumb and first finger and, using a paintbrush, handle as a miniature rolling-pin. Start rolling the paste retaining a thick part at the end nearest to you. Then roll from the left and right hand sides in order to thin the paste evenly all the way over, but leaving it thicker at one end.

2. Cut out the leaf or petal. The base of the cutter should be over the thicker part of the paste.

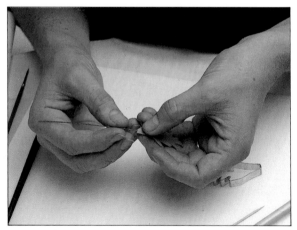

3. Take a piece of 28- to 30-gauge green covered wire in your right hand, dip the hooked end in a little egg white, then pick up the leaf holding firmly between the thumb and first finger of your left hand. Push the wire into the leaf, the pressure ensures that the wire goes in straight and stops it from piercing through the paste. The wire needs to go in about 6mm (¼in).

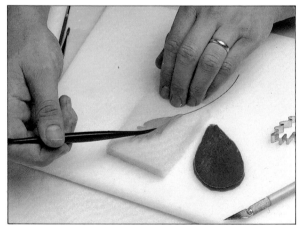

4. Take the leaf and place on a rubber or plastic veiner. Then place on a piece of sponge rubber and, using a veining tool, mark the central vein to give the leaf more character. Vein on both sides.

Colouring Flowers

1. For certain flowers you will need a greater density of colour than dusting alone can give, for these you need to paint the petals. Mix a little petal dust or paste colour with some clear spirit (gin or vodka). Spirit is used for this purpose as it evaporates and dries quickly and does not soften the paste. However, mix only small quantities of colour as it too will evaporate while you work. Here the dots are being painted on the throat of a foxglove using a plum colour and a No00 paintbrush.

2. To get a soft overall effect on your sugar flowers you will need a soft round No4 brush. Here a honeysuckle flower is dusted a creamy-yellow shade; note how the plate is used like an artist's palette to mix the colours.

3. If a stronger density of colour is required on the outer edge of the petal only, a short, firm, flat brush should be used. Work with a gentle stroking movement from the outside of the petal to the inside. Using this principle, the spray carnation can have a contrasting colour on the petal edges.

4. Here a blackberry leaf is dusted prior to varnishing, again a flat, firm brush has to be used. The copper colour is used to give a little depth to the leaf and is brushed down one side of the leaf only.

5. There are several ways to achieve a shiny surface on foliage. The method used here employs a commercially available confectioner's glaze used in the bakery for varnishing marzipan and chocolate for display purposes. It is edible but has an unpleasant taste. Brush the glaze over the surface of the foliage and stick the wire in a stand for about 15 minutes to dry. Two other methods you can use for shining the surface of the paste are painting with gum arabic glaze, or the leaves may be held in the steam of a kettle for a few seconds. This gives a gloss finish but it is prone to going matt in damp or humid weather.

6. Here confectioner's glaze is being used on blackberry fruits. Once you have finished using your brush, clean in a spirit based cleaner, such as white spirit or dry cleaning fluid.

Daffodil Leaf

Leaves may be made very quickly and effectively using floristry tape. This tape is available in a variety of shades and may be coloured with dust.

1. Cut a piece of wire approximately the length of the leaf you want, and a slightly longer piece of floristry tape.

2. Take the floristry tape and stretch it, this opens up the tape releasing a glue so it sticks to itself.

3. Place the tape on the work surface, lay the wire on to it and then bring the long end back on itself over the top of the wire.

4. Now run your finger over the surface of the leaf to stick the two sides together.

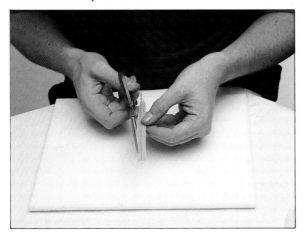

5. Take a pair of small sharp scissors and cut out the leaf shape. This is a daffodil so it is a long, thin leaf with a pointed end.

6. The finished daffodil leaf with its two cut sides.

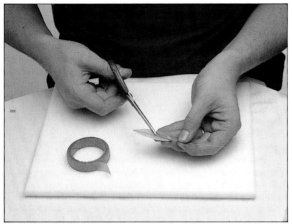

7. Here is a mimosa leaf made in the same way, but it has a more regular leaf shape. Take a pair of sharp scissors and make cuts at an angle up the leaf.

8. Continue until you have cut both sides and achieved a feathered effect.

9. Twist the leaf in a spiral to give a 3-dimensional effect.

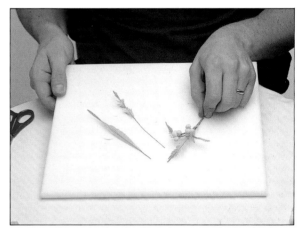

10. Here the finished two leaves and a finished spray of mimosa.

LESSON 15

Pulled Flowers

Pulled and Finger Flowers

Hand-moulded flowers are usually known as pulled or finger flowers. They are the easiest flowers to start with as little special equipment is needed.

This lesson begins with pulled basic blossom which is the easiest flower to master and progresses to more complicated flowers like the snowdrop. The more difficult flowers are featured towards the end of the chapter so if you have never made any pulled flowers before, it is best to begin with those at the beginning of the chapter. Remember that the smaller the piece of paste that you begin with, the smaller the finished flower and the more fiddly it is to perfect. It is better to start off with a larger piece of paste, perfect the flower, then reduce down the size rather than risk becoming frustrated and disappointed working with tiny petals. Making evenly shaped petals and perfectly balanced flowers comes with practice, and the more practice you have the better your finished flowers will be.

EQUIPMENT
Sharp modelling knife
Wooden modelling stick
Dowel or end of paintbrush
Modelling tools
Petal dust
Paste food colouring
Wire
Floristry tape
Stamens

Basic Blossom

1. Take a pea-sized piece of flower-paste, this should be thoroughly kneaded so that it is soft and warm.

2. Mould into a small cone shape, dip the pointed end of your dowel into cornflour (cornstarch) and insert into the thick end of the cone.

3. Taking a sharp modelling knife make five equal sized cuts for the five petals. The cuts should be one-quarter to one-third of the total length of the cone.

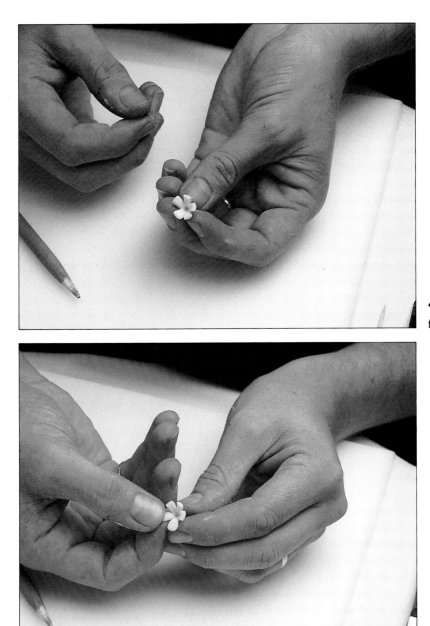

4. Remove the dowel and open up the flower by pushing your finger into the centre.

5. Taking each petal in turn process by squashing, pinching and pulling.

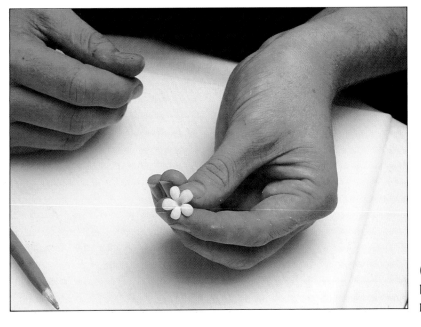

6. You should end up with a flower with five equal petals, but remember this will only be perfected with practice.

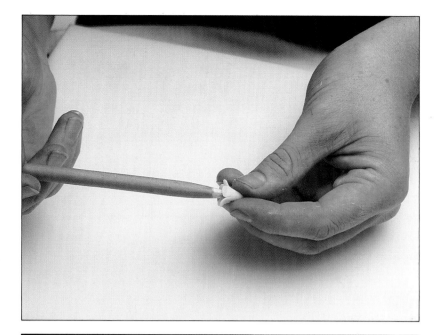

7. Place your wooden stick back into the throat of the flower and pull the petals up slightly to produce a nice shaped flower. Remove the stick.

8. Take a piece of 28 or 30-gauge covered wire. The wire usually comes in packs with long strands, cut each one into four to give lengths of wire suitable for most flowers and sufficient to wire the flowers into sprays without being wasteful. Bend the wire to make a small hook on one end, dip the hooked end into a little fresh egg white and thread through the throat of the flower, as shown.

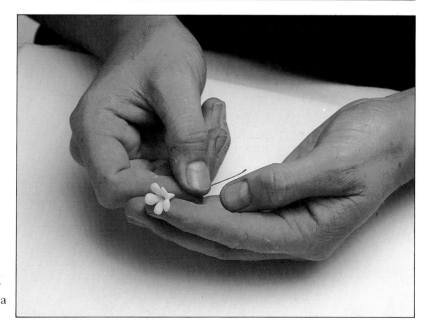

9. Pull the wire through until it sits into the soft paste at the back of the flower. Squash the flower back around the wire. You now have a finished blossom on wire.

Winter Jasmine

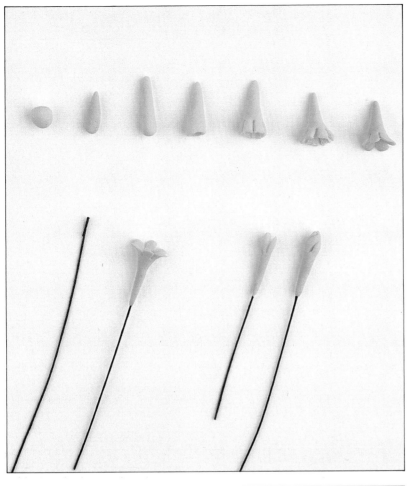

Colour some flower paste golden yellow, roll into a ball then into a long thin cone. Stick your dowel into the thicker end of the cone. Cut six petals and remove from dowel. Squash, pinch and pull each petal. Take a piece of 30-gauge covered dark green wire, make a hook and slide down the throat. Place a single white stamen into the throat (refer to picture below for positioning). To make the buds, roll a thin cone, stick the hooked wire into the thin end, cut approximately one-third of the way down with scissors and then twist the two pieces together like a spiral.

Finishing

Dilute some dark green, paste food colouring with clear spirit and paint calyxes on each of the flowers and buds using a small, fine paintbrush and leave to dry. Tape the flowers and buds in clumps on to a piece of 26-gauge wire which then acts as the main stem.

Winter jasmine is a most attractive flower to use in winter sprays and contrasts with the usual red and green Christmas cake spray.

Daisy

Take a small ball of white paste, mould into a cone, press a dowel into the thicker end. Cut eight petals, and open up the flower. Squash, pinch and pull each petal then pinch each one in to a slight point. Make a hook on a piece of 28-gauge dark green wire, dip in egg white and thread down the throat of the flower. Take a piece of dark yellow paste, roll into a tiny ball and holding it on your first finger, press some tulle over the top, to flatten and mark it. Remove the tulle and insert into the centre of the daisy with the patterned edge uppermost. Using a small calyx cutter, cut out some thin green paste. Thread up the wire and stick this onto the flower.

Finishing
Dust a little green petal dust into the centre of the daisy. Daisies are an attractive flower to use on many types of cake and are particularly suitable for spring or summer weddings.

Primrose

Colour some paste to a creamy lemon-colour, roll into a ball then into a long cone with a slightly bulbous end. Stick a dowel into the bulbous end, cut five petals then make a further five cuts in the centre of each petal but half the length of the first cuts. Open up and you will have five heart-shaped petals. Run a cocktail stick over the surface of each petal. Make a hook on a piece of 26-gauge mid-green wire and thread through the throat of the flower. Place a small ball of green paste into the centre of the flower and using a cocktail stick, make a small hole in the centre of the green piece and use to position a white stamen. Roll out some green paste and cut a calyx using a mini 8-petal daisy, cup on a piece of sponge and thread up the wire. Stick around the base of the flower squashing around the base.

Finishing
Dust a little green into the centre of the flowers. To make a stem more in scale with the flower, two additional wires are taped to the original one. Primroses are ideal for spring cakes, particularly Easter cakes or country-style weddings.

Violet

Colour some paste violet and roll into a ball. Mould into a cone and stick a dowel into the thicker end of the cone. Cut one petal to a quarter of the total circumference of the paste and four petals from the remaining three-quarters. Open up the flower and run a cocktail stick over each petal in turn. Make a hook in a piece of 28-gauge green wire then bend a hook at right angles, as shown and dip the hook in egg white. Thread the wire through the throat and push so that the wire pierces the top of the back of the cone behind the top two petals, making sure that the larger single petal is at the bottom. Cut off any excess paste and then bend back the wire. Roll out some green paste, cut a diamond shape and then cut each side almost in half to make the calyx. Place over the violet as shown. Make an orange stamen and insert into the centre of the violet. Mark a vein down the centre of the large petal.

Finishing

Dust with dark violet petal dust. Mix a little white petal dust with some clear spirit and paint a few lines into the centre of the violet.

Violets are a common flower connected with springtime and Easter. They look attractive on Easter cakes, eggs and birthday cakes.

Heartsease

Colour some paste to a pale ivory-colour and roll into a ball. Form into a cone shape and stick a dowel into the thicker end of the cone. Cut one petal from a quarter of the cone and four equal petals out of the remaining three-quarters. Squash and pinch but do not pull each petal, then roll a cocktail stick quite firmly over the surface to thin out rather than to frill the petals. Place on the wire in the same way as for the violet. Squash to elongate the petals and to push up the top layer. Once on the wire insert a small ball of paste into the centre and make a cavity in it using a small ball tool or the end of a glass-headed pin. Tuck the bottom of the large petal under to make it into a heart shape. The calyx is the same as for the violet.

Finishing
Dust the top two petals mauve or violet and the other three yellow, the backs should be dusted in the same colours. Put a touch of mauve and violet on the bottom petal for detail. Mix some black paste colouring with some clear spirit and paint the central lines using a very fine brush. To finish, dust a little green into the centre of the flower.

Heartsease is a wild pansy and comes in a range of colours. They are dainty colourful flowers making them suitable for many types of cakes and sprays.

439

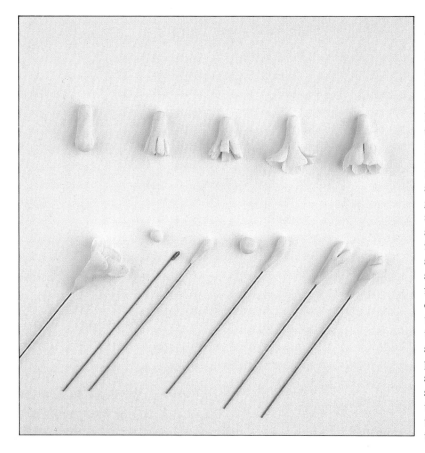

Freesia

Make a dumbell shape in ivory paste and stick a dowel into one end. Cut into six equal petals; squash, pinch and pull and roll a cocktail stick over each petal. Place onto a piece of sponge and cup each one stroking the ball tool from the outside to the inside of the flower. Push your ball or dog bone tool down the centre of the throat to stretch it slightly. Take a piece of 26-gauge mid-green wire, hook and dip in egg white and thread through the throat. Take a small ball of paste and place inside the flower to act like a plug to stop it from sliding down the wire. Using a cocktail stick make a small hole in the plug and fold together three 2.5cm (1in) pieces of cotton or stamen cotton and push the folded ends into the hole using the thumb and first fingers of both hands squash slightly. Move three alternate petals inwards and others outwards, squash just below the petals. To make sure the centre three stay in position, the outer three are then gently eased up to sit as a second row on top of the first three petals.

The buds are made in various sizes, the smallest are just tiny cones placed on wire and rolled down between the fingers to form a long, elegant bud. The twisted buds are made in the same way as the winter jasmine buds.

Finishing

Once dry, dust with pink or any other appropriate petal dust, as freesias come in a wide range of colours. A little green petal dust is brushed into the centre and around the base of the flower. The buds are lightly dusted all over with green while the twisted buds are half green and half pink. You will need graduated flowers as well as buds to make a spray.

Mix a little green food colouring with some clear spirit and paint a calyx on each bud and flower. Paint a small single leaf shape on either side using a fine paintbrush and allow to dry. Assemble starting with the smallest bud and placing the others to the right then to the left all the way down.

Snowdrop

Roll a small ball of white paste and make into a cone, then stick a dowel into the thicker end and cut six petals. While still on the stick, make a smaller cut in the centre of three alternate petals as for the primrose. The three smaller petals are a smaller version of the primrose. Squash, pinch and pull all of the petals, roll a cocktail stick over each of them. Cup both sets of petals on a foam base. Stick a ball tool into the centre and roll the flower about to make a bulbous cavity above the petals. Make a hook on a piece of 30-gauge dark green wire and thread through the flower; bend over so the snowdrop hangs like a bell. Slide a small ball of paste along the wire for the calyx, sticking in position with egg white. The three heart-shaped petals sit in the centre, with the three large plain ones on top similar to the petal formation of the freesia. Roll out some green paste and cut a thin pointed strip, stick the square end on to the wire and mould around the base of the flowers.

Finishing

Mix some green colouring with clear spirit and paint some very fine feathery lines on to the three heart-shaped petals. The snowdrop being so very small is the most fiddly flower to make and only practice will enable you to manipulate tiny petals.

Snowdrops have a limited use, but look very attractive on a winter or early spring wedding cake, especially if the wedding is in a white and green colour scheme.

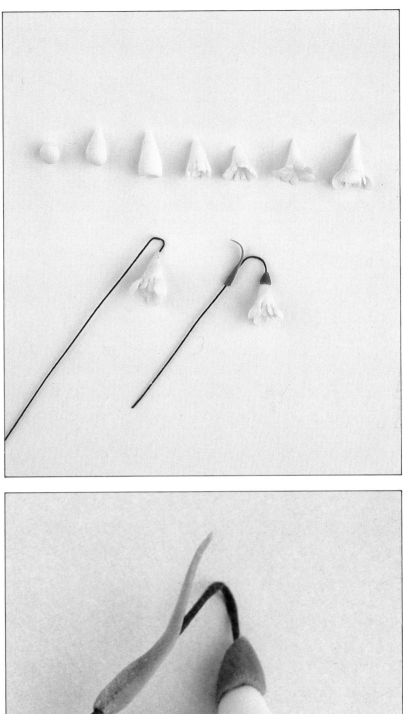

Bluebell

Colour some paste bluish-mauve and roll into a ball. Mould into a dumbell shape, stick a dowel into one end and cut six petals. Place each petal onto a piece of sponge and cup using a ball-tool stick, then insert a ball tool up into the centre of the flower to make a bulbous cavity. Using tweezers, pinch the flower as shown to produce a ribbed effect on the side. Tape two white stamen ends onto a piece of wire, and wrap round extra tape to stop the wire coming back through the flower. Thread the wire and stamens through the flower. The buds are made by making a small cone, pinched with tweezers.

Finishing
Brush with a mixture of blue and violet dusting powder. Tape the buds and flowers onto a main stem as shown starting with a bud in the centre then setting another to the left then the next to the right and so on. You can make a long spray by using five to seven buds and five to seven flowers. Bluebells look attractive bunched together with other spring flowers.

Many dozens of flowers can be made using the techniques shown and once the technique is mastered you should be able to look at almost any flower and be able to make it by deciding which of the skills will be necessary to use. The flowers covered in this chapter may be used in a wide variety of sprays and floral arrangements. The following provide just a few ideas to get you started.

Baby's Booties

A pair of small china baby's booties filled with pastel-tipped petal blossom would be a suitable gift for a new arrival or for a christening cake. Fill the booties with white sugarpaste; make some figure-of-eight double loops in lemon and white. Place the ribbons in position then arrange an assortment of sizes of basic five petal blossom and buds in the booties using a pair of tweezers. Tie two lemon bows and stick these on to the front of the booties with royal icing or a rubber based glue.

Posy of Pulled Blossoms

A posy of pulled flowers would make a delightful decoration on any cake and could be made in a variety of colour combinations. For this posy you will need fifteen to twenty five-petal blossoms and about eight buds and frilled blossoms. When dry, these have been dusted with blue and peach petal dust and arranged with blue and peach 6mm (¼in) figure-of-eight double ribbon loops and placed into a small, white post holder. For instructions on wiring flowers into a spray refer to page 236 which covers the posy wiring technique step-by-step.

Peach and Blue Anniversary Cake

The same peach and blue posy on an Anniversary Cake. The cake is a 20cm (8in) heart-shaped and royal-iced in peach with shells and running S scrolls piped with a No42 tube then with a No2 and overpiped in blue using a No1 tube. A blue polka dot ribbon has been attached around the side with a bow on the front. An inscription, a small feather butterfly and the posy finish the top decoration.

Silver Vase

This flowing vase is filled with dozens of pulled blossoms and buds. Make five identical legs and wire into a posy with double figure-of-eight loops and stick into a silver vase. This would be an ideal top decoration for a three tier wedding cake. (refer to Lesson 19 for information on wiring flowers into posies. The principle is like the reverse S or crescent spray).

Garden and Wayside Cake

Cover a long octagonal board with wild silk or an alternative fabric. The edge has been finished with a velvet ribbon around it. Cover a small oval cake in pink sugarpaste. Transfer on to the board with an oval piece of waxed paper between the cake and board so as not to strain the fabric, making it possible to reuse the board. Pipe a small shell around the base. A 3mm (⅛in) ribbon is placed above the shell and then forget-me-nots are piped freehand over the sides of the cake. A spray of flowers is placed into posy pick with a butterfly and inscription to finish off this unusual floral cake.

LESSON 16

Cutter Flowers

Flowers Made Using Cutters

Numerous varieties of flowers may be made from the many cutters now on the market. Cutters for flowers and foliage come in lots of sizes and makes, some metal and some plastic. Every manufacturer produces a slightly different shaped cutter for the same flower and they all make slightly different looking flowers. For some of the flowers shown, you will have to modify the shape of a cutter.

The Rose

The rose, symbol of eternal love, peace and serenity, is the most popular cutter flower. The one shown here works equally well as a three, four or five level petal formation.

Method
Colour some flower paste to the required colour, here peach has been used. For the best results prepare graduated shades of the colour, use the darkest shade at the centre and lighter shades for the outer petals. If matching pastes to bridal fabrics, match your darkest shade paste to the fabric.

Roll the paste into a ball, then into a cone. Make a hook on a piece of 26-gauge mid-green wire, dip into egg white and stick into the thick end of the cone. Mould around the base to cover up the hole. Leave to dry for a day.

Roll out some paste until it is translucent, cut six petals. The cutters shown come in a set of five, the middle three cutters of the set have been used to make the rose shown, the first six petals have been cut with the second smallest cutter. Brush some egg white on the top of the cone, place the first petal like a peep bonnet on to the cone, tuck the left-hand side in and wrap the right-hand side on top of this.

Continue the second row by placing another petal on the join of the first petal, stick with a little egg white, leaving the right-hand side of the petal open. The next petal sits inside the last and overlaps on top of the neighbouring petal, so now there is one petal in the centre and two petals on the next row. Continue on to the next row, this time

adding three petals. Place in an overlap formation creating a spiral appearance. The first six petals are now in position, no frilling or softening of petals is needed for the first six petals. Do not try to cover the cone, if you look at the picture the petals only come about two thirds of the way down the cone.

Lighten the paste by adding white paste to a ratio of two parts coloured paste to one part white. Remember if you are making more than one rose, place the first six petals on all your roses before adding white to the paste. Roll out some of the lighter paste, cut four petals using a slightly larger cutter, soften these four slightly using a cocktail stick, position these petals using an overlap, spiral formation.

Add further white paste to the peach for the final row. Roll out the paste, cut five petals with the next cutter up in size, frill with a cocktail stick and attach. Usually you will have to do this with the rose hanging upside-down so the petals do not flop back.

Take a piece of green paste, make

into a cone with a flattened bottom and place a piece of flattened white paste beneath this, as shown.
Roll out using a paintbrush as a mini rolling-pin and cut out using a calyx cutter. Cut feathers on the legs, as shown, turn over and, using a large ball tool, make a cavity for the rose to sit in. Slide up the wire, sticking with egg white and mould into the rose.

To make the leaves, squash a piece of green paste and roll out retaining a thicker area. Cut out with the thickest area at the base of the leaf. Hold firmly between your thumb and first finger and insert a piece of hooked wire. Press into a veiner; roll a cocktail stick along the edge and clearly mark the central vein. Support in a natural position until completely dry.

Dust with a mixture of brown and yellow petal dust. When dry, dust the rose with a peach and pink mixture when dry to lift it slightly. The rose and leaves are then wired together to form a spray.

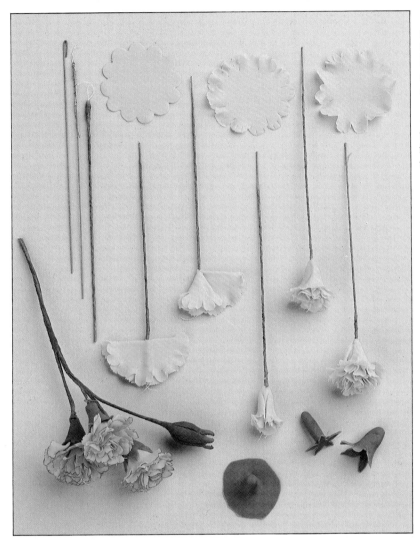

Roll out some paste but do not roll it until it is translucent as you would for the rose, as for double frilling it should be a fraction thicker. Cut out the carnation shape using the carnation cutter.

Using a sharp modelling knife, cut on the indentation and two or three times on the curve of each scallop. To frill the petal, take a cocktail stick and working with a firm rolling movement, start frilling the paste keeping it moving all the time so that it does not stick to the work surface. Continue until frilled all the way around. Turn over onto a piece of thin foam, brush egg white all over the surface up to the frilling.

Thread the wire through the centre, fold in half, remove from sponge, brush egg white over the centre third of one side and bring the left-hand side third over; repeat on the other side by turning it over and bring from the side to the centre so it is an S shape if looked at from above. Squash firmly onto the wire.

Continue by rolling, cutting and frilling two further petals. These are turned over, brushed with egg white and slid onto the wire. Hang upside-down supporting between your two thumbs and first fingers. Squash all around to get an even finish.

Make a small cone, known as a Mexican hat, rolling from the inside to the outside using a paintbrush. Cut out a calyx and then, as for pulled flowers, stick a wooden dowel down the centre to open it up. Slide this up the wire and attach to the carnation with egg white.

To make the bud, surround a yellow cone with a piece of green paste and cut through the green using a modelling knife to reveal the yellow underneath. Place onto a piece of wire. Dust the petals with a flat brush using a contrasting colour and wire with the bud into a spray.

Spray Carnation

Spray carnations are a very lovely, delicate flower to use on any celebration or wedding cake and can be finished in some interesting colour combinations.

Method
Take a piece of 26-gauge mid-green wire, put a hook on one end and hook a piece of cotton or thread on to this, squash with pliers and wrap a piece of fine rose wire around the top piece. Using a thin piece of floristry tape, wrap around the top and tape down to the base of the wire.

Clematis

The clematis is an attractive climber. The one illustrated is Montana, a small four petalled variety that flowers in abundance. There are many books on clematis or look in a seed catalogue as these usually include full colour pictures of clematis and other flowers. Clematis would be very dramatic on a wedding cake and, as many men grow them, could be used on a man's cake along with the foliage.

The cutter for Clematis Montana is made by squashing a Christmas Rose cutter. Only bend cutters if you plan to do the flowers on a regular basis, if not use a cardboard or petal template, (see page 227).

Method

Roll out some pink paste and cut four petals. Place on a veiner like a violet leaf, hibiscus, or any with fan-shape veining. Turn over and using a veining tool or cocktail stick, mark two curved lines then turn over so the lines are underneath and inverted on the top.

Take a small, circular piece of paste and make a hole in it. With the end of a paintbrush, squash slightly and sit inside a wooden curtain ring. Assemble the four petals onto the tiny centre ring sticking with egg white and using the curtain ring as a support. Stick some white stamen cotton pieces around the centre. These have been dusted a mauve colour in places to produce a striped effect.

Take some yellow cotton, wrap round the tweezer ends that should be about 12mm (½in) apart, wind around 13 times and then twist some wire around the centre to form a figure-of-eight with the wire in the centre. Cut the two loops and trim off the excess wire and stick into the centre of the clematis to make the mass of yellow in the centre. Allow to dry before finishing. Dust with a stripe of darker pink down the centre of each petal and dust a little green around the base of the petals.

Petunia

Petunias with their floppy flowers come in many colours, including pink, mauve, lilac, red and striped effect ones. They would be nice on a summer birthday or get well cake because they are a cheery flower.

Method

Make a cone and place flat end on to work surface; roll using a paintbrush until you have a central node and a refined outer area. Cut out using a petunia cutter. Place a wooden dowel into the centre of the flower and rotate it to stretch the throat open. Holding the back of the flower, place each petal down on to a leaf veiner to vein the petals, then holding on the edge of your work surface, frill the petal edges with a cocktail stick. Tape five white stamens together with floristry tape; make a hole at the base of the flower and stick the stamen piece into the throat threading through the back. If making an unwired petunia, trim off the excess stamen ends once the flower is dry. If wiring the petunia, slide a small hollowed cone of green on to the back and tape the stamens to a piece of wire with mid-green floristry tape. Dust with two shades of pink to get a striped effect with a little green in the centre.

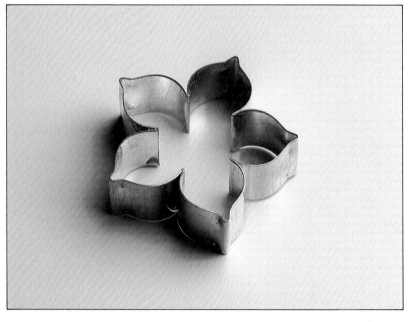

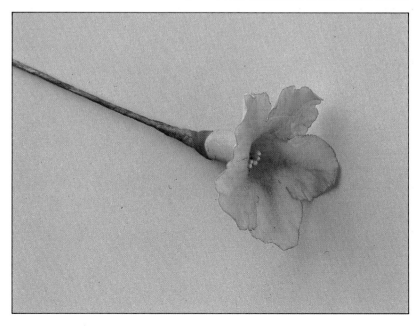

Fuchsia

Fuchsia are a dramatic summer garden flower hanging in clumps like ballerinas in the sunshine. They come in hundreds of colours. It is best to pick some real fuchsias to achieve naturalistic colouring, or have a book with colour photographs at hand. For the best effects, show them hanging out of a vase as they do naturally.

Method

Take six stamens in dark pink with one longer than the other five. Wrap a piece of 28-gauge green wire around them. Squash a piece of paste around the wire and a piece of paste on the longer stamen. Roll out some paste and cut six petals using a rose petal cutter. Lay three in a fan, sticking with egg white. There are ten wrapped around the small cone of paste. Stick the further three petals, after frilling them slightly, overlapping the joins in the first row of petals. Roll out some more paste and, using a pansy sepal cutter, cut out four petals. Put on to a veiner to give some detail to the petals. Roll a cocktail stick over the edge to frill them. Place the four on as shown. Make a Mexican hat shape in a second colour, rolling with a paintbrush, and cut out the back piece of the flower using a fuchsia sepal cutter. Vein each petal and cup upwards on a piece of foam. Make a cavity in the centre for the first stage to sit into; slide the prepared centre up through the back piece sticking with egg white. Stick a calyx on to the back, and dust according to colour scheme and also dust the long stigma green. Tape on to a piece of 26-gauge wire for support if wiring several into a spray.

Sweet Pea

Sweet peas are a very popular garden summer flower. They come in a lovely assortment of pastel shades as well as dark velvety colours. They can be made in a white or pale cream and dusted or painted in a colour.

Method

Take a small pea of paste. Hook a piece of 26-gauge mid-green wire and stick the pea of paste on to the hook that has been dipped in egg white. Flatten the pea of paste slightly. Roll out some paste and cut out a rose petal using the second smallest petal in the rose set. Place on to a piece of sponge, brush a little egg white down the centre and down one side of the petal. Then with the point of the petal towards you, take the flattened piece of paste on the wire and place the thin edge into the centre of the petal; fold both sides over and squash together. Pull the top piece back at a slight right angle.

Roll out some more paste and cut out the first main petal. Roll a cocktail stick around the petal to frill, place on a piece of sponge and vein the centre. Place the prepared wired inner petal into the centre of the main petal with the tiny right angled piece hooked over the top gap in the petal. Squash at the back as shown. Roll out a little more paste, cut out the second main petal and shape. Frill this slightly, put on a piece of foam, vein the centre then turn over so the veining is inverted. Stick the prepared piece to this new petal using egg white. As the sepals start to set you can move them about. Roll out some green paste, cut out a calyx. Place on a piece of sponge, cup and slide up the wire, sticking with egg white. The tendrils are made by wrapping pieces of wire around the handle of a paintbrush. Dust when dry and assemble into a spray.

Sweet peas tend to look best on their own because they are flat flowers. They do not mix well. A natural type of buncl arrangement suits them best.

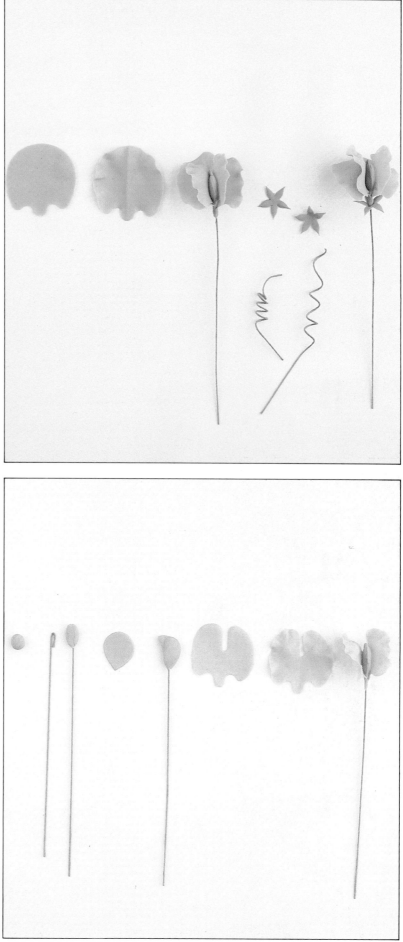

451

Longiflorum Lily

These elegant trumpet-shaped lilies look very attractive on a large wedding cake.

Method

Roll out some white paste and cut six petals using a lily cutter. Soften each petal slightly using a cocktail stick; vein on the reverse side of the petal. Stick with a little egg white into a fan shape. Roll into a hollow cake pillar to dry. This is ideal to support the shape of the lily. For the stamens and stigma make a hook in a piece of 26-gauge Nile green wire; take five lily stamens and use fine pieces of floristry tape to cover the white cotton underneath but leave the lemon top exposed. The stigma has a small cone attached to the top and is divided into thirds. Brush the lemon lily stamens with egg white and dip in dark yellow or gold petal dust; leave to dry. Bend the stamens with tweezers and tape all five in a ring to the longer stigma. Once the lily is dry, slot through the lily base – if wiring, tape the end of stamen arrangement to a 24-gauge wire and slide a small ball of green paste up the wire to fill in the end of the lily. Dust with green in the form of lines down the centre of each petal.

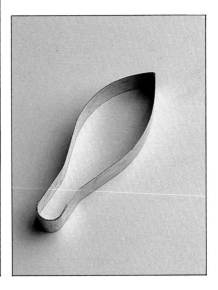

Cymbidium Orchid

Cymbidiums come in hundreds of colours and various shapes. A medium sized cutter was used to make an orchid suitable for use in a corsage or in a large spray. The step-by-step assembly of the Cymbidium orchid is covered on page 242. Cymbidiums are popular in autumn wedding bouquets.

Method

Roll out some paste retaining a thicker part as for leaves. Cut out a petal and insert a hooked piece of 30-gauge wire, vein on a sweetcorn leaf or other suitable veiner. Three large and two Cymbidium. One large sepal is set against a piece of dowel or tube, the other four sepals, two large, two smaller, are all laid over the curved surface. Leave to dry. To make the throat, hook a piece of 26-gauge wire and place a medium cone with a bulbous end on the wire. Roll out two small wing shapes using a paintbrush handle. Make a small cut with scissors underneath each wing and vein both sides along the length of the column. Bend over, make a small cavity and place a tiny, yellow ball split in half in position sticking with egg white. Roll out some green paste, cut out the throat petal, then cut two small pieces out with a modelling knife as shown. Frill the scalloped end of the petal only, then cup the two side sections of the petal on a piece of foam. Vein the centre using a veining tool. Brush a little egg white at the base of the petal and place the column in position. Wrap the sides of the petal over to meet, then stick the throat petal about one third of the way up the column. Place a small piece of foam rubber into the throat to stop it collapsing while drying, (this has been removed from the photograph to show the detail).

Place on an orchid former, or support on a piece of foam rubber allowing the orchid to hang over the edge. Leave all parts to dry. The assemble and finishing is covered in depth on page 242.

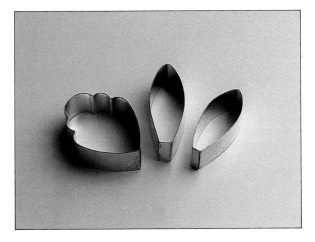

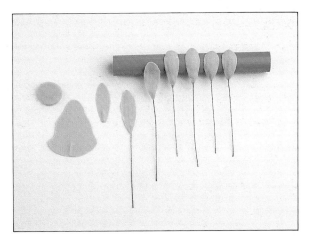

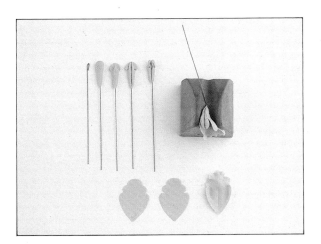

Cattleya Orchid

The Cattleya orchid, known as the bridal orchid in America, comes in shades of cream, pink, mauve, lemon and white highlighted with various pastel colours; it is a very feminine orchid with its frilly petals and is always a popular choice. The assembly of the Cattleya is identical to that of the Cymbidium.

Method

Roll out some white paste using a paintbrush, retaining a thicker part at one end. Cut three long, thin petals and two that are slightly shorter and wider. The thin ones have a deep, wide veining on the backs of the petals; one is set-off against the tubing and the two wider petals are both frilled and veined and set-off over a curve. All of these petals go on 30-gauge green wire.

Begin the throat by making a column, which is shorter than that for the Cymbidium. Vein down both sides. Make a small yellow ball and cut in half, this is then placed into a small cavity. The throat petal is cut out and veined on any fan formation leaf veiner, alternatively you can buy orchid throat veiners. Frill all the way around. Place the throat petal on a piece of sponge rubber and position the column at the base of the petal, yellow ball side downwards; bring both sides up to meet at the top sticking with egg white. Support in an orchid throat former or over the edge of some thick foam. Dust with a pale pink and lemon petal dust.

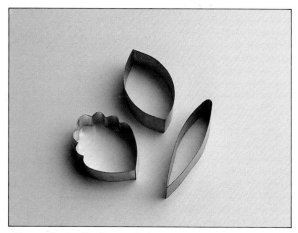

Cutters for the Cattleya orchid.

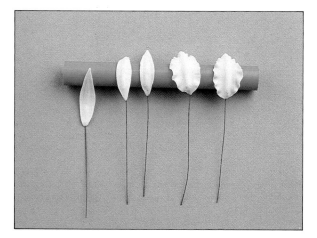

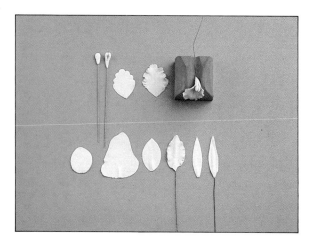

Miniature Cymbidium

Miniature Cymbidiums look very delicate on a tiny birthday cake or in a spray as a filler in conjunction with larger orchids. They are quite fiddly and quite time consuming to make.

Method

Make a tiny hook on a piece of 28-gauge wire. Place a small cone on one end, graduate its shape to form a bulbous tip. Vein on both sides, then bend the top over slightly. Roll out some pink paste and cut the throat petal. Frill the bottom edge and cup the two sides, then attach to the prepared column with egg white as shown. The sepals on this type of cutter are all in one; roll out some pink paste and cut out the petals. Vein each one down the centre. Cup one petal, then turn over and cup the other four, when you turn the petal over again they will curve backwards. Slide the throat into the centre of the petal sticking with a little egg white; leave until dry. Dust with a darker pink and paint a few delicate spots using petal dust mixed with clear spirit.

Doris Pink

Doris pinks are a popular flower especially with the older generation. They are a mid-summer flower and part of the Dianthus family. Pinks can be used like carnations in sprays or used in a natural bunch on a cake tied in a bow with a piece of ribbon. Using the smaller cutter you can make French marigolds using the same method.

Method

Hook a piece of 25-gauge Nile green wire; make a medium-sized cone of green paste. Dip in egg white and insert the wire into the finer end of the cone. Make a cavity in the top of the cone for

the petals. Roll out some pink paste and using a medium primrose cutter, cut out the petal, make a few tiny cuts around

each petal and frill with a cocktail stick. Dust with dark pink powder straight away. Brush a little egg white into the cavity of the calyx, place the first petal in position and repeat with a further three or four petals until the flower is finished. The centre petal should be squashed up to fill the centre cavity.

Marigold

Use the cutter which is the next size down to the Doris pink and use dark, yellow paste with orange dust. The calyx has tweezer pinches down it and has a touch of burgundy petal dust put on when dry.

Gypsophila

Gypsophila is a dainty flower favoured by many brides for their bouquets. Making these tiny flowers in flower paste is very time consuming, but worth the trouble, it softens harsh flowers and fills in sprays beautifully.

As it is almost impossible to tape wires successfully to such a dainty skeleton of branches, it is better to place the sugar buds and blossoms onto real gypsophila stems.

Method

Buy a piece of gypsophila and dry by hanging in a dry place for 3-4 days. Alternatively, place sprigs in the microwave on defrost setting for about 3-4 minutes. This draws the moisture out, it then only needs a day of hanging. When dry, the flowers will be

crispy to the touch. Cut these all off so you are left with just the stems. Roll tiny balls of white paste and stick on to some of the branches. Most of the branches are in threes so you can use either two buds and one flower or two flowers and one bud on each. Roll out some white paste, cut out two flowers at a time using a small blossom ejector cutter; cut each scallop of the petal in half and frill the whole blossom like a miniature carnation.

Take two cut, frilled blossoms, stick together with egg white and make a tiny hole in the centre. Using a cocktail stick, thread on to the end of a stem, as with the spray carnation, fold in half like a fan, then into an S shape. Squash with tweezers. Continue all over the sprig of stems covering with flowers. This size spray would take about 30 minutes to complete. When finished, dry for a while then mix some green paste colouring with some clear spirit and paint the calyxes on each bud and flower with a fine paintbrush.

Ivy Leaf

Ivy leaves are a useful foliage suitable for year round use. They are, however, particularly useful for Christmas cakes. The ones shown are variegated ivy but the principle is the same for all foliage.

Method
Take a piece of pale ivory–coloured paste and roll into a ball. Squash, and roll with a paintbrush, retaining a thicker part at one end for the wire. Cut out the ivy leaf positioning the base at thicker part as shown; hold firmly between your thumb and first finger and insert a 28-gauge green wire that has first been hooked and dipped in egg white. Place on an ivy leaf or violet leaf veiner or use a real ivy leaf. Vein on both sides. Run a cocktail stick over the edge to soften slightly. Place on a sponge and vein the centre of the leaf using a veining tool or cocktail stick. Pinch the bottom slightly and leave to dry. When dry, dust the back green, then work the variegation by using two shades of green. Brush the lighter shade on first using a flat paintbrush and brushing from the centre to the outside of the leaf, then using a darker shade, dust on top of the lighter colour, again working from the centre outwards.

Periwinkle

The periwinkle has been made in the same way as the variegated ivy using the same cutter as clematis, but the green has been painted on by mixing green colouring with spirit. Start off with a very pale green for the background, slowly build up the colour with two stronger shades. Dry before using.

Foliage

Here several varieties of foliage have been made in the same way as the ivy. They have been coloured in various shades of green either by dusting, painting or varnishing to show the different effects.

Ferns

This picture shows sword and maidenhair fern. Make a wire skeleton and cut out the leaf shapes, stick on with softened flower paste which acts like strong glue. Dust or paint green.

Heart-shaped Wedding Cake

This elegant cake with its spray of roses and Cymbidium orchids is shown step by step on page 245.

Instructions

Marzipan and cover a 25 and 15cm (10 and 6in) heart cake. Place on boards and leave for a few days. During this time the flowers can be made and assembled and the lace pieces piped. Make a paper pattern for the side by measuring from the front point to the back. Fold the strip in four and draw an equal scallop in each division, scribe onto both sides of the cake to end up with eight scallops in total. The embroidery may be worked free-hand but the shaping could be included in the original pattern and scribed on at the same time as the scallops. Stick the tiny cutout hearts onto the cake using a little egg white. Pipe a shell around the base with a No42 tube then pipe a scalloped line along the scribed line and attach the lace, place the miniature bows above the points. Using a posy pick stick, make a hole into the top tier and place the spray into position, (page 247). This cake has a perspex cake divider instead of traditional pillars.

Wild Flowers

Wild Flowers

Making wild flowers allows all your creative instincts to come into play. There are very few cutters available, so it is a matter of experimenting with the different principles you have learnt to create the flowers of your choice.

Use the flowers in this lesson as guidelines to get you started. However, if you are starting from scratch you will find it essential to have either a real flower model to hand, or detailed photographs or illustrations of the anatomy of the flower in question. When looking at the flower you wish to model, try to imagine other flowers that are similarly constructed and if these are covered in this book, then you will know which method to follow.

Honeysuckle is made using the finger flower method. As this is quite an advanced flower, you have to work quickly to complete before the long sepal dries. First attempts may be disappointing because the petal starts to dry before all stages are finished, but with practice you will become quicker.

Honeysuckle

Wild honeysuckle in soft tones of cream, yellow and pale orange grows freely in the hedgerows in the summer months. It can be used in amongst other flowers or on its own. For a dramatic effect use a spray of three or four pieces of honeysuckle trailing over the edge of the cake.

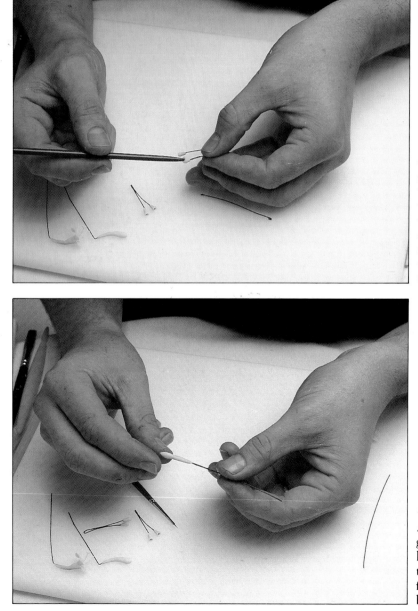

1. Using ivory flower paste start off with the sprocks in the centre. Take three pieces of 30-gauge green wire, put hooks on both ends of two pieces and just on one end of the third. Dip the hooks in egg white then place a tiny cone of paste on each. Use the end of a paintbrush, as shown, to make a cavity in the thicker end of each cone to expose the tip of the wire.

2. To make the buds, make hooks on five to seven pieces of 30-gauge wire. Roll a ball of paste into a long thin cone and then stick onto the first hook, roll between your two first fingers to get a long elegant bud bringing the top to a slight point.

3. Taking the bud in between your thumb and first finger, curve both the bud and wire gently. Take a pair of tweezers, bend at the neck as shown. You will need to repeat steps 2 to 3 with the remaining buds, but graduate the size of the buds to finish with three or four different sizes.

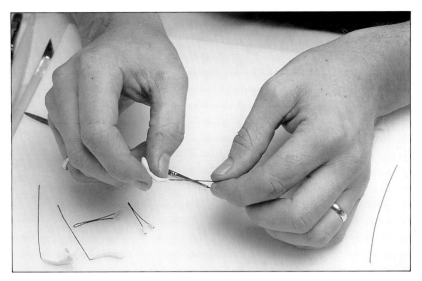

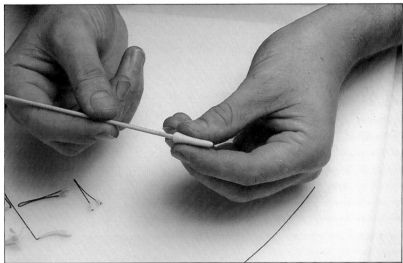

4. Take a piece of paste and roll into a long thin cone. Using a satay stick, insert this into the thicker end, as for pulled and finger flowers, and rotate the stick so it moves freely.

5. Cut a thin strip to form a petal by cutting two straight lines near each other then make a slight angled cut either side of this as shown. The remaining piece is cut into four. This is clearer in picture 7.

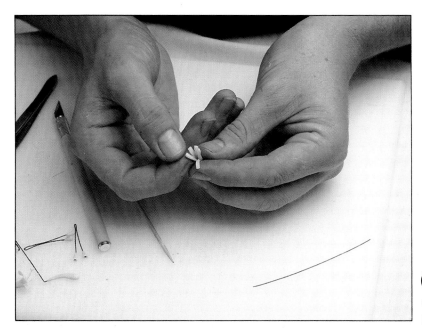

6. Open up the flower by bending each petal backwards. Roll a cocktail stick on each of the four top petals to frill them slightly.

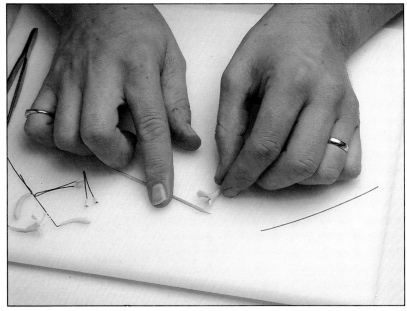

7. Roll the single petal to approximately twice its original length using a cocktail stick, be very gentle as too much pressure will cause the petal to break.

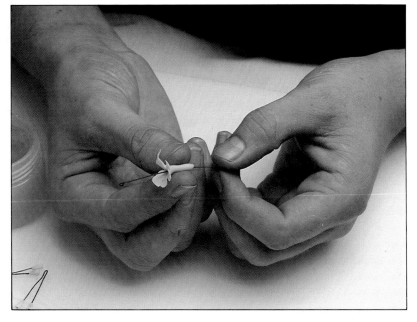

8. Curl petal under using a ball tool. Make a hook on a piece of 30-gauge wire and thread down through throat of the flower.

9. Roll between your fingers to make a long tubular back; lay over a wooden dowel with the single long petal downwards, and push on top with your finger curving the flower and wire at the same time.

10. Take three double fine white stamens, fold two in half and one irregularly to end up with five the same length and one longer one. Run a pair of scissors along the cotton to curl them slightly, then insert into the centre of the flower with tweezers. If you do not have fine stamens, use button-thread instead.

11. Squash the centre to make sure the stamens are secure. To make a spray, you will need three to five flowers.

To make a spray, you will need three to five flowers.

Finishing
Dust with a soft, round brush and a mixture of orange and yellow petal dust to produce the soft apricot tones. Dust the longest stamen, the centre of the flower, and base of the flower soft green. The buds are dusted green at the base and yellow at the top. The sprocks are dusted green. Tape the two folded sprocks into the single one then, working in a clockwise movement, gradually increase the size of the buds as you progress. Finish off by placing the flower in position as shown.

Foxgloves

These tall flowers with their hanging heads are an excellent way to give height to a spray. They are made without cutters so it will take a little practise to produce a consistent shape, however, the sizes need to be graduated to be most effective.

1. Mould a piece of creamy pink paste into a cone with a sloped side, insert a wooden dowel into the end and rotate so that the stick moves freely.

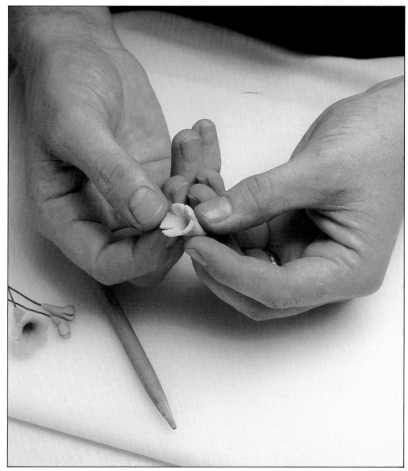

2. Cut one petal from one-quarter of the circumference and the remaining three-quarters into four equal petals, just like the heartsease; squash, pinch and pull each petal.

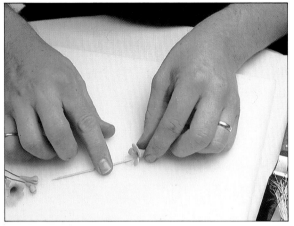

3. Roll a cocktail stick along each petal to thin rather than to frill.

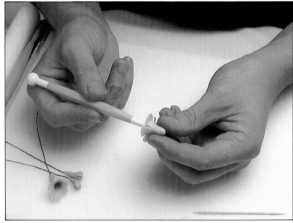

4. Stick a ball tool into the throat of the flower to open it up slightly.

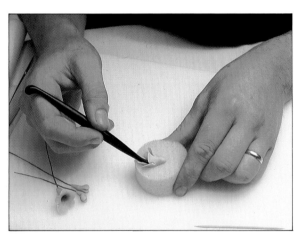

5. Using a dog bone tool on sponge, stretch the throat of the foxglove so it cups slightly.

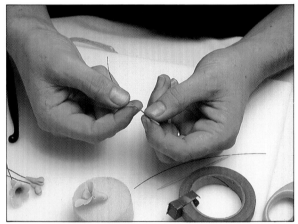

6. Make a hook on a piece of wire and taking a piece of floristry tape wrap over the hook and tape down the wire.

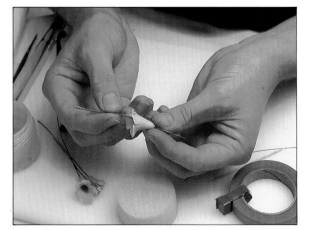

7. Thread down through the flower, the thicker end piece stops the wire coming right through the foxglove flower.

8. To finish the foxglove, dust with pink dusting powder. A white petal dust is dusted on the inside of the flower. Mix some burgundy petal dust with some clear spirit and paint the spots on the throat.

Blackberries

Blackberries are a very attractive late summer or autumn fruit wired in a spray, as shown. They look most appealing on a man's birthday cake perhaps with a paste butterfly, ladybird or dragonfly on one of the leaves.

To make the blackberry, make a cone of blackish-violet paste. Place this on to a hooked 26-gauge wire; roll lots of tiny balls of paste and stick these all over the surface of the cone until it is completely covered. Roll out some green paste and cut a calyx; slide this up the wire and stick to the base. For the under-ripe blackberries, make in the same way but in mid-green paste.

The leaves are made the same way as the rose and ivy leaves featured in the previous lesson, but vein using a metal veiner for a strong veining effect. Make the flower in the same way as the buttercup using a small rose cutter with a cluster of yellow stamens in the centre of the flower.

Finishing

Dust the under-ripe blackberries dark green one side and red the other. Varnish. The flower is dusted with a little green in the centre, while the leaves are dusted with a touch of copper-coloured petal dust, these too are varnished.

Acorn

Acorns can be used on a man's cake or on a box of chocolates as a change from flowers; they can also be used with autumn flowers to make an unusual spray.

For the cup of the acorn, make a cone in mid-brown and mark with the end of a No. 2 tube to get a scalloped effect on the cup. The acorn is made by making a cone in green with a tiny tip of brown placed on the top. Stick into the cup using egg white. To make a wire acorn, mount a cone onto a wire and hollow out the cup, the wire should be at right angles to the cup; place the acorn in as before. The leaves are made as instructed on page 196.

Paint the acorn with green colouring mixed with clear spirit to give a natural effect to the acorn. Paint the leaves in a mixture of green and autumnal colours. Wire into a spray.

470

Bess Rose

The Bess Rose is a small wild rose. It is a very dainty variety ideal for use on wedding, birthday and celebration cakes; it can also be adapted to make a Christmas Rose, green dust should then be brushed into the centre instead of using pale pink dust all over.

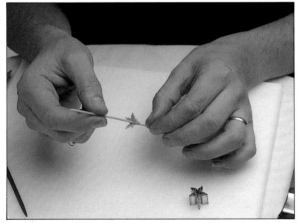

1. Make a Mexican hat and roll out the base using a paintbrush. Place the small calyx cutter over the top of the node and cut the calyx.

2. Make a hook on a piece of 26-gauge wire. Dip the hook in egg-white and thread through the calyx, pull through so that it embeds itself into the calyx.

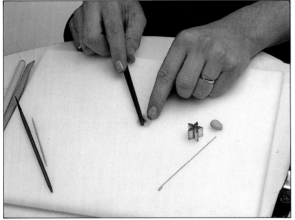

3. Make a small ball of paste, place this on top of the hole made when the wire was inserted to act as a plug. Make a hole in the centre of the plug for stamens.

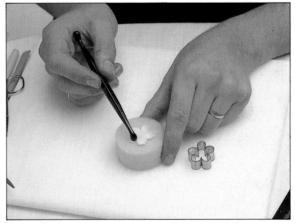

4. Roll out some white paste and cut out a five petal blossom. Place on a sponge and cup each petal slightly using a dog bone tool.

5. Brush some egg white on the calyx and turn the petal over; stick the calyx as shown onto the back of the rose.

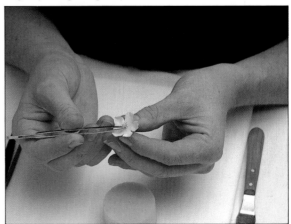

6. Cup each petal onto a piece of foam to give it a cupped shape to the flower. Place some yellow stamens into the centre hole

Forget-me-nots

Forget-me-nots with their cheery blue and yellow faces are useful in sprays based on a blue colour scheme.

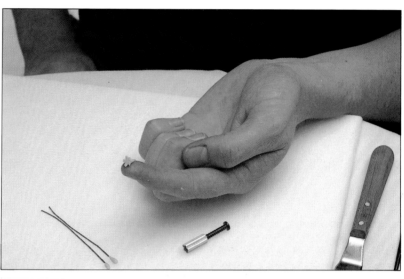

1. Make some buds by putting some little, elongated blue rounds on pieces of 30-gauge wire and shape into a tiny cone. Cut out small-sized blossom using an ejector cutter.

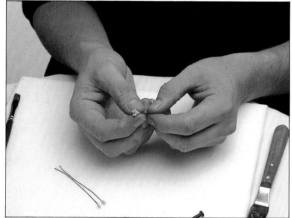

2. Thread the blossom onto a piece of 30-gauge green wire which has been bent into a hook at one end.

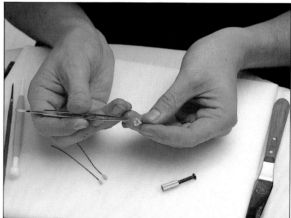

3. Roll out a little yellow paste and cut a miniature yellow blossom shape, insert into the centre of the blue forget-me-not using tweezers and a little egg white. Make a tiny hole in the centre using a cocktail stick.

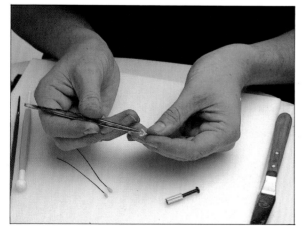

4. Take a white stamen in a pair of tweezers. Place the stamen into the centre of the flower.

Finishing
Wire into a spray as shown. You will need five to seven buds and three to five flowers per spray.

Buttercups

Buttercups with their bright, yellow flowers give warmth to a spray and mix well with most other wild flowers.

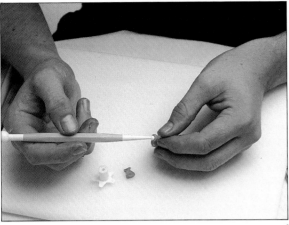

1. Mould a cone of green paste. Place onto a piece of 28-gauge green wire which has already been hooked. Make a cavity using a ball tool as shown.

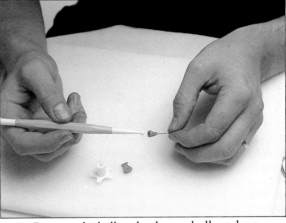

2. Remove the ball tool to leave a hollowed out cavity.

3. Roll out some green paste and cut a small calyx. Lift up on the modelling tool.

4. The finished calyx with its top piece in position, stick this with egg white.

5. Roll out some dark, yellow paste and cut out five petals using an apple blossom cutter.

6. Vein each petal and frill the edges gently with a cocktail stick.

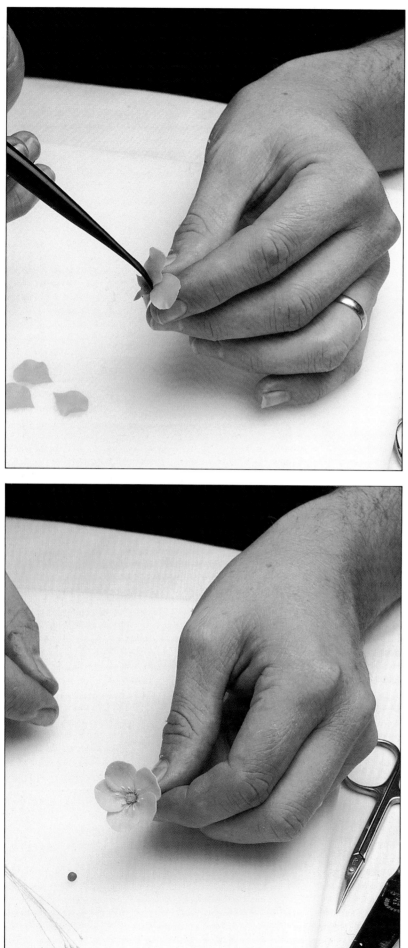

7. Using a little egg white, stick the petals into the centre of the prepared calyx overlapping each one in turn.

Finishing
To finish the buttercup place a ring of fine yellow stamens around the centre, then, taking a small ball of green paste roll in yellow semolina and stick into the centre. When dry, dust with a mixture of dark yellow petal dust and gold lustre to give a golden sheen to the petals.

Making Flowers from Fresh Samples

Using Fresh Flower Samples

Sugar flowers may be made from fresh specimens by using a wide variety of techniques.

To begin with, it is important to use simply constructed flowers. Pick fresh flowers from the garden after the dew has been dried by the morning sun or, if buying from the florist, check on seasonal availability as some varieties may need ordering in advance. Many florists will give you the odd head or leaf as it often seems unnecessary to buy a whole bunch of flowers when you only want one sample.

An assortment of orchid formers that can be made from empty drink tins cutting out the desired shape using floristry scissors. The ones shown are, at the back, an unwired Cymbidium orchid, front left, the Phalonopis (moth) orchid and the front right, the Dendrobium.

Dendrobium Orchid

This orchid, also known as the Singapore orchid, comes in the off-white as shown and shades of pink and mauve. It is one of the many flowers for which there is no cutter available, but it is possible to reproduce this and many other flowers without cutters.

1. A spray of fresh Dendrobium orchids. Pick off a suitable flower to use as a model for the paste flower.

2. Using a modelling knife carefully disect the flower, you will notice that the Dendrobium has seven sections. Start working with the column, this is the small piece that comes into the throat; mould one in paste using your fresh one as a guide. To make the throat, roll out some paste and, using the fresh throat petal as a template, place onto the paste and cut round with a modelling knife. Remove the petal and support on foam to achieve the same soft shape as the fresh petal. Alternatively, lay on top of the fresh throat to set.

The two sepals or wing petals are cut from rolled sugarpaste again using the fresh petals as templates, veining the centre of each.

The main part is the back three sepals which are made in one piece. Cut out the shape from an empty drink tin and bend in the same shape as the fresh part. Roll out the paste and cut this piece again using the fresh petal as a template, then place on a former to dry.

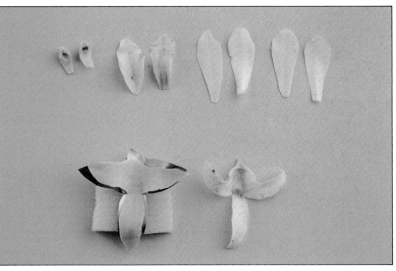

3. This final picture shows the fresh and sugar orchids together, the sugar one is on the right. It has been assembled when dry using softened flower paste as a glue. When set, the orchid is dusted with a yellowish green petal dust.

Alstromeria

Alstromeria or Peruvian lily comes in many colours including red, yellow and cream as well as the pink shown. It is made using the individually wired petal principle used for orchids and foliage in Lesson 16.

1. Here the fresh spray of alstromeria with its delicate centre detail. Pick off a suitable flower as a sample.

2. As with the Dendrobium orchid, the fresh petals are used as templates. Take some pink paste, roll into a ball then squash, roll out using a paintbrush, retaining a thicker area towards the centre at one end. Place the petal on the paste so that the base covers the thicker part and, using a modelling knife, cut round the petal. Vein using the back of the real petal as the veiner and then place the piece of hooked 30-gauge wire into the thicker part. Place on sponge and mark the two curved veins and then turn over so the veins are on the back but in relief on the front of the petal. You need three large petals in pink and three of the smaller ones in off-white.

To make the stamen centre, squash grey paste onto six pink stamens and tape a piece of pink stamen cotton on to the end of a piece of wire, cutting in half lengthways to get a feathery top. Tape the grey tipped stamen onto the wire as shown. Dry along with the petals.

3. Dust and paint the flower taking the colours and the detail from the fresh petals to get the colouring correct. To assemble, take the centre stamen piece and place the three smaller petals in a triangular arrangement, then arrange the three outer petals in the gaps taping tightly to make sure they stay in position.

Rubrem Lily

This large fragrant lily with its dark dense colouring looks attractive on a wedding cake and creates a very dramatic effect.

1. This picture shows the spray of fresh lilies. Pick a bloom and cut off the petals carefully with a modelling knife.

2. To make the lily petal, take the fresh petal left and use as template. Dust and paint as fresh sample.

Scabious

This attractive summer garden flower comes in shades of blue and mauve making it an easy colour to use with pink, creams and lemons.

1. The fresh Scabious head with its soft frilly petals.

2. Remove a fresh petal and uncrumple it, lay on a piece of thin card and draw round it, then cut out to make a card template. Roll out some white paste, cut the petal shape. Using a modelling knife, cut the edge with tiny slits like those made for a spray carnation, then frill the edge, as shown. Dust in a blue or mauve shade straight away. After pleating the petal, as shown, place onto a cut out green daisy shape. Support with foam rubber sticking with egg white in the centre, continue all the way around, then make thin strips of white rolled paste, frill one end and then ruche up like french pleats. These sit inside the main petals. The stamens used were green matt-headed ones with tiny pieces of blue cotton placed in between them.

3. The sugar and real flower, side-by-side. The sugar flower is dusted blue and the fresh one shows one of the many shades of the Scabious.

480

Fresh Flowers

Fresh flowers were commonly used before sugar flowers became popular. Most royal iced wedding cakes would have a bride and groom or a silver vase filled with fresh flowers as a top feature decoration and these are still frequently requested.

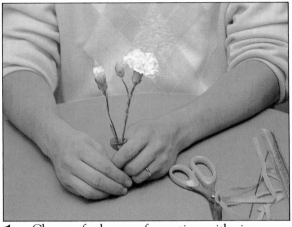

1. Choose a fresh spray of carnations with nice strong stems and a good shape.

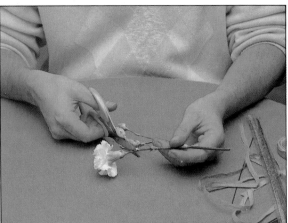

2. Cut off the head about 2.5cm (1in) down the stem behind the back of the flower ; if using buds or slightly open flowers, cut as for full blooms.

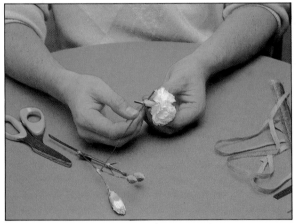

3. Taking a piece of anealed floristry wire, pierce the back of the calyx by pushing through the wire.

4. Bend the wire over to double up. Be careful to support the stem to stop the wire breaking the back of the calyx.

5. Taking a piece of 1cm (½in) wide floristry tape, tape down the wire starting on the calyx.

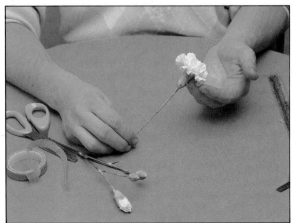

6. The finished wired spray carnation with a flexible wire stem.

Ivy Leaf

The principle shown here for wiring an ivy leaf may be applied to any type of foliage.

1. A sprig of ivy is cut off the leaves, leave a little piece of the stem at the base of the leaf.

2. Take a piece of fine rose wire and thread through the leaf as if using a needle and cotton.

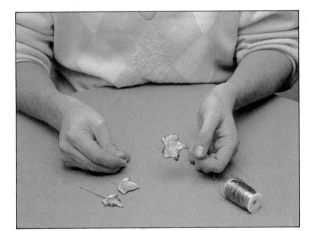

3. Wrap the smaller piece of wire around the stem and the first piece of wire.

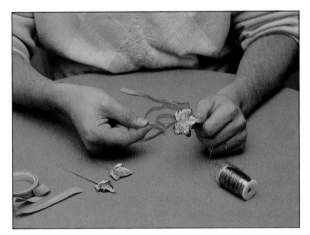

4. Using a piece of 1cm (½in) wide floristry tape, tape down the wire to finish off the leaf.

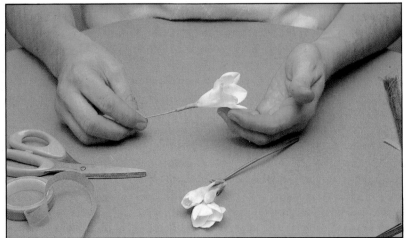

Freesia

Cut off the separate freesia blooms with a pair of floristry scissors. Thread a piece of medium-gauge wire through the flower, bend the two pieces down and twist the smaller piece around the longer one. Tape down the flower and wire starting where the first wire was inserted.

Fresh Flower Bouquets, Sprays and Posies

1. This posy is suitable for a large cake or as a spray for a bridesmaid. Wire into a posy in the same principle as the wired sugar posy in page 236. The posy is finished with a hand-made crochet posy frill and flowers include Doris pink, mauve and white freesias, Nigella (Love in a Mist), asparagus fern and gypsophila. The tails are made in white and lilac 3mm (⅛in) wide ribbon.

2. The two tier wedding cake shown here has a medium-sized bridal bouquet as a feature decoration. If a wedding is being done on a budget, a specially designed bride's bouquet could be put into the posy pick on the cake as the main decoration as she arrives at the reception. The bouquet features pale peach roses, white freesia, Dendrobium (Singapore) orchids, gypsophila, asparagus fern and miniature daisies.

Silk and Fabric Flowers

Fabric flowers have many uses in cake decorating. Attractive and dramatic effects can be obtained using them on celebration and wedding cakes. Department stores, florists and cake decorating shops all stock an enormous array from tiny blossoms to large lilies and orchids, but only some of these are of a suitable size and shape for cake decorating.

The most realistic, but the most expensive, are the silk flowers, although many of the man-made fabric polyester type are now made to a high standard. Fabric flowers are also useful to use to perfect an arrangement that is to be made in sugarflowers as these are fragile to work with. Most fabric and silk flowers come on thick wire stems that have to be replaced with thinner 26 to 30-gauge wire which is wrapped round a piece of existing stem to make them more flexible. You can even colour fabric flowers; use white flowers from which delicate shades can be achieved with a firm-haired paintbrush and petal dust. Silk and fabric flowers can also be used on wedding cakes instead of sugar flowers particularly when time or money is short.

Silver Vase

This picture shows fabric flowers arranged into vases. The smaller is in fact a silver cake pillar that has been upturned and filled with dry floristry foam or sugarpaste. The flowers used in the arrangement are lemon and white carnations, blossoms, gypsophila and foliage.

The larger silver vase is filled with an arrangement of pink and white fuchsias, carnations and foliage.

Bridal Bouquet

1. This large bridal bouquet is arranged in the same way as the green and peach orchid and rose in Lesson 16. reproduced on a larger scale and placed into a posy pick on a wedding cake offering an alternative to sugar flowers.

Flower Sprays & Corsages

Sprays & Posies

The Victorian posy always has a rose as a central focal point with rings of flowers and foliage working out, or a more natural arrangement with five small leg sprays tapered out, with the cavities filled with ribbons and more pulled blossoms.

The flowers and foliage needed to produce the following posy and straight spray are: three spray carnations, sixteen five petal basic pulled blossoms, nine buds and five medium ivy leaves.

1. Using floristry tape cut in half, start by taping three blossoms together all on the level.

2. Then make one pink and one green double ribbon loop from 3mm (⅛in) ribbon and position either side of the blossoms. Place a bud in between each ribbon. Note how the posy is being worked in triangles at this stage.

3. Now place another blossom behind each bud, shaping into a slight curve. It is important not to place the flowers too low. If you do, you will end up with a cone shape. The curve on a basin bottom is approximately the angle you should be working towards. Note the dominant triangle shape.

4. Take the spray carnations and place one in each of the gaps between the blossoms; tape tightly. Make two pink and two green medium-sized double figure-of-eight loops and position alternately green and pink around the edge. The shape now changes from a triangle formation to a circular.

5. Place the remaining blossoms and buds at random around the posy where needed.

6. To finish the basic assembly, tape the five ivy leaves spaced at regular intervals around the posy. In between two of the leaves, tape two loops with double tails. These are single figure-of-eight loops, but with extra long tails. The tails are the front of the posy.

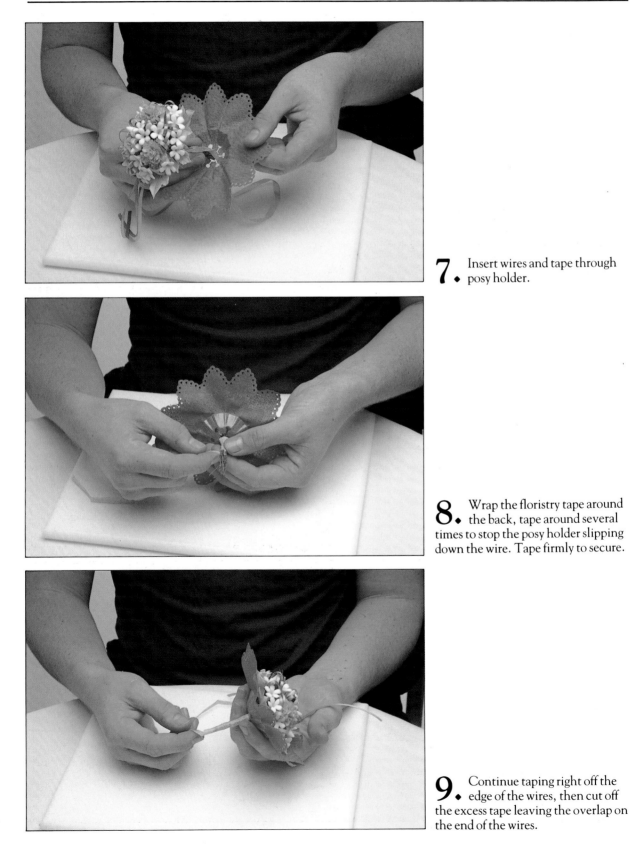

7. Insert wires and tape through posy holder.

8. Wrap the floristry tape around the back, tape around several times to stop the posy holder slipping down the wire. Tape firmly to secure.

9. Continue taping right off the edge of the wires, then cut off the excess tape leaving the overlap on the end of the wires.

10. Fold the excess flap over to cover all the ends so as not to leave sharp wires exposed, then tape back up the handle until you run out of tape.

11. The finished posy.

12. Here is the same posy shown in a tiny floristry posy holder, it has been carefully cut around the edge to produce an attractive scallop.

Inverted V Sprays

The flowers shown are those needed for both the inverted V and reverse S curve sprays. They consist of five spray carnations, seven ivy leaves, twelve buds and about twenty-eight blossoms.

1. Begin by making the two legs of the spray which are both identical. First of all position a pink swallow bow and then two buds followed by five blossoms and a double green loop.

2. Continue with buds and flowers and place a carnation centrally, finish with pink double figure-of-eight bow. Repeat to make the second leg.

3. Make a posy as previously described using the remaining flowers, a double bow and three figure-of-eight loops.

4. The four ivy leaves are positioned together at the top and the remaining ivy leaf at the base of the posy leaving a gap either side for the legs.

5. Tape the first leg into the posy, taping tightly so it does not move.

6. Tape in the third leg and bind all wires firmly together. The finished inverted V spray would be placed in a posy spray pick, if being used on a cake.

Corsage

Corsages nowadays are used mainly as a decoration on garments for weddings, but several years ago they were given by gentlemen when taking a lady out to dinner. Sugar flower corsages are suitable for small cakes or knife sprays or they may be given as a gift.

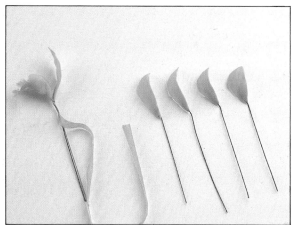

1. Make all the pieces from the directions given on Page 203. Start off by taping the back cupped sepal to the throat as shown.

2. The two small sepals sit with their curved sides upwards either side of the cupped back sepal. Place the two larger curved petals at the bottom of the flower as shown. Make a small sausage in yellow paste and stick into the throat and vein in half.

3. Dust some yellow petal dust into the centre of the throat. Mix a little plum petal dust with some clear spirit and paint some fine feathery lines around the frilled part as shown. Finish off the painting with some spots on the throat.

4. Using a soft pink petal dust, brush around the throat and at the base of the sepals.

5. Take one Cymbidium orchid, one piece of gypsophila, two leaves, a yellow bow, plus a tulle bow.

6. Tape together as shown.

Spray Carnation Corsage

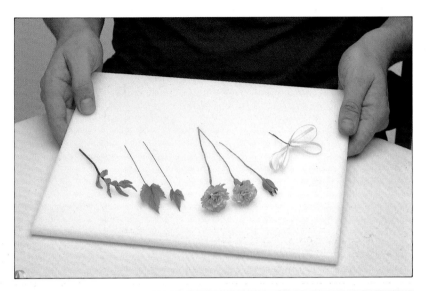

1. You will need two carnations, one bud, two ivy leaves, one piece of sword fern and a double figure-of-eight bow.

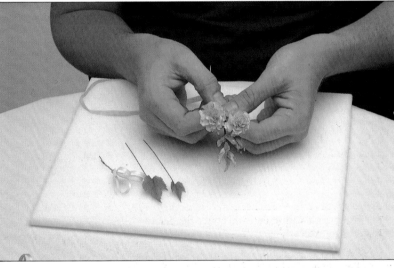

2. Start off with the sword fern, then the carnations and continue with the other pieces.

3. The final stage is the positioning of the ribbon bow. This can be in a contrast colour, as shown, or the same shade as the flowers.

Blackberry Box

A spray of blackberries makes an alternative to a spray of flowers on a chocolate box. This is ideal for a Father's day or Mum's birthday gift. It would also be suitable for a husband and wife as a joint gift.

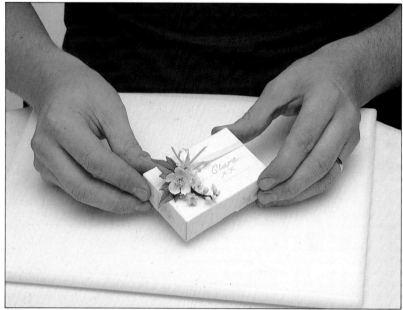

Gift Box

A lovely idea is to make a small spray of flowers to be attached to a small cake box used when people are unable to attend a wedding or celebration. It has been tied with a 3mm (⅛in) powder blue ribbon and then has a small spray of Bess rose, forget-me-nots and ivy leaves. The silver writing adds the finishing touch to the box.

Knife Spray

When decorating a wedding cake, it is a lovely touch to make a knife spray to match. Make a small straight spray in flowers to match those used on the cake. Take a piece of 30-gauge covered wire and thread through the spray twisting at the back of the spray. Bring the wires around the side of the knife where the blade meets the handle, bring to the centre back and twist the wires together tightly. Cut off excess wire and fold back towards the spray.

Bridal Bouquet

This large spray, based on a small bridal bouquet, is wired in the same way in fresh or silk flowers. This size spray is suitable as shown for two or three tier wedding cakes and can be made up to two or three times this size if required. There is a lot of initial preparation as you will need several hours to make the flowers. This spray contains Cymbidium orchids, roses, pulled blossoms, ivy and various foliage and gypsophilas but other flowers could be used, if desired. Usually this type of spray does not include ribbons.

1. Make the flowers shown. The main ones being five Cymbidium orchids, four roses, two rose buds. You will need several sprays of gypsophilas, two to three dozen pulled blossoms and an assortment of variegated ivy and other foliage.

2. Start off with a small ivy leaf, then add the first buds. The two rose buds are progressively opening up as you work along the spray.

3. Place the first orchid in position. You will have to tape this firmly. Make sure the taping is really tight as large flowers need supporting.

4. Then place another rose and orchid. Note the zig zag effect going from one side to the other. Leave aside at this stage and go on to the separate posy.

5. Now you need to wire a separate posy for the top. Start off as shown with the remaining two roses and another orchid.

6. Finish off by using the last orchid and all of the remaining flowers and foliage.

7. Tape the posy to the first part of the spray, make sure to tape these firmly together using full width floristry tape.

8. The finished bouquet.

9. This type of spray and most of the others show should be put into a posy or spray pick. This is a white food-grade plastic vial; the one shown comes with a little base so that once the base is cut the spray can be removed and the vial placed back into its stand to hold the spray. Stick the pick into position on the cake. This spray is placed at an angle but be careful not to place too near the edge of the cake or the flowers will look unbalanced, spoil the effect, and may crack the paste.

10. Continue pushing the vial in until it is level with the top of the cake surface. Fill the cavity with sugarpaste to hold the wires in place. On no account must the wires go straight into the cake. For a small spray, the top from a fibre tip pen can be used in place of a posy pick.

11. The top tier of the wedding cake with the bouquet in position. Because a larger spray will trail below the board it is best to take the bouquet to the reception separately and then insert into the pick once the cake is set up. If this is not possible, you will have to bend the spray then, once in position, it will have to be carefully pushed back into shape.

Wired Sprays

Having mastered the art of flower-making, it is time to go on to combine them in the form of sprays and arrangements.

There are a great variety of wired sprays and corsages in many different styles to choose from. Those covered in this chapter include the basic types that are suitable to use on celebration and wedding cakes. The principle is not unlike that used by a florist when producing bridal bouquets, posies and corsages for a wedding in fresh flowers. The only difference is that fresh flowers are easier to arrange because you can undo the spray if not happy with it, but sugar flowers do not like that sort of treatment as the petals and calyxes get broken. Generally sugar flowers have to be treated with loving care, and should not be packed too densely or they crack and break. Once the cake is covered or even before it is baked, it is best to have a visual idea of what type of spray you are going to put on the cake. The most important elements are colour, shape and proportion.

Colour
When flowers are put together the overall colour scheme tends to become more intense. When using dark colours, try to make the smaller flowers in the dark colours rather than the large focal flowers as this would make the overall effect too dense. Generally a florist would use not more than two or at the most, three main colours so bear this in mind too. A flower arrangement nearly always includes some foliage as a finishing touch and this is equally true for sugar sprays. Ribbons may be an important addition and again can dramatically change the finished effect. Choose neutral coloured ribbons as these blend best with the flowers. If using several colours together always place them together off the cake and see if they tone in with each other before arranging.

Shape
The shape of a spray of flowers can dramatically change the overall appearance of the cake, but with practice you will be able to look at a cake and assess the best type of spray to use.

Proportion
The proportion of the flowers is a very important point to consider. There is nothing worse than a spray with all the flowers out of proportion and when combining several different flower types, it can take some time to work out. The easiest solution is to make the sugar flowers the same size as the fresh ones, alternatively, make all of them to half scale. Pulled and finger flowers are useful as you make these to whatever size you require, while you can be a little restricted when using cutters as there may not always be a cutter of a suitable size available.

If you are new to wired flower arranging, start off with fabric flowers as you can bend these and squash them without breaking them. Once the basic shape has been mastered you can then duplicate it using sugar flowers. Most silk and polyester flowers are on thick wires unsuitable for small sprays so you will need to cut the wire off leaving about 1.5cm (⅝in), then tape a piece of 26-gauge wire to this and bind with floristry tape. Fabric flowers can be repeatedly used in the same or different sprays.

Once you have made your chosen flowers, dust to the required shade and bind with floristry tape. The Nile green colour is suitable for most sprays, but dark green and white are also used from time to time. Depending on the size of the spray and flowers, cut the tape in half or quarters lengthwise. If you have made a mass of flowers and have two or three sprays to make for a wedding cake, split the flowers up before beginning the first spray so that all the sprays will be equal and you will not run out of flowers.

If new to sugar flower arranging, it is advisable to work on a sheet of foam then you can lay the spray down in between stages or if you drop anything it will not break. When taping, tape firmly, if not the flowers will move about and you will have problems creating and maintaining a shape.

Ribbons
Ribbon loops play an important part in making posies and sprays. For further information on making loops and tails, see lesson on Ribbons in Book 1.

Competitions & Commissions

Cake Commissions

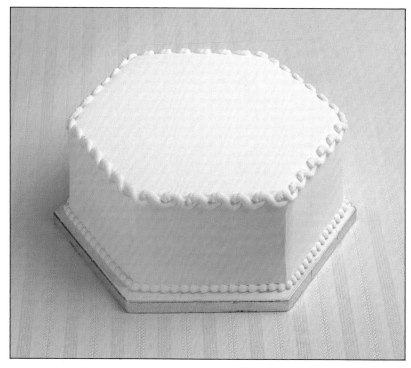

Portions from a Cake

If the cake is commissioned you will have to find out the number for the wedding breakfast, the evening reception and any additional pieces for people unable to attend or to be sent away. Once you have these numbers add them together to give you a number to calculate the size on.

For further information on portions from a cake, see lesson on Designing a Cake in Book One of this series.

Pricing Cakes

How much do I charge? This question causes so many problems and it is always a difficult one to answer because many factors have to be taken into account when pricing a cake.

There are two main types of cake produced: the commercial cake – this would be the type of cake your local baker produces. He usually works out his expenses on the ingredients for the cake itself, then adds the labour costs and his mark up. This is fairly easy to do as he has all his invoices in front of him, he knows how much everything costs, how much he pays his staff and what his profit margin should be.

Secondly, there is the home commissioned cake – this includes icing a cake for a commission, friend or family. A commercial cake should be easy to produce and not terribly labour intensive. Most people at home spend a lot longer icing a cake, often doing a little at a time rather than completing the cake in a day from start to finish. Pricing becomes even more difficult when friends or family are involved. Often the cake is given as a gift but when you work out the cost of the ingredients alone you will find you are being more than generous. Listed below are some different ways of structuring your prices.

Work out the total cost of all the ingredients and add two or three times that amount depending on the

complexity of the design and the hours spent working on the cake. The price can be worked out per kilo or pound for the basic cake coated and decorated and then charge extra per spray of flowers or for special features. Alternatively, the costing may be made on all the ingredients, then work out an hourly rate for labour, remember shopping, washing-up and clearing-up time, all these things add up and should be taken into consideration.

Do not under-estimate yourself. Many people feel that they cannot charge a reasonable fee because they are not professional. Today that does not mean much, professional is only a term for someone who has been to college and works in industry full or part-time.

Many people work from home and produce work of a very high standard. When you give a quotation for the price of a cake, cover yourself by saying it is only approximate. We all learn from our mistakes and often someone chooses a design from a book which you think is going to take about an hour and it ends up taking a whole evening to do and you must be sure that you do not lose out. If a customer is making their own cake it can sometimes take two to three hours to level it off and to fill-in large holes and cracks. All these things will affect the final price.

It is nice to offer the hire of a knife and stand. Although it is an initial outlay, by charging a hire fee you will soon be able to recover your costs and then be able to buy some new shapes maybe a perspex, spiral or S-stand. Make sure you have your stand and knife insured, and that your name is clearly marked on the base. Often they are put into the kitchen at the end of a reception and it is easy for them to get lost in a busy hotel kitchen.

Commission Form

When taking details for a cake commission it is advisable to have a standard form prepared so that you are sure to get all the details from the client. Use the following example as a guide.

Wedding Cake Order Form		
Name of customer:	Shape of cake:	Number of tiers: Sizes:
Address: Telephone:	Cutting cake yes/no	
	Base colour:	
Date of wedding:	Secondary colour:	Other themes in wedding (eg. bows, birds, butterflies etc.)
Viewing date:	Board type:	
Design roughs submitted by:	Swatches of bridal material provided yes/no	
Costings Finished cake:	Flowers (type and colour):	Special instructions (eg. inscriptions, runouts, lacework etc.)
Stand and knife:	Florist's name:	
Delivery charge:	Address:	Knife spray yes/no
Deposit paid:		Stand and knife hire yes/no
Balance due on approval at viewing:	Telephone:	

Competition Cake

Entering competitions is a very challenging, yet most satisfying aspect of cake decoration and sugarcraft. Many hours can be spent on any one part of a cake, whether it be the coating, linework, figure-work or the lettering. To give yourself a good chance of winning, total dedication to your work is required. This can be very demanding on your time, so do ensure you are able to allocate sufficient to do justice to your exhibit. It could be many weeks before you see any reasonable work worth entering, but persevere and hopefully you will achieve your aim.

Understanding the Schedule

First of all check that you are eligible to enter the class you wish to exhibit in. It may be a novice or open class, or it may be that you need to be a member of a particular body or organisation. It is important to read the specification very carefully and to be aware of what the class is requesting in terms of size, cost, presentation, and the accepted use of edible or non-edible decorations. Note also whether you need to use a real cake or if cake dummies are allowed in the particular class you wish to enter.

Remember to complete and return the entry form with the entry fee if required. Check the date of the competition and the time of delivery for your exhibit; give yourself extra time on the actual day in case of delays or breakages.

Designing the Cake

Try to be as original as possible with your cake design, do something to attract the eye of the judges. Numerous ideas can be gleaned from greeting cards and gift wrapping paper, not only for the motif, figure or animal, but also for ideas on lettering styles and inscriptions. If you intend to use any templates for off-pieces, for example runout collars, it is better to measure your cake after the final coat and then design your collar to fit exactly. Otherwise, work to accurate dimensions and templates throughout the production of the cake.

Materials

Use good quality ingredients to give you a good quality exhibit. In the case of royal icing use a fine bridal icing (confectioner's) sugar. Strain the egg white or reconstituted albumen before mixing to remove any fine lumps or impurities which could affect coating. Sugarpaste cakes need a good coating to win points, so use the paste recipe or product which you know works best for you. Keep a record of colours used for your various materials in case you need to re-match. Royal icing can be weighed and a set number of drops of colour added, make a note of the ratio and use it again if necessary. Sugarpaste can also be colour matched by mixing a strong shade of the eventual tint you require, a portion of this mixture can then be weighed and mixed into a decided weight of white paste. For example 30g (1oz) of coloured paste to 1kg (2lbs) of white sugarpaste.

Cake Dummies

Use the highest quality cake dummies you can afford. A smooth unblemished surface to start with will make coating and covering much easier. If you have to use a real cake for your exhibit, do ensure that you achieve a good smooth coating of marzipan on which to work with your icing or sugarpaste. Coat the cake dummy and board separately to create a good finish on both. The two can be brought together when assembly of all the various parts of the cake commences.

Hints and Tips

For royal icing coating, add a few drops of cold water to the icing for each coat. This will soften the icing and help achieve a smoother finish. The final coat should be very thin, working with considerable pressure on the side scraper and straight edge for the top surface.

Smooth down the surface of your coatings with a sharp knife or sandpaper – except on the final coat, when scratches would be visible. Try to cover the take-off mark on the side of your royal iced cake with a linework panel or other parts of the side decoration.

Use fine tubes when outlining runout pieces or collars to give a degree of delicacy to your work.

Ensure a good sheen on runout work by placing the units near a gentle heat immediately after flooding. Use an anglepoise lamp.

Linework is an important part of the finish of your cake and can mean a considerable amount of points towards your final result. Use No1 and No0 tubes along with some work done in No00. For curved lines a slightly softer consistency of icing will create a better flow. Ensure good joins are made on linework and pipe an equal distance from the adjacent line. As a rule for piping, the distance between lines should be similar to the thickness of the tube you are using at that particular time.

Packing and Exhibiting

Once your cake is completed, attach your staging tickets to the cake board with a little glue, do this neatly and keep the labels straight and clean. Place the cake carefully into a good strong cake box with a secure lid. Many serious exhibitors have wooden carrying boxes made with a foam covered sliding base section to make positioning in the box easier, these carrying boxes should also have a strong handle with which to carry them.

Label your exhibit box, especially if you have more than one, making staging easier on arrival at the competition venue.

Well before leaving for the venue, check that you have the schedule for reference, and your admission tickets.

On arrival at the venue, don't remove the cake from the box until you have found out exactly where to place your exhibit. Then stage your cake in its allocated space, being careful not to damage other exhibits that may already

be on the table. Place the cake in the correct viewing position, so that the judges first look is the one you want them to see.

After the judging, whether or not you are a winner, try to find the judges of your cake and discuss your exhibit with them. Most of them will be quite co-operative in this way. By talking to the judges you can make notes about aspects of your cakes that could be improved, or altered. Do not be discouraged by the fact you do not win anything for your first entry, or even subsequent entries. Keep trying, use your experiences and put the judges comments to good use to improve your skills, knowledge and ability.

The Wedge Cake

The wedge cake was popular at one time and you may get an occasional request to do a cake with a wedge. This is when a wedge of the cake is cut out then tied with ribbon and replaced. The wedge must be taken into consideration when designing the cake, for example, a continuous run-out collar could not be used. It is best to decide on the basic design before cutting the wedge as most designs are worked out upon six, eight or twelve repeating segments and the wedge would represent one whole section. Work out a pattern so you know the size

of the portion to be cut. Find the centre of the cake after two coats of icing using a compass or a circle of paper folded into quarters, and then mark the edge of the cake in the two places it is to be cut. Using a sharp knife and a rule, mark a line from the centre dot to each of the outer lines then hold the ruler vertically up the side and mark the two down lines.

Cutting through the sugar and cake

It is very important to use a saw bladed knife to cut the wedge. Use an even sawing action to cut through the icing on the top then move onto the side and repeat the sawing action holding the knife vertically against the cake. Once the icing has been sawn through use a fine bladed sharp knife and cut through the marzipan and the cake using a gentle sawing action making sure that the knife is straight. Take care not to cut into the cake board. Remove any crumbs and give the cake a final coating of icing. Once this final coat is dry you only need to saw through the icing to release the wedge.

Tying with ribbon

Take a piece of satin ribbon 3-5cm (1½-2in) and 70-100cm (24-36in) long. This can either be in white or in a shade to match or contrast with the coating of the cake. In order to prevent the ribbon being stained by the cake it should be sandwiched in between a

folded strip of greaseproof (waxed) paper. The paper should reach up to the start of the marzipan and be long enough to wrap round both sides of the wedge. Once replaced into the cake only the front of the ribbon should be showing and the paper should not be visible. Place the wedge back into the cake and tie the ribbon in a bow with trailing tails, trim the end of the tails to equal lengths and cut into an inverted V-shape. With the wedge in position the cake can be decorated. Use paper clips to clip the rolled up tails onto the ribbon so they do not get in your way when decorating the cake. The bride and groom can then simply release the piping and remove the customary wedge. Some competitions, especially when a percentage of points are given for the cake itself, will ask for a wedge cake. This makes it easier for the judges to remove the wedge for inspection and tasting. It will always state in the schedule if a wedge is required.

Specialist Work

If you are entering modelling or flower work for a competition it is advisable to invest in a display case. Covering an exhibit helps protect it from being touched and consequently damaged, it also protects it from dust. A small dish of silica gel inside the case helps to keep the atmosphere around the exhibit moisture free.